THE BONE GATHERERS

An Early Christian Woman's Rome
Sites Associated with Women Founders and Saints

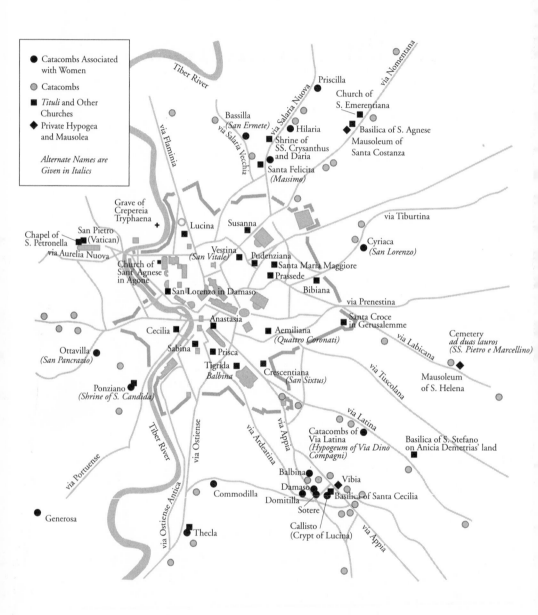

Legend:
- ● Catacombs Associated with Women
- ○ Catacombs
- ■ *Tituli* and Other Churches
- ◆ Private Hypogea and Mausolea

Alternate Names are Given in Italics

Tiber River

via Nomentana

Priscilla
Church of S. Emerentiana

Bassilla *(San Ermete)*
via Salaria Nuova
via Salaria Vecchia
Hilaria
Shrine of SS. Crysanthus and Daria
Basilica of S. Agnese
Mausoleum of Santa Costanza
Santa Felicita *(Massimo)*

via Flaminia

Grave of Crepereia Tryphaena

Lucina
Susanna

via Tiburtina

Chapel of S. Petronella
San Pietro *(Vatican)*
via Aurelia Nuova

Cyriaca *(San Lorenzo)*

Vestina *(San Vitale)*
Pudenziana
Santa Maria Maggiore
Prassede

Church of Sant' Agnese in Agone

San Lorenzo in Damaso

Bibiana

via Prenestina

Anastasia

Santa Croce in Gerusalemme

Cecilia
Aemiliana *(Quattro Coronati)*

via Labicana

Cemetery *ad duas lauros (SS. Pietro e Marcellino)*

Ottavilla *(San Pancrazio)*

Sabina
Prisca

Tigrida *Balbina*

Crescentiana *(San Sixtus)*

via Tuscolana

Mausoleum of S. Helena

Ponziano *(Shrine of S. Candida)*

Tiber River

via Ostiense
via Ardeatina
via Appia

via Latina

Catacombs of Via Latina *(Hypogeum of Via Dino Compagni)*

Basilica of S. Stefano on Anicia Demetrias' land

Balbina
Damaso
Vibia

Commodilla
Domitilla
Sotere

Basilica of Santa Cecilia

via Portuense

Generosa

via Ostiense Antica

Thecla

Callisto *(Crypt of Lucina)*

via Appia

Map Drawn by Bruce Jones Design Inc.

The Bone Gatherers

The Lost Worlds of
Early Christian Women

NICOLA DENZEY

Beacon Press, Boston

Beacon Press
25 Beacon Street
Boston, Massachusetts 02108-2892
www.beacon.org

Beacon Press books
are published under the auspices of
the Unitarian Universalist Association of Congregations.

10 09 08 07   8 7 6 5 4 3 2 1

This book is printed on acid-free paper that meets the uncoated paper
ANSI/NISO specifications for permanence as revised in 1992.

Text design by Yvonne Tsang and composition by Susan E. Kelly
at Wilsted & Taylor Publishing Services

Library of Congress Cataloging-in-Publication Data

Denzey, Nicola Frances
    The bone gatherers : the lost worlds of early Christian women / Nicola Denzey.
        p. cm.
    Includes bibliographical references and index.
    ISBN-13: 978-0-8070-1308-3 (hardcover : alk. paper)   1. Women in Christian-
ity—History—Early church, ca. 30–600.   2. Christian women—Rome—History.
3. Women—History—To 500.   I. Title.
    BR195.W6D46 2007
    274.5'63201082—dc22   2006039315

For my mother

CONTENTS

ABBREVIATIONS

AA.SS	*Acta Sanctorum.* Edited by Socii Bollandiani. Paris, 1863–.
ACW	*Ancient Christian Writers.* Edited by J. Quasten and J. C. Plumpe. New York: Paulist Press, 1946–.
AHR	*American Historical Review*
AJA	*American Journal of Archaeology*
ANF	Library of the Ante-Nicene Fathers. Edited by Alexander Roberts and James Donaldson. 24 vols. Buffalo, N.Y., 1867–1872.
ATR	*Anglican Theological Review*
BHL	Bollandist Hagiographical Library. 68 vols. Brussels, 1885–1970.
Bull.Arch.C	*Bulletino di Archeologia Cristiana.* Rome, 1872–.
CCSL	Corpus Christianorum Series Latina. Turnhout: Brepols, 1947–.
CIAC.Atti	*Atti del Congresso Internazionale di Archeologia Cristiana.* Vatican City, 1894–.
CIL	Corpus Inscriptionum Latinarum. Berlin, 1863–.
CJ	*Codex Justinianus.* Edited by G. Härtel and F. M. Kaufmann. Leipzig: Reclam, 1991.
CQ	*Classical Quarterly.* London, 1907.
CSEL	Corpus Scriptorum Ecclesiasticorum Latinorum. 95 vols. Vienna, 1866–1957.
CTheod	*Codex Theodosianus.* Edited by T. Mommsen and T. Meyer. Hildesheim: Weidmann, 2000.
DACL	*Dictionnaire d'archéologie chrétienne et de liturgie.* 15 vols. Paris, 1907–1953.
Digest	Justinian, *Digest of Roman Law*
ED	*Epigrammata damasiana.* Edited by A. Ferrua. Rome: Pontificio istituto di archeologia cristiana, 1942.
Festus	Festus, *De Verborum significatione quae super sunt.* Edited by Carl Müller. Hildesheim: Olms, 1975.

GCS   Die griechischen christlichen Schriftsteller der ersten drei Jahr-
           hunderte. Berlin, 1891–.

HE   Eusebius, *Ecclesiastical History*

HTR   *Harvard Theological Review*

ICUR   *Inscriptiones christianae urbis Romae Septimo Saeculo antiquiores,*
           new series. Edited by A. Silvagni and A. Ferrua, 12 vols. Vatican City,
           1922–1981.

ILCV   *Inscriptiones Latinae Christianae Veteres.* Edited by E. Diehl. 3 vols.
           Berlin: Weidmann, 1925–1928.

ILS   *Inscriptiones Latinae Selectae.* Edited by H. Dessau, 3 vols. Berlin,
           1892–1916.

JAC   *Jahrbuch für Antike und Christentum*

JECS   *Journal of Early Christian Studies*

JFSR   *Journal of Feminist Studies in Religion*

JRS   *Journal of Roman Studies*

LCL   The Loeb Classical Library

LIMC   *Lexicon Iconographicum Mythologiae Classicae.* 9 vols. Zurich: Artemis
           Verlag; Düsseldorf: Patmos Verlag, 1981–1999.

LH   Palladius, *Lausiac History*

LP   *Liber Pontificalis.* Translated and edited by L. Duchesne. 2 vols. Paris,
           1986.

MEFRA   *Mélanges d'archéologie et d'histoire de l'Ecole française de Rome,*
           Antiquité. Paris, 1881–.

MGH AA   *Monumenta Germaniae Historica. Auctorum Antiquissimorum.* Edited
           by T. Mommsen. Berlin, 1892.

MH   *Martyrologium Hieronymianum.* Edited by G.-B. De Rossi and Louis
           Duchesne. Brussels: Typis Polleunis et Ceuterick, 1894.

NPNF   Library of the Nicene and Post-Nicene Fathers

PL   Patrologia Latina. 217 vols. Edited by J. G. Migne. Paris, 1844–1855.

RivArcC   *Rivista di archeologia cristiana*

Samm.   *Sammelbuch Griechischer Urkunden aus Aegypten.* Edited by
           F. Preisigke and F. Vilabel. 2 vols. Göttingen: Hubert, 1952–1962.

SC   Sources chrétiennes. Paris, 1988–.

SEG   *Supplementum Epigraphicum Graecum.* Leyden, 1923–.

VC   *Vigiliae Christianae*

INTRODUCTION: THE BONE GATHERERS

At a flashpoint in tensions during three tumultuous years of persecutions and pogroms from 249 to 251 CE, Rome's bishop, Cornelius, faced the fearsome Decius, the first emperor to launch a systematic and cruel hunt for Christians in Rome and abroad. Decius had already put to death Cornelius's predecessor, Fabian, in 250. The papal seat sat vacant for nearly a year as the Christian population of Rome roiled against the emperor and fractured under the force of external and internal pressures. Cornelius had been elected against his wishes, for 251 was a dangerous year to become the bishop of Rome. Decius himself had declared that he would rather vie with a claimant to the imperial throne than tolerate another bishop of Rome (Cyprian, *Epistle* 55.9).

Two years later, Cornelius was dragged outside the city to a Temple of Mars and ordered to throw a pinch of incense on an altar in honor of the emperor and the gods of Rome. Cornelius stood his ground and refused. The imperial response was swift: the bishop was summarily decapitated. His body lay in pieces, unmourned, until it was brought back to the city by a hero as unlikely as she is unknown—a "blessed" (*beata*) Roman Christian woman by the name of Lucina. Lucina brought the pope's body to her lands that adjoined the public Christian Catacombs of Callixtus, and she buried the pieces in her family crypt. She ordered his grave to be marked only with a simple marble slab and the Latin inscription "Cornelius, bishop and martyr." The stone exists still, unearthed from Rome's soft soil in 1849.[1] Ancient sources record the date of Cornelius's burial: September 14, 253 CE.

Lucina was Rome's first bone gatherer of pious literature, a woman of substance and means who collected the bodies of the saints to give them a proper burial. It was this same Lucina who had earlier carried the body of a far more powerful saint than even the pope and martyr Cornelius to sanctuary on her lands. Before Cornelius's martyrdom, she was his friend, and she had exhorted him to exhume the bones of the city's patron saints Peter and Paul. They deserved, after all, far better than the relative ignominy of a temporary catacomb burial outside Rome's southernmost circuit. Lucina wanted them to be glorified, brought closer to the sacred spots where the apostles had so long before forfeited their lives. Cornelius took Peter's bones to the Vatican Hill, where they still lie under the main altar of St. Peter's (*LP* 1. 66–67). But Lucina herself moved—so the story goes—the bones of Saint Paul. She piously "translated," or carried the holy relics, to a peaceful spot along the long road that led to Rome's port city Ostia, the Via Ostiensis. There, she had them buried close to the place where, according to tradition, Paul had been beheaded, on a piece of property that belonged to her.[2] With that, Lucina was allied with the pope as his twin conservator of Rome's paired saints and as, in a real sense, the "owner" of Paul's relics. Cornelius had Peter's bones, but Lucina's prize—buried on her own property—was no less worthy of reverence. Lucina's ownership of Paul's bones, along with her ability to influence the bishop of Rome, would have made Lucina a powerful figure—arguably the most powerful of the lay Christians of Rome. At least, this is what we might be inclined to think.

If we look through the annals of the early Roman Catholic Church, through the letters and martyr acts and inventory lists and pilgrims' guides that provide our earliest accounts of the history of the church at Rome, more and more bone gatherers like Lucina appear, though none quite as spectacular and influential as she. They are always women. The young virgin Viatrix collects the bodies of her brothers Simplicius and Faustinus—flung off a bridge—from the shallows of the Tiber and buries them on the lands of the matron Generosa at the sixth milestone of the Portuan way.[3] A matron named Hilaria gathers the bones of Daria, a vestal virgin converted to Christianity, after she is immured.[4] The wealthy widow Cyriaca provides a burial space for the martyred saint Lawrence.[5] Octavilla gathers up Saint Pancratius's body to bury in her own lands by the Via Aurelia.[6] The devout matron Cecilia gathers the bodies of her martyred husband and her brother-in-law, Valerianus and Tiburtius, and takes them to her own land.[7] Pope Damasus (366–384 CE) recounts how a noble lady, Lucilla, translated the sacred relics of the martyrs Peter and Marcellinus from relative ignominy on Rome's Via Ardeatina to a "more suitable place" off Via Labicana, Rome's cemetery known as *ad duas lauros,* "by the two laurel trees."[8] Church records and legends—for some *are* fictions—preserve scores of similar tales of women and bones and burials on women's lands.

What do we make of this pattern? In one important sense, the bone-gathering motif harkens back to the ends of the four New Testament gospels, where the sole narrative function of a group of women—differently constituted in each gospel—is to provide Jesus with a proper burial.[9]

The women come to anoint Jesus's body, to tidy up the areas in front of his grave, to make sure the tomb hadn't been violated, to grieve. They are resigned to the reality of death. They cannot hope for the Resurrection, because they are mired in the conviction of death's inevitability. Even the unnamed woman of the Gospel of Mark who comes to anoint Jesus's feet and head in preparation for his death has it wrong: she sees only the descent of the flesh into end, only body that must be prepared, not its possibilities for Resurrection. She is a symbol for faithful devotion, but not of hope and belief and full understanding.[10]

The gospel stories of Jesus's mourning women—and these early Roman Christian accounts of women bone gatherers—make inherent sense to us, because we assume that women are somehow more profoundly of the flesh and more directly connected to the cycles and rhythms of life. We see them as natural caretakers, the first to mourn, and the ones who mourn most deeply. In the vast range of Christian art, perhaps the only scene more moving than the sight of Jesus's mangled, lacerated body hanging from the cross is the *Pietà*, the limpness of Jesus's corpse spilling over the lap of his sorrowing mother. We perceive the connection between women and death as so natural that we scarcely stop to see what it might conceal. Why does Mary Magdalene go to Jesus's grave to grieve, but the male disciples to receive the revelation of the Resurrection? Why is it Lucina, of all people, who takes Paul's body tenderly to her own lands or sees to the decent burial of a flayed and decapitated pope? And why does the importance of the women bone gatherers end just there, with their having fulfilled their limited role in Christian stories as mourners and caretakers of the dead? Who, after all, tells us that women were assigned this role, and only this one? How was it that we come to remember—and in the case of Lucina, even forget—the early Christian women of Rome as mourning women?

If we move past the "naturalness" of a woman gathering the body of a dead saint to bury it and think instead on the meaning of this action in its historical context, we see something different. The phenomenon of Rome's bone gatherers reveals the importance of Roman Christian women as female patrons—*patronae*—of the church. Scholars of the ancient world have certainly recognized the importance of lay patronage in culture making.[11] Robin Lane Fox, a British historian of Rome, observes: "The motives and achievements of these donors were central to the civic culture within which Christians lived. It was they who financed the amenities of life and from them civic culture was delicately suspended."[12] Lane Fox speaks here of the pagan *men* who established the civic infrastructure that enabled the social networks and religious organizations of the city to flourish. But pagan women—barred from most other forms of public political and social engagement—could be equally generous in their civic beneficence. And following their example, female patrons of Christianity could also become powerful custodians and arbiters of meaning, of the holy.[13] Just as Mary Magdalene's presence at Jesus's tomb made her the first witness to the Resurrection and thus (to some) the foremost of the apostles, so does Lucina's donation of her lands for burial—and her status as owner of Paul's bones—make her one of Christian Rome's first bearers of the holy.

Medieval historian Patrick Geary has challenged us to think of the bones of saints, apostles, and martyrs not just as sacred objects but as commodities in the economic world of late antique and medieval Europe. Bones are unique; they are simultaneously people and things.[14] The roles and status of late ancient and medieval women in this trafficking and commodification of people as things have not received the attention they might. In a culture in which wealth was inherited and goods acquired by purchase, theft, or gift, wealthy women could be formidable allies to a pope—or equally formidable adversaries. This book, then, is partly about the vital—yet largely hidden—role of women as religious and economic agents, commodity brokers in the spiritual marketplace that was the newly Christian city of Rome.

But let us return to our bone gatherer Lucina. If we seek to learn more about her, we immediately meet with some puzzling elements to her story. She appears in ecclesiastical records again and again. In a fifth- or early-sixth-century martyr text called the *Passio Sebastiani*, she fishes up the body of its hero, Saint Sebastian, a soldier from the first cohort of Praetorian guards, from the sewer into which it had been thrown.[15] In this account, Saint Sebastian himself appears to her in a vision and spurs her on, begging to be buried *ad catacumbas, iuxta vestigia apostolorum:* in the catacombs, next to the remains of the apostles Peter and Paul.[16] The year, we learn, is 290 CE, under the long persecution of Rome's next-to-last pagan emperor, Diocletian. But here, a problem of logic emerges: by that time—according to our accounts concerning Lucina's burial of Pope Cornelius in 253 CE—Lucina had *already* moved Paul's body to the Via Ostiensis.[17] But there is no mention of this event in the *Passio Sebastiani*. As far as its author was concerned, in 290 CE the bones of the apostles still resided in the catacombs off the Via Appia. And in another martyr account, the *Passio Processi et Martiniani*, it is Lucina, again, who transfers the bones of Processus and

Martinianus to her land.[18] But Processus and Martinianus were the legendary jailers of Peter and Paul at Rome's Mamertine prison, and the setting for this *passio* is the late first century, the age of Jesus's own eyewitnesses and apostles. In the final reckoning, Lucina appears in no fewer than eleven ancient sources. Each time, she appears as a bone gatherer. But the sources disagree on whose bones she collected and when precisely she lived. Apparently, she was alive, gathering bones, in the first century, and still alive, gathering bones, two hundred years later.

Perhaps, then, Lucina never existed. At least one historian of late ancient Christianity, Kate Cooper, dismisses her as a "pious fiction."[19] If this is the case, what of her sister bone gatherers, the women whose acts of generosity and piety laid the physical foundations for Rome's cult of the saints, the women patrons of Christianity who donated their time and their lands? Some of these certainly existed. In the town of Velletri, not far from Rome, archaeologists have unearthed a dedicatory stone dating to the fourth century stating that a woman named Faltonia Hilaritas had founded a Christian cemetery there.[20] The inscription, at the very least, should make us wonder if women bone gatherers were merely literary inventions. Unfortunately, archaeological evidence itself is generally opaque; in the absence of supporting literary or epigraphical sources, we cannot tell from excavating a cemetery who, definitively, founded it. Faltonia Hilaritas left us a dedicatory inscription—but it is the only one.

On the other hand, many of the bone gatherers have very suspect histories. For example, the wealthy bone-gathering matron Lucilla, who moved the bones of the saints Peter and Marcellinus, seems to be but a variation on Lucina. Kate Cooper calls her, in fact, Lucina's literary twin or *Doppelgänger*.[21] And as for Lucina's legend—that she moved Paul's bones in the 240s CE to her own lands on the Via Ostiensis—we know from earlier sources that by the year 200 CE Paul's bones were venerated at a small shrine called a *tropaion* on that road.[22] Perhaps Lucina lived much earlier than the 240s and had moved Paul's bones to her land sometime before ecclesiastical historians noted the *tropaion* in 200 CE. Or perhaps—just perhaps—she never existed at all.

The question of whether Lucina ever really existed is of vital importance to understanding the nature of early Roman Christianity generally and the role of women in Roman Christianity specifically. It is not a question easily answered; nor can we be sure either way, given the state of the evidence. If we look for evidence for women's activities as influential patrons of the early Roman church, no source preserves this better than visual and archaeological sources. This book tells the story—or really, the stories—of these lost and forgotten women. It takes seriously the possibility that fictive characters like Lucina might conceal real women such as Faltonia Hilaritas who inspired these narrative re-creations. And it looks to a set of sources different from those that scholars conventionally read (or write about) to illuminate and amplify their lives: the visual, archaeological, and epigraphical sources that preserve vital evidence for women's history, activities, piety, and influence in early Christian Rome. The relevance of these sources for reconstructing ancient women's lives is only just beginning to be recognized. In 1985, the scholar Margaret Miles was the first to emphasize their significance:

> If we were, for the moment, to put all of our historical literary texts back on the shelf, to shelve even our knowledge of them, and to reconstruct a history of Christianity on the evidence of visual texts alone, we would see immediately that from the earliest Christian images there is a continuous depiction of women and the development of subjects and themes based on the experience of women.[23]

Miles is absolutely correct, though perhaps not daring enough. If we were to "shelve" our knowledge of literary sources and turn only to the neglected visual evidence, we would still have only a partial, imperfect picture of ancient history. To round out that picture, we must dare to read all extant sources together, remembering all the while that they were in some sort of meaningful—though often implicit—dialogue with one another. But that is not all I have done here; I have often pushed beyond or through the sources to bring to bear the full weight of my knowledge of the ancient world, and to explore largely unknown territory concerning what the lives of individual women were like. There are no fictions in this book, but the reader will come across something akin to feminist midrash—that is to say, like some Jewish feminist theologians, I want to sing stories of these lost women's lives. I want to write these women back to life. This process involves not just listening and looking intently, but engaging the imagination, reconstructing, drawing connections, making assumptions, looking again, walking and rewalking through a space, actively wondering and pondering, holding these women's bones in my hands, and sitting in front of their images for many, many hours.

I have endeavored to make this book *experiential*—that is to say, I am primarily interested in what late ancient Roman women experienced in their lives and how they thought about themselves. To do this is not merely to pore through documents and to look at pictures; it's also about, I believe, experiencing and re-creating for readers what late ancient Rome was like and what ancient women likely saw, thought, felt, and lived in the city's dark, private spaces. Each chapter of this book, then, highlights not just one or two "lost" women, but also a specific place. These places can be seen—indeed, experienced—today, and I have spent much time in them all. I hope readers of this book will go to Rome and will stand in front of Veneranda's image or Turtura's fresco or the Velata's grave to ponder these women and their places deeply, whereas they might before just have passed by, unseeing.

Although nearly two millennia separates us from the lost women of ancient Rome, I remain convinced that their lives can become more vibrant to us if we pay attention to the experience of seeing what they left behind for us to see. For this reason, I have delved into theoretical work on the history of response and have been most engaged by scholars (especially art historians) who are less concerned with ancient brush or building techniques than they are with the question of viewer-centered responses to art.[24] Those who commissioned a catacomb painting, I assume, were less concerned with artistic technique than they were with conveying information. We can work backward from the catacomb painting to try to figure out what that information was. There are plenty of clues to help us: we can compare similar paintings; we can understand that painting in relation to the space that houses it, or consider the painting in its fullest social and cultural context. After that work has been done, we can try to bring in an understanding of our own responses to a painting in a space. What do we see, and why? What colors the way we see, and how is that likely to be like or unlike what an ancient viewer saw, or what an ancient *patrona* of art and architecture intended?

In telling the story of these lost and forgotten women, this book grapples with the problem of powerful women for the early Christian church in Rome. It explores why—as the church grew in power and influence—women came to be most valued within specific, narrowly defined social roles and why, for the most part, real women came not only to be marginalized but to be rendered virtually invisible. There is no simple tale here of the oppression of women. There is a tale to be told, but it is one of the church's creation and manipulation of collective memory and of subtly shifting perceptions of women and femaleness in the process of Christianization. It is about the process of recollection and remembrance and the role of seeing in the construction of institutional memory. I am interested in instances in which real women were sometimes "made male" in ecclesiastical and scholarly perception—like the women of some catacomb banquet paintings who are later repainted as unambiguously male figures, as I discuss in chapter 4. Not uncommonly, we find that women were simply obliterated through the process of male-centered remembering, made absent in the face of overwhelming evidence for their active presence in a variety of early Christian roles. By the time that Lucina and her bone-gathering sisters appear on ecclesiastical imaginative horizons during the fifth and sixth centuries, they are no longer anything but mere literary refractions of real, influential women who once marshaled their considerable resources into a church that gave them no other avenues for their active agency in shaping the notions of "tradition" that would come to form the backbone of Catholicism.

This book is not a sweeping history of the Roman Catholic Church, nor even of women in the history of Catholicism. Instead, I focus on only a handful of "case studies" of forgotten women, most of whom lived within the same span of around a hundred years (ca. 250–350 CE), all within the city of Rome. I have imposed these chronological and geographical limits on the mass of historical sources that remain from a period that historians call "late antiquity" (or, more recently, "late ancient Christianity")—that is, the late third to the eighth centuries—because such narrow focus makes this book feasible; otherwise, it would be a far bigger task than I might hope to complete in a single, readable volume. It also zeroes in on a century when Catholicism began to take shape in earnest. The conversion of the emperor Constantine in 312 CE initiated a new era for the church. But recently, scholars have acknowledged that a good part of the shaping of a newly Christian Rome had to do with the efforts of the city's people and their own competing visions of Rome as a new City of God.[25] The fourth century, then, witnessed the success of the papacy over rival factions of Christians in the city—a victory that came, in no small part, from its strenuous efforts to create and manipulate Christian historical memory. *Catholic* self-identity—and *Catholic* concepts of "tradition"—began to stand for *Christian* self-identity and tradition as a whole. It is also a century in which the roles of women in the church begin to coalesce into forms different from those previously seen. It is the age that witnesses the rise of the virgin and the martyr, the age in which powerful Christian widows are limited and censured, and the age immediately prior to the rise of women's monasticism, the first proponents of which were drawn—almost implausibly—from a tight circle of Roman aristocratic families. Those women—the ascetic aristocratic women of late-fourth-century Rome—have been much discussed.[26] Their immediate predecessors, however, have not. It is to these women that I turn my attention.

To find the lost women of third- and fourth-century Rome, one must look in unexpected places. As I've noted, historians traditionally turn first to textual sources. This inclination reflects our training as historians and our own comfort with reconstructing history from text. But the written sources for women during this time period have been read and reread countless times in the past few decades; they get us only so far. There are remarkably few of them, and the evidence they yield is invariably from the upper classes. To find nonelite women, we need to look elsewhere. The best place to look, as it happens, is at archaeological sites, which in this case are the burial places of Rome: the catacombs. This is because death provided the only opportunity for hundreds of thousands of otherwise unknown Roman women or their loved ones to leave some sort of physical record of their existence. This record may be a grave or the body itself; it may be an epitaph or a portrait. Most of the material remains we have from the late Roman period are, in one way or another, products of commemorating the dead. To cite a figure from only one type of evidence, fully 75 percent of the hundred thousand or so inscriptions left by the Romans, chiseled into stone or marble, are tombstones. Properly used, they represent an untapped gold mine of information about ancient women. Remarkably, no single book exists that examines women's lives in early Christianity based on the material and physical evidence that women left behind, whether it be a tomb, an epitaph, or a funerary image. This book moves in the direction of filling that lack.

It must be said, however, that visual, archaeological, and epigraphical evidence from Rome's Christian catacombs rarely preserve authentic women's voices. What this type of evidence *does* provide is some limited but fascinating evidence for what women were doing, how people (men and women) wanted to preserve women in memory (and which aspects of their identity were important to preserve for memory), and what was important for people outside the most powerful circles of Rome's ecclesiastical and aristocratic elite to remember and show about themselves and the women in their families. It is important to remember that these sources, too, are refracted through lenses of both class and gender; they represent male obsessions with commemoration and status at least as much as they do women's own lives and self-representation. Despite all this, however, they do often show women's activities differently—and in different proportion—to what we find in the church's official textual record. The reason for this is partly one of scale—catacomb art and inscriptions were simply too prolific for the church to expend much energy on. Second, commemorative art, tombs, or inscriptions for ordinary women were not public statements issued by the church that might be read by outsiders. In that sense, they were not "official" documents crafted to shape public response. Thus this book reads together some of those official textual sources from the period with this visual and archaeological evidence to find, highlight, and ponder the women of the third and fourth centuries. It aims to interrogate our evidence anew— not just with suspicion, but with more knowledge of alternative visions and voices.

Many people are interested today in what ancient women's lives were like and what opportunities women had. Some scholars have offered an attractive, even inspiring image of how these ancient women were our sisters in emancipation, paving the way for the historical and political struggles of women today.[27] These scholars are not necessarily wrong. Women's roles in the early church were in marked decline from the first to the fourth centuries. It is indeed possible to massage the ancient sources to show women in the roles of leaders, priests, men's equals, but only if we ignore evidence from the third and fourth centuries. Lest this book disappoint those seeking powerful Christian women priests, I answer that the "lost women" in this book, although they did not exercise the sort of power that we use to define terms like "successful" or "independent" or "leader," nevertheless actively participated in forms of power and authority. They were women with agency—rallying their sometimes substantial financial resources to participate actively in the dominant discourses of religion. Furthermore, they left records of this participation: monuments, inscriptions, and images of themselves.

I've elected to start our visits to Rome's lost fourth-century women not with a Christian but with a young pagan freedwoman (that is, a member of something like the "middle class") who lived in the third century. I'm interested not so much in what she believed, but in things more visceral—in what her death tells us about the way that Romans thought about important things, from marriage and women's bodies to how to carry on when people we love die. Chapter 2 delves into the mind and heart of an anonymous freedwoman of the mid-fourth century who kept to her ancestral rites in a Christian Empire even as she buried her Christian daughter. The example of the woman I have named "Proba" alerts us to the challenges that women faced to exercise religious agency in a patriarchal social structure (particularly nonelite women, whose options were more limited than were those of their elite sisters)—and the considerable ingenuity with which nonelite women carved a small but sure place for themselves within the late Roman world. In chapter 3, I look at the same woman's own grave and compare her distinctive use of visual rhetoric with that of her contemporary and social equal, a Christian woman buried at the Catacombs of Priscilla. I see both these women—however different their religious convictions and daily lives—as simultaneously engaged in genuine efforts to portray themselves as learned and active participants in the culture of fourth-century Rome. Their poignancy, for me, lies in the degree to which their efforts were in vain.

Chapter 4 explores one of the jewels of early Christian art and architecture, the Greek Chapel in the Catacombs of Priscilla. Its famous image of a meal scene has been one of the most controversial in early Christian art, if only because different factions of scholars and viewers have invested so much in their debate over whether its participants were women. I use the meal scene painting to speculate on what seems to me clearly an example of women's sacred space. Chapter 5 visits the grave of Veneranda, a fourth-century Christian woman who venerated Saint Petronella, the legendary daughter of Saint Peter. Chapter 6 investigates two more spaces: the church of the matron martyr Saint Cecilia in Rome's Trastevere district and the church of the virginal child martyr Saint Agnes, far beyond the city's walls to the northwest. Both chapters contrast what late ancient Christian women *did* with how they came to be remembered. The final chapter, 7, reads the pontificate of the highly controversial pope Damasus (366–384 CE) as a triumph not just of Catholic unification and clarification of vision and purpose, but a concerted effort of an all-male institution to deliberately masculinize Christian Rome—to the detriment of Rome's female patrons and sponsors.

To understand what the women featured in this book might mean for us today, and to learn what we can from them, we need to take women such as the pagan "Proba" (chapters 2 and 3) or her Christian contemporary Veneranda (chapter 5) on their own terms, and to seek to understand them in their full historical context. This is to listen attentively to what they have to say, to elevate them from historical obscurity, and to avoid distorting them into our own models of idealized womanhood. We're left with a complicated, lively world—full of equally complicated and lively women.

CHAPTER I

DEATH TAKES A BRIDE

What joys await your new lord,
What pleasures during the dark night
or even at midday. But the day is waning.
Come forward, new bride.
—Catullus, "Wedding Hymn"

Nights like these, my little sister grows,
Who was here and died before me, so small.
Many such nights have passed since then.
She must be beautiful by now. Soon someone
will wed her.
—Rainer Maria Rilke, "From a Stormy Night, #8"

I n the spring of 1889, Rome was all abuzz with the discovery of yet another ancient relic: a beautifully carved marble sarcophagus, still sealed with heavy lead clamps, buried in the heavy blue river clay of the Tiber's banks. It was inscribed only with a woman's name: Crepereia Tryphaena. The coffin had been unearthed by workmen building the foundations of the monumental Palace of Justice on the west side of the Tiber, across from the final resting place of the first imperial family, the Mausoleum of Augustus. The workmen had been having trouble with the foundation. The particular site that had been infelicitously selected for the Palazzo was outside the ancient Campus Martius, outside the *pomerium* or enclosure that girdled the city's most sacred ground, and outside the circuits of the ancient Servian walls—thus, in an area where ancient burials had been allowed. So full of tombs, and thus so friable was the land on which the Palace of Justice's foundations were to sit, that it collapsed in on itself often during the course of building; in fact, the Palazzo shifts and cracks so threateningly still today that it sits empty along the banks of the Tiber, a giant white elephant, too dangerous to occupy fully.

The workers, coming across the sealed sarcophagus, alerted the authorities immediately and cordoned off the area from the eyes of the curious. The privilege of breaking the seals on an ancient tomb fell to only a few men in the city, the *Conservatori*, who conducted their archaeology—and, in effect, their plundering of antiquities to the city's Capitoline collections —in secret, or at least far from the "excited and sometimes dangerous crowds."[1] But this particular sarcophagus was far too heavy to be spirited away. The marble itself weighed a substantial amount, and over the course of the centuries, water had dripped in through a tiny fissure in the lid, filling the coffin with groundwater from the Tiber. Everyone recognized, too, that the sloshing of water inside the box whenever it was moved could only disarrange its contents. Thus one of the city's most celebrated archaeologists, Rodolfo Lanciani, was quickly dispatched to the Palazzo di Giustizia to be the first human being to gaze on Crepereia Tryphaena's remains in nearly two millennia.

Lanciani was a heavy-set, intense man with a passion for antiquities and an immense knowledge of the topography of ancient Rome. A photograph from 1894 shows him dapper in a bowler hat and handlebar moustache, holding court for a bevy of enthralled ladies.[2] At the time of the discovery of Tryphaena's sarcophagus in the Tiber's mud, he was only forty-four years old, but he had already been secretary of the city's Commissione Archeologica Comunale for seventeen years. He also held a prestigious chair in Roman topography at La Sapienza, the University of Rome, which he would continue to hold until two years before his death in 1929. First and foremost, Lanciani was a scholar, not a man of the cloth. Unlike most of his peers at the Vatican's Commissione di Archeologia Sacra—the other major group involved with trawling the city's ancient heritage—Lanciani had never taken a priest's vows. But one wonders what competition he must have felt with the Vatican's black-clad clutch of archaeologists, as each vied to re-own and reinterpret the city's ancient past.[3]

In front of a crowd of construction workers and fellow scholars early on the morning of May 12, 1889, Lanciani ordered the brass seals clamping the sarcophagus shut to be broken. The workmen eased aside the heavy stone lid. Straining to get the first glimpse of the coffin's contents, Lanciani and the crowd drew a collective gasp of amazement. Inside the box lay the skeleton of a young woman, her long thick brown hair swirling around her body in eddies of crystal clear water that submerged her. Such a prodigious quantity of hair she appeared to have that Lanciani and his colleagues, intrigued, ventured closer for a further look. But it was not hair that curled and drifted around her; it was long strands of algae that had adhered to her skull, a river crown of mud-green tresses floating to the surface, glossy in the warm May light. "The news concerning the prodigious hair spread like wildfire among the populace of the district," recalled Lanciani in his *Pagan and Christian Rome*—a sort of auto-archaeological memoir—"and so the exhumation of Crepereia Tryphaena was accomplished with unexpected solemnity."[4]

Lanciani's description of Tryphaena's body—at once clinical and subtly emotive—is worth repeating here in full:

> The skull was inclined slightly towards the left shoulder and towards an exquisite little doll, carved of oak, which was lying on the scapula, or shoulder blade. On each side of the head were gold earrings with pearl drops. Mingled with the vertebrae of the neck and back were a gold necklace, woven as a chain, with thirty-seven pendants of green jasper, and a brooch with an amethyst intaglio of Greek workmanship, representing the fight of a griffin and a deer. Where the left hand had been lying, we found four rings of solid gold. One is an engagement ring, with an engraving in red jasper representing two hands clasped together. The second has the name PHILETVS engraved on the stone; the third and fourth are plain gold bands. Proceeding further with our exploration, we discovered, close to the right hip, a box containing toilet articles. The box was made of thin pieces of hard wood, inlaid *alla Certosina,* with lines, squares, circles, triangles, and diamonds, of bone, ivory, and wood of various kinds and colors. The box, however, had been completely disjointed by the action of the water. Inside there were two fine combs in excellent preservation, with the teeth larger on one side than on the other: a small mirror of polished steel, a silver box for cosmetics, an amber hairpin, an oblong piece of soft leather, and a few fragments of a sponge. The most impressive discovery was made after the removal of the water, and the drying of the coffin. The woman had been buried in a shroud of fine white linen, pieces of which were still encrusted and cemented against the bottom and sides of the case, and she had been laid with a wreath of myrtle fastened with a silver clasp about the forehead. The preservation of the leaves is truly remarkable.

Tryphaena's grave goods were detailed and unusual enough to reveal, if not the circumstances of her death, the circumstances of the last part of her short life.[5] She lived in the third century, perhaps during the tumultuous reign of Caracalla (212–217 CE) or maybe a bit earlier, under Septimius Severus (193–211 CE). Like most inhabitants of third-century Rome, she was not Christian. Nor was she, despite the quality of her jewelry and her finely carved marble sarcophagus, of noble birth. Her first name was Greek, not Roman, indicating that her family had once served as slaves to the noble Creperei family before the Creperei granted one of Tryphaena's ancestors his freedom. And so Tryphaena was from an evidently wealthy family of Roman freedpeople, part of an emergent "middle class" granted citizenship during Caracalla's reign, despite their immigrant and servile origins. Freed-people were known for their elaborate, often ostentatious graves, as they strove to make an enduring mark on a culture where status was conferred by high birth, not by money or aspirations.[6]

The items buried with Tryphaena give us precious clues about her life. At the time of her death, she had been newly married. We know this from her red jasper ring, which was carved to look like the *dextrarum iunctio* "joining of the right hands" rite that sealed a marriage. Many similar, authentic Roman *dextrarum iunctio* rings still circulate on the antiquities market, slipped off the skeletal fingers of long-dead brides by enterprising grave robbers. A second ring had been engraved with the name of her fiancé Philetus. The two plain gold bands were wedding bands, to be worn on the third finger of her left hand; in fact, we have the Romans to thank for our "modern" custom of wearing gold wedding bands on the ring fingers of our left hands. But if Tryphaena had been married, she was evidently not married for long. Her husband, or more likely her parents, chose to have her buried in her wedding gown, wearing on her head not the wreath of laurel with which Romans customarily crowned their dead, but a wreath of myrtle—the traditional headdress of the Roman bride, the *corona nuptialis*. Even more poignant was their choice to include Tryphaena's doll, toward which Tryphaena inclined her head in her stone bed. It was not merely because Tryphaena was still in her early teens when she died but because, on her wedding day, a Roman girl customarily offered up the favorite doll of her childhood to the goddesses Venus or Diana.[7]

In the case of Crepereia Tryphaena, we do not know if hers was a story of triumph over disease and disfigurement and her fiancé Philetus was her true love, or whether she was merely a pawn in a larger game of social positioning. My guess would be the latter, less romantic scenario. Evidently from a wealthy family, she would have had a substantial dowry to offer—no small incentive for a man in a social class where the transmission of wealth could come not from earning money but only from dowries and inheritances. What she lacked in physical soundness and beauty, in other words, Tryphaena may have made up in other more practical assets.

Tryphaena's unexpected emergence into the modern era marks her as unusual, but her life was probably much like those of countless other third-century Roman women interred in less desirable bits of land. Three similar ancient burials have been found around Rome, all dating between the first and third centuries. A twenty-year-old Roman woman was found in 1887 near Vetralla, just outside Rome. In 1954, a very young girl was found at Mentana (ancient Nomentum), dressed in a white tunic embroidered with gold thread, adorned with gold jewelry. And in 1964, roadwork on the Via Cassia unearthed the burial of a girl of perhaps eight, with her earrings, necklace, ring, and ivory doll.[8] These burials stand out for two reasons: first, burials (as opposed to cremations) were unusual in Rome's first two centuries and so, presumably, had to have been both unusual and special at the time; second, all these girls were buried with substantial amounts of jewelry—an ostentatious, even wasteful practice. Why Romans apparently confined such lavish burials to female children or young women remains a mystery. I suspect that they stood apart for their pathos; theirs, perhaps, was the most tragic death: Death's abduction of his child bride on the cusp of her earthly wedding.

A Roman man mourned the death of his daughter in ways deeply shaped and limited by his culture's obsession with masculinity. At least, the genre of consolatory literature—in which one man publicly extolled the virtues of another man's deceased wife or daughter—belonged resolutely to the male conceptual domain. We still possess one striking example of a nubile Roman daughter's tragic death seen from this quasi-public male perspective. The first-century author Pliny the Younger (63–113 CE) penned a letter to his friend Marcellinus upon the untimely death of his friend C. Minicius Fundanus's daughter, Minicia Marcella. She was not yet thirteen. She had died, like Tryphaena, just before her wedding—the invitations had already been sent out. Pliny marvels to Marcellinus at the composure with which Marcella bore her fatal illness: "She complied with all the directions of her physicians; she spoke cheerful, comforting words to her sister and her father; and when all her bodily strength was exhausted, the vigor of her mind sustained her. That indeed continued even to her last moments, unbroken by the pain of a long illness, or the terrors of approaching death" (*Letter 54*). Above all, the Fates had made a cruel joke of their decision to tear Marcella away from her own wedding:

> Oh, melancholy, untimely loss, too truly! She was engaged to an excellent young man; the wedding-day was fixed, and we were all invited. How our joy has been turned into sorrow! I cannot express in words the inward pain I felt when I heard Fundanus himself (as grief is ever finding out fresh circumstances to aggravate its affliction) ordering the money he had intended laying out upon clothes, pearls, and jewels for her marriage, to be employed in frankincense, ointments, and perfumes for her funeral. (*Letter 54*)

Given the substantial power of this letter, we can imagine the mix of Lanciani's emotions when he came upon, in another one of his famous excavations, Marcella's grave, unviolated for seventeen hundred years, high on the summit of Rome's Monte Mario.[9] Her simple epitaph records only that she lived twelve years, eleven months, and seven days.

Tryphaena, like Marcella, is known best from her death. Let's consider, for instance, her sarcophagus; it has a few things to teach us. The word "sarcophagus" derives from two Greek words, *sarx* or "flesh" and *phagein,* "to eat" or "to swallow" (as in our English loan-word *esophagus*). The word was not merely metaphorical. The stone or marble boxes Romans used for burial were literally flesh-eaters. The best sarcophagi were imported from the eastern Roman Empire and were said to have contained a high percentage of lime, which may have hastened the decomposition of a corpse. In the first century, the Roman naturalist Pliny the Elder (23–79 CE) spoke wonderingly of sarcophagi as marvelous flesh-eaters that consumed every part of a corpse but the teeth (*Natural History* 36.131). This was not exactly true, yet Pliny's account does reveal that for first-century Romans the sarcophagus was something of a menacing novelty. Romans had routinely cremated their dead until, for reasons scholars continue to dispute, burial came to replace disposal by fire.[10] When precisely this switch from cremation to inhumation happened is difficult to pinpoint, but by the time of Emperor Hadrian (117–138 CE) no more *columbaria* (hypogea built to house cinerary urns) were built. Bodies were buried next to cinerary urns in older columbaria, and then in hypogea or underground chambers.[11] By the time of Tryphaena's burial, setting bodies in elaborately carved stone coffins had become more customary for Romans of means and good taste. These sarcophagi were cozied into niches within tombs or hypogea, or they were sunk directly into the ground, as in Tryphaena's case.

After the second century of the common era, sarcophagus burials appear to have been favored by the middle class. The very poor had little choice about what would happen to their remains; their bodies were simply thrown into massive pit graves or *puticuli* (from the Latin *putescere*, "to stink," and *putor*, "stench"), many of which lie today under the busy intersection of Via Carlo-Alberto and Via Mazzini in downtown Rome by Termini, the city's main train station. A mixture of human and animal corpses and ordure were tossed in the pits together "in revolting confusion," as Lanciani put it.[12] So vile was this mixture that when Lanciani excavated the *puticuli* nearly two thousand years later, he had to give his workers frequent breaks to escape the nauseating stench produced by the "uniform mass of black, viscid, pestilent, unctuous matter" that had once been the city's poorest inhabitants.[13] On the opposite end of the scale, the emperors, along with their immediate family, appear to have been cremated up until the fourth century, at which point Constantine decided to break with ancient tradition and have himself interred in an elaborate mausoleum along with the collected remains of all of Jesus's twelve disciples. In Tryphaena's day the imperial families still aspired to the glory of the pyre, and cremation was reserved for them alone.

The third century, during which time Tryphaena's family buried her, marked a transitional phase in Rome's mortuary customs. Freedpeople and aristocrats had themselves interred, choosing sarcophagi as finely carved as they could afford to hold their mortal remains. Ideally, there would be a symbolic connection between the subject of the carving and the patron buried within. Some of the finest sarcophagi bore mythological friezes cunningly suggesting a relationship of analogy between their human inhabitant and some ancient hero; thus hundreds of coffins of men display condensed myths of Dionysius, Meleager, Achilles, or, if its inhabitant were female, Atalanta, Niobe, Alcestis, or Persephone—forming what art historian Richard Brilliant calls a "metonymous tableau" between ordinary human existence and the life of gods and heroes.[14] A myth didn't need to fit the life of the deceased point-by-point. Romans felt free to pick and choose from a relatively broad palette of themes: a girl's life cruelly cut short (Persephone); a mother in agony for her dead children (Niobe); a proud, independent daughter who prizes her virginity and spurns her suitors (Atalanta). These mythological sarcophagi betrayed Romans' predilection for tragic stories of death and disaster, as well as a new fondness for drawing analogies between the circumstances of their own lives, qualities, and premature ends and those of mythic heroines and heroes. Metonymous tableaux were visual and visceral more than learned and precise; for instance, many sarcophagi that husbands commissioned for their wives show Penthesileia's corpse draped in the arms of her sorrowing lover, Achilles. In the story from which it is drawn, Achilles himself had slaughtered Penthesileia—but this is hardly to say that the Roman men who chose to place this scene on their wives' coffins were all guilty of murder. Elements of the myth, as well as the true "back story" of a death—were alternately expressed and suppressed through the heroic, tragic visual moment of a grieving husband bearing his wife's body home.[15]

The historian Paul Veyne once found in Roman carved sarcophagi a way for Romans to aestheticize death to escape its bitter melancholy.[16] But it could equally have been the case that sarcophagi, like any other element in the commemoration of the dead, gave melancholy free rein. The public display of sorrow—and sarcophagi were for the most part public objects, meant to be displayed and admired—still draws new participants into its spectacle; it neither suppresses nor exorcises grief. Who could fail to be moved by the recollection of Alcestis's self-sacrifice for her husband, or Niobe's shuddering sorrow at the death of her children, or by any human life cut short? Indeed, the very nature of inhumation gave new opportunities for personalizing, perpetuating, and broadcasting grief. Roman cinerary urns for human ashes were relatively small, and although sometimes beautifully adorned with stone garlands or vines, were too tiny to be covered with mythological or figural scenes. The switch to inhumation presented much bigger, even "life-sized" spaces to tell some sort of story about the deceased on the sides of these massive stone boxes. This, perhaps, is why we still occasionally find human ashes and bone fragments in some sarcophagi; the families who cremated and then interred their loved ones may have appreciated the extra space on the outside of the sarcophagus to tell a good tale of pathos and tragedy. In the public world of the Roman Empire, there was no such thing as death without story—not for those with even a little bit of money. As the Harvard classicist A. D. Nock once wryly observed, "Death was a serious business; and yet it called for any magnificence which you could command."[17]

Not all sarcophagi were adorned with mythological scenes that made thinly disguised allusions to the virtuous and tragic lives of their inhabitants. Many sarcophagi circumvented symbolism and directly recorded snippets of the ordinary lives of those whose bodies they devoured: the ag-

onies of birth, the sweet joys of a child's first steps or games, the last lingering moments of a wake. These moments were prosaic, not heroic. And yet,
even here, aesthetics were pressed into the service of broadcasting virtue,
inviting spectators and sympathizers. Such was Tryphaena's sarcophagus,
simply carved with her name and scenes from her own death.[18] Although
they are generally more common for adult men than for women, a few other
spectacular instances of these *vita humana* sarcophagi for young women remain. In the British Museum, a small sarcophagus is carved with a girl's
lying-in-state. She lies on a funerary bier not flat on her back, but turned
three-quarters toward the viewer. The oddness of the angle makes it clear
that we are her intended audience; she is lying this way not because the
scene accurately conveys reality, but because we are meant to see her fully.
A young woman—presumably a slave—arranges the pillow at her head,
and a cat sits curled beneath the bier. The girl looks peaceful, as if only nap-
ping. On either side, though, sit her parents, their bodies contracted in grief.
They mirror each other in pose, heads covered, each with a hand propping
up a heavy, inclined head. Though their grief is palpable, it is constrained by
the measures of symmetry and balance in the overall composition. Still, it's
difficult to move one's gaze off the dead child for long.

But let us not forget about Crepereia Tryphaena. Did she suffer an untimely
and sudden death on her wedding day? How did she die? Her skeleton reveals that she suffered from scrofula, an ancient form of tuberculosis to
which Romans assigned an ugly word that means "brood sow," probably
because of its ability to disfigure its victims by swelling their necks
grotesquely. Tryphaena's skeleton, Lanciani tells us, still bore the marks of
scrofular lesions and twisted rib bones; she was evidently ill for long enough
for the disease to attack her skeletal development. And so Tryphaena likely
lived her short life in substantial pain and misery, but she did manage the
one achievement that was the goal for all Roman girls: to find and marry a
husband of her own.

From her birth, a well-born Roman girl's existence was oriented toward
her marriage. It was the most important social contract in the vast network
of social relations that governed the empire. Indeed, the first Roman emperor, Augustus, had instituted a series of laws that made marriage a legal
obligation for all citizens. These marriage laws remained in place until the
first Christian emperor, Constantine, struck them down in 320 CE. The
pressures of mortality—and of producing a viable heir before death's grip
snatched away the mother—necessitated early marriage. After the age of

twelve, a girl was considered legally nubile, that is, marriageable; after fourteen, she was considered fully a woman.[19] This is why Crepereia Tryphaena moved in one swift night from a child who played with dolls to a myrtle-crowned bride, expected to participate fully in the requirements of a sexual existence. She may not even have begun menstruating; it was not considered a condition for marriage or for sex. In fact, some Roman doctors maintained that regular sexual intercourse before the onset of menses made menstruation easier when it did start, usually around the age of fourteen or fifteen. But the famed doctor of the second century, Soranus, disagreed; he cautioned fathers against marrying their daughters before they had had their first period. If the fathers were impatient, he recommended for the girls a regimen of massage, gentle exercise, a daily bath, and a special diet to induce menstruation "spontaneously and if possible before the first experience of intercourse" (*Gynecology* 1.5.25).

Even Soranus believed that it was necessary for girls to begin their sexual lives as soon after puberty as possible, so as to head off later health problems, including weight gain from something called the *plethora*—an unhealthy physical condition brought about by an overabundance of unreleased sexual energy—or other female troubles, including hysteria (a physical or psychological condition brought about by a rebellious uterus, which in Greek is called a *hustera*) or even just an improperly functioning uterus, which many believed might abandon its ordinary placement and wander unmoored around the body, causing a host of problems (*Gynecology* 1.25).[20] Because a sexual life, furthermore, could only licitly unfold within the bonds of marriage, a teenage girl who felt sexual desire was surely ill-raised and headed for disaster. It was safer for all concerned, Romans believed, to rein in the appetites of desire early and within the confines of conjugal life.

If male Roman doctors were grievously misinformed about the nature of the female body and the technical details of sexual intercourse and fertility, women themselves were not necessarily more enlightened. Needless to say, married at such a young age, Roman girls came to the marital bed with virtually no knowledge of sex—let alone any practical experience in such matters—except (and this we do not know with any certainty) what they may have heard from their mothers, nurses, or older married sisters perhaps only just the night before their weddings. In the fourth century, the church father Jerome warns the young virgin Eustochium against keeping the company of married women, lest she overhear details of married life inappropriate to virginal ears (Letter 22). Leaving the state of chaste virginity required some gentle coaxing of the new bride on her wedding night, perhaps even by the gods themselves. A striking painting of the second century CE known as the *Aldobrandini Marriage* now resides in the Vatican Museums. In it, a timid bride sits tremulously on her wedding bed, while the goddess Persuasion tries to help her steel her resolve. The god Hymen, meanwhile, reclines at the end of the bed, half hidden in the room, waiting to claim the part of the young virgin's body that is consecrated to him. His body is youthful and taut with sexuality, his posture a masterful combination of languor and impatience. The scene plays out the emotional reality of a young bride's wedding night: her innocence was not to last long. Her new husband may not have deflowered her on their wedding night out of respect for her chastity, but he made up for his self-restraint by sodomizing her instead.[21] How women—girls, really—felt about this, we have no idea. And we also have little idea about how a young bride like Tryphaena must have felt on her wedding day. It's difficult to imagine that she had much affection for her new husband, a man she may scarcely have met and certainly never spent time with alone.

How did Roman women die? By modern standards, Romans were often unhealthy and usually died early.[22] In a world in which the life expectancy lay between twenty and thirty years, death threatened at any age.[23] Rome's shockingly high mortality rate reflects what we presume must have been a very high occurrence of infant deaths; it does not mean that people reached the natural end of their lives in their mid-twenties. If you survived infancy and childhood, you stood a fair chance (not a good chance, mind you) of reaching adulthood. Statistical analyses of ages of death recorded on pagan and Christian epitaphs from Rome reveal that children between the ages of one and five faced the greatest danger from premature death, with the number declining gradually after age five but still remaining high between ages six and twenty.[24] After the age of twenty, death rates declined sharply.

But there was no age at which an individual could be safe from disease or epidemic. Death from pulmonary tuberculosis, for instance, peaked in one's early twenties. In fact, tuberculosis likely claimed most of its victims between the ages of five and twenty, if we compare data from early-twentieth-century China.[25] But it wasn't just the well-known diseases such as tuberculosis that threatened the Roman populace. Afflictions such as minor infections or inflammations—merely a nuisance to us in an age of antibiotics—could well become fatal in a hot, crowded, and filthy city, particularly in the summer months, when mortality rates peaked.[26] July to October were Rome's most dangerous months of the year, felling otherwise healthy people in only a few days. Bacillic dysentery, too—easily controlled in the modern world with antibiotics—ran amok through urban populations. Consider that in Egypt up until the twentieth century, dysentery had a fatality rate of between 20 and 30 percent.[27]

To make matters worse, Rome's urban conditions precipitated other waves of epidemic that ravaged the populace, including cholera, typhoid, and malaria. Its location along the low-lying banks of the murky Tiber made the city a prime breeding ground for water- and mosquito-borne diseases, particularly endemic falciparum malaria—a form of malaria characterized by high fever, jaundice, renal dysfunction, and pulmonary edema.[28] Most of the city's inhabitants were captive, possessing neither the money nor the opportunity to escape to healthier climes.[29] Then, too, Roman military incursions had rendered Rome sicker: they imported to the city from farther east epidemics against which the population had no natural immunity. The worst of these scourges to arrive in Rome, beginning in the second century, was smallpox. We don't know how many it killed, but one classicist estimates that there were as many as three hundred thousand deaths in the year 166 CE alone—equaling one third of the city population or several thousand deaths a day.[30] Comparative figures from early-twentieth-century China indicate that smallpox could bring with it a child mortality rate of up to 40 percent.[31] Even the comparatively less fearsome measles could cruelly ravage an unsuspecting and unprepared population. The historian William McNeill in his masterful *Plagues and Peoples* (1977) identifies measles as the scourge that virtually leveled Rome in a massive pandemic in the 250s and 260s CE—just after Tryphaena's death.[32] As painful as a life with scrofula must have been, Tryphaena was lucky to have escaped measles. To a population with neither natural immunity nor vaccines, measles can be more terrifying than smallpox. The World Health Organization recorded 30 million to 40 million cases of measles in 2001, and 745,000 fatalities as a result of measles.[33] Although measles primarily attacks the young, its effect on women—the primary, housebound caregivers of Rome—would have been profound, and its effect on pregnant women deadlier still.

Who died earlier or more often in Rome: men or women? The question is actually fairly difficult to answer. In the United States in 2003, women had a statistical edge over men, living on average 80.1 years to men's 74.8.[34] The ancient world was different. Parents' preference for male children apparently encouraged the abandonment, even murder, of female infants, although our evidence for this is not directly from the city of Rome.[35] Walter Scheidel, a demographic historian of Rome, speaks of "femicide and 'benign neglect'" of female infants and children, which may have lessened women's chances of survival.[36] It was not that Roman parents casually throttled or exposed their daughters at birth—this is a monstrous misconception of Roman attitudes—but that girls' nutritional and psychological needs were considered to be very different from boys'. The physician Soranus, for instance, thought that girl babies were constitutionally tougher, thus they could get by with less (*Gynecology* 2.21.48). Roman governmental schemes for rations and food allowances to poorer families allotted girls a smaller share of food, in the mistaken belief that female children required less nourishment than male children.[37] Girls were not exactly starved to death, but they may have suffered malnourishment and malnutrition more frequently. This, in turn, may have affected fertility levels. There is some evidence that these were not particularly high. In the first century, the Roman poet Martial composed an epigram in honor of a woman celebrated at Rome's famed Secular Games (celebrated, ideally, only once a century) who gave birth to five sons and five daughters—all of whom were still living at the time of her death. There's no wonder Romans sought to honor her: Scheidel puts the odds of ten siblings outliving their mother at a thousand to one.[38]

In 1963, the demographic historian Henric Nordberg analyzed more than eleven thousand Christian epitaphs of third- and fourth-century Rome. By collating information on ages of death recorded on these tombstones, he determined the average age at death for men as 23.8 years, but only 22 for women.[39] Scholars set to the task of explaining the apparent disparity. Beyond the hypothesis that female children were disproportionately killed or left to die, the simplest explanation—though by no means the only one—is that death resulting from failed pregnancies, including the consequences of an abortion gone terribly wrong, skewed the numbers against women's favor. The historian Gillian Clark suggests that abortions in Rome were not uncommon; doctors used "purges, diuretics, massage, violent exercise, and hot baths after drinking wine." She continues, "If these ancient equivalents of gin, hot baths and jumping off the kitchen table failed, there seem to have been back-street abortionists using the knitting-needle technique."[40] The Christian apologist Tertullian describes in blood-curdling terms a third-century doctor's abortion kit along with techniques for partial-birth abortion (*A Treatise on the Soul*, 25); it is far from clear, however, whether the source reflects actual medical practice. We must keep in mind that heirs were valued (the production of heirs was the entire point of marriage), and a woman of means would have little reason to abort a child unless it were a product of adultery. If she undertook such a thing without her husband's consent, she put her own life at risk not just from a septic procedure but also from Roman law, which stipulated death for adulterers and wives who destroyed a fetus (since it was, technically, a husband's property). If, on the other hand, her husband had forced her to abort, such willful destruction of an heir could only be the result of the husband's suspicion that the child she carried was not his. A woman of lesser means, on the other hand, would hardly have been able to afford the expense of a doctor. She would likely have employed some sort of herbal or medicinal abortifacient. The mortality rate for these "cures" would have been significantly lower than for surgical, late-stage abortions. Romans realized that infanticide (by way of exposure) was preferable to partial-birth abortion, because it carried less risk for the mother and less shame for the family. Death from abortions gone wrong, then, was likely not a major cause of the shorter life expectancies of Roman women.[41]

But what about death in childbirth, or as a consequence of childbirth? Romans rarely noted cause of death on tombstones, and death resulting from childbirth was never stated as such. We can only *infer* that it happened. Among Christian epitaphs, for instance, Henric Nordberg notes the tombstones of eighteen people who died within the first few years of marriage. Of these, at least sixteen were women. Nordberg surmises, "It would surely not be too much to assume that most of these died from some sort of illness connected with or resulting from pregnancy.[42] Certainly, pregnancy and delivery would have put women at significant risk. In 2004, six hundred thousand women across the globe died in childbirth. Of these, 99 percent were in underdeveloped countries. In Sierra Leone, Mozambique, Somalia, Rwanda, and Ethiopia, women have about a one in seven chance of dying in childbirth.

How does a woman die in childbirth? The leading cause is hemorrhage or loss of blood, followed by toxemia (sudden maternal hypertension or high blood pressure), and embolism—a blood clot that travels through the system until it blocks an artery. Less common, but still alarmingly possible, is rupture of the uterus and septicemia (blood poisoning). In the United States in the 1920s, about 40 percent of maternal deaths resulted from sepsis, including infection following illegal abortions. We could project a similar figure for Rome, where the need for a sterile environment was neither known nor met. Caesarean sections were performed in Rome, though usually on women who had already died in labor, to free the struggling newborn from the womb. "Lifestyle factors" also contributed to fatal pregnancies: the ingestion of alcohol, inadequate intake of food, poor nutrition, and emotional and physical stress. It is little surprise that Roman women of all classes visited the shrines of a wide variety of deities who oversaw pregnancy and safe delivery: Carmenta, to whom pregnant women would come to offer sacrifices at her double altars (one to Postverta and one to Prorsa, who oversaw regular and breech births); Eileithyia and Leucothea; Juno Lucina (Juno associated with light) and Juno Opigena (Juno who gave help, *ops*, to women in childbirth); Deverra; Diana; Alemona; Nona; Decima; Partula; Antevorta; Egeria (whose name was interpreted as from *e-gerere*, to "push out [a child]"); Fluonia; Uterina; and Intercidona.[43] Three statues of the Nixi Di, the "straining gods" that together oversaw labor, stood before the shrine of Minerva on the Capitoline hill, right in the very heart of the city.[44] Roman historian Peter Garnsey wisely draws our attention to the meaning behind the proliferation of childbirth deities; it reflects "a community engaged in a desperate battle against hostile powers to reproduce itself."[45]

It was also the case that women could die simply from having too many children too often. Here, we have no direct evidence from women of the lower and middle classes but some compelling data from elite Roman women. The emperor Marcus Aurelius's wife Faustina gave birth to thirteen children, including two sets of twins. Eight of these died while still children; not a single one made it past forty. Faustina herself died, exhausted and heartbroken, at forty-six, grandmother to none. From the seventeenth to the fortieth years of her life, Faustina endured between ten and twelve deliveries. Walter Scheidel calculates the mean interval between her children's births as only 2.1–2.6 years. He also provides evidence for other such short intervals among Roman imperial women: Julia, the wife of Marcus Agrippa, had five children in nine years. Vipsania Agrippina, the wife of Germanicus, gave birth to nine children in twelve or thirteen years. She might have had more but for Germanicus's death only a year or two after the birth of baby number nine.[46] The emperor Arcadius and his wife, Aelia Eudoxia, had five children between 395 and 404 CE with an interval between pregnancies that ranged from three to seventeen months. The shortest interval that Scheidel notes is for Heraclius's wife Eudocia, who gave birth to their daughter only nine months after their marriage and to a son ten months after that. She died three months after her son was born.[47]

Baldly, then, evidence from the late Roman Empire suggests that women simply died more frequently and younger than men. Even the material remains seems to support what the literary and epigraphic sources hint. Sir Moses Finley, a historian of Rome, cites the case of a family hypogeum in continuous use during the second and third centuries containing the bodies of sixty-eight wives buried by their husbands, but only forty-one husbands buried by their wives.[48] But the apparent outpacing of dead wives to dead husbands may point to cultural factors, not startlingly high mortality rates for women. Women were commemorated more often than men not because they died more frequently or tragically young, but because men commemorated women for a male public culture. These might be wives, or they might be daughters; in a sense, it hardly mattered. The elaborate verbal, literary commemoration of the dead—whether in an epitaph, a funeral oration, or a letter of consolation, was a male-oriented, male-dominated genre.

A highborn man's struggle to come to terms with a daughter's premature death is captured poignantly in the letters from the Roman orator Marcus Tullius Cicero (106–143 BCE) upon the death of his daughter, Tullia, in childbirth at age thirty-two. By that time, Tullia had been married three times. She was first engaged at twelve, married at sixteen. Her first husband, much older than she, had died when she was only twenty-two. She married again at twenty-three, divorced her second husband—carefully selected for her by her father—at twenty-eight, and chose her third husband, Dolabella, herself a year later. But even this marriage of love had not been a happy one for Tullia; her father disapproved and considered intervening to end the marriage. Dolabella had been caught having an affair and besides, Cicero was straining to meet the dowry installments. At the time of her fatal pregnancy, Tullia found herself separated from a husband once more.

Although Cicero had not approved of his daughter's third marriage, it is clear from his correspondence to his friend Atticus that, at her death, he fell completely to pieces:

> I have isolated myself, in this lovely region, from all human conversation. In the morning I hide myself in the dense, impenetrable forest and don't emerge until nightfall. Next to you, solitude is my best friend. My only form of communication now is through books, but even my reading is interrupted by fits of weeping. I resist as best I can these urges to cry, but I am not yet strong enough. (Letter 248, in Cicero, *ad Familiares* 4.5)[49]

We have a letter from another of Cicero's friends, the orator and jurist Servius Sulpicius Rufus, who sent the orator an elegant letter of condolence: "When I received the news of your daughter Tullia's death, I was indeed as much grieved and distressed as I was bound to be, and looked upon it as a calamity in which I shared" (Letter 554, in Cicero, *ad Familiares* 4.5). But despite overtures toward empathy, Servius soon retreated into a "pull-yourself-together" sort of a stance. Given the tragedy that was the end of the Roman Republic, the death of a woman paled: "Are you so very sorrowed if we lose the frail spirit of one poor little girl?" He tried to put his friend's grief into context:

> She lived as long as life had anything to give her; that her life outlasted that of the Republic; that she lived to see you—her own father—praetor, consul, and augur; that she married young men of the highest rank; that she had enjoyed nearly every possible blessing; that, when the Republic fell, she departed from life. What fault have you or she to find with fortune on this score? (210–211)

Rufus's words fell on deaf ears, no doubt. He would have done better to heed the words of the fourth-century rhetorician C. Julius Victor: *pauculis consolare, quod ulcus etiam, cum plena manu tangitur, cruentatur* ("Consolations should be brief, because a sore is bloodied when touched with the whole hand") (*Ars Rhetorica*, 27).

After the passing into death's dominion of a woman like Tryphaena in the third century, the Roman ritual process of death would have been, so far as we know, the same for women as for men. The family gathered around the deathbed; someone stooped to bestow a last kiss to catch the soul, the eyes of the corpse were closed (*oculos premere*), and the dead was called upon loudly by name to ensure that death had taken hold (*conclamatio mortis*). The body was taken from the bed and placed on the floor (*deponere*)—a reverse ritual from the *tollere* or *suscipere* of the *paterfamilias* that initiated a child's entrance into family life;[50] it was a symbolic return to Tellus, mother earth. Her corpse was then washed, anointed, dressed, and shrouded in wool or linen by her slaves and nurse—Roman mothers had less of a "hands-on" relationship with their children than we might expect. It might have been embalmed, in a fashion, or else it would have been sprinkled with lime to hasten its decomposition. It was then buried—quickly. A group of Christian epitaphs from third- and fourth-century Rome giving both dates of death and dates of burial indicate that in the majority of cases, people were buried within a day of their deaths—two days at the most.[51] Rome's close heat and humidity precluded any sentimental lingering over the dead. That's not to say that the proper obsequies, and an attractive death scene, did not have their time and place. So Tryphaena's family probably refocused their energies, transforming her wedding feast into her funeral. Her dowry likely went to pay her funerary expenses, as Roman law stipulated. No expense appears to have been spared: a beautifully carved sarcophagus was ordered, featuring a frieze of Tryphaena's funeral. And then her coffin was set directly into the muddy earth in a plot that, fifteen hundred years later in this city "constantly being rewritten," seemed to someone to be just right for a Palace of Justice.

The Roman funerary process for private families we know virtually nothing about, especially women's funerals; all our surviving textual evidence is for noblemen, who would have been laid in state on a specially constructed bier and surrounded by family, friends, supporters, and hired mourners. But it does seem—from the visual evidence, at least—that grief leveled any perceived differences in the way that the dead should be honored. Women and men were given the same obsequies, the same elaborate funerals, and the same time lying-in-state.[52] This process of lamentation was ritually prescribed, controlled, and limited by law. One carved relief from the early-first-century tomb of the noble Haterii family shows a lying-in-state scene for a dead woman. She lies on her back in the open atrium of her house, garbed in an elaborately draped *stola*. Rings adorn her left hand, and she wears on her head a wreath of flowers. Her couch is set high on a platform, surrounded by torches, incense burners, and candelabra. Mourning women accompany the body, some of whom have loosened their hair in a potent show of grief; they all beat their breasts in sorrow. Of this retinue of women, some are paid mourners, some are family members, and others are slaves, formally freed as a condition of the deceased woman's will. But this Haterius woman was from one of Rome's finest families. The funerary process for a third-century young freedwoman we know scarcely anything at all. Would her body—or her effigy or portrait—have been carried through the streets, as we find in the funerals of Roman nobles? Would her husband have taken her portrait bust to bed with him to console him in his solitude, as we hear that bereaved wives sometimes did? Would she have had professional mourners, the *praeficae?* We only know that as a last stage in the process of caring for her body even after death, Crepereia Tryphaena was arranged prettily in her coffin with her best jewelry, her wedding head-dress, and her dolls. It made a touching, even heartbreaking, tableau.

Lanciani gives us another remarkable story about dead women that merits repeating here: the discovery of the body of an embalmed woman of the high empire, perhaps a century or two before Tryphaena. Unlike Try-phaena, however, the embalmed woman was not Lanciani's own discovery —though he was much interested in her story and records its details in his *Pagan and Christian Rome*.[53] The date was April 16, 1485, during the pon-tificate of the Renaissance pope Innocent VIII. Monks from the diocese of San Francesca Romana, excavating an area of tombs near the Via Appia south of the city, happened upon a mausoleum with a sarcophagus embed-ded into its foundations. The heavy sarcophagus was socked in concrete so thoroughly that it had proved too bothersome for tomb raiders to rob out. Besides, the lid was sealed with molten lead. Thus, rather unusually, after more than a thousand years, the burial inside was still intact. The monks ex-cavated the sarcophagus and broke its seals, perhaps moved by a reverential passion for Rome's antiquities that seemed—at least in Lanciani's mind— to characterize much of the city's populace. This time, the most curious el-ement of the event was an unfamiliar odor that wafted up from the unsealed tomb—"like turpentine mixed with myrrh." The mysterious scent burning in their nostrils, the monks moved in closer for a look.

What they discovered inside the Via Appia sarcophagus was even more remarkable than the body of Crepereia Tryphaena. Lanciani transcribes de-tails from the diary of Antonio di Vaseli, an eyewitness:

> The body seems to be covered with a glutinous substance, a mixture of myrrh and other precious ointments, which attract swarms of bees. The said body is intact. The hair is long and thick; the eyelashes, eyes, nose, and ears are spotless, as well as the nails. It appears to be the body of a woman, of good size; and her head is covered with a light cap of woven gold thread, very beautiful. The teeth are white and perfect; the flesh and the tongue retain their natural color; but if the glutinous substance is washed off, the flesh blackens in less than an hour. Much care has been taken in searching the tomb in which the corpse was found, in the hope of discovering the epitaph, with her name; it must be an illustrious one, because none but a noble and wealthy person could afford to be buried in such a costly sarcophagus thus filled with precious ointments. (295–296)

A second contemporary account, from a letter by Daniele da San Sebastiano, dated 1485, confirms di Vaseli's details, though with slightly less scientific disinterest:

> One of [the coffins] contained a young girl, intact in all her members, covered from head to foot with a coating of aromatic paste, one inch thick. On the removal of this coating, which we believe to be composed of myrrh, frankincense, aloe, and other priceless drugs, a face appeared, so lovely, so pleasing, so attractive, that, although the girl had certainly been dead fifteen hundred years, she appeared to have been laid to rest that very day. The thick masses of hair, collected on the top of the head in the old style, seemed to have been combed then and there. The eyelids could be opened and shut; the ears and the nose were so well preserved that, after being bent to one side or the other, they instantly resumed their original shape. By pressing the flesh of cheeks the color would disappear as in a living body. The tongue could be seen through the pink lips; the articulation of the hands and feet still retained their elasticity. (296–297)

Such a sensation was the discovery of the embalmed woman that "the whole of Rome, men and women" flocked to San Francesca Romana to view the body. After some deliberations, the Conservatori moved her body to the Capitoline hill in the center of the city. (A German eyewitness remarked rather cynically: "One would think there is some great indulgence and remission of sins to be gained by climbing that hill, so great is the crowd, especially of women, attracted by the sight.")[54] The body lay on display for three days before exposure to the air and the crowds took its toll. Apparently, someone had removed the protective layers of ointment that covered the body, and soon enough the exposed skin of the corpse's face and hands turned black. The body quickly putrefied. And then, in the middle of the night, the body disappeared from view. No one knows what happened to the body of the unnamed woman whose burial was so carefully preserved and arranged. Rumors circulated that the pope, irritated by and perhaps jealous of the attention that the lifeless and blackening corpse of an ancient pagan woman was garnering, ordered the Conservatori to secretly bury her body at the foot of the city walls beyond the Porta Salaria. Others held that Innocent had merely ordered the body to be ignominiously dumped into the Tiber under cover of darkness, so as to stifle the superstitious curiosity of the populace.

The visual, verbal, and even corporeal commemorations of women that I have included here, as tender as they may be, should not make us lose sight of the fact that we are left behind with the sentimental memory portraits carefully composed by men, in letters and laudations and inscriptions and carved into stone for other men, circulating in a world of men. Witness the lengthy verse epitaph of the fourth-century senator Vettius Agorius Praetextatus to his wife of forty years, the noble Aconia Fabia Paulina. After an introduction to Paulina's immaculate character, Praetextatus addresses her directly:

> Paulina, partner of my heart, source of modesty, the bond of chastity and pure love and trust born in heaven, to whom I have entrusted the secrets enclosed in my mind; a gift of the gods, who join the marital bed with loving and chaste bonds; with the devotion of a mother, conjugal grace, the ties of a sister, the modesty of a daughter, with the great trust by which we are jointed to friends; by the experience of years, agreement in religious devotion with faithful yoke and simple harmony, helper of her husband, industrious, cherishing him.

We are moved by such tender words, lovingly arranged. But then Paulina herself is made to speak:

> The luster of my parents gave me nothing greater than that I seemed even then worthy of my husband. But the name of my husband, Agorius, is all splendor and distinction, who born of proud stock has adorned country, senate and wife with the integrity of his mind, his character and industry, and has attained the supreme pinnacle of virtue. (*CIL* 6.1779, trans. Lewis/Reinhold [1990], 370–371)

Paulina, from her grave, can speak only of her husband, and not of herself.

Tryphaena's body, though probably arranged by the women around her, weeping as they dressed her in her wedding gown to meet her unexpected new husband Dis Pater in the underworld, drew pathos as the tragic sacrificial victim in a man's world of arranged marriages and tender child brides. And our nameless embalmed woman, glistening naked under her blanket of myrrh and aloe, stirred not only sentimental romanticism; she became a macabre, erotic draw for her male observers so many centuries after her death. We wonder at them, as they in turn wondered at the still-moist fullness of the dead woman's lips and tongue and the languor of her heavy lidded eyes, and as they wrote of her beauty that still moved them, though more than a millennium old.

Just as men had their own visual and verbal discourses of grief, they had their own models of a "good death," starting perhaps with Plato's death of Socrates, or even earlier, in the heroic warrior deaths of Homer's *Iliad* and *Odyssey*.[55] The death of a philosopher was a measured, reasoned death faced with courage and resolve in the company of disciples and friends, the Socratic death. The death of a warrior, the *kalos thanatos*, embraced notions of both valor and pathos—a discomforting mix that gave birth to Aristotelian notions of tragedy: the simultaneous experience in the viewer (or reader) of two opposite emotions that, taken together, engendered a new experience Aristotle called *catharsis*. But there was no model of a good death for women to follow. What would that have looked like, after all, and how might it have been different from that of men? Four hundred years of Roman literature preserves for us no woman's deathbed scene.

Let us consider, for a last moment, all the ways a woman of the third century in the prime of her life could die: disease, neglect, accident, suicide, abuse, or childbirth gone wrong. Chances are, most of those deaths would not have been met with a husband hovering tenderly nearby. Women— even married women—most likely met their deaths at home, in a world of women. For them, the image of a man's controlled death, a reasoned surrender of the soul in the presence of his disciples and compatriots, would have been almost unimaginable. Instead, the only model for women's death was the "untimely" death (even when men die young in battle, it is not untimely, because it is heroic, sacrificial, redemptive, glorious). Women, in dying young, are wrenched out of the domestic roles for which they were destined, into an otherworldly existence where they can only rest as incomplete: not yet brides, not yet mothers, not yet adult, not yet finished with their toil. Both Christians and pagans were apt to use on women's graves a line borrowed from Virgil's *Aeneid: Abstulit atra dies et funere mersit acerbo* ("Cut off by a black day and buried in an untimely grave" [6.426–429]).[56] Those who died unmarried were prevented from fully crossing over into the dark underworld, and so remained in the liminal space of the restless shades. This notion of an unfinished life harkens back to ancient Greece, where we first find poignant epitaphs for lost virgins and brides. Classicist Richmond Lattimore, in his compendium of Greek and Latin epitaphs, cites two from the third century BCE: "Weep for my untimely, unwedded youth" and "In my bridal raiment, for I died untimely."[57] The theme continues in Greek drama, where heroines such as Antigone, Polyxena, and Iphigeneia all perish just before their weddings. As the heroine Antigone laments:

> Soon the sun will go out
> On a silent, starless shore
> And Hades will step aside.
> He will give me to Acheron,
> Lord of the pitch-black lake,
> And that bridegroom's cold hand
> Will take my hand in the dark.
> (Sophocles, *Antigone* 810–813, 87)

By the Roman period, the untimely dead became known by the Greek term *ahoroi:* those "taken out of their hour [to die]." Death out of one's time brings an eternal restlessness that breeds not only a sense of pathos, but also a primal fear: that the dead will be angry and shiftless, vengeful in their incapacity to finish in their life after death what they had started in their short lives. It is this sense of "not being finished yet" that made Romans bury new brides in their wedding dresses, or with their dolls, or as carefully preserved objects of love and desire. It is the same sense of not being finished yet that provoked the ritual restraint of women's corpses—the tying up, dismembering, and ritual preventing of the dead from returning to finish what they had started. Women's graves could be hedged in by curses, like this one from third-century Rome:

> [I curse] Rufa Publica: her hands, her teeth, her eyes, her arms, her belly, her tits, her chest, her bones, her marrow, her belly, her legs, her mouth, her feet, her forehead, her nails, her fingers, her belly, her navel, her cunt, her womb, her groin. I curse Rufa Publica on these tablets.[58]

One of Rufa Publica's jilted lovers carefully inscribed these bitter words on thin metal sheets, then slipped them into the cinerary urn that held her last remains. Not all memory glorifies the dead; sometimes it excoriates them or seeks to obliterate them.

The classical anthropologist S. C. Humphreys connects ancient Greek concepts of a good death with concepts of virtue, for there is virtue in the heroic death.[59] The word "virtue" itself stems from the Greek word for man, *vir*—thus "virtue" is connected etymologically with male power and behaviors. A death on the battlefield epitomizes masculinity, the power of maleness, the power of the *vir*. Although less connected with concepts of aggression, the death of the philosopher still emphasizes the (male) power of control—a control that extends even into trumping the chaotic powers of death, in that the philosopher deliberately chooses the moment of his death. But womanly virtue is passivity, compliance, subordination. Death takes her, but the paradox remains as to whether or not it is virtuous to accede. The answer to the paradox is that death itself becomes gendered male. Death is the husband for whom the young bride is arrayed; death, too, is the rapist who carries away the maiden into the dark underworld.

CHAPTER 2

PROBA AND THE PIGLET

Sprinkle wine and perfumed oil on my ashes,
O guest, and add balsam to the red roses.
My unmourned urn enjoys perpetual spring.
I am not dead; I have only changed worlds.
—Ausonius (310–395 CE), *Epitaphs*, #31

T he problem was the pig. The woman had had enough problems in these years of famine, upheaval, and misery. The gods were angry as it was, and clearly, the woman had things to do to recalibrate her relationship with them. The sacrifice of a vigorous young piglet would be a fine place to start. The unknown woman—grave robbers would efface the last traces of her recorded name, so let's call her Proba, a fine late-Roman name—was the proud keeper of ancient traditions: a pagan in a newly Christian empire, and a devotee of the goddess Ceres. But Fortuna had been cruel to Proba: she was also a recent widow and the grieving mother of a dead child, a daughter snatched away in the bloom of her youth. Now she was left with two dead family members, angry gods, and ancient rites that had to be performed under daunting circumstances.

The pig was a problem because of Roman law and tradition. These ancient laws stipulated that for family members to cleanse themselves from the ritual state of pollution that came from contact with a corpse, a pig had to be sacrificed. This pig, the *porca praesentanea*, was sacrificed to Ceres, Proba's favorite goddess.[1] In fact, the sacrifice of the pig was necessary for a number of reasons beyond the cleansing of symbolic pollution. The act was mandatory, the legal responsibility of an heir; it had to be performed for an inheritance to be received. The sacrifice also transformed a place where a corpse lay—a tomb—into a sacred place, a *res religiosus*. Tombs themselves were not sacred until a body had been placed within them and the funerary rites carefully observed, including this slaughter of a pig.[2] The sacrifice also had to be performed—at least in part—in the presence of the corpse. Though Proba's husband, a pagan, likely would not have questioned this, their daughter—a Christian—may not have been so sanguine.

By the middle of the fourth century, sacrifices had become dangerous things to undertake. Constantine had banned nocturnal sacrifices, but prominent pagans lobbied to have areas of the empire excluded. In Rome, one could still honor the gods with sacrifices, provided one were cautious and discreet.[3] Proba, being a woman and thus technically ineligible to carry out the messy task of animal slaughter herself, might have been relegated to word-of-mouth arrangements and back-door dealings.[4]

And what was a pious mother to do, after all? Would she uphold ancient traditions—as one of the last "Romans of Rome"—and have a pig slaughtered in the Stygian gloom before her daughter's lifeless body? Would she simply do it herself? Or would she neglect ancient rites at the risk of forfeiting her own life, as her contemporary, the writer Festus, put it, so as to respect her daughter's religious faith?[5] Should she choose for her family burial vault a private hypogeum, where such rites might have been countenanced, or a private section of a public Christian catacomb, where the desperate squeals and wriggles of a pig destined to meet his Maker would have scandalized any Christians who caught wind of a blood sacrifice on Christian ground?

First things had to be first. Proba, a woman of means, set about procuring for her husband and daughter a final resting place. I imagine she wanted somewhere lovely—somewhere where her life could be revealed in all its tragic pathos, through pictures rather than clumsy words. Like any Roman, she would have wanted a place to which she could return each year at the annual days of commemoration for the dead, to pick up that tenuous thread of connection between her and her beloved departed family. And given the scale and grandeur of her graves, she apparently wanted something impressive, something in keeping with a life lived in interesting times.

The nameless woman I call "Proba" lived in the late Roman Empire, sometime during the perilous fifty years between the brief pagan "revival" of the Emperor Julian (361–363 CE) in an empire then "officially" Christian for nearly fifty years, and the sack of Rome in 410 CE. There is much about her that we no longer know: her name, her birth and death dates, where she lived, whom she married, who her friends were—all the precise contours of her life. Historians of ancient Rome face this problem of unknowing all the time; it is why general histories are written, of wars and politics or of the literary productions of elite men. In the case of the woman I have called Proba, we know her only from her own attempt to create and manipulate memory and tradition, to tell us what of her was the most important thing to leave for posterity. Proba chose a grave. In fact, her family's grave constitutes one of the finest examples of late Roman funerary art to have survived until today.

Proba purchased for her family, at considerable expense, space in an underground complex. The hypogeum lay a short distance beyond the Aurelian walls, along the Via Latina that runs southeast from the city. Like most roads leading out of Roman cities, the Via Latina was lined with tombs, sober reminders of death's proximity. All burials in the Roman Empire, by law, lay outside the city walls. As long ago as the fifth century BCE, this law had been inscribed on the tenth bronze tablet of the Twelve Tables, Rome's most ancient and hallowed law code: *hominem mortuum in urbe ne sepelito neve urito* ("no person may be buried or burned within the city [walls]").[6] With a population density greater than that of modern-day Calcutta, such a law made good, practical sense in an ancient *urbs*. As Rome expanded in the third century of the common era, the old Republican walls that girded the ancient city had to be replaced; the emperor Aurelius (270–275 CE) built sturdier walls encircling a much larger area. These Aurelian walls still stand today, their massive girth punctuated by fourteen monumental gates that mark the principal roads out of the city.

And so Romans used the lands directly outside the city walls as burial grounds, since the dead needed to be put somewhere, and since cremation was both too costly and, by the second century CE, too passé.[7] Those who had the money to buy up the prime real estate directly on the road constructed elaborate tombs, sometimes multistoried, modeled in the Greek style after houses for the living, or, more accurately, after temples. In fact, tombs—properly consecrated, of course—*were* temples, legally and literally.[8] Their *res religiosus* status ensured that tombs were as sacred as altars. Thus violations of tombs were serious offenses, and tomb violators were as loathed as murderers or necromancers. Clattering out of Rome in horse-drawn carriages, horses' hoofs striking black basalt paving stones, inhabitants of Rome gazed reverentially upon these temples of the dead as they passed along the major routes that led out from the city like the support threads of a giant spider's web.

So what sort of arrangements needed to be made after someone had died, in a world without funeral homes and morticians?[9] How did Proba go about finding a place to inter her beloved? In Rome, as elsewhere in the empire, funerary *sodalitates* "brotherhoods" or *collegia funeratica* (funerary, burial guilds) sprang up in response to the problem of death—or more specifically, the problem of burial in a city with generally weak social and familial networks and soaring real estate prices. To ensure a proper burial in a city with a shortage of space and high costs for mortuary care, men of modest means could join a funerary brotherhood, or *collegium funeraticum*, paying dues either in money or in goods to secure a place in a collectively owned and administrated burial complex.[10] These *collegia* took their names from adherence to a deity, or to their founders. Roman women could—and did—independently establish *collegia*. In the Galleria Lapidaria at the Vatican Museums, there remains an inscription of a guild, a *collegium quod est in domo Sergiae Paulinae* founded by a woman called Sergia Paulina, which met at her house.[11] But *collegia* that specifically convened to enable the burial of their members customarily excluded women, probably because women were banned from carrying out the animal sacrifices that were a necessary component of Roman funerary practice.[12]

The Christian church—first organizing itself into a formidable institution under Constantine's imperial patronage (306–337 CE)—also provided burial space for its members. Already by the third century, it controlled sprawling cemetery complexes outside the city, the Catacombs of Sebastian, Domitilla, Commodilla, Priscilla, and Callixtus. Christians opened these complexes, it seems, as the burial sites of *collegia funeratica*. Women were not excluded, partly because no one (male or female) had to perform animal sacrifices as part of Christian funerary process. The *collegium funeraticum* status, however, did give the church the right to exclude pagans and heretics.[13] Into the first category, of course, came Proba and her husband. As defenders of an increasingly diminishing and persecuted ancient tradition, their burial in Christian catacombs may or may not have been particularly welcomed. If pagans were not welcomed, it was the legal responsibility of the tomb owner to state so categorically; the *paterfamilias* or head of the family had the right to restrict or allow the burials of any others in the graves he had purchased within the catacomb grounds, provided the terms were made public and permanent. Such exclusionary clauses intended to keep pagans out of Christian burial chambers do in fact show up occasionally on epitaphs and tomb closures.[14]

Numerous Christian catacombs, however, preserve both Christian and pagan burials side by side, including the Catacombs of Priscilla, Domitilla, and Sebastian.[15] In the case of tombs with multiple owners—and often in catacombs this was the case—the law stated that a co-owner of the tomb could not be refused burial for having a different religious affiliation (*Digest* 11.7.41). Thus the Christian catacomb of Saints Peter and Marcellinus shared space with the pagan cemetery of the *equites singulares,* the imperial horse guard.[16] Pagan burials dated as late as 249 CE joined Christian tombs of the pious at the *memoria apostolorum,* the tomb shrine dedicated to Peter and Paul near the Via Appia south of the city.[17] Still now, under St. Peter's Basilica at the Vatican, Christians and pagans slumber together in third-century graves adorned with emblems of Jesus or images of the Egyptian god Horus. All these instances of "mixed" burial tell us that perhaps rather often, families of third- and fourth-century Rome were divided along religious lines, but also that we have no reason to imagine that this division was necessarily difficult territory for a family to negotiate.

Proba did not choose a Christian burial site for her family. Instead, she selected one of the dozens of private burial complexes that dotted the countryside. These private hypogea were smaller, more intimate, than the massive Christian cemetery complexes with their anonymous graves and miles of labyrinthine galleries. Such private hypogea were sometimes also attached to *collegia,* but more frequently, families established them for themselves, as well as for their slaves and clients. These private burial chambers were often elaborate, enduring monuments that required the mobilization of significant resources to construct. Death in Rome was a thriving enterprise. Tombs were bought and sold, traded, promised to progeny, and occasionally illicitly reused despite dire threats against postmortem squatting. A pagan grave from the Via Portuense warns that even on dark nights, someone is always watching:

> Sacred to the Spirits of the Dead. Aurelius Niceta made this [grave] for his well-deserving daughter Aurelia Aeliana. Beware, gravedigger, do not dig [here]! God's eye is great; beware, [for] you too have children.[18]

Another, from the Christian Catacombs of Sant'Agnese, wishes a more biblical fate on tomb violators:

> Come to a brutal end; be thrown from the grave and never resurrect! You will have the [same] fate as Judas, whosoever might violate this grave.[19]

Such contracts and curses were carefully but permanently incised on gravestones themselves. In other words, even in the world of the cata-

combs, death was not a charity but a business. Tombs were built and purchased by those who could afford posthumous display. In the end, it mattered little, in the world of conspicuous commemoration of the dead,
whether you were Christian or pagan, so long as you could afford to pay.[20]

The Roman dead were not just tossed in slag heaps, unless of course
they were very poor indeed, or if the crowd of corpses from a famine or
plague overwhelmed the labor and resources needed to bury them decently.
In 2006, Vatican archaeologists were shocked to come across over a thousand skeletons still garbed in elegant togas but stacked like cordwood in the
Catacombs of Peter and Marcellinus on the city's ancient Via Labicana—no
doubt remarkable testimony to the hasty disposal of bodies during one of
Rome's plagues or natural disasters.[21] Ideally, however, all burials had to be
duly noted and registered. Tombs in Rome fell under the highest religious
authorities in the empire, the *pontifices* or College of Pontiffs (*CTheod.*
9.17.2). The head of the college, the *pontifex maximus,* was the emperor
himself—a practice that continued through the Christian emperors until
one of them, Gratian, finally refused the office in 384 CE. All burials were
registered with the pontiffs, even into the Christian period; a letter of the
prominent Roman nobleman Quintus Aurelius Symmachus (340–402 CE)
speaks of their role in Rome as late as 385 CE (*Epistle* 2.36). The business
dealings were the work of *fossores,* or grave diggers, who became important
enough to the economic and religious structure of the early church that they
constituted, by the fifth century, a class of clergy, not merely drones digging
endlessly in the subterranean tunnels honeycombing the land outside the
city.

It's not clear why this woman I've called Proba chose this particular hypogeum on the Via Latina. It may have been close to her home. She may
have known of the *fossor* selling spaces there, or it may have contained the
bodies of people she knew—perhaps more distant members of her family.
It may have belonged to a *collegium.* She may have been impressed, upon
visiting the complex, by the quality and number of its paintings, which were
surely unusual. And, as a pagan woman in a Christian empire, she may have
appreciated that in this particular hypogeum, everyone's choice of religious
affiliation was respected even after death; at the Via Latina hypogeum,
pagans and Christians lay in adjoining rooms, each room decorated to reflect its owner's convictions.[22] At any rate, by the time Proba purchased and
commissioned space there, the hypogeum complex had already existed for
nearly a century and contained the bodies of nearly four hundred people.
And it was exclusive: one section—probably the last to be built—contained

the bodies of as few as eleven adults of considerable wealth and discerning tastes; these may have been Proba's relatives—some pagan, some Christian, just as her immediate family was.

Compared with the Christian catacomb complexes that together came to hold the remains of an estimated six million dead, the Via Latina hypogeum was tiny, tidy, and intimate.[23] At the woman's behest, two chambers were hewn out of *tufa*, Rome's soft brown volcanic soil, plastered over, and richly decorated with paintings that Proba herself commissioned—an ambitious "special order" that tested the strength of her excavators and the repertory of her hired artists.[24] But the results were spectacular, and she must have been very proud.

The Via Latina hypogeum holding Proba's family crypt was carefully dug following a logical and elegant plan of long vaulted galleries and thirteen individual family chambers or *cubicula* (from the Latin *cubiculum* or "little dormitory").[25] At the farther ends of the complex—the parts dug between around 350 CE, the long galleries seem to blossom into cubicula following a plan of considerable geometrical beauty and order. The complex was fortuitously rediscovered in 1955 under the crossroads of the Via Latina and the Via Dino Compagni.[26] Yet another great boom in urban expansion had seen the renovation of an apartment complex aboveground, and the contractors had sunk building supports directly through the catacomb, rudely puncturing its forgotten silence with concrete and steel. Luckily, someone alerted the Vatican, and the Pontifical Institute of Sacred Archaeology quickly dispatched its leading archaeologist and secretary, a bespectacled Jesuit by the name of Father Antonio Ferrua, to conduct excavations—though apparently not without drawing the ire of thwarted land developers. Such is often the liability of building the new upon the very ancient in Rome. Ferrua conducted painstaking excavations, assigning the catacomb's rooms letters of the Italian alphabet, from A to O. Proba's family reside in cubicula N and O, the last of the hypogeum to be dug, probably somewhere between 350 and 370 CE.[27]

The Via Latina hypogeum was started around 315 CE, in the wake of Constantine's violent accession to sole power. On October 28, 312, Constantine fought and vanquished his last remaining rival in the West, the emperor Maxentius, on the Milvian Bridge just to the north of the city. Many modern scholars have questioned the depth of Constantine's subsequent "conversion" to Christianity and his true commitment to the faith, but there is no question that he helped Christians to gain legal and social legitimacy.[28]

Such newfound openness or boldness of an openly Christian ruling class is reflected in the Via Latina hypogeum, which contains some of the most elaborate and therefore expensive wall paintings in an expanding corpus of Christian funerary art. The Christian crypts from the Constantinian period, Cubicula A, B, and C, were painted with finely rendered scenes mostly from the Old Testament: Moses leading the Israelites across the Red Sea; Jonah reclining; the sacrifice of Isaac; Job sitting in misery, his wife holding her nose against his stink. In these chambers were places for twenty or so bodies, although many more were added in the next sixty years, rudely cut into the painted scenes, or gathered in collective pit burials. Along the galleries more burial slots were cut into the walls, mostly those of children, each commemorated by brief epitaphs: "To Maximus, in peace, who lived for ten months," or "[Here lies] Proclus, who lived six years and twenty-two days. He was placed here on the third of the kalends of October."[29] The quality of these epitaphs, crudely carved on the backs of bits of pilfered marble, and the names of the children (Simplicia, Maximus, Proclus) mark these graves as those of the have-nots or *humiliores*, perhaps the slaves of those Christians buried in the more elaborate chambers. It is not clear if they were Christian too. It seems not to have mattered much.

If chambers A, B, and C in the Via Latina hypogeum were commissioned by Christians, then D, E, and F were commissioned by a mixed group of Christians and non-Christians, perhaps a few decades later in the mid-350s.[30] The sole person to be buried in Cubiculum E—in all likelihood a woman—lies beneath a lovely and evocative portrait of the goddess Tellus, Roman goddess of the earth. Tellus reclines on the ground with the relaxed ease of a goddess, swathed in dark fabric only from her waist down. A faint round halo glows behind her head. She raises her right hand as if in greeting, gazing off to her right. Beside her, an asp crawls along the ground, winds its way around her left arm, and snakes out toward her exposed breast. The provocative pose of the snake puzzled Father Ferrua; he suggested that the reclining female figure might be Cleopatra, choosing an asp's bite as her preferred death.[31] But Cleopatra in a Roman tomb didn't make a lot of sense. Others surmised that the image was meant to represent Isis.[32] But the recumbent goddess, Ferrua concluded, is surely Tellus.[33] Like other Tellus images, she lies upon the ground. She is surrounded by Tellus's attributes: the snake and long stalks of wheat and poppies. No Roman could have mistaken her for anything else, except perhaps the goddess Ceres, with whom she was often equated. Maybe it was the Tellus cubiculum that told Proba, a devotee of Ceres, that she had found the right spot for her family's final resting place. Maybe she was related to the woman buried under Tellus's image, or maybe they both belonged to a *collegium* loosely organized around Tellus's cult in Rome. In either case, they were some of the last prominent women in Rome to honor the goddess who had been revered in the city for a thousand years.[34]

In the middle of the fourth century, Rome was still a substantial urban center and was still—at least on the face of it—pagan. Contemporary gazetteers or *regionaria* give us a sense of how cosmopolitan it must have been; they list 28 libraries, 8 bridges, 11 public baths, 18 aqueducts, 9 circuses and theaters, 15 fountains, 80 golden statues, 74 ivory statues, 36 triumphal arches, barracks of army, police and fire brigades, 290 granaries and warehouses, 856 private baths, 254 bakeries, and 46 brothels. Its inhabitants occupied an astonishing 44,000 apartment buildings (*insulae*) and 1,790 private houses.[35] Nevertheless, these gazetteers capture Rome in a state of urban decline. By the middle of the fourth century, its population had diminished from more than a million to perhaps eight hundred thousand. The city had ceased to be the beating heart of the empire; only rarely after the third century did the emperor reside in the city for any length of time. After the death of Constantine, the new city he had established and christened with his own name, Constantinople, remained the administrative headquarters of the empire. Thus it was left to the members of Rome's ancient nobility, both pagan and Christian, to negotiate together the range of civic and religious duties involved in the care of their city and its people.

There was little in the fourth century to help draw the lines between what was a "Christian" civic duty and what traditionally Roman. In 323 CE, Constantine noted with concern that members of the Christian clergy had been compelled to carry out sacrifices by people "of different *religiones*" (*CTheod.* XVI. 2. 5). Willing or not, these bishops and presbyters could see the sense in obeying ancient Roman law and serving the religious needs of the populace. Perhaps, at that time, a Christian presbyter's sacrifice of a pig in the presence of a corpse would not have brought the opprobrium that it would fifty years later. But despite his voiced concern, Constantine ordered no campaign against the ancient traditions of Rome. Christian bishops and elders might still carry out sacrifices if required. The official cults of Rome continued as they had since the founding of the city, their priesthoods filled, though, with increasing difficulty. The ancient temples were maintained and repaired as needed for two more centuries. But by the 370s, some pagans may have feared that the writing was on the wall. In 382 CE, the emperor Gratian stopped imperial support for all non-Christian cults in the city. Special privileges for the vestal virgins and other priesthoods were revoked or abolished, and their lands were confiscated and put to new use. Whether Proba lived to see what for her may have been very dark days, we do not know.

It was in this atmosphere of civic transformation around the time of Constantine's sons and successors in 350 CE that Proba prepared a crypt, what was called in Rome a *sepulchra familiaria,* for her husband and, when the time came, for her own burial.[36] The purchase of such family vaults was commonplace, and there was little morbid about such planning and foresight.[37] Women often enough took on this responsibility themselves; in a society in which elite men married women ten to fifteen years younger than themselves, the phenomenon of widows commissioning and paying for graves must have been common enough to have passed in most instances without comment. That Proba herself commissioned the vault (and not her husband) is virtually certain from the images she selected, which highlight the grief suffered by a virtuous wife for her dead husband and which invoke the powerful presence of Ceres, the deity who oversees women's rites of passage including marriage, childbirth, and death.[38]

The construction of a family vault had to reflect Proba's family's status—or if we choose to be cynical, the status to which it aspired.[39] Diggers, plasterers, and painters were brought in. The crypts were enhanced with marble architectural features: to the columns hewn out of Rome's soft tuff were added Ionic capitals and bases in fine marble imported from Greece; specially cut low marble screens called *transennae* offered the only form of doorway or threshold between Proba, her husband, and their daughter in the adjoining room. All the surfaces were plastered, whitewashed, then carefully painted. To decorate the tops of the barrel vaults over the two graves in Cubiculum N, artists reproduced with paint and plaster an elaborate Greek key pattern drawn directly from the ceiling mosaic on the mausoleum of Constantine's daughter Constantina. If Proba could not afford a mosaic ceiling for her grave—and few in Rome could—she could at least imitate the most beautiful and stylish Roman imperial mausoleum.

A Roman hypogeum was not a vault to be sealed up and forgotten. It was a sort of memory theater, a space set on the margins between ordinary life and another realm, a place where one could meet the dead halfway.[40] The powerful combination of portraits, likenesses, and scriptural and mythological scenes enlivened by the soft light of flickering oil lamps not only rekindled a longing for one's beloveds, it confirmed their place in sacred history.

"Proba's" special-order rooms at the Via Latina catacombs. On the left, we look into Cubiculum O, her daughter's tomb chamber; the niche at right is part of Cubiculum N, where her own body probably lay. Note the carved architectural details and the elaborate decorative painting.

At the same time, a visit to a subterranean tomb was no exercise in pleasant nostalgia. It was an ordeal: bodies, though limed and sealed away, nevertheless reeked in the damp, barely circulating air. Vials of perfume set into the walls and tomb closures could not keep the smell in abeyance. Catacombs and hypogea were not places to linger without good reason. In his final piece of writing, the elderly church father Jerome—a contemporary of Proba and, for a time, her fellow inhabitant of Rome—recalled his days exploring the catacombs with his friends as a schoolboy:

> And often I entered the crypts, dug deep in the earth, their walls on either side lined with the bodies of the dead, where everything is so dark that it almost seems as if the psalmist's words were fulfilled: "Let them go away in terror into their graves" (Psalms 55:15). Here and there the light, not entering through windows but filtering down from above

through air shafts, relieves the horror of the darkness. But again, as one cautiously moves forward, the black night closes around, and there springs to mind Virgil's lines: "Surrounding horrors all my soul affright. And more, the dreadful silence to the night." (*Commentary on Ezekiel* 12.40.5–13 = *CCSL* 75: 556–557)

Schoolboys don't change from millennium to millennium, so we can still smile indulgently at Jerome and his pals' appetite for chilling experiences. But there were other, more formal occasions for visiting graves at the many annual feasts of the dead. Romans held days to honor their ancestors, such as the *Parentalia* (February 13–21), when families came bearing offerings of wine, salt, oil, water, milk, and honey, and festooned tombs with flowers. There were the *Nonae*, the *Rosalia* (May 10), and the *Dies Rosarum* (May 23), when rose petals were sprinkled on graves. There were days that recognized, too, the potentially baneful influences of the roving, hungry dead, such as the *Lemuria* (May 9, 11, and 13); the *Feralia*, when old women were called up to placate the restless shades (February 21). And then there were the days specific to each family, privately marking out its rhythms of death. The third, ninth, and thirtieth days following a death necessitated their own set of rites, and the yearly anniversary of a death would again bring families underground in rites of commemoration.

The most important and most frequent visitor to Proba's family grave would have been Proba herself. We have no indication that she had any other, surviving children. Nor did she choose to remarry. She emphasized her self-imposed devotion to her husband even after his death with allusions to uxorial fidelity painted on the *arcosolia* of both her own and her husband's graves. Proba was a *univira*—literally, a "one-man woman." The deaths of her husband and her daughter—whether at the same time or of the same cause, we cannot know—left her rich but desolate. This was her life's drama, and if the tomb was a memory theater, its most significant audience was the chief actor herself. Thus called underground several times a year by days of recollection and remembrance, Proba descended a staircase into the darkness, where at the far, far end she could just see, penetrating the gloom, the flickering light of four heavy oil lamps hanging from chains above her daughter's grave.

Each grave in a hypogeum complex such as the Via Latina catacomb could recount its own drama, its own particular story that shaped the itinerary of its visitors.[41] And people brought their own ways of seeing with them, as they moved through the darkness, their eyes roving from one picture to another. The infinitely variable and complex combinations of reader and "text"—to think for a moment of wall paintings in catacombs as a sort of visual text—renders it impossible for us to be sure, in any absolutist sense, what any of the images meant.[42] This is not precisely to say that absolute meaning deteriorates in a sort of infinite regress of relativity or subjectivity, but that what Proba experienced as she made her way to the back of the complex, what she thought as she passed by the tomb of the Tellus painting or by an image of Christ teaching Peter and Paul, was specific to her own life and character. Did she loathe Christians and Christianity? What did she think about the sweeping Christianization of Rome during her lifetime, or of the brief, dramatic reversal that the emperor Julian "the Apostate" brought in his attempts to reinstitute paganism to the empire? Did she indulge her daughter's decision to convert to Christianity or try to prevent her? And now, with both her husband and her daughter gone, as she pushed through the darkness toward their graves, what did she feel as she looked at Christian images: Jesus raising Lazarus, or Adam and Eve standing by the serpent and the tree? And what was in her mind as she selected the images, both pagan and Christian, to adorn the tombs of her lost ones? What message did she intend to convey, and for whose benefit? Many of the keys to these questions she took to the grave with her.

Fortunately for us, we have that grave.

The Via Latina catacomb—sometimes also known as the Catacomb of the Via Dino Compagni—is today closed to the public, in large part to protect paintings so fragile they can crumble under a hot breath. And so, few modern visitors to Rome will ever stand in Cubiculum O, Proba's daughter's tomb chamber. But this is what you would see: a small, richly adorned space, dominated by a large, gray bardiglio marble sarcophagus at one end. With its heavy texture and color, the coffin seems oddly out of place; interrupting the harmony of painted tufa, it immediately draws the eye. As far as Roman sarcophagi go—the finest examples of which are gorgeously carved—this one is unspectacular. It bears no carved effigy of the deceased, nor any other scriptural or mythological scenes. Its very plainness moves this woman's status away from Rome's top-drawer elite, which could afford to commission far more elaborately carved coffins. Since other sarcophagi in the complex are very similar, they all probably came from the same local studio, where the carver held some sort of general contract with the grave diggers. The simple carving is religiously neutral, a sort of "off-the-rack" stock item designed to be generic enough to suit all customers. The only thing that would have been carved to order was the front panel reserved for the deceased's name. We imagine that it was duly filled out when Proba's daughter passed away. But at some time, her name was thoroughly scoured off. The point of such defacement was probably not personal. Rather, in the brutally utilitarian world of the late empire, someone else subsequently thought the grave would be a pretty nice place to be buried, too. It may have the same person or people who also cut the rude gashes of new grave slots into the paintings of the Parting of the Red Sea and the Raising of Lazarus on either side of the chamber. Death carried on its relentless march, and corpses needed to go somewhere.

Behind the daughter's sarcophagus is an arched recess called an *arcosolium,* simply decorated with the image of a peacock hovering over a niche painted to look like a shell. Peacocks were a standard favorite of the Via Latina painters, a religiously neutral ornament they used to adorn other cubicula in the complex as well. To either side of the peacock, winged *putti* grasp garlands, as if to drape them over the body. This too was a standard order. Farther out from the *putti,* two winged female personifications of Victory stand, each with an arm upraised, flanking the recessed niche. All the decorative elements painstakingly painted on the plaster walls drew from conventional Roman funerary art, part of a catacomb painter's stock-in-trade.[43]

But then, alongside all the *putti* and garlands and flowers and birds one would expect to find in a Roman painted crypt, we find something rather unexpected: a series of large, well-rendered scenes from the Old and New Testaments—Moses leading the Israelites across the Red Sea; Daniel in the lion's den; Jesus raising Lazarus; the feeding of the five thousand; Noah in his ark. Their jarring presence and prominence here in a pagan grave makes it quite clear: although Proba herself was pagan, her daughter had died a Christian. In fourth-century Rome, it was not unusual for well-born women to convert to Christianity, often to the dismay of their families. The phenomenon is well attested from literary and epigraphic evidence. What was unusual, however, was Proba's choice to articulate her own and her daughter's different religious choices in the curiously quasi-public, quasi-private space of a subterranean catacomb. Also unusual, as we shall see, is the degree to which the two crypts reflect deeply felt connections between mother and daughter, human and divine.

Readers unfamiliar with the world of the fourth century may be surprised to learn that Proba and her daughter lead us into largely unexplored territory.

Most scholarship this century has proceeded from the assumption that by the fourth century, Rome was predominantly Christian, with only a few intransigent pagans stubbornly swimming against the powerful riptide of Christianity. The intransigent pagans of whom we have most knowledge happen also to have been male. Thus the representative pagan resistance to Christianity most often invoked are two men of senatorial class: Quintus Aurelius Symmachus and Vettius Agorius Praetextatus. Pagan women of the period slipped away unnoticed from historical record; they are named but almost entirely silent, like Praetextatus's wife, Aconia Fabia Paulina, whom we know almost exclusively from the sorrowful verse epitaph she composed for her husband's grave.[44] This absence of pagan women of influence stands in sharp contrast to noble Roman Christian women of the same century. A great deal has been written in the past twenty or so years of Paula and her daughters, Blessilla and Eustochium, the Anician women Faltonia Betitia Proba and Anicia Faltonia Proba, and Melania the Elder—all of whom lived in Rome at the same time as Proba.[45] Did Proba and these noble Christian women know each other? Almost certainly not. Rome was still a big place, Christian aristocracies still small, and pagan aristocracies apparently smaller still.

Scholars who have studied fourth-century Christian women cast them as central players in the transformation of Rome into a Christian empire. Although pagan men maintained civic allegiances to the *mos maiores*—Roman traditions passed down for centuries—they seem often enough to have married openly Christian women. The Caeionii clan offers a case in point. In the fourth century, four of the noble Caeionii sons—all strong proponents of Rome's traditional cults—each took a Christian wife. These Christian wives were influential enough ensure that their daughters were raised in their own tradition, not that of their fathers. Two of their granddaughters, Melania the Younger and Paula, joined the ranks of the most powerful Christians in the late empire, forging relationships with Jerome and Augustine that were preserved in correspondence we can still read today.

The case of fourth-century "mixed marriages" of pagan husbands and Christian wives has led some to speculate that these noble Christian women may have acted as Christianity's vectors. In 1961 the foremost historian of late antiquity, Peter Brown, advanced his "pillow talk" conversion hypothesis: Christianity did not triumph in the post-Constantinian period because of the mobilizing force of imperial edicts or mass conversions following powerful public sermons; instead, it moved horizontally and intimately, as Christian women compelled, wheedled, threatened, and cajoled their husbands into joining them in the faith.[46] This paradigm of a slow, inexorable, and intimate conversion of the empire, conjugal couple by conjugal couple, has been so widely accepted that a fourth-century woman asserting pagan beliefs which she apparently shared with her husband continues to confound explanation. The early-second-century author Plutarch's suggestion that husbands compel their wives to follow them in their choice of gods as of friends may explain why a woman should choose not to become Christian, but Plutarch's advice gives the impression that a woman's choice not to convert to Christianity was motivated entirely by a desire to please her husband (*Moralia* 140D). Traditional Roman religious choices apparently offered nothing compelling for women. Proba's case suggests otherwise.

Scholars have tended to take for granted that prominent women of the fourth century were predominantly Christian or, if not Christian, crypto-Christian or cowardly coerced pagans, compelled by uxorial pressures to walk behind their husbands in matters of religion. But recent studies have paid more attention to women's religious lives and options in Rome, illuminating behaviors, practices, and faiths in which Roman women led lives as meaningful and rife with possibilities as anything that Christianity provided. One of these religious options, as it turns out, is that which Proba herself had embraced, the cult of Ceres. What appeal Ceres held for Proba we will soon see; for now suffice to say that the choice apparently had little to do with her husband's wishes. It did have, however, a great deal to do with understanding the nature of daughters—even Christian daughters. And so Proba set about commissioning a grave chamber that featured Jesus and Moses alongside Ceres and Ceres' daughter, Proserpina. The choice of such a juxtaposition was not haphazard but deliberate, even brilliant.

Because Proba commissioned her daughter's burial chamber and likely selected the choice of subjects painted on the wall, it's worth trying to figure out what drove her to select the particular images she did. All the art historians who have worked on the chamber's provocative juxtaposition of pagan and Christian imagery have assumed that the Christian ones were dominant; that is to say, that the person who commissioned this art was himself Christian, with the pagan images used in only an ancillary or superficial manner. The art historian William Tronzo, whose work on Via Latina is the most extensive and the most highly regarded art historical treatment, argues that Cubiculum O was commissioned by a Christian of a sort of bourgeois or "new" sort who employed pagan imagery to his own ends to show a fondness for archaic Roman traditions.[47] "In the case of cubiculum O and related monuments," Tronzo writes, "the pagan motifs chosen seem to be those that either made a passive reference to Christianity—in the wheat and the grapes—or embodies themes like personal salvation, eternal life, and the blissful afterlife that corroborated Christian notions." He goes so far as to conclude, "The images in O do not spring from an internally coherent, pagan system of values; they are generated in response to Christianity itself."[48] Tronzo has said much about Via Latina that is very helpful, but here, I'm afraid he is wrong. The images in O were *not* generated in response to Christianity in any sort of a cultural vacuum. Nor are the pagan images in the chamber lacking an "internally coherent, pagan system of values." What is remarkable in Cubiculum O, in fact, is the manner in which its imagery reflects not only coherence but subtle intention, intelligence, and one woman's desire to articulate the values that mattered most deeply to her family.

When art historians seek to uncover the logic of a series of images in one particular space—what is called an "iconographic program," they turn to the sources Christians had before them: the Bible, popular sermons or homilies, perhaps early collections of prayers used for the dead. Tronzo and Jaś Elsner, another renowned art historian to have written on Cubicula N and O, both approach the question of the chamber's iconographic programs from the assumption that the patron was a male Christian.[49] But if we imagine that it was a pagan woman who had selected the Christian images, we are left wondering if she had any firsthand knowledge of what went on in a Christian basilica or a smaller *titulus* church, or if she had much patience for the scriptures. We can't turn to textual sources and traditions to uncover the logic of this woman's choice.

A choice of images in a series also have iconographic or artistic precedents, however, such as other examples of funerary art, or even the handbooks that catacomb painters must have had with them as guidebooks. Perhaps, then, this woman's artist—whom art historians surmise was Christian—suggested to her which ones his Christian clients especially favored—except that some images appear here for the first time or only infrequently, and others we might expect to see are missing. In terms of earlier artistic precedents, these certainly existed, and it is surely no coincidence that we find in Proba's daughter's cubiculum two of its most prominent images—Jesus raising Lazarus and the Parting of the Red Sea—in the same place and almost identical to an earlier chamber, Cubiculum C. But this conspicuous "borrowing" of imagery doesn't explain why only two of the nine Christian images replicate Cubiculum C. What was the inspiration, the logic, for the other paintings? Why Daniel? Why the three Hebrews in the fiery furnace? Why the miracle of the feeding of the five thousand? Why did Proba assent to her artist's replication of only two of Cubiculum C's images, and then diverge from the model at hand?

Here's why, I believe: Proba loved her daughter and sought to understand her. And her daughter must have explained to her mother at least something of what Christianity "meant" and why it drew her. She may have used language and concepts that her mother was likely to understand, as a pagan—not because she was stupid but merely to lessen the space between them—to explain what to Proba may initially have seemed an obstinate and unfathomable choice of religious adherence. Chances are, all that Proba knew about Christianity as she set about choosing the paintings for her daughter's grave she had learned from her daughter herself, in those lost conversations on the things that separated them and the things that drew them close.

These are speculative thoughts, of course, perhaps overly sentimental for some historians who refuse to look beyond proof and paper trails and smoking guns. But women's history grants few of those, more often offering only silences from which to extrapolate lives and relationships and moments. Proba wasn't silent; she merely spoke through a symbol system that has remained largely opaque. To hear her talk, it's easier to start with a simpler part of the code than her choice of Christian imagery. Let's begin with the ceiling of Cubiculum O.

Surrounded by garlands of grain and flowers, two seated female figures mirroring each other in pose and gesture sit head to head. They are arranged so that when one enters the chamber, a visitor clearly sees one seated figure directly over the daughter's *arcosolium*, holding a cluster of grapes. As one turns to exit, over the threshold into the chamber where Proba herself lies, one sees the mirror image of another almost identical figure, this time holding a handful of grain sheaves, pointing down toward the ground. The seated figure with the grain sheaves is clearly Proba's beloved Ceres; in a range of Roman art from wall paintings at Pompeii to a wide range of coinage from the high empire, Ceres sits in this precise posture, holding grain sheaves in one hand and a long scepter in her other.[50] If the first seated figure over the entrance to Proba's grave is Ceres, the second seated figure over her daughter's grave would most naturally be Ceres' daughter, Proserpina. Unlike Ceres, Proserpina has no standard iconography. But a number of Roman portrait statues and reliefs feature Ceres and Proserpina as virtually identical seated goddesses, one larger and one smaller.[51] The grapes held by Proserpina over Proba's daughter's grave may have been an allusion to the wine of the Eucharist, or to Jesus as the True Vine—or perhaps to something else now lost.[52] Whatever the meaning of the grapes, the ceiling itself—the only one of its kind in the entire corpus of Roman funerary art—surely reflects Proba's connection to her daughter. She chose to articulate this connection through Ceres and Proserpina, each one carefully arranged in the physical space of the catacomb, to point the viewer to Ceres the mother and Proserpina, the daughter whom she would follow even into Hades.

Of all the goddesses in the Roman pantheon—and there were many—Proba chose Ceres to adorn the cubicula she commissioned. Ceres is not the best known Roman goddess, yet she was well loved and well known among the women of Rome. Her worship was far older than the already ancient city. Even her name betrays her ancient origins; it shares its etymological root with such verbs as *creare* ("to create, beget"), *crescere* ("to grow"), and *gerere* ("to bring forth fruit, produce"). Her role as a deity of grain, particularly spelt, gave rise to our English word "cereal." A number of epithets in Roman literature assert Ceres' centrality to agriculture and the fertility of the land; she was Ceres *fertilis* ("fertile"), *fecunda* ("fecund"), *frugifera* ("she who brings the crops") and *genetrix frugum* ("progenitress of the crops").[53]

Ceres' cult in Rome took both public and private forms. She stood at the center of two annual festivals: the Cerealia and the *sacrum anniversarium Cereris*. Rome's oldest calendar or *fasti* mentions the Cerealia, which was celebrated on April 13. The second festival was imported from Magna Graecia (Sicily) in the third century BCE; centering on Ceres and Proserpina, its celebrations were open only to women (Ovid, *Metamorphoses* 10.431–436; *Amores*). In Rome, Ceres was worshiped at the temple of Ceres, Liber, and Libera. (Liber was a form of Bacchus, the Roman god of wine. Libera is another name for Proserpina, who also is called "Kore" in Greek.) We don't know where this temple was located; ancient sources indicate that it may have graced the Aventine hill, overlooking the Circus Maximus. In that spot today stands a lovely orange grove, nestled in next to the basilica of a very different holy woman, St. Sabina. Or the temple may have been in the low-lying lands of the Forum Boarium, the cattle market between the Tiber and the forum. The spot is close to where stands today the church of Santa Maria in Cosmedin, with its iconic Roman sewer cover, the open-mouthed and ominous *bocca della verità*. Rites for Ceres were also performed at the Temple of Tellus as well as the Altar of Ceres Mater and Ops Augusta, constructed by the first emperor of Rome in 7 CE.

The cult of Ceres, Liber, and Libera was officiated by men, probably Rome's *aediles* and tribunes of the plebs. But there were in the cult of Ceres and Proserpina priestesses of Ceres. The right of the female *sacerdos Cereris* or priestess of Ceres in Rome to administer public funds for a cult, the *sacra publica,* she shared only with her more famous sisters the vestal virgins. Unlike the vestals, who were consecrated to Vesta at age six and remained celibate throughout their thirty-year tenure, priestesses of Ceres were generally married. Was Proba a priestess? Unfortunately, we cannot know. Traditionally, there was only one Ceres priestess appointed at a time, drawn from the ranks of Rome's nobility. Plutarch, in the second century, called the priesthood of Ceres the highest honor to which a Roman *matrona* could aspire (*Parallel Lives,* 26). Her priestesses were known to hold special duties and to perform their own sacrifices with special sacred knives.[54] But it is impossible to know how the situation had changed by Proba's day. On the one hand, sacerdotal offices needed desperately to be filled as the number of eligible pagans steadily diminished in the city. On the other hand, despite her aspirations and wealth, Proba may not have been of high enough birth to compete. The classicist Amy Richlin's study of pagan priestesses revealed that of 147 priestesses known from epigraphical sources, 81 were freeborn, and an additional 38 were most likely freeborn. Only 10 of the 147 were lower-status freedwomen, although one of these, Prima Vestina, was indeed a priestess of Ceres.[55] Unfortunately, we cannot know if Proba's piety to the goddess reflected that of a sworn representative or merely a passionate devotee.

To honor Ceres the fertile grain-goddess, Proba commissioned her artists to festoon the architraves, arches, and ceiling vaults of both her crypt and her daughter's with garlands of wheat, pomegranates, and poppies—all symbols of the goddess's agricultural abundance. In fact, so distinctive and constant is the symbol of cereal or grains in Cubicula N and O that perhaps Proba and her husband didn't just propitiate the grain goddess; perhaps they chose her as a sort of patron or protector because they themselves were involved with Rome's grain dole, the *Annona.* Ceres was not just the goddess of grain; she also oversaw its cultivation and importation. And for hundreds of years, the noble families of Rome arranged for grain (primarily from Egypt, the "breadbox of the Mediterranean") to be brought up the Tiber to be distributed to the needy. The *Annona* was therefore a respected and highly visible form of public service that brought substantial prestige to its officers (the *praefecti annonae*), including the emperor himself. Another late fourth-century employee of the *Annona*, a man by the name of Leo, chose to be buried in a similarly elaborately painted Christian cubiculum across the city in the Catacombs of Commodilla, broadcasting his important status in civic affairs.[56]

There is some indication that Ceres was thought to preside over the *Annona;* the grain dole may even have operated out of the Temple of Ceres, Liber, and Libera, which was still open in Proba's time. Alongside the remains of a great temple in the Forum Boarium—the building many scholars surmise was the Temple of Ceres, Liber, and Libera—a great portico was built during Proba's time, which partly adjoined what is now the church of Santa Maria in Cosmedin. A number of inscriptions found near this portico bearing the names of *praefecti annonae* suggest that the structure might have served as a *statio annonae* or grain distribution center.[57] Proba's chambers were painted sometime between 350 and 370 CE. In 359 CE, storms and other calamities held up the Mediterranean grain trade, bringing a short but disastrous famine to the city of Rome. One historian of the period, Ammianus Marcellinus—himself a "Roman of Rome"—speculated darkly that the famine had been brought about by a failure to honor the traditional gods of Rome (*History* 19.10.3). One wonders if Proba's abundant grain motifs stood as ironic in a time of starvation and the emptying of the grain stores, or as a form of acknowledgment and thanks to the goddess who restored abundance to Rome. And one wonders if the image of the feeding of the five thousand in Proba's daughter's *arcosolium*—rare in early Christian art—might have been an apt (or hopeful) choice in times of famine, one well suited to a member of a family involved in the benevolent distribution of bread to a hungry city.

Even if it is merely fanciful to imagine that our fourth-century family had anything to do with Rome's *Annona*, there were other symbolic associations involving Ceres that could just as satisfactorily explain her presence in Proba's daughter's vault. By the imperial period, Romans invoked Ceres in their funerary rites. Publius Papinius Statius (45–96 CE) calls her *inferna* and *profunda*, two epithets associated with the underworld (*Thebaid* 4.460; 5.156). Her image is common on funerary reliefs of the imperial period; she stands alongside the other deities of the underworld: Dis Pater (the Roman father of the underworld), Hermes (a god who conducted souls of the deceased through the netherworld), and Proserpina. Many carved Roman sarcophagi of the third and fourth century were adorned with images of Ceres driving her chariot, with snakes in place of horses, in pursuit of Pluto and Proserpina.[58] These might even be personalized, with portraits of the bereaved and the deceased carved into the faces of Ceres and Proserpina.[59]

Anyone who visited a stone carver's studio to pick out a sarcophagus would have learned that Ceres was a popular choice in funerary imagery. Curiously, though, Ceres' standard iconography on sarcophagi does not match that which we find in Cubiculum O. There, a fine, large image of Ceres was placed not in either of the cubicula themselves, but in the narrower transitional space between the two rooms. She stands alone, not driving a chariot but holding a torch, her gaze directed at Proba's daughter's grave. This kind of an image of Ceres was far from the standard order for burial spaces. In Roman funerary art, Ceres drives her chariot down to the underworld— what we have here, by contrast, is a sacred, cultic image of the goddess—as you would have found her in her temple, not on a narrative sarcophagus. But why would Proba have commissioned *this* kind of an image, rather than a painting of Ceres chasing Pluto into Hades?

Proba was, if nothing else, eager to demonstrate her erudition, her antiquarian knowledge of Roman and Greek cultural traditions.[60] And we ought to take this erudition seriously when we consider how Ceres is presented in this crypt, and where those images were located. In the case of the large, standing image of Ceres in the threshold between Proba's own grave and her daughter's chamber, it was surely not a coincidence that Ceres was for the Romans a "liminal" deity associated with thresholds or margins (Latin: *limen*). An ancient Italian tablet, the Tablet of Agnone, associates Ceres with two goddesses, Anterstataí ("She Who Stands Between") and Líganakdikeí Entraí ("She Who Bears the Laws Between").[61]

As the classicist Barbette Stanley Spaeth has brilliantly demonstrated, Ceres' status as a liminal goddess connects her with human rites of passage, marking the transitions from one life-phase to another, including birth, marriage, and death.[62] Ceres also stood at the threshold between the world of the living and the world of the dead. In the city of Rome stood a monument known as the *mundus* ("world"), the opening of which was a state ritual. On the days when the *mundus* stood open, all public business in the city was halted. No one dared to idly wander the streets in search of revelry. The city stood in a state of ritual suspension, since incautious actions could bring unfortunate consequences. When the *mundus* stood open, the spirits of the dead were free to roam in the world of the living. This *mundus*, Festus tells

Fresco of Ceres standing, from the passageway between Cubicula N and O.

us, was called "of Ceres."[63] The late Roman writer Macrobius associates the *mundus* with Dis Pater and Proserpina, the *tristes atque inferni dei* ("sad and infernal gods") (*Saturnalia* 1.16.16–18). Spaeth comments, "To the Greeks and Romans, the purpose of these festivals was to propitiate the dead by allowing them to briefly visit the world of the living."[64] Just as Ceres controlled the opening of the *mundus,* the ritual boundary between the living and the dead, so did she stand at the threshold between Proba's own burial chamber—commissioned while she was still alive—and the room that held her daughter's body.

There was another, telling reason Proba chose to include Ceres imagery in her daughter's tomb. Both the mythology of Ceres and the rites offered to her articulated a mother's desperate search for her daughter. During the time of the Late Republic (first century BCE), Ceres came to be conflated with the Greek goddess Demeter, a sister of Zeus and the chief agricultural deity of ancient Greece. Greek sources tell of Demeter's beautiful daughter Persephone who was worshiped in Rome by the Latinized form of her name, Proserpina. While gathering spring flowers from a meadow one day, Persephone was seized by Hades, the god of the underworld, and dragged through a chasm in the earth back to his infernal kingdom. Demeter, overcome by sorrow at the rape and disappearance of her daughter, roams the earth far and wide in search of her. The story is told in the ancient *Homeric Hymn to Demeter* from the late seventh century BCE:

> Sharp grief seized her heart, and she tore the veil
> on her ambrosial hair with her own hands.
> She cast a dark cloak on her shoulders
> and sped like a bird, over dry land and sea,
> searching. No one was willing to tell her the truth,
> not one of the gods or mortals;
> no bird of omen came to her as truthful messenger.
> Then for nine days divine Deo roamed over the earth
> holding torches ablaze in her hands;
> in her grief she did not once taste ambrosia
> or nectar sweet-to-drink, nor bathed her skin.
> (4, lines 40–50)

While Demeter, the goddess responsible for the fertility of the earth, searches in grief, the land grows fallow, and an eternal winter descends:

> For mortals she ordained a terrible and brutal year
> on the deeply fertile earth. The ground released
> no seed, for bright-crowned Demeter kept it buried.
> In vain the oxen dragged many curved plows down
> the furrows. In vain much white barley fell on the earth.
> She would have destroyed the whole mortal race
> by cruel famine and stolen the glorious honor of gifts
> and sacrifices from those having homes on Olympus,
> if Zeus had not seen and pondered their plight in his heart.
> (18, lines 305–313)

The situation is dire, and so a council of the Olympian gods is quickly convoked. Eventually the great Zeus relents and heeds his sister's desperate pleas; Persephone would be returned to the world of the living. But because Hades had tricked her into consuming the fruit of the underworld—a luscious red pomegranate—she cannot fully be released from its grasp. She must stay with her husband for one third of the year—the deepest winter. But Persephone may join her mother each spring for the remaining two thirds of the year. This myth, recorded so long before in the Homeric hymn, was certainly known in the late Roman Empire; Augustine alludes to it in his *City of God* (ca. 410 CE) as the myth that undergirds not the story of Demeter and Persephone but, in his account, the rites of Ceres and Proserpina. He invokes the myth to explain the etymology of Proserpina's name, which he says derives from the verb *proserpinare*, "to spring or come forth," since Proserpina's return marked the beginning of spring. Later, in the fifth century, the rape of Proserpina inspired the late Roman poet Claudian to compose an epic poem, *De Raptu Proserpinae* ("The Abduction of Proserpina"). Clearly, the archaic Greek myth of the earth's fertility as connected to a mother's love for her daughter made a deep and lasting impression on late ancient Romans as well.

The story of Ceres' search for her daughter was not merely a myth to be casually told and retold. By the second century, it was a sacred drama ritually enacted under the carefully controlled conditions of a Roman mystery cult. A "mystery cult" or "mystery religion" was an ancient set of religious behaviors rooted in Greek practice. Romans chose to be initiated into secret rites and revelations, called "mysteries." Their aim was a sort of conversion for the individual, what classicist Walter Burkert calls "a change of mind through experience of the sacred."[65] Ceres' mysteries, particularly the important *initia Cereris* (also called the *sacra Cereris*), were unusual in that initiations were often restricted to women members.[66] These rites, imported from Greece in the third century BCE, were based on the Greek Thesmophoria, the ritual drama involving Demeter's search for Persephone. That Proba herself was initiated into the *sacra Cereris* is virtually certain from the numerous allusions to the goddess she placed throughout the grave chambers. Such ritual initiations into the cult of Ceres were not frequent in the Christian empire, but certainly did still take place; an inscription of the fifth century CE mentions a female initiate of Ceres.[67] Aconia Fabia Paulina, the wife of the renowned pagan intellectual Vettius Agorius Praetextatus, had, during Proba's lifetime, been initiated into a number of Ceres' mysteries, including the Eleusinian mysteries, the *sacra Cereris*, and the rites of Liber,

Ceres, and Kore at Lerna.[68] Like the *sacra Cereris,* the Eleusinian mysteries enacted the drama of Ceres' search for Proserpina.

Proba commissioned her artist to paint an image of the goddess at the threshold between her own grave and her daughter's cubiculum as Ceres Eleusina, or Ceres associated with the mysteries of Eleusis. The large Ceres painting in the threshold of the final two grave chambers of Via Latina shows the goddess standing with her weight on one hip in a graceful sway. She is crowned and veiled, carrying a torch in her left hand and a bundle of wheat in her right. Behind her on the ground sits a *kiste,* a basket that held the *sacra* or sacred emblems of the goddess carried from Eleusis to Athens during the festival of her mysteries. A monumental marble statue of the Eleusinian Demeter in a similar pose dating from the second century still stands in the Round Room of the Vatican Museums today, although the *kiste* is now missing. This *particular* depiction of Ceres as Ceres Eleusina was another indication that Proba herself placed this image on the wall not merely as decoration drawn from the standard funerary iconography of Ceres, but to commemorate her initiation into the goddess's mysteries. But the mysteries may not have been the Eleusinian mysteries. The presence of the wine amphorae in the picture—the emblem of Liber, god of wine—suggests that the sacred rites into which Proba was initiated may have been the mysteries of Ceres, Liber, and Kore at Lerna, the same rites into which Aconia Fabia Paulina had been initiated.

Aconia Fabia Paulina's tombstone—on which her epitaph proclaims her initiation at Lerna—proves for us that in the fourth century, pagans of Rome still saw fit to announce their initiatory "pedigree" on their graves. Proba chose to do it visually, with a potent, wordless image of the goddess on her own hypogeum that would have meant only one thing to its ancient viewers: the initiation of the person buried there into Ceres' mysteries. Had she merely wished to make a visually poetic metaphorical statement concerning the premature death of her daughter as a form of unjust rapture by Hades—and we can find numerous examples of this scene on Roman sarcophagi—she would have followed their iconographic precedent, commissioning an image of Ceres driving her serpent-drawn chariot hard after Hades and the hapless Proserpina.[69] Instead, Ceres shows up in the threshold of Cubicula N and O not as enraged mother, but in her more benevolent and arcane "cultic" form, a goddess of hidden mysteries.

A second image directly faces the painting of Ceres in the passageway. Some have identified this second image as either Proserpina or Ceres, but I believe they are wrong.[70] The painting depicts a matron clad in a purple tu-

Fresco of a female devotee of Ceres holding first-harvest offerings. This image is some-times identified as Ceres or Proserpina, but the woman lacks any indicators of divinity; she lacks a crown and scepter but wears the jewelry and the stola *and* palla *garments of wealthy Roman women. This may be a portrait of "Proba" herself. It directly faces the image of the standing Ceres (page 47) in the passageway between Cubicula N and O.*

nic, pearl necklace, and a white *stola* standing in a pose similar to that of the goddess but holding a bunch of wheat sheaves pointed toward the earth, one in each hand. Unlike the image of a crowned Ceres, who holds her traditional accouterments (the torch, the wheat sheaves, and the *kiste*), the matron stands in the white garment of initiation, holding the first-harvest offerings traditionally offered to Ceres. Ovid, in the first century, wrote about such a ceremony in Book 10 of his *Metamorphosis:*

The time of Ceres' festival had come
in duty kept by mothers every year,
When, robed in white, they bring their firstfruit gifts
    Of wheat in garlands (*primitias frugum dant spicia serta suarum*)
      and for nine nights count
    Love and the touch of men forbidden things.
(238, 10.431–436)

Although popular consensus has identified this figure as Proserpina, I like to think it is a portrait of Proba herself, as she wished to be remembered, honoring the goddess.[71]

It's time to return to the Christian images Proba selected for her daughter's grave. Why did she make the choices she made? Some are easier to interpret than others. The large image of Jesus raising Lazarus, for instance, makes obvious sense in a Christian grave, and seems provocatively counterposed against the image of Hercules leading Alcestis to her husband in Hades on the same wall of Cubiculum N. The theme is not just the fate of the deceased after death, but the osmotic quality of death; given the assistance of a higher power, one could, while still living, move into the realm of the dead—or else be called back, resuscitated from the tomb. In either case, death was a temporary change of state for those emboldened by a god. Less easy to interpret is the second large painting in the room, in which Moses leads the Israelites across the Red Sea. The image depicts a clatter of Egyptian soldiers, shields, and horses to the left and an orderly procession of fourteen male Hebrews on the right, who glance over their shoulders toward the Egyptians. Between them stands a large, beardless Moses in a toga, reaching across the breached seas with a wand. It is essentially a replica of an older painting in the same hypogeum. But what frames this image in Cubiculum O is unique; on one side of the parting of the Red Sea stands a menacing depiction of an Egyptian soldier in full armor wielding a spear. Directly opposite him, an unarmed Israelite stands, his arm raised in a defensive posture to ward off a blow. These images appear to speak to one another, but the conversation is difficult to discern. Still, the theme, like that of the opposite wall, is essentially that of transition, even transformation.

    Smaller images, of Noah in his ark and the three Hebrews in the fiery furnace, adorn the sides of supporting walls and tufa-hewn square pilasters. The symbolic connection here may have been the sacrament of baptism, the hidden language of Christian initiation. The Hebrews' passage through the

Red Sea, too, became in the interpretive world of early Christian art a visual code for baptism, the sacrament by which an individual made the transition from a previous, profane existence to a life in Christ. But the initiatory symbols water and fire were not exclusive to Christianity. The pagan writer Festus notes that in traditional Roman wedding rites, participants carried a torch "in honor of Ceres; the new bride was accustomed to be sprinkled with water, either so that she might come chaste and pure to her husband, or so that she might share fire and water with her husband."[72] The appearance of the torch in Festus's description here reminds us of the torch-bearing Ceres who leads the way into the daughter's chamber. Through the symbolic language of fire and water, and their connection to both pagan wedding rituals and Christian initiation rituals, Proba may have seen her daughter's espousal of Christianity as a sort of symbolic marriage.[73] Indeed, it was commonplace to talk about a virgin consecrated to Christianity as a "bride of Christ." The daughter herself might have used such language to explain to her mother her decision not to marry. I suspect that Proba made her peace with her daughter's decision, which in the absence of any surviving siblings would have brought about the end of her family line. It's provocative, at any rate, that the torch-bearing Ceres leads viewers who enter Cubiculum O bearing their own torches and lamps into a sort of wedding chamber, a space whose imagery conveys allusions to an initiatory process of sacred marriage.[74] This process, furthermore, would be manifest to those visitors to the tomb who, like Proba, had already been initiated into the symbolic system that unlocked the meaning of the grave chamber. Otherwise—and I suspect Proba was fully aware of this—as an uninitiated viewer was led down into the silent earth and moved by torchlight through this series of images and space, she became herself one of the initiated. Given that Proba arranged this at the very time in the evolution of the empire when the traditional rites—including the mystery religions—were being forced "underground," as it were, our fourth-century Roman of Rome had found a way to draw others, secretly but surely, into an ancient religious experience at its most esoteric and profound.

When she chose to have images of Jesus raising Lazarus alongside an image of Ceres, Proba was not heralding the triumph of one religion over the other. Yet neither did she fail to distinguish between a pagan image and a Christian image. There was her religious commitment to Ceres and her daughter's devotion to Christ. Her task, as a bereaved mother, was to reflect both of these commitments while also drawing out the common ground between herself and her child.

Mothers and daughters, in Roman art, are rarely depicted together.[75] To convey their bond, then, Proba chose to draw a symbolic equation between herself and her daughter, and Ceres and Proserpina. This symbolic language of connection was common enough in ancient Rome; we need to understand it as a move more profound than simply the egotism of self-divination. Proba is not telling us she and her daughter were like gods— rather, she is telling us that the gods are like us. The profound loss and wrenching grief of burying her own child found Proba thinking mythologically—and this, I think, is a human trait. In an essay of extraordinary perceptiveness and sensitivity, the Roman art historian Susan Wood ends her analysis of Demeter and Persephone imagery in Greek and Roman culture with a glimpse at our own.[76] She reminds the reader of twelve-year-old Polly Klaas, who was abducted at knifepoint in her own home in California and later raped and murdered. Invoking a piece by journalist Noelle Oxenhandler titled "Polly's Face" in *The New Yorker,* Wood draws a connection between the posters of Polly's face and Roman cult images before quoting Oxenhandler:

> And here we touch upon the cosmic horror of this crime: kidnapping has to do with the invasion of the "bright" world in which children chatter and play . . . by another world, the dark world of unspeakable sorrows, the underworld. Part of the horror of Polly's story is how swiftly these two worlds connected, how easily the dark world made its claim—as when, in the ancient myth, a crack opened up in the earth, and golden-haired Persephone, who had been happily playing with her companions, vanished with the dark figure of Hades into the ground. "The child is the light of our lives," Polly's mother was quoted in the newspaper as saying—speaking the language of Demeter, goddess of earth and growing things, who when her daughter vanished cast the shadow of drought upon the whole world. The photographs of Polly show a child as beautiful as Persephone: flowing hair, soft, dark eyes; a radiant, dimpled smile. . . . And as those of us who remain here grow accustomed to her face, which everywhere denotes her absence, we cannot help participating in her transfiguration. Even as we refuse to give up hope for her return, we find ourselves going in and out of the bank, the post office, the bookstore, turning a girl into a goddess.[77]

We have only the very general outlines of what Proba experienced when she was initiated into Ceres' mysteries. Initiates were sworn to a deep secrecy that remained unbroken for more than a thousand years. But we do know from Ovid that initiates carried torches in a nocturnal ceremony, probably as a ritual reenactment of Ceres' search for her daughter (*Fasti* 4.494). And we know that women initiates to the mysteries of Ceres and Proserpina, the *sacra Cereris*, enacted the role of Ceres, uttering a ritual wail of grief, calling out to their daughter in the underworld (Servius, *Commentary on Verg. Aen.* 4.609). The next day of the rites was spent fasting in mourning, ritually sharing in Ceres' sorrow at losing her daughter.[78] If Proba had already lost her daughter by the time she came to be initiated, we can imagine with what anguish she must have carried through a mourning rite that for her cut to the bone. But if her daughter passed away into the darkness after Proba's induction into Ceres' deepest mysteries, it was that profound experience of initiation into a goddess's sorrow that helped her to articulate and to bear her grief.

Unfortunately, we do know how Proba solved the problem of the pig. Perhaps by invoking the presence of Ceres at the mouth of her daughter's grave, and by having her own portrait stand in front of her—bloodless offerings in hand—Proba tried to circumvent ancient ritual tradition. If so, it would be an unprecedented case of a pagan neglecting the primary way to express religious devotion. As the classicist Clifford Ando has noted, religiosity among fourth-century Roman pagans was expressed most properly through ritual, since it was "through ritual that men interacted or united with the divine."[79] Proba would have had to recuse herself from what Ando calls the "clarion call" that rallied the last generation of Roman pagans: "Verily do I promise that I will maintain and preserve, so long as I am able, that which has been handed down and sanctioned by antiquity."[80] Without the proper and due sacrifice of a pig, Proba risked compromising a relationship with Ceres that sustained and formed a large part of her identity, both public and private. Pagans of the fourth century were acutely aware that such a neglect of tradition had lasting and ominous consequences. At least one, the late antique historian Zosimus, drew a dark connection between the sack of Rome in 410 and the citizens' wanton neglect of the gods (*Historia Nova* 5.38–40).

Still, once each year on the anniversary of her daughter's death, as was the custom for pagans and Christians alike, the woman would enter the dark stillness of the hypogeum in memory of her daughter and stand before her grave. She passed by her husband's grave too—he would be remembered on his own death anniversary, and in a different way—and the space prepared for her own body, someday. As she passed through the narrow arch-

Looking up toward the top of the arch over the sole grave of Cubiculum O, the portrait of the deceased becomes visible. It is the only portrait tondo in the entire catacomb complex, and hers is the only burial in the entire elaborately decorated chamber. Although she was probably Christian, her mother chose to have her depicted in this fresco in the guise of Persephone, the young maiden abducted by Hades to be his bride in the underworld.

way between their cubiculum and their daughter's, her torchlight danced off the wall, revealing Ceres standing with her own torch, lighting the way into the underworld, revealing to her the way to lost daughters. For a moment, the goddess's image shone back like a mirror. Proba and Ceres stood at the same place, in the same pose, with the same determination to enter the jaws of Pluto if only to see their daughter again. For what difference was there, really, between Proba's experience as an initiate of Ceres—undertaking nocturnal rites by torchlight, calling out in the gloom Proserpina's name, weeping and fasting—and her experience as a bereaved mother, making a similar journey into the bowels of the earth, mourning not the ethereal and fair-ankled daughter of a goddess, but her own flesh and blood, her only child? Over her head on the painted vault, Ceres still presided, seated holding a scepter and her wheat. Over her daughter's grave sat Persephone, in the pose of her mother, holding a *thyrsus*—the wand of the initiate—in one hand, and a bunch of grapes in her extended hand. And if one drew very close to her grave, down on bended knees by the sarcophagus, and looked up in grief and imprecation, there was a lost daughter, ringed by red flowers, haloed like Proserpina, with the sad, sideways gaze of a soul in the underworld.

CHAPTER 3

WAITING IN THE AFTERLIFE

But hers was considered so great a sacrifice, not only by humankind but also by the gods, that in recognition of her magnanimity it was granted to her—and among all those who have done many noble deeds there is only the smallest handful to whom such a boon has been given—that her soul would rise once more from the Stygian depths.
—Plato, *Symposium*

W ho waits for us in the afterlife? When we think of what happens to us and to our loved ones after death, where do we get these ideas? Do we imagine that we will be reunited with them? Does marriage continue in heaven, or do we all live as genderless angels, hovering free from the earthly bonds of love and jealousy?

Christian theologians often present Christianity as revolutionary because of its promise of universal salvation: *all* souls of the pious will be admitted to heaven, without the exclusivism of Roman religious systems that were geared to an increasingly diminishing elite. Such a view, however, effectively flattens the background of Roman religions, which were rich and diverse enough to include a variety of afterlife scenarios geared to a variety of different inclinations and convictions.[1] Yet one thing shared by these Roman views of the afterlife is that families—and in particular, husbands and wives—would find one another once more in the world beyond. The bonds of marriage were as enduring as they were comforting.

By contrast, we can witness in the growth of Christianity and the cult of the saints the dissolution of Roman ideas of enduring familial bonds in heaven. The idea that earthly marriage would be transcended in heaven was an ancient one in Christianity; in the Gospel of Matthew, Jesus cannily responds to the "trick question" of the scribes and Pharisees concerning the details of marriage in the endtime: "In the Resurrection they neither marry nor are given in marriage, but are like angels in heaven" (Matt 22:30). Thus men, women, and children populate Paradise, forming communities of celestial faithful disconnected from the earthly fetters of family—or perhaps, more accurately, communities of individuals bonded to a new and enduring family of saints. The North African church father Tertullian (ca. 160–225 CE) writes that the Christian awakens in heaven not to her assembled family of long-departed beloveds, but to the luminous face of her angel (*de Anima* 53.6).

The answer of who was waiting for you in the afterlife, then, depended on whether you were Christian or pagan—just not in the way that many people think. Despite what many assume—that Christians more or less stormed Rome with the "revolutionary" idea that life continued beyond the grave—few citizens of the fourth century believed that death simply snuffed out a human existence. Surely, death meant different things to different people, as did the general concept of continuity beyond death. Some adhered to the Aristotelian notion that the production of progeny constituted the only form of immortality possible for human beings.[2] One could also believe in a sort of conceptual afterlife—that eternal forms or virtues far outlived the vicissitudes of human flesh. Or people might embrace a more hopeful, forward-looking eschatology of a Life Beyond. The bones of a married couple garbled together into dust in a single sarcophagus was one type of immortality. Envisioning the afterlife as a paradisiacal garden in which the blessed cavorted together amid the trees was another, and Romans felt relatively unconstrained to play with a number of different scenarios.

Two particular funerary chambers, both designed to contain the bodies of formidable women, elegantly reflect two different philosophies of death embraced by their occupants. We might ponder what we can learn from the women for whom they were designed. One was Christian, one was pagan. The pagan woman, as it turns out, we have already met. The woman I have named Proba still has much to tell us, particularly about how she felt about marriage, life, and death. And we might imagine her in conversation with a contemporary, a Christian woman whose name has also been lost although her image and grave remains. But let's start with Proba's own grave chamber, which scholars have located in Cubiculum N in the hypogeum of the Via Dino Compagni, better known as the Via Latina hypogeum.[3]

In her daughter's tomb chamber (Cubiculum O), as we have seen, Proba manipulated physical space, employing a visual rhetoric to express a profound and connective relationship between herself and her daughter. The base "text" for that rhetoric, expressed in images she probably commissioned, was the myth of Ceres and her lost daughter, Proserpina. Naturally, the woman drew on a different set of narratives for what she wished to convey about her relationship with her own husband. Her own tomb chamber was no less lavishly adorned than her daughter's; it featured sculptured columns, finely painted peacocks and leaping goats; in honor of her favorite goddess, Ceres, the ceilings were festooned with garlands of wheat being reaped by miniature *putti*. And then she commissioned her artist to paint over the room's tombs two scenes loosely figured on a timeless Greek drama still performed today.

The playwright Euripides (480–406 BCE) composed his drama *Alcestis* in 438 BCE—more than seven hundred years before an unknown Roman matron sat and devised the decoration for her and her husband's final resting place under Via Latina. The play opens with a monologue by the god Apollo, who explains that Admetus, the king of Thessaly, had become a cruel pawn in the contestations, jealousies, and vengeances of the gods. On Admetus's wedding day, he learns that he is to be seized by Death and taken down into dark Hades before his appointed time. Apollo had intervened to prevent the cruelty of such a premature death, we learn, but he persuaded the Fates only to accept a bitter compromise: Admetus could escape his fate if he could convince someone else to forfeit his or her life in Admetus's stead. "One by one he tested all his friends," Apollo intones in his opening monologue, "and even his father and the old mother who had brought him forth—yet found none who would die for him and never more behold the light of day" (*Alcestis*, lines 15–18). Only one person in all of Thessaly offered to make this bravest and most selfless of sacrifices: Admetus's wife, Alcestis, daughter of Pelias.

For Romans, as for Greeks, the figure of Alcestis conveyed the theme of untimely death. But that was not all. There could be no better story to celebrate an idealized Roman marriage that outlasted death itself. Alcestis herself was, in the symbolic universe of fourth-century Rome, the paragon of a dutiful wife, selfless and devoted. Proba thus chose her deliberately, to illustrate in grandly symbolic terms her relationship to her husband.[4] So in one wall painting, Admetus lies on his deathbed, attended by a group of six mourners, five of them male. A female mourner, slightly oversized so as to

Lunette fresco from the back of one of the two arcosolium *graves in Cubiculum N, depicting a scene from* Alcestis. *Here, Heracles (center) leads Alcestis out from the underworld and back to her husband, Admetus, who sits in an attitude of mourning.*

draw the eye, stands at the foot of the bed to the far left of the image, her arms upraised, her veil pulled up over her head. Another woman, presumably Alcestis, bends solicitously over Admetus. Given that Romans had a predilection for figuring themselves mythologically in funerary art, there can be no doubt that Proba meant the viewer to see in this scene an only loosely disguised allusion to her own ministrations and devotion at her husband's bedside.[5]

In Euripides' play, Admetus implores his wife to stay with him and their children: "Rouse yourself up, poor woman, do not abandon me! Pray for pity to the gods who have you in their grasp!" (*Alcestis*, lines 250–251). But Alcestis remains steadfast in her promise to die for him, and makes the perilous journey to the world beyond: "I see the two-oared boat in the lake. Charon, the ferryman of the dead, his hand on the boat pole, calls me now . . . someone is taking me—don't you see him?—away to the court of the dead" (lines 252–255, 259–260). Death claims Alcestis, but one of the gods—Heracles—will intervene. He draws her back into life, leading her from the world of the shades into the sure light of day. The triumphant conclusion to this drama is figured in the wall painting directly above the main grave in Cubiculum N, which perhaps once held Proba's bones. In it, Admetus sits at the right of the painting; his slumped figure, passive and mute, exudes grief—even confusion. To his right, Heracles approaches with the fierce, many-headed dog Cerberus, guardian of the underworld. With his hand on her shoulder, Heracles guides Alcestis out of the dark cave of the shades. The scene is at once allegorical and metonymous; although it alludes to a drama, it also points forward to a life moment and to Proba and her travails. We are best not to take it literally—that is, that Proba went to death's door or beyond to "redeem" her husband. The point is that she considered herself fully capable of such selfless devotion.

Proba's decision to cloak herself in the guise of Alcestis was not especially innovative. Since Alcestis's central drama involves the ultimate uxorial sacrifice, Greeks and Romans conventionally invoked the story either on women's sarcophagi or burials, or else on the sarcophagi of married couples.[6] To give one example, an Alcestis sarcophagus dated to between 161 and 180 CE that was found at Rome's port, Ostia, once held the bones of a husband and wife, Caius Junius Euhodus and Metilia Acte.[7] For the coffin that would hold both their bodies, the couple selected scenes from Alcestis that best highlighted the virtues of both husband and wife.[8] The theme of the sarcophagus, to which the myth of Alcestis is made to service, is marital virtue and the unity of the couple even after death.[9]

C. Junius Euhodus and Metilia Acte commissioned their artist to carve their faces, aging and homely, onto the youthful bodies of Admetus and Alcestis. On the sarcophagus's principal relief, Alcestis collapses back on her couch, while her husband presses toward her, his hand outstretched. Other family members, including two small children, weep at the scene. But this scene of evident, palpable pathos leads the eye to the scene immediately to the right. Here, Heracles firmly grasps Admetus's hand before a low, arched doorway; and Alcestis, heavily veiled, inclines her head as she stands, a mute shade, behind Heracles. Behind her, Proserpina stands resting her left hand gently on the shoulders of her husband, Pluto. The presence of Proserpina here on this Ostian sarcophagus brings us back to Proba's design choice of two centuries later, where the myth of Alcestis in her own tomb chamber introduces the myth of Proserpina in her daughter's crypt. Evidently, the two women—the woman I call Proba and Metilia Acte— thought in similarly mythological terms of their own life dramas. Roman women were, some have observed, myth-makers—certainly to the same degree as Roman men.[10] In any event, the point made was identical. As the art historian Susan Wood notes, "Metilia Acte, like Alcestis, has earned victory over death by her virtue and wifely loyalty."[11]

Yet another wealthy woman of late ancient Rome chose to feature Alcestis in her funerary chamber in order to convey that she herself had been an exemplary wife. The freedwoman Vibia was a pagan contemporary of Proba's, the widow of a priest to the god Jupiter Sabazius. She and her husband commissioned their grave paintings at almost the same time that Proba's cubiculum was prepared.[12] Above Vibia's *arcosolium*, an artist painted an elaborate image cycle. In one fresco, Alcestis escorts Vibia into the afterlife.[13] In another, Pluto, god of the underworld and his child bride, Proserpina (here labeled by another one of her names, Aeracura), rule from high thrones; in still another, Pluto drives Vibia off in his *quadriga* chariot as Mercury, leader of souls into the underworld, stands poised nearby. The image is labeled ABREPTIO VIBIES ET DISCENSIO ("Vibia's abduction and descent"). In the next scene of the cycle, a figured labeled "the good angel" (*Angelus Bonus*) seizes the right hand of a heavily veiled Vibia and leads her to a banquet in the afterworld, where her deceased husband is already seated, waiting for her. The scene is labeled INDUCTIO VIBIES and BONORUM IUDICIO: the "Introduction of Vibia" and "The Judgment of the Good." For the pagan woman Vibia, the afterlife would be primarily a social affair, with a banquet of the blessed complete with servants and wine. And there amid the celestial symposium, in the fullness of timelessness, Vibia would again take her place at her husband's side.

What Proba wished to convey to those who visited her grave was not so different from what Vibia had depicted explicitly. Two things, above all, were important to broadcast. First, she drew a direct analogy between her own experiences and identity in her own time—the late fourth century—and the classical Greek past. It was not merely that she wanted to show off that she was learned: she was one of the last bearers of that past as the city moved inexorably toward becoming fully Christian. I suspect that she took that role fully to heart. Second, as with Vibia, her duty to her husband defined her very identity. Given a voice, an opportunity to speak, Proba exalted her marital status and the virtue that comes from being a good wife. She was no different from many other Roman women of her day; again and again, what late Roman women tell us of themselves on scores of inscriptions, epitaphs, funerary paintings, and sarcophagi, and even in the modes of their burials (as we saw with the case of Crepereia Tryphaena in chap. 1) is that marriage was important enough both to define women's life duty, even to survive death itself.

From the first to the fourth centuries, marriage and death were—for women's lives, at least—intrinsically and symbolically interconnected in a way that is difficult for us to comprehend. It is not as simple as to say that the two rites of passages were the only virtual certainties in women's lives, nor that a woman's mortality was imperiled by the demands of marriage; her chance of dying in childbirth made marriage as dangerous as it was inevitable. Nor was the connection between marriage and death purely or merely symbolic—that, for instance, marriage caused a sort of "social death" in a woman's freedom or visibility. Married women enjoyed a fairly high degree of social autonomy, particularly compared to what they had as unmarried girls under the *potestas* or authority of their fathers. Upper-class married women or *matronae* constituted a special class or order in Rome, the *ordo matronarum*, which carried with it distinctive privileges such as the right to be carried in a special litter (called a *pilenta* or *carpenta*) or to wear gold jewelry and purple clothing. The bodies of *matronae*, as the classicist Amy Richlin points out, were treated with particular deference. One late Roman author notes that *matronae* could not be moved aside on the streets even by magistrates, "lest they should seem to be pushed or handled, or pregnant women be jostled."[14]

The positive, "upwardly mobile" acquired status that *matronae* enjoyed sat uncomfortably with relatively liberal Roman views of marriage. Wedding ritual was simply not laced with the language of finality, the "until death do us part" of modern Western marriage vows. Just as for us in North America, marriages in Rome ended in divorce almost as often as they ended in the death of a spouse. Divorce was simple—the process marked only by the coldly dismissive words of a husband: *tuas res tibi habeto* ("Take your things").[15] Marriage to one man over the course of a woman's life was praised as a feat of virtue, but divorce carried little social stigma. A woman was also as free to divorce her husband as he was to divorce her.[16] Indeed, much to men's chagrin, women could even divorce and legally remarry if their husbands went off on too long a trip without them.[17] This "free marriage" (free because the wife was not under her husband's control or *manus*; she remained under her father's *manus* while he was still alive) marked a change from earliest Roman law, according to which a husband could divorce his wife only for three crimes: poisoning his children, counterfeiting his keys (apparently to his wine cellar), or infidelity. If he divorced his wife for any other reason, half the husband's property was forfeited to her, the other half consecrated to Ceres. The language of the ancient law even darkly insinuates that the husband himself could be made into an offering to Ceres and the other gods of the underworld.[18]

Marriage, as a social and cultural institution, did not remain conceptually fixed over the Roman Empire's duration. That is to say, most modern classicists perceive a progressive movement from marriage in the earlier Roman Republic, characterized by duty, sober practicality, and the idealized submission of a young wife to her husband and overlord, to a more altruistic partnership of something more like social equals in the empire—what we call "companionate marriage."[19] Such trends are difficult to chart objectively, of course, without reading in a great deal of our implicit convictions about what marriage should be. But we do find a marked shift in language indicating that Romans of the first century CE saw marriage differently from their ancestors. A Roman citizen of the high empire who chose a wife took her legally as his *uxor*. The word denoted a legal relationship central to the transmission of land and property to heirs. But as time progressed, the preferred word for "spouse" became *coniunx*, a word that means, literally, "yoked together" like a pair of oxen. The word lives on in the English adjective "conjugal." *Coniunx*, as a word, implies a burden equally shared.

Romans after the time of the emperor Marcus Aurelius (161–180 CE) held three social virtues particularly dear: *clementia, concordia*, and *pietas:* clemency toward enemies, concord at home, piety to the ancestors and state.[20] All three could be broadcast on the smooth "billboard" space of a sarcophagus. A man might show clemency for a prisoner of war in a military scene painstakingly carved on his coffin; and he might demonstrate *pietas* through a scene of a sacrifice to the gods. But to illustrate *concordia*, a man needed a wife. Concord was best and most evocatively symbolized by the married couple—usually at the moment of their wedding.[21] Livia, the wife of the first Roman emperor, Augustus, established a shrine to Concordia as gratitude for her long and harmonious marriage; consequently, hundreds of years later, couples still celebrated weddings before Livia's statue (Ovid, *Fasti* 6.645–646). As the historian Peter Brown observes, "the married couple came to appear in public as a miniature of civic order."[22] Social order was best represented, then, by domestic peace and order. "The *domus aeterna*," notes the classicist Brent Shaw, "became a replica of the *domus temporalis*."[23] In other words, the model of the earthly household with the conjugal couple at its core was projected as an ideal, an exemplar of a higher order.

As yokefellows in domestic and civic duties, Roman spouses of the high empire presented a public face of harmony and partnership. Marital virtues were carefully displayed on shared sarcophagi. We find a variety of friezes, paintings, sarcophagi, and even glasswork commemorating if not precisely happy, at least peaceful couples at their wedding, their heads inclining ever so slightly toward one another or actually touching, their right hands joining their bodies together in the graceful arc of joined right hands called the *dextrarum iunctio*. In the third century, the custom of joint burials of husband and wife in a single sarcophagus became popular. These sarcophagi often featured a central *clipeus* or circular portrait window in which the couple are presented together, wordlessly, often in some sort of comfortable display of affection—perhaps one resting a hand softly on the other's shoulder or arm. In fact, the imagery was so commonplace that sarcophagus workshops produced them en masse, leaving the couple's facial features uncarved and amorphous so that they could be personalized after purchase. After all, the particularity of the image—the portrait's ability to convincingly memorialize real people—was subordinate to its symbolic meaning as an idealized portrait of concord. That symbol remained fixed, even if the details of features and likenesses varied from coffin to coffin.

The public face of Roman marriage wasn't merely about expectation and display. Marital concord became a potent psychological goal in its own right. But how men met their end of the bargain within the bonds of matrimony was not the same as how women met theirs; Amy Richlin has shrewdly noted that a harmonious marriage, in the Roman social context, was one in which the husband was pleased.[24] Roman women of the upper classes were expected to visit the shrine of *Dea Viriplaca*, a deity whose name literally means "goddess husband-pleaser," which stood high on the Palatine hill near the imperial palaces. They were also expected to honor Venus *Obsequens* (the goddess who reminded women of their marital duties) and Venus *Verticordia* (Venus "Changer of Hearts," who could turn women's hearts away from dangerously unvirtuous thoughts to pure, chaste virtue).[25] Numerous tombstones record lengthy marriages in which concord was manifested primarily as uxorial submission: "Caecilius, a husband, makes this epitaph in memory of Cecilia Placidina, the finest wife, with whom he lived well for ten years without any quarrels."[26] These harmonious relations were condensed into short expressions found again and again on the epitaphs of wives: women brought to their marital unions an acquiescence *sine ulla querella, sine ulla contumelia,* or *sine ulla offensa:* "without a quarrel," "without insult," or "without offense."[27] A tombstone to a freedwoman named Clodia Secunda dated to a period shortly before Crepereia Tryphaena's demise, reads:

> Sacred to the spirits of the dead. To Clodia Secunda, the sweetest, well-deserving wife who lived 25 years, 10 months, 14 days and was married to me without any complaint for 7 years, 4 months, 18 days. Lucius Caelius Florentinus, centurion of the 10th urban cohort, set this up for her. She was born on August 4th when Mamertinus and Rufus were consuls [182 AD]. She died on June 17th while Aper and Maximus were consuls [207 AD].[28]

We can't recover the "real" Clodia Secunda from this epitaph that commemorates her. All we know of her character draws from stock blandishments: "sweetest," "well-deserving," passive. And there are scores of similar epitaphs, both Christian and non-Christian. One pagan husband commemorates his physician wife, whom he married when she was only fourteen: "To Primilla, a physician, daughter of Lucius Vibius Melito. She lived forty-four years, of which thirty were spent with Lucius Cocceius Apthorus without a quarrel. Apthorus built this monument for his best, chaste wife and for himself."[29] Another from the Christian Catacombs of Domitilla muddies the line between Christian and pagan but retains the conviction that wifely submission characterized the best possible marriage: "To the gods of the underworld. For Flavia Speranda, a most holy, incomparable wife, a mother to all, who lived with me for 28 years, 8 months, with no bitterness. Onesiforus made this [inscription] for his noble and well-deserving wife."[30] To be sure, this language of uxorial acquiescence could also be co-opted by women setting up epitaphs to their husbands: "To the noble Aurelius Agapitus Dracontius, a most sweet and incomparable husband, who lived with me for thirty years without any quarrels. Aurelia Amazonia made [this stone]. Rest in peace."[31] But such cases were unusual. Most of the time, women were remembered for their fertility, beauty, industry, self-sacrifice, fidelity, and chastity. These were qualities that defined women's lives in a man's world. As the art historians Diana Kleiner and Susan Matheson note, whether women "actually possessed such characteristics in life was never the point."[32]

"Forgotten wives and evanescent children, such is the constant rubric of mortality at Rome." So wrote the late Ronald Syme, one of Britain's foremost historians of ancient Rome.[33] Syme was usually right; but here he was wrong. Wives were not so easily forgotten in Rome. To begin with, a woman's life in third- and fourth-century Rome was not lived in *purdah*. Women were publicly visible and active.[34] They shopped, visited their friends, ran businesses, endorsed and patronized political candidates, participated in civic activities, and even fought in the gladiatorial arena. But ordinary women became most visible for us today through the traces left behind of their lives, and those traces were likely to be more deeply chiseled for women who married than for those who didn't. This is because when women died, they were most likely to be commemorated by their husbands. Our largest group of epitaphs in Rome (both pagan and Christian) comes from husbands to their wives.[35] This is curious, when one considers that given the age difference between men and women at marriage, women probably often outlived their husbands. Yet if they did, we would expect to find a higher proportion of tombstones from children to their mothers than from husbands to wives. The curious (and perhaps sad) fact remains: if Roman women died as widows, no one was likely to commemorate them.[36] In terms of affective familial bonds, then, the strongest bond appears to have been between husbands and wives, followed by parents to children. On the basis of this and other evidence, Roman social historians have noted that the Roman *familia* was rather different from our modern notion of family; there was no simple nuclear unit of father-mother-child.[37] The marital bond, though attended within the household by slaves, patrons, freedpeople, wet nurses, nurses, and pedagogues (something like nannies), remained the chief affective relationship that a highborn woman would experience in her lifetime.

If it were not precisely the case that a woman's closest emotional connections were neither with her parents nor with her children but with her husband, this is certainly the impression that has been created for us from the extant records of women's lives, particularly the visual or epigraphic records. In these, marriage—not motherhood—defines a woman's social identity. This is why we find a woman's marriage consistently recorded on her epitaph, whether she died in the Roman Republic of the first century BCE or in the Christian empire of the fifth century CE. But whether she was a mother, or how many children she bore, was often not significant enough to record for posterity. Indeed, many women's epitaphs, both Christian and pagan, include the length of the marriage but not the age of the wife at death. A successful life, then, was measured not by how many years a woman had lived or how many children she bore, but how many of those years were lived in matrimony. By the fourth century CE, it became fashionable for husbands to note the length of marriage on their wives' epitaphs not just in years and months, but also in days, even hours. In one brief inscription from the Catacombs of Callistus, for instance, a husband laments the loss of his wife, with whom he lived "well" for twenty years, ten days, and one hour.[38] Wives were even more likely to carefully record the length of their marriage on their husbands' epitaphs down to the hour, as in this inscription from the Christian Catacomb of Bassilla off the Via Salaria: "Silvana to her well deserving husband Nicatius, with whom she lived three years, two months, and eleven hours."[39] It's possible, of course, that Silvana—one of Rome's poorer inhabitants—didn't know her husband's age, and so didn't ask for it to be recorded. What is more likely is that even if she did, the length of their marriage was far more important a detail to record for posterity.

A curious argument among classicists has concerned the degree to which we can extrapolate Roman emotional lives from our own, as if profound human emotions emerged only with modernity. Still technically an open question, for example, is whether Romans loved their children ("the way that *we* love our children" remains unvoiced, but it is there). Whether Roman spouses loved each other is even more debated. Marriages for love did happen in Rome, clearly.[40] One tombstone from Rome records a freedwoman's sad elegy to her departed husband:

> To the sacred spirits to be worshipped, a sacred thing to the spirits of the dead, I, Furia Spes, a freedwoman, dedicate this to Sempronius Firmus, my husband, most dear to me. When I met him, as a boy and girl we were joined equally in love; I lived with him for too short a time and in the time we should have lived, we were torn apart by an evil hand. Therefore, I ask you, most sacred spirits, that you protect my dear husband whom I entrust to you and that you be willing to be most indulgent to him in the night hours, and that I might see him [in a dream?] and also that he might want me to persuade fate to allow me to come to him more sweetly and quickly.[41]

If we can wonder if Roman couples loved one another, we can wonder, too, if they grieved when one partner died. It's not that there isn't abundant proof that Romans mourned, it's that funerary epigraphy is so standard as to raise suspicions. Wives are commemorated time after time with a few platitudes: *dulcissima* ("most sweet"), *cara* ("dear"), *incomparabile*. So standard epitaphs offer no reliable barometer of true sentiment, one could argue, because their language is so highly conventional. Almost all tomb-stones of the third and fourth centuries, for instance, describe the deceased as "well-deserving." The Roman historian Keith Hopkins remarks, "The very act of transforming feelings into words automatically channels them along conventional lines. Language is a set of conventions."[42] True enough. But as Hopkins notes, grief isn't any less potent just because it is channeled into a set of social conventions and commemorative habits, particularly when it comes to death.

Many epitaphs by women to their husbands still exist. Strikingly, most withhold details of sentiment. Perhaps such language was inappropriate, or perhaps widows had other, more pressing concerns. In the Christian Cata-combs of Bassilla, for instance, a young widow named Elia Ebantia erected a remarkable epitaph to her husband that still resonates with the horror of her situation. Married for only nine months to a very sick man, their union had nevertheless produced a daughter, Faustina. By the time that the wife composed her husband's epitaph, their child was only a few days or months old, and Elia Ebantia felt compelled to explain: "Of the nine months of our marriage, he was sick the whole time but for 39 days." It was in that period that she had conceived her child—not outside the confines of marriage as wagging tongues, no doubt, conveyed. One feels for Elia Ebantia, the young widow and mother, struggling not only against her circumstances but against those who muttered that such a short marriage to such a sick man was not likely to have produced a legitimate offspring.[43]

On the other hand, thousands upon thousands of funerary inscriptions from husbands to their wives decry the cruel hand that fate had dealt them by dragging their spouses to an early grave. "I have lost my wife. Why should I stay any longer now? If I had been fortunate, my Piste would have been alive. I am gripped by grief, alive when my wife is dead. Nothing is so miserable as to lose your whole life, and yet to go on living."[44] These epi-taphs attest, most baldly, that to mourn one's wife was perceived as an im-portant Roman social virtue.[45] For the same reason, Roman husbands of the third and fourth centuries took much more care to record the precise length of their wives' lives—even to the hour—than did any other family member or relative.[46] But they also assume that passers-by, reading the epitaphs, would empathize with the sad plight of a bereaved husband and would join him in sorrowing for a love cut short by the Fates.[47]

What all this tells us is that the precise quality and degree of grief that one spouse suffered upon the death of the other is difficult to discern di-rectly from inscriptional sources. No doubt Romans *did* mourn, in different degrees depending on the texture of each marriage. Complicating an already complex landscape of personal grief, then, were various "commemorative habits" that affected the choice of language, visual and verbal, to express emotion. It would be unwise to surmise that Roman women loved their husbands less just because three times as many husbands left us epitaphs for their wives than wives for their husbands. Men commemorated their wives more often partly because they had more wealth at hand to do so, and partly because commemoration of wives became a public virtue in and of itself. Setting up a tombstone brought men social merit; it also constituted what Roman historian Brent Shaw calls a "cultural act—even more artificial than the relationships and sentiments it recorded."[48] The precise language of commemoration carefully etched for public consumption followed the ideals for women that were, as Sir Moses Finley notes, "formulated and imposed by middle- and upper-class Roman males."[49] It does not mean that women necessarily behaved in exemplary ways, or that marriages were so consistently a picture of harmony. Finley likens the women who emerge from epitaphs as "anonymous and passive fractions" of a family, "for the virtues which were stressed were decorum, chastity, gracefulness, even temper and childbearing." He gently reminds us not to believe everything that husbands said of their wives, for public memory, after their deaths.[50]

But the same was true of what wives said of their husbands, and indeed, what wives said of themselves. Let's return to the case of "Proba." From the standpoint of modern feminism—a perspective by which we would be quite unfair to judge her—Proba undercut her own autonomy by choosing to emphasize her own marital fidelity as the most significant marker of identity. But women have always participated in such public and social discourses of respectability. Besides, she did so with considerable—and, I think, characteristic—élan, as we shall see.

Proba's grave chamber features two fine renditions of dramatic moments in the story of *Alcestis*—one, the initiation of the dramatic action as Admetus lies dying, and the second, the final moment of triumph as Heracles returns Alcestis from the underworld to her grieving husband. What interests me most here, though, is the way Proba and her artist altered the script. Proba invokes *Alcestis*, but she *disremembers* it. Here, strikingly, Heracles touches Alcestis gently, and the two form a visual unit. By contrast, in other depictions of Alcestis on Roman sarcophagi, it is Admetus and Alcestis who touch, to hold hands.[51] The symbolic gesture on these sarcophagi—the *dex-*

trarum iunctio—connotes marriage, and thus it would have been natural, expectable even, to find Alcestis and Admetus holding hands here. Once again, Proba—or her artist—has broken from convention. But why?

There *is* a logic here, but it is difficult to penetrate. The theme of marital vows continuing beyond death also figured in Proba's other choices of wall paintings in Cubiculum N.[52] Next to the painting of Admetus on his deathbed, we find a large image of Heracles and Minerva. What had escaped the notice of most modern observers is that Heracles and Minerva also stand in the *dextrarum iunctio* position that, as we have already seen, often signifies a married couple whose bond will extend beyond life itself.[53] It's a curious gesture for Heracles and Minerva—they were never married—and a clear sign that the identity of the figures was less important than the symbolism of the pose.[54] Minerva was a half-sister to Heracles, his protector and, in a sense, his patron; it was with Minerva's assistance that Heracles completed some of his assigned labors, particularly the return of the famed apples of the Hesperides. Perhaps the handclasp signified Heracles' gratitude and nothing more.[55] Sometimes a handshake is just a handshake.

But something else is curious. On standard Alcestis sarcophagi, Heracles draws a heavily veiled Alcestis out of the world of the shadows to her husband. Thus Alcestis on Metilia Acte's sarcophagus resembles a ghost, but also a Roman bride who came to her husband heavily veiled, demure.[56] The image may hearken back to early Greek variants of the myth, where Alcestis meets her death on her wedding day. In fact, the art historian Susan Wood observes that almost every figure in Alcestis's return on Metilia Acte's sarcophagus finds a parallel in a typical Roman wedding scene. Alcestis's *palla* drawn over her head resembles the *flammeum* or saffron-colored veil of the bride. The couple—Alcestis and Admetus—stand together, rejoined, clasping right hands in the *dextrarum iunctio*. But in Cubiculum N, Proba wanted something different. Above her grave, Heracles leads Alcestis out of the looming cavern mouth of the underworld. He turns back to face her, gently guiding her toward her husband. This is no scene of happy reunion, of a marriage, of equal partners coming together in a moment of celebration. There is only a pale, absurdly naked, and effeminate husband on one side, and facing him, the wife and her new partner, the brave and virile Heracles who has rescued her from the jaws of death. One wonders what Proba meant by it all, really.

Perhaps Proba's choice to feature Heracles in her family grave chamber was both deliberate and provocative. A recent article by H. Gregory Snyder explores the layers of meaning behind the choice of images in Via Latina catacombs. Snyder notes that in the fourth century, Heracles was interpreted in a variety of ways. On one level, he stood as a pagan "answer" to Christ—he too could save his followers from death. Proba might, then, have been making a pointed allusion to the richness and continued potency of Greco-Roman intellectual and spiritual traditions in an environment in which these were losing significant ground to Christianity. But it seems to me that Proba was up to something else. As Richard Brilliant notes, certain images require "prior knowledge or preunderstanding" (*Vorverständnis*) to be effective.[57] Part of this *Vorverständnis*, for ancient Romans, entailed recognizing Heracles as an ironic hero or, even further, as a buffoon. In Rome, the number of serious dramas featuring Heracles was a mere trickle compared to the torrent of satyr plays, farces, and comedies in which he entertained his audiences with a delight which, to borrow classicist Karl Galinsky's words, seemed not to have known a saturation point.[58] And though we tend to regard *Alcestis* as a tragedy, we are quite wrong. It was, rather, a type of farce. In it, for instance, Heracles appears as somewhat of a buffoon—the comic relief. He chastises those who take life too seriously, for "this is no life at all, but rather, a botched job" (line 800). Such a cavalier attitude has Heracles that he shows up at Admetus's household, gets blindly drunk, and sings boisterously, out of tune (lines 748–761). The indiscretion is highlighted even more by dramatic irony—although he does not know it, he is drunk and disorderly within a household hushed and occupied with preparations for Alcestis's funeral.

At the culmination of the play *Alcestis*, Admetus, too, comes across as a fool; he fails to recognize that the silent, veiled woman whom Heracles leads to him is his wife. He accepts her as his new bride, thereby breaking his promise to Alcestis that he will not remarry if she consents to die in his stead. Only after he has taken his new bride does he realize it is actually his old bride, and he is caught, awkwardly, in his lie. This supposedly triumphal scene here at the grave, therefore, would have recalled to a Roman audience not merely an example of extraordinary uxorial devotion and Herculean triumph over death, but a hilarious "gotcha" moment in which a humiliated husband's trustworthiness was revealed to be merely a sham.

As a farce, *Alcestis* had a potentially subversive quality, perhaps one especially appreciated by female viewers. This was recognized by the early-second-century Roman satirist Juvenal, who complains, "Our wives look on at Alcestis undergoing her husband's fate; if they were granted a like liberty of exchange, they would gladly let the husband die to save a puppy-dog's life" (*Satire*, 6). There is comedy and irony in the depiction of the idealized wife who is, at once, silent and subordinate to Admetus, then to Heracles, but who emerges as the heroine of this set-piece room. I very much doubt that this was all lost on Proba. As classicist Carlin Barton writes about the miming and staging that formed part of a Roman funeral, "the categories of tragedy and comedy dissolve: all life becomes a paradoxical hilarotragedy."[59] Proba, in her use of a farce that masquerades as a tragedy to convey the values and drama of her own life, becomes a trickster—a role not unknown among female performers in late antiquity. In her study of women mimes and dancers in late antiquity, Ruth Webb notes these women used "trickery to attain their ends. What is more, they use the female body as a potent means of expression and, of course, persuasion."[60] Proba here uses images of herself-as-Alcestis-as-Minerva to "trick" but also to persuade her viewers that she was the true heroine here. It is far from clear, in the end, whether her husband's death constituted Proba's tragedy, or her moment of ironic realization of men's potential duplicity and dissimulation.

Ancient viewers visiting Proba's grave chamber may have experienced an "ironic amusement" and, perhaps, a sense of resignation or nostalgia for things past and passing.[61] And they may have appreciated this patron's sense of humor and her firm belief that of herself and her husband, she was the more formidable. She had her husband depicted as a passive and foolish Admetus afraid to die. She commissioned bold paintings of an ironic and unlikely savior—one who could knock back too many drinks and then go on to throttle Death himself ("beside the very tomb, seizing him with my hands," as Heracles boasts). And then she had herself depicted both as Alcestis, the dutiful wife, and as Minerva, the goddess of war—and wisdom. It was the final, visual testament of a formidable Roman widow in the late empire. She, as the paragon of virtue both feminine and masculine, would herself breach Death's dark barricades, moving in and out between realms with the sure knowledge of their permeability.

We are with Proba, traversing Rome's streets, perhaps on the way outside the city walls to visit the temple of Fortuna Muliebris—a privilege afforded only to *univirae*, women who had taken only one husband in the course of their lives. As we walk—or better still, ride in our litter (for good heavens! this is Rome, after all)—we pass by another woman, about the same age, hurrying off in the opposite direction with darting, downcast eyes. She's Christian, and she has a prayer meeting to attend. The wind wrings her long, striped red dalmatic around her ankles and for a brief instant, we can only just see the outline of her body inside the shapeless, boxy garment as she smoothes down her tunic . . . and then she's disappeared around a corner, a blur of bright green afterimage scorched onto our retinas in the sunshine. Were they to talk—for a moment, or even for a long while—what would the two women discuss? First, let's consider the things that connected them: they lived in the same turbulent decades in the same vibrant city. They had both been married, and both were mothers. Both likely came from the same social class—not top-drawer elite, but the socially ambitious. Both were ordinary and insignificant, destined to be almost forgotten—to be almost entirely absent from the historical record—but for their graves. Yet both were convinced, although in very different ways, that what they achieved in their lives would earn them a certain kind of immortality. Still, the process of the Christian woman's entrance into Catholic memory and tradition was governed by a different set of historical circumstances and ideologies of recollection. Unlike Proba's grave in Cubiculum N—undiscovered until the 1950s—the Christian woman's burial chamber has been long known and long interpreted, though almost always by male clerics who drew meaning out of her image in a way that reflected not *her* life, but their own concerns and beliefs. It is fair to say that these interpreters failed to listen attentively to what she had to say about who she was. But it's time to pay her a visit.

In the Catacombs of Priscilla under Rome's Via Salaria Nuova in the northern suburbs, there exists a small, finely decorated cubiculum known from its extraordinary central painting as the Cubiculum of the Velata ("veiled woman").[62] The painting fills a lunette high above a central arch (or *arcosolium*) grave. Still clearly visible—thanks to expert restoration—are three separate scenes. On the left, three figures are arranged together. A woman garbed in a yellow, striped dalmatic stands at front, nearly facing the viewer. She holds in her hands a scroll, although rather than looking down at it, her gaze is directed off to her right. To her left and slightly behind her, a smaller male figure stands ready with something that looks like a piece of fabric, perhaps a veil or a robe; he too looks off to the right. The largest figure in the frame is a seated, older man. He sports a curly gray beard and a long white dalmatic with stripes on the sleeve. Extending his right arm, he rests his hand lightly on the woman's right shoulder. No one quite knows what this dramatic and significant visual moment commemorates, though many things have been proposed.

In the middle scene that dominates the composition, a woman—proba-

Lunette fresco from the back wall of the Cubiculum of the Velata at the Christian Cata-
combs of Priscilla, showing three scenes in the life of the deceased woman buried in the cu-
biculum's main grave. At left, we see the woman between two men in a moment some have
identified as a wedding scene and some as her consecration to a life of virginity; in the cen-
ter, the woman prays in an attitude known as an orans; at right, the same woman sits in a
high-backed chair holding a small, naked child on her lap.

bly the same woman as the one figured on the left and right—stands with
both arms upraised, raising her eyes heavenward. She wears a dramatic dark
red dalmatic with patterned, brocade stripes and a white veil with dark
stripes. The viewer's attention focuses on her hands, which are disproportionately, strikingly large and open toward the heavens. On the right side of
the lunette, the same woman sits on a chair almost identical to the one on
which the old man sits at left; she is gazing to the right, too, holding a small
naked child high on her lap, almost awkwardly.

The burial chamber in which we find these remarkable scenes is diminutive, and it contains a number of simple slot-graves next to the central
arched grave that almost certainly contained the burial of the Velata, the
Veiled Woman. The space has been so heavily restored over the centuries,
however, that it's difficult to tell how many graves had been in the room and
what precisely the Velata's grave had looked like. Her bones may once have
rested in a sarcophagus under her image, or perhaps in a slightly more hum-

ble *arcosolium* or arch grave dug down into the cool volcanic soil. But hers was still the focal point in a small room of simple graves. There are other paintings in the room too: to the left, there's the sacrifice of Abraham (Gen 22:9–10); to the right, three Hebrews (Dan 3:15–29) raise their hands heavenward in the fiery furnace. A dove appears above them bearing a branch. The ceiling vault has a fine painting of the Good Shepherd hoisting a lamb aloft his shoulders; there is also a painting of Jonah being disgorged from the mouth of the whale. Because of the early Christian imagery (and also because these catacombs themselves are entirely Christian) we know that the Velata was certainly Christian, certainly devout, and certainly a woman who commanded a great deal of respect.

But let's return to the central painting and its story. Since the catacomb's rediscovery in the sixteenth century, all three "moments" or tableaux in this painting have been subject to considerable discussion and interpretation. The right-hand scene of a woman holding a child in her lap was for generations of interpreters read as the Virgin and Child.[63] Although the other tableaux were interpreted as scenes from a woman's life, no one seemed to be particularly curious as to why the Virgin and Child would be figured so prominently next to images of an actual woman. Wouldn't it have been simpler to imagine that that image of a mother and child in a woman's grave was a portrait rather than a sacred image? Catholic scholars answered that early Christian art was primarily symbolic—therefore the best and truest reading of the scene was one that privileged the symbolic over the literal. But look what happens then: the image of a mother and child, interpreted as the Virgin and Child, becomes a symbol not of *maternity*, but of *virginity*— to which, these interpreters imagine, our Velata aspired. One important Christian archaeologist of the last century summed up the Catholic view: "This group is of the greatest importance because it proves that the Virgin Mary was represented by the first Christians not only as a subject of veneration, but also as a model of virtue to be imitated."[64]

Why virginity, though? Was the Velata a consecrated virgin? So generations of male observers have suggested. They saw the scene at right as her consecration ceremony.[65] The Velata stands with the bearded male bishop behind her, his hand on her shoulder. To her side, standing behind her, a man stands holding the veil that will mark her entry into the church's order of virgins. In the central image, the new virgin in Paradise raises her hands in prayerful devotion, her head veiled. To the right sits the model of the eternal, blessed handmaiden of the Lord—to inspire and edify the Velata.

This is one way of reading the image, but it carries with it some problems. First, we have no descriptions—either visual or textual—of a virgin's ordination ceremony, so we don't actually know if this is what we see here. It was likely the case that consecrated virgins were *not* veiled—at least, Tertullian in the third century was angered by the insolence of Christian virgins who believed that their piety and devotion meant that they did not have to hide behind the veil—because they had nothing to conceal nor to fear. And so another explanation for the images was sought. As early as 1895, the art historian Otto Mitius argued that what we have in the Cubiculum of the Velata was not the consecration of a virgin, but a Christian marriage scene.[66] Claude Dagens, who made a thorough study of the cubiculum in the early 1970s, concurred.[67] And so catacomb guides now describe what we see as a wedding scene:

> On the left a bishop gives his blessing at the dead man's wedding, while the youth at his side hands him the nuptial veil; the scroll in the bride's hands is the *tabula nuptialis,* a document enumerating marital duties. The woman as mother is shown on the right with a baby in her arms, a group which was thought in the past to represent the Madonna and Child.[68]

It's not entirely surprising that although the grave painting features three prominent images of women—or rather, the same woman three times—the Vatican-published guide interprets this as a wedding scene for the unnamed "dead man" who hovers in the background of one of the three vignettes. Further, the author emphasizes the action of the *men* in this scene: the bishop, the groom, and the attendant. All the bride does is hold the tablet that supposedly details her marital duties. No mention is made of why the husband seems so overshadowed by his wife, nor is it noted that the bishop places his hand on the *woman,* not the man. The guide offers a stunning, yet typical, example of the masculine gaze, which reduces all activity to the sphere of male significance.

But there is another problem. The hypothesis that what we see here is the Velata's wedding is every bit as problematic as was the argument that this is her consecration into the church's order of virgins. Indeed, there's even *less* argument to support it. Why would the bride stand in the foreground, with the groom so small and relatively unimportant, behind her? For centuries, Roman wedding iconography featured husband and wife standing beside one another, their right hands joined. It was the standard way to depict a marriage, even a Christian marriage.[69] And there are other things that seem not quite right. The "nuptial" veil held in the hands of the young man could just as plausibly be a virgin's veil, or even a clerical veil or *pallium*. For a nuptial veil, though, it's all wrong. The Roman nuptial veil was bright flame-yellow, from which it took its name, the *flammeum*. The veil here is white, with a thin red stripe at bottom.[70] Third- or fourth-century Christians rejected the *flammeum* as too "pagan" in association and replaced it with the *velum* or *velamen*, but this covered both the bride and the groom.[71] The pose we see here—with the bishop laying his hand on the woman's shoulder—is also unprecedented for marriage scenes, whether Christian or pagan. In the third century, Clement of Alexandria reported that a priest consecrates a couple by laying his hand on *both* the bride and the groom.[72] And then there is the mystery of the scroll (Latin: *volumen*). People often hold scrolls in Roman funerary art; it was a sort of short-form symbol for the wearer's high status. But Catholic interpreters see it here as a *tabula nuptialis* or document "on which the duties of the husband and wife are listed."[73] This interpretation is rather telling, for Augustine reports in the early fifth century that the *tabula nuptialis* listed not domestic duties, but the details of the dowry. It was read in the presence of wedding guests. Augustine continues that the new wife assents to the document "whereby her husband has become her lord (*dominus*) and she has been made his handmaid or slave (*ancilla*)."[74] Even still, Roman depictions of marriage all feature the husband holding this *tabula matrimoniale*, not the wife.[75]

Iconographic standardization is important: it ensures that when viewers look at an image, it conveys what the artist or commissioner wishes to convey. If the Velata (and her husband) wished to convey to viewers that her marriage was significant, then surely they would have ensured that the painting of their wedding looked, well, like a painting of a wedding. Why would they—or she—have broken from a standard convention? And even if the person who commissioned this image had been a man, why would he have shown himself as a young boy, standing quietly and subserviently behind his slightly older wife at their own wedding?

Neither explanation—that the scenes in the cubiculum of the Velata represent her consecration as a church virgin or her wedding ceremony—accounts for the nature of the iconography here. The images retain their mysteries. But the insistence in official literature of the catacombs that the scenes represent one of only two possible options crowd out other, woman-centered or women-oriented readings. They do not allow the Velata to speak—which is ironic, since the art above her grave was clearly intended to convey what, of her, was most important.

———

Let us return to a largely unexamined assumption: that one of the scenes on the Velata's grave features her wedding. We've arrived here partly by the process of elimination; the accompanying vignette depicts her with a child, thus it's a good guess she was married (and a fair guess that she was not an official, consecrated virgin). For ordinary people in the late empire, the slow Christianization of the populace did nothing to change the conviction that a woman's highest aspiration was to be a good wife. The highly influential biblical texts known as the Pastorals—1 Timothy, 2 Timothy, and Titus—make clear that women may be saved only by being submissive, silent wives and mothers:

> And Adam was not deceived, but the woman was deceived and became a transgressor. Yet she will be saved through childbearing, provided they continue in faith and love and holiness, with self-control. (1 Tim 2:14–15)

If anything, late antique Christianity only further narrowed a woman's domestic horizons. An early Christian epistle dated to the late first to mid-second century, titled 1 Clement, adjures an unknown cleric to maintain the domestic status quo:

> You directed women to accomplish all things with a blameless, respectful, and pure conscience, dutifully loving their husbands. And you taught them to run their households respectfully, living under the rule of submission, practicing discretion in every way. (1 Clement)

In the Pastorals, women are confined to the domestic sphere because they do not deserve freedom; they are too weighted down by sin. They are spiritually and morally continuous with Eve, inexorably caught in the snares of the flesh.

In the world of the second and third centuries, sin was not an abstract principle but a sort of genetic flaw lodged inextricably in the fibers and sinews of the human body. One wonders, then, if women's inherent connection to the flesh and to sin made them more connected to death in late antique Christian ideologies—their bodies were vehicles for pain, death, and guilt, for which they were expected, as Eve had, to suffer more acutely through the pains of childbirth. Death had entered the world through Eve, and women bore the responsibility for this reality more viscerally than men. The only sort of immortality that they might confer came from bearing children; the only sort of salvation for them came from the same—but of course, it was not true salvation. Only death might free them from the dissolute burdens of their flesh. This was true for men, too, of course, but to a lesser degree—it was not men's fault so much as it was women's that the body aged, corrupted, and passed into bone and worm-ridden tissue; the process could be traced back to Eve's perverse willingness to disobey. Bodily corruption and death were therefore, in patristic theology, the natural order of things only after the Fall, the consequence of women's intrinsically rebellious nature.

But if this is so—and certainly this is the impression that third- and fourth-century Christian theological writings provide—the images of women that speak to us in the material and visual evidence from the catacombs tell a radically different story. The Christianization of the *polis* had little effect on material culture, particularly in the way that women were commemorated. Wives still gained immortality through their husbands' graven praises on their gravestones. This epitaph from the Catacombs of Bassilla could just as plausibly have been written by a pagan as by a Christian:

> Sempronius Eunomius to his well-deserving wife Coccia Rufina, with whom he lived for twenty-one years, more or less. [She was] incomparable; concerning whom so much boldness was drawn out for the benefit of all, that behooved the feminine yoke; from which [marriage] I prayed often with so many prayers to have for myself one child from her womb. Goodbye, in peace.[76]

But nowhere do we see any indication from Christian funerary inscriptions that women stood closer to death, nor that their flesh had been vitiated by sin. Indeed, Christian husbands commemorated their wives as "most faithful" and "most darling" no more nor less than did pagans; even their claims that their wives were "most chaste" pointed not to strenuous attempts to contain the violent impulses of sin endemic within female flesh, but rather to the centuries-old Roman valuations of chastity and fidelity as the ideal qualities of a wife.

In terms of Christian funerary art, the only thing we can say about the connection between women, sin, and death is that we find in the Christian catacombs a remarkably disproportionate number of images of dead women. No one has ever commented on the phenomenon; it's safe to say that women are, in the dark spaces of communal graves, overwhelmingly present without having a presence. We see them everywhere as we walk through the labyrinthine galleries and cubicula of the catacombs, but their presence is never remarked upon—neither in the voluminous literature of early Christian art, nor in the cheerful, constant patter of the catacomb guides who lead modern visitors through the subterranean gloom. It's also curious that images of women never stand juxtaposed with images of Eve. Given the ardent attempts of fourth-century fathers of the church to connect ordinary women to their spiritual mother, we might expect to find their images somehow linked or juxtaposed. But no such attempt was made. Instead, the dead women of the catacombs tell a rather different story about women's status, their social and spiritual possibilities, and the nature of salvation. But then, considering that women played active roles as patrons of burial lands, it perhaps comes as little surprise that they are featured as prominently in catacomb art as they are.

In remarkable ways, the catacombs came to represent women's sacred space—a fact never recognized anymore. The Velata's burial art is one fine example of the once active presence of powerful women, and yet catacomb guides will tell you only: here is a painting of a woman or perhaps really a symbol of a pious soul; here is a painting of the Virgin and Child or perhaps only an ordinary woman and her child; here is the image of that woman's wedding. And then you will move on in the gloom, to wonder at our earliest surviving painting of the Madonna, just a little bit farther down the corridor. No one asks why there are so many images of women at the Catacombs of Priscilla; no one asks, either, why in this one catacomb we find so many early, fine depictions of the Virgin. Was there a reason, in the late ancient world, for this emphasis on the feminine?

In most Christian catacombs in Rome, cubicula contain burial spaces for an entire family. Their decoration, we suspect, consciously replicated the *domus* or Roman house. Yet these family "bedrooms" are decorated with images not of the entire happy family group—as one might expect from Roman mausolea—but, more often than not, of the matron alone surrounded by decorative or typological figures. In their isolation of the powerful woman, catacomb images such as the Velata's often provide a sort of "flip side" to the information on most Christian funerary inscriptions, where women are defined primarily by their uxorial devotion. Whether this absence of the marital couple in art is played out in the burials of the grave chambers themselves remains an intriguing question. Where are the men and children in these family graves? Where are all their likenesses? Did women commission artists to place their own images in cubicula, keeping pious vigil over those whom they loved? Or was it an act of male devotion to feature a wife or daughter so prominently, to the exclusion of others? Or are all these lone women who peer out at us from the catacomb walls powerful widows who were commemorated for their activities on behalf of the church: learning, teaching, modeling appropriate behavior, even donating their resources to the church? Could, for instance, the image of the Velata standing with scroll in hand, the bishop putting his hand on her shoulder, record the Velata's financial donation to the church and not her submission to her husband?

So let's return to look again at the images over the Velata's tomb. In them, she appears as a married woman actively engaged in various activities, but apparently without her husband. The remarkable isolation of a woman from her family that we find here is hardly unusual in Christian funerary art. And yet we might compare this isolation with the numerous funerary effigies—dating from the Republican period on—that lined the roads out of Rome, where families, or at least husband and wife, were portrayed together.[77] Remarkably, in the corpus of third- to fifth-century Christian catacomb frescoes, precious few images exist of women with their husbands or with their children. We may wonder what to make of the curious absence of family in these images, the lack of referents, in fact, to practically *all* such relationships. There was a decision made somewhere, whether by the artist or, more likely, the patron(s), to deny or obliterate these horizontal familial bonds.

The image type of the solitary woman in a family grave acts as the visual counterpoint to certain contemporary ideological writings that emphasized the sacred bonds of Christian matrimony. Even the austere church father Tertullian—an advocate of virginity although himself securely married—presented the married couple as a paradigm of domestic piety:

> How beautiful, then, the marriage of two Christians, two who are one in hope, one in desire, one in the way of life they follow, one in the religion they practice. . . . [T]hey pray together, they worship together, they fast together; instructing one another, encouraging one another, strengthening one another. Side by side they face difficulties and persecution, and share their consolations. (*Ad Uxorem,* 2.8; pp. 35–36)

Catacomb images, by contrast, rarely if ever emphasize devotion through domestic harmony. Instead, women are disproportionately represented as solitary figures, often in the *orans* pose that the Velata assumes in the central, dominant image on her grave. Whatever this pose (and its isolation) meant, the church officials who oversaw the catacombs evidently did not consider these paintings of solitary, prayerful women either illicit or inappropriate.

But if the images of solitary and apparently powerful Christian women in the catacombs were not *theologically* troubling, in the world of third- and fourth-century Roman Christianity, the phenomenon of the solitary woman *was socially* troubling. Confining women to the domestic realm in canonical texts such as the Pastoral Epistles only exacerbated already potent disagreements in late ancient Christianity concerning women's spiritual opportunities and religious authority. As the historian Philip Rousseau observes, "Seeing the household as the arena of redemption provoked anxieties about sexuality, marriage and the place of women."[78] Christianity, he continues, provoked "a desire to embed sexuality within a protective set of community structures." Consequently, virgins were at once highly respected and carefully curtailed in the limits of their authority. As Rousseau notes, these same tensions prompted respect for widows, "offering them more than a choice between remarriage and oblivion."[79] Given the marked absence of Christian epitaphs to widowed wives, the social oblivion that faced widows was all too real. Whenever possible, remarriage after widowhood offered women the surest way to be immortalized, if only in clumsy words carved in stone.

How can we allow the Velata to speak? How can we listen attentively to what she says, rather than just assume that she belonged, submissively, to the church and/or her husband, body and soul? Indeed, there is little about the imagery that suggests that the Velata considered herself submissive. The images above her grave are bold, costly, and rare. They feature her in three different life moments, or as three significant personae. One is the Velata as a mother. No father or husband figure is present in this vignette—and his absence is telling. If it were a domestic scene of an earlier century—an ordinary, garden-variety Roman funerary relief—it would feature husband, wife, and child. The Velata's solitude here is a clue that her *maternal* status was valued more highly than her *uxorial* status. The second vignette that balances the image of her as a mother depicts her as the sole woman in the company of two men, where she is the center of the action. A seated, bearded man places his hand on her shoulder, and she reads from a scroll that she herself holds. Behind her, a slave or attendant stands at the ready, holding a veil. The third and most central vignette features a large, veiled portrait of the same woman, her arms raised, perhaps in prayer. All the images are somehow related, although they do not say the same thing in the same way.

If we remain skeptical about the theory that the left-hand scene depicts a marriage or the ordination of a virgin, we are left to explore what interpretation might be equally or more plausible. Two art historians, Philippe du Borguet and André Grabar, have suggested that the scene features the Velata's catechetical instruction. She holds in her hands a scroll—not listing her marital duties, but on which are written the Christian scriptures that she is learning in preparation for her baptism.[80] The pose conveys, at once, the Velata's piety and her learnedness. These last two are *qualities,* of course, and thus do not much help us interpret the scene—and yet they are more helpful than seeing a wedding scene in something that is only a wedding because Catholic interpreters want to find one here. The Velata tells us not that she is married, but that *she can read,* and that her act of public reading was even endorsed by a bishop at a moment in her life she found significant enough to record on the walls of her grave.

In a fascinating article on images of women on Christian sarcophagi, the British art historian Janet Huskinson gives us a new way of reading images such as the Velata's—particularly the central *orans* image and the so-called wedding scene. She reads such poses not as conveying a *symbol,* but specific *actions:* "Now the emphasis seems to fall on processes of intellectualization, of learning, reading and praying, in which women are shown to be expert practitioners."[81] Interpreting one particular carving from a Christian sarcophagus, Huskinson observes that the woman portrayed is "properly active in pursuit of the texts that were a characteristic of contemporary Christian culture: she listens to them attentively as they are expounded by Christian teachers, and she holds, or reads from, a scroll or codex of her own. The content of what she reads and hears must be an important part of her self-formation, confirming her in her Christian identity."[82] Huskinson's words help us to understand what the Velata found most important to convey about herself. She saw herself (as her family or her community saw her) as both learned and pious.

Intellectual women like the Velata found a home in Christian circles. This is not to say that pagan women of equal means were not also intellectually engaged, as the case of the woman I call Proba demonstrates through her eloquent use of visual rhetoric. But Christianity of the third and fourth centuries presented at least some women with the opportunities to learn and to lead within small communities and study groups. The third-century bishop of Rome Hippolytus, for instance, wrote to and for a female audience (*Comm. In Daniel* 1.22). A century or so earlier, the Syrian Christian Tatian defended learned Christian women. After speaking against Greek views of women, he writes, "I want to mention these women so that you may not think that we indulge in strange activities, or jeer at the women who philosophize among us" (*Oration to the Greeks,* 33.2, p. 63). By the fourth century, the intellectual activities of a certain class of women—particularly as scriptural experts—had a considerable influence on Christian visual culture. Huskinson comments, "The image of the learned woman had become an acceptable stereotype. . . . [T]heir range and number suggest that Christian art opens up the intellectual role of women in relation to men even further than its recent antecedents had done."[83]

To think of Roman Christian women as intellectuals or philosophers is very different from the dominant Catholic interpretation that tends to classify ancient women not by activity but by life stage: thus women conventionally fall into the categories of virgin, matron, or widow. Instead, we might measure women by the type and quality of their activities. The Velata, like Proba, wanted primarily to be depicted after her death as learned, in a culture in which learning the scriptures was tantamount to virtue. The learned woman was not entirely unusual; the fourth-century Roman *patrona* Melania the Elder, for instance, impressed the church historian Palladius with her erudition:

> Being very industrious and loving literature, she turned night into day, perusing every writing of the ancient commentators including 300,000 lines of Origen and 250,000 of Gregory, Stephen, Pierius, Basil and other standard writers. Nor did she read them through only once and casually, but laboriously went through each book seven or eight times. (*LH,* 60)

Paula and her daughter Eustochium—whom we will meet more fully later in this book—mastered Greek and even Hebrew so as to work alongside the great scholar and translator Jerome. Certainly (provided they were not explicitly instructing men) there was nothing inherently shocking or shameful about women displaying their learnedness. The Velata—or whoever commissioned her image—did so by choosing a visual rhetoric widely employed by late ancient women.

The visibility of women such as the Velata in the Christian catacombs suggests a number of possibilities. First, the powerful women who commissioned paintings may have endeavored to create *memoriae* for themselves.

Or there may have been a movement to reinsert deceased women into the fabric of the family and community through the creation of a specific, family- or community-centered "cult of memory." It is possible that some of these communities were primarily composed of women—we know from the Council of Elvira that women up to then often held all-night prayer vigils for the deceased—in which case images of women may have provided powerful visual encouragement and models for imitation. In the funerary vigils of women, deep in the catacombs, we can imagine that catacomb images of richly adorned matrons in the act of prayer—perhaps even of prophecy or public learning—likely challenged nascent patriarchal ideas of gender, status, and power.

We also know from the funerary evidence of women's inscriptions and images that with virtue, properly exercised, came sure immortality. What differed between Christians and pagans was the definition of "virtue." For pagans, when it came to women, "virtue" was inseparable from "wifely virtue." For late ancient Christians, virtue came to lie almost exclusively in chastity. This chastity could best be demonstrated, perhaps, by visual isolation into a world of women. To what degree a pagan woman such as Proba considered herself to be "immortalized" by marital virtue—or her family apotheosized—we cannot say.

Let us return to Proba and her grave chamber. Just as she chose for her daughter a myth of Ceres and Proserpina—a myth with a happy ending, since the mother successfully lobbies for her daughter's return to the world of the living if only for a portion of the year—so does the myth of Alcestis share the same parabolic arc, the same pattern of *descensus ad infernum,* the descent into hell. Consider, for a moment, the religious dimensions of this story. Proba chose to paint her own life through Alcestis just as Christianity took a sure, inexorable hold on Rome. The classicist Beverly Berg argues that there is no battle between Christianity and paganism in Proba's cubiculum: "The decoration of the tomb chamber was chosen to celebrate the devotion of a wife to her spouse and to display the painter's artistry, rather than to make a statement about the divinity, Christian or pagan."[84] But I'm not so sure. Christianity also centers itself around a *descensus ad infernum:* of Christ into death and back into life to redeem humanity. The ancient story of Alcestis, however, genders sacred duty differently. Given the curious mix of Christian and non-Christian imagery in the Via Latina hypogeum, it's intriguing to think that the figure of Alcestis—like the figure of Proserpina painted triumphantly over a young Christian woman's grave in Cubiculum O—may have been deliberately chosen by a pagan woman to stand defiant against Christianity's Redeemer. If so, the woman I call Proba revealed her thoughts on Christianity with a complicated series of implicit statements about the relative antiquity of Alcestis to Christ; the interplay of love, sacrifice, and duty; and the capability of women to act as redemptive figures. The images at Via Latina therefore reflect a battle—not so much between Christianity and paganism, but over *remembering*. The biblical images in the catacomb, like all biblical images, were meant as "clues" that brought to viewers' minds the events of Christian sacred history; Proba's images brought to mind a different myth, and a different remembered experience. As for Proba herself, in effect, we encounter her harrowing hell not once but twice: once to ransom her life for her passive, naked husband, and once to fetch her apotheosized daughter, the new Proserpina. It is Proba's own heroic efforts as a dutiful and loving wife and mother that broke death's sure bonds. But what does that say about her idea of an afterlife? Only that she acceded to its existence as some sort of mythological space, and that its boundaries were osmotic, permeable.

Who waits for us in the afterlife, then? The answer shines down from the walls of all Roman burial chambers. In their deep gloom, the mix of real and imagined, of the remembered and the invoked, must have thrown third- and fourth-century viewers—the family of the Velata, or of Proba—into the liminal space between the world of death and a better, promised place. It was a world in which civic and domestic virtue was as surely rewarded as was a steadfast and single-minded devotion to the Lord. We can imagine the Velata's family making their way through Priscilla's labyrinthine catacombs and standing, gazing upon her image. In the darkness, seeing her taking her place among those whom God had rescued from the jaws of death, the Velata's solitary figure became a symbol of her enduring presence, comforting her family from paradise.

CHAPTER 4

PRAYING WITH PRISCA

Just north of Rome's Aurelian walls along the Via Salaria Nuova and the spacious grounds of the Villa Ada park, a small convent of Benedictine sisters nestles among ocher- and rust-colored buildings. The convent's not particularly easy to find; like many religious houses in Rome, it is tucked away in a residential quarter few tourists bother to penetrate. But within the convent's stolid gray walls, a small community of sisters entrust themselves to a life lived in prayer, contemplation, and obedience. For their service to the church, they embroider exquisite liturgical vestments with fine silken thread. And when the sisters come together each day in their chapel for the celebration of the Holy Mass, they gather under a huge, glittering mosaic few in the outside world ever see. It features six people at a scimitar-curved table. At one end, a bearded priest, his arms outstretched, breaks bread for a celebration of the Eucharist. The image is somehow at once solemn and joyful, and the nuns regard it with pride. It was a gift of thanks to the Benedictine sisters, one sister told me, from a Jewish family in 1954 for offering them a place of sanctuary during the Roman pogrom of World War Two.

Nuns, of course, are not priests, and so they cannot conduct a Eucharistic service. Thus in this hushed world of women, as in every other Catholic convent in the world, a priest must visit the sisters to help them celebrate Catholicism's most holy sacrament. The mosaic directly before their eyes confirms this sacred reality: men stand in the natural hierarchical order one step closer to Christ, and women—though welcome to share in Christ's body and blood—cannot themselves bodily mediate the divine. They may not offer up the mystery of the Transubstantiation, the moment during the Mass at which the host is transformed into Christ's very substance, his sacred body. That this "natural order" has always been operative in Christianity is likewise proved by the mosaic, which is no modern invention: it is a faithful reconstruction of a Christian wall painting seventeen hundred

Mosaic featuring a modern reconstruction of an ancient fresco. Seven figures sit at a curved table sharing a Eucharistic feast. This large mosaic adorns the central wall behind the altar in the chapel of the Benedictine convent on top of the Catacombs of Priscilla. The sisters are in charge of leading visitors down into the catacombs.

years old that rests far underground directly beneath the sisters' feet. Visitors are welcomed to see the original for themselves.

The Benedictine sisters, in cooperation with the Pontifical Commission on Sacred Archaeology, administrate the Catacombs of Priscilla, which extend more than seven miles underground from their property well into the Villa Ada grounds. The catacombs count among Rome's largest. They originated as a disconnected series of Christian and pagan burial sites that had, over the course of a century or so, so grown that they merged together, the way that villages merge together over time to form cities. Parts of the catacombs, later reused for the burials of the very poor, were carved out of what had been quarries and water cisterns. Parts had been the cemetery grounds of wealthy ancient Roman aristocrats. Parts had been used to house the sacred burials of the holy martyrs; so many martyrs' bones did the Catacombs of Priscilla hold, in fact, that Renaissance explorers dubbed Priscilla "the Queen of the Catacombs." And today the sisters are happy to take visitors down for a brief tour, along well-worn circuits, past some of the jewels of early Christian art: the earliest known painting of the Virgin Mary, the Cubiculum of the Velata, and the small subterranean chamber

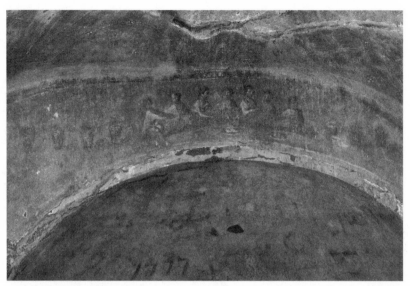

The original "Fractio Panis" image from the Greek Chapel at the Catacombs of Priscilla, upon which the mosaic at left is based. Are the figures male or female, or a combination of both? And what do their actions commemorate?

known as the Greek Chapel with its image of six people waiting eagerly to accept the Eucharist from the outstretched hands of the bearded priest—the image that has become the sisters' icon, the symbol of their ministry and the very beating heart of Catholic Church order.

On my first visit to the Catacombs of Priscilla, I looked with wonder and tender awe at the ancient paintings, until we reached the Greek Chapel. There I stopped short, gazing at the image of devoted Christians sitting at table fellowship, receiving the Eucharist. What struck me with some degree of force was that as far as I could see, all the figures seated at the table—*including* the figure "officiating" at the left—were *women*. But how could this be? Could women have received—and offered—the Eucharist in the late third century, at the time when scholars guess that this image was painted?[1] I had to find out. And I had to find out, too, why what I saw in this fresco was so clearly at variance with what others saw when they looked at it, from the sisters of Priscilla upstairs to my learned guide standing beside me. Indeed, what I discovered was that no other image in all of early Christian art had generated such a maelstrom of controversy, as scholars and people of faith disputed the true meaning of this image almost two millennia old.

The discovery of the Greek Chapel with its controversial meal scene has its story. The great excavator of the catacombs, Commendatore Giovanni Battista De Rossi (1822–1894) was a contemporary of Rodolfo Lanciani's—but unlike Lanciani, De Rossi was resolutely a man of the cloth. With the virtual explosion of building and excavating that marked late-nineteenth-century Rome, the cleric encouraged his senior students to further uncover Rome's lost secrets. By De Rossi's era, the Catacombs of Priscilla had already been rediscovered for two centuries—but not in their entirety. In 1888, De Rossi found a portion of the catacombs in absolute ruin. It was clear that the mere passage of time could not have wreaked such havoc; someone (or some group of people) had willfully broken into that portion and utterly destroyed it. The archaeologists doubted it was the work of ancient barbarian invaders. Lanciani discovered that two Renaissance popes, Innocent X (1644–1655) and Clement IX (1667–1670) had ordered excavations of Rome's ancient funerary lands on the Via Salaria, searching for hidden treasure. He quotes the memoirs of the seventeenth-century archaeologist Pietro Sante Bartoli:

> The hope was frustrated; but, deep in the bowels of the mound, some crypts were found, encrusted with white stucco, and remarkable for their neatness and preservation. I have heard from trustworthy men that the place is haunted by spirits, as is proved by what happened to them not many months ago. While assembled on the Monte delle Gioie for a picnic, the conversation turned upon the ghosts who haunted the crypt below, when suddenly the carriage which had brought them there, pushed by invisible hands, began to roll down the slope of the hill, and was ultimately precipitated into the river Anio at its base. Several oxen had to be used to haul the vehicle out of the stream. This happened to Tabarrino, butcher at S. Eustachio, and to his brothers living in the Via Due Macelli, whose faces still bear marks of the great terror experienced that day.[2]

The catacombs had been discovered, then, as early as the 1650s, and had been repeatedly and thoroughly ransacked since then. Apparently, the incident of the ruined picnic by the Anio convinced people that the catacombs, haunted by evil spirits, needed to be destroyed. By the end of the nineteenth century, they were a mess and almost entirely caved in.

Fortunately, the catacombs proved much larger than people had counted on, and thus by the time De Rossi resumed a more scientific excavation, much work had still to be done on areas untouched by superstitious and destructive visitors. A young De Rossi protégé by the name of Josef Wilpert persuaded his master to allow him to try a new chemical compound to dissolve the lime that had encrusted the walls of one chamber, seeking to reverse two thousand years of mud and mineral deposits. Wilpert's special interest was early Christian wall painting and the interpretation of early Christian art more generally, which he viewed as proof of the purity and antiquity of Catholic sacramentalism. In 1894, the discovery of a meal scene in this ancient, double-roomed chamber was a triumph. De Rossi himself heralded it as the "pearl" of catacomb paintings. For him, it proved beyond a doubt the antiquity and orthodoxy of the Catholic devotional life, for there, in the scene, were "six men and one woman," celebrating the Eucharist.[3] The image had even captured the key moment in the rite: the breaking of bread representing the body of Christ. Wilpert dubbed the image the *Fractio Panis,* the "breaking of bread."

Few Catholic scholars since Wilpert and De Rossi have questioned whether the figures in the fresco are celebrating a Eucharist, nor have any considered that the gender of the seated figures might be anything other than male (with one token, veiled woman in attendance). On my last visit in the summer of 2005, a very delightful and learned nun by the name of Sister Martha showed me both the mosaic in the upstairs chapel and the original painting; for her, neither element of the picture was in dispute. The truth was self-evident: the figures were "clearly" all male except for the sole veiled female, and the scene was unambiguously a Holy Eucharist. She had tired of all the visitors who claimed otherwise; could they not clearly see for themselves? But no, visitors do not always see what was so plain to Sister Martha.

The intriguing thing about the *Fractio Panis* fresco is that we are initially so sure of what we think we see. In truth, the image itself presents a dizzying range of interpretive possibilities. Perhaps the officiating figure is a male priest, or perhaps not; perhaps the officiating figure is actually female, or perhaps not; perhaps the figure is not actually breaking bread, but doing something else; perhaps the figure is officiating, or perhaps is merely a slave offering bread at an everyday meal; perhaps the breaking of bread is a Eucharist, or perhaps it is just the starch course. All these possibilities remain equal and viable possibilities, but we, the viewers, bring with us our own interpretive screens that filter out certain interpretations and encourage others. Images have such power. As the art historian and classicist James A.

Francis has recently noted, "Images subvert our illusion of rationality and control. We repress what we find disturbing in them by ignoring it, explaining it away . . . or outright insisting that we see something else."[4]

We cannot trust what we see. The eye tricks us. We see what we want to see, what we are inclined to see from years of habituation, cultural programming, wishful thinking. Experiments of modern psychologists alert us to the trickiness of the eye and the brain: the brain's ability to entirely block out information that doesn't belong. In one remarkable experiment on visual cognition, researcher asked their subjects to watch a brief videotape featuring several people playing basketball in a relatively small area.[5] The subjects are asked to carefully track two basketballs, to watch how many times they are handed off from one player to the other. "Watch carefully," the researcher says, "it's tricky." The subjects watch carefully, and count. The ball is whizzed back and forth, behind people, in front of them, between legs. The videotape ends, and the subjects are questioned. How many passes? Most reach the same answer, give or take a few, but that's not the point of the exercise. The researchers rewind the videotape, and ask the subjects to watch again—this time, without tracking the ball. Here's what they see: in between the whizzing and bouncing of the ball, a large man in a gorilla suit wanders in between the players, dodging them, even pausing to cheekily beat his chest directly at the camera. The subjects, watching the tape again, are stunned: surely there's some trick! The tapes were switched! There was no man in a gorilla suit in the first videotape! But there was. The brain, focusing on what it *can* or *must* do—watch the ball carefully—completely fails to register what is right in front of the eyes.

So what, then, *do* we see?

A controversial book first published in 1993 by the American scholar Karen Jo Torjesen, titled *When Women Were Priests: Women's Leadership in the Early Church and the Scandal of their Subordination in the Rise of Christianity*, includes a reproduction of the *Fractio Panis* image. The photo's caption reads: "A woman breaks bread at an early Christian Eucharist. The clothing and hairstyles worn by the participants suggests that most of them are women."[6] Similar observers have also claimed that the image records women—or a mixed audience of men and women—celebrating a Eucharist led by a woman.[7] The controversy over whether or not the *Fractio Panis* delivers proof that in early Christianity, women could act as priests has spanned both sides of the Atlantic. In 1973, Joan Morris discussed the painting rather conspiratorially in her book *The Lady Was a Bishop*.[8] She claimed there, among other things, that the clear evidence for women's ministry in the church had been intentionally covered up by a century of male clerics, beginning with the defacements secretly undertaken by Wilpert himself. Although the book did not meet widespread acceptance, it had an influence. In the United Kingdom, a brief pamphlet by Thomas F. Torrance titled *The Ministry of Women* (1992) finds in this banqueting scene clear evidence for women's ministry in the early church.[9] Torrance's work was invoked on a BBC Sunday broadcast, *The Hidden Tradition,* produced by the Reverend Angela Tilby in 1992, which featured a lay minister, Lavinia Byrne of Cambridge, England. The radio program ignited a firestorm of controversy in the United Kingdom and abroad. In the United States, a theologian by the name of Dorothy Irvin wrote an article titled "The Ministry of Women in the Early Church: The Archaeological Evidence" in 1980.[10] She claimed that the *Fractio Panis* had been overlooked—even intentionally suppressed, she hinted—as powerful evidence for a woman's priesthood or ministry in early Christian Rome.

Irvin's landmark attempt to bring "women's archaeology" to the fore in contemporary debates concerning women's ordination was systematically decimated in a fierce rebuttal by another scholar, K. M. Irwin.[11] In what can be charitably called an unusually fraught academic exchange, Irvin and Irwin debated the degree to which we might be able to uncover evidence for what real women did in the early church based on the visual evidence they left behind. Joining the fray were Patrick Henry Reardon, pastor of the St. Anthony Orthodox Church in Butler, Pennsylvania, who wished to "pay his respects" to Torrance while at the same time arguing vociferously that the Catholic Church never allowed women as clerics. About the controversial meal image, he writes, "Even now, looking at a photograph of that fresco over and over again, I discern no trace of what he [Torrance] and some other people say they see."[12]

All those who see the *Fractio Panis* as an authentic but undiscovered "record" of women's ordination face the weight of nearly two thousand years of Catholic teachings that insist that women have never exercised priestly authority. The specter of a vast Catholic antifeminist conspiracy and cover-up has been raised. But what is the truth? Let's return to the meal image for a closer look. In its original setting (as in the mosaic reconstruction), the image hovers as if in space. Against a deep red backdrop, six figures sit upright on their long cushion (called a *pulvinum*) behind a curved table. To either side of the table, seven baskets sit on the ground. On the table lie two platters and a goblet. All the figures seem engaged in conversation; at the extreme left we find a figure who appears, oddly, to be squatting on the table itself, in the act of breaking bread with long, outstretched arms. It's extremely difficult to discern the sex of any of the figures with the exception of the figure fifth from the left. She wears a veil and inclines her head slightly, her right arm held up, as if gesturing while speaking.

If the ambiguous gender of the figures in this image mark it as controversial, the scene itself is not particularly unusual. Meal scenes such as this one are very common in catacomb art. They appear in both pagan and Christian burials, and they conventionally depict both men and women actively sharing a meal.[13] In the case of the *Fractio Panis* image, however, scholars are divided. Some argue that it records an actual practice of the Christian community that used the space; others maintain that the image offers an idealized type—a scene of a heavenly banquet that would await the deceased in the afterlife. The key concern in this debate hinges on whether the banquet depicted was *funerary* (following Greco-Roman practice) or *sacramental,* such as a Eucharist.[14]

Funerary banquets were commonplace within the Greco-Roman world and were divided into various types. For instance, the *silicernium* was performed directly after a burial, while the *novemdiale* was performed nine days following. There were also annual banquets to celebrate the dead, such as the feast of the *Parentalia* on February 22. A late-fourth-century Christian text known as the *Apostolic Constitutions* indicates that Christians freely embraced these ancient customs; it advocates that the third, ninth, and thirtieth day after death ought to be commemorated with ritual meals and observances.[15] All these ceremonial meals were customarily consumed near the burial site. It seems reasonable to suppose, therefore, that the meal depicted at the front of the Greek Chapel represents a funerary meal or *refrigerium,* given its immediate context. Far from celebrating a Eucharist, the guests were toasting their dearly departed.

Yet if meals were held in the Greek Chapel, there is no material or architectural evidence for them. Funerary banquets were usually not celebrated underground, but in the yards or areas adjacent to the tombs, as numerous examples from nearby necropoleis indicate.[16] The image itself, too, contains no obvious visual referents to a funerary meal that we find in other meal scenes; missing are necessary accouterments such as tripod stands, beverage heaters, or amphorae of wine. Often funerary paintings of meal scenes also include servants coming and going, and some include painted words recording the speech or "toasts" to the dead.[17] A funerary banquet in ancient Rome—even ancient Christian Rome—was a relatively "secular" affair, which is not to say that the gods were not invoked. But they could be lively, with the guests well into their cups by the end. Augustine and other ancient Christian writers chastened their congregations for such unseemly displays of public drunkenness near the tombs: "I know that there are many worshippers of tombs and pictures. I know that there are many who drink to great excess over the dead, and who, in the feasts that they make for corpses, bury themselves over the buried and give to their gluttony and drunkenness the name of religion" (*De moribus ecclesiae catholica* 1.34.75). Some tomb inscriptions even plead with boisterously plastered visitors not to urinate on graves as they tottered their way through miles of tombs with nary a public latrine in sight.[18] As for the *Fractio Panis* image, all the figures seem engaged in conversation rather than solemnly focused on the figure breaking bread. The lively casualness of their poses seems to militate against reading this painting as sacramental or Eucharistic.

But other interpreters—most of them Catholic—have staunchly maintained along with Wilpert that the *Fractio Panis* depicts a Eucharist.[19] Indeed, the seven figures surrounded by seven baskets have suggested to at least a century's worth of viewers a Eucharistic feast.[20] The art historian Robert Milburn, for instance, reads the Greek Chapel's meal scene as commemorating or recording the actual liturgical practice of a community.[21] More recently, however, interpreters such as Fabrizio Bisconti, a Vatican specialist in early Christian art, and Robin Jensen, an American art historian, find the central meal scene "symbolic" rather than actual.[22] Bisconti bases his interpretation on the manner in which the images seem to float against the background, part of a characteristic style he likens elsewhere to "cut-outs."[23] The number of the figures and baskets likewise suggests the scene was intended to be symbolic rather than historical or actual, what Bisconti terms a "celestial *convivium*" or dining scene.[24] Similarly, Jensen argues that meal scenes such as the one in the Greek Chapel are meant to represent a Christian vision of paradise based on Jesus's promise of a celestial banquet for the blessed in Matthew 26:29 ("I tell you, I will never again drink of this fruit of the vine until that day when I drink it new with you in my Father's kingdom") rather than any earthly practice; the figures should be understood as "dining in heaven."[25] Jensen bases her argument predominantly on patristic accounts of the Eucharist, which she argues was formalized by the third century and would have included the whole community, "not just a handful of members reclining on couches."[26] It's also likely that celebrants would have been standing, not sitting. The significance of such a scene, she argues, lies in its implications for the community or individuals who commissioned it. Their intention was to depict themselves—or their loved ones—as blessed, participating in a sacramental life with their Savior in the hereafter.

The question of what type of meal is being celebrated in the *Fractio Panis* bears directly on another debate: the sex of the figures. To my eye, the figures all look female, with the possible exception of the figure at the far left, which is too faded to be seen distinctly (the same figure is unambiguously male in the mosaic reproduction). Artistic and social conventions support my judgment. First, the figures all have the neatly coiffed hair of Christian (and pagan) women of the third century; hairstyles remain an important "clue" in identifying both the sex of figures in Roman art and the date of paintings and portraiture in general.[27] Second, all the figures sit upright on the same *pulvinum*. Roman men, by contrast, ate in a reclining position, on special benches known as *klinae* (in fact, a Roman dining room was called a *triclinium* because it had three of these benches: *tri-klinae*). But if all the figures are female, why would only one be veiled?

It's difficult to discern what the woman's veiled head signified. It could have indicated that the veiled woman was the only married woman present. It could have meant that she was of lower status than the others. Or if we believe that the scene reflects the sacramental life of a church community, the veil could mean that she played some sort of prophetic role. A letter from the first-century apostle Paul to his community at Corinth in Greece records that Christian women were encouraged to veil themselves during the act of prophesying (1 Cor 11:5). But if, by contrast, we interpret the meal as funerary, the woman's veil would be an indication of mourning.[28] In other words, there are many reasons why only one woman in a group would be veiled; the veil is a marker of *status*, not of *gender*. Not all women would have worn one all the time—and thus, while we can say that the veiled woman is almost definitely the only one of the figures we can securely identify as female, this does not mean that the other, unveiled figures are not also female.

But who was the veiled woman, in this image, and who might she have represented? If you look closely at her pose, you see that she may at one time have held a chalice or goblet aloft in her right hand as she gazes beyond the table, directly away from the figure breaking bread. In other words, she may at one time have been offering up a toast. Both she and the person at the far left, in fact, direct their gestures not at the food in the center of the table, nor even to one another, but to a point or moment not recorded within the meal scene itself. Again, what precisely the veiled woman's actions signify remains unclear, but it is possible that she—not the "male" figure breaking bread at the left—was the focal point of the ancient painting. What happened to the ancient chalice—if there was one—is yet another mystery.

But what about the "breaking bread" figure? The Benedictine sisters, remember, regard it as the bearded male priest, the bringer of the salvation of Christ's body and blood. This identification goes back as far as Wilpert in the late nineteenth century, who first identified it as the male "host" seated at the place of honor.[29] Because the figure is smaller than the other figures, however, and also curiously perched alongside or even *on top of* the table, I would surmise that it is a slave. No priest—not even an ancient one—would put his feet on the same level as the body of Christ. He or she wears some sort of tunic so that the knees are visible through diaphanous fabric, but it is difficult to tell how long the garment extended. If it were short, it would be male dress; if it were floor-length, women would have worn it.[30] Scholars have also long debated whether the figure is bearded, but it is clear only that the red background paint behind the figure's head has rubbed off, resulting in the chin area appearing lighter than the rest of the face.[31] Whether this defacement (literally!) was intentional—the deliberate work of some pious male cleric attempting to make a female priestly figure more unambiguously male—we can only speculate.

The furious debates over the sex of the figures in the Greek Chapel's *Fractio Panis* painting really hinges on what they are all doing in the meal scene. Many theologians and Catholic faithful actively resist interpreting all the figures as women. The reasoning has been: either the figures include men and the small figure breaking the bread (thus "officiating") is male, or else the feast is not Eucharistic but some other type. The theory that the meal offers an idealized depiction of "dining in heaven" serves the same ends; all these interpretations deftly skirt the possibility that the image may reflect the active and autonomous participation of women in Christian sacramental behavior. On the other hand, feminist Christians who see the figures as exclusively female tend to find in this image proof for women's active role in offering the Eucharist in the early Christian church. Both groups see in the scene what they wish to see, but neither group, in fact, stands on very solid ground. The image, as it fades, takes its secrets with it.

Is this painting early evidence for the Catholic sacrament of the Eucharist? And are these *women* celebrating the Eucharist? In truth, we do not know. The form of the Eucharist came to be fixed only in the fourth century, making it difficult for us to determine what a third-century Eucharistic feast (the most likely dating of the *Fractio Panis* image) looked like. That it could have included women, however, is certain; that certain communities would have had a Eucharistic feast led by women is at least plausible. Dorothy Irvin suggests that Tertullian's oft-quoted declaration that no woman be allowed to speak in church "even to teach, to baptize, or to discharge any man's function (Latin: *virilis muneris*), much less to take upon herself the priestly office" (*De Virginibus velandis* 9.1) was likely an attempt by an early third-century church father to control women's behavior that he—and other men—clearly found offensive. For this reason, Tertullian advocated that women should strive to become priestesses—not of the church, but of modesty—as *sacerdotes pudicitiae* or "modesty's priestesses" (Tertullian, *De cultu feminarum* 2.12.2–3).

There is a way to reconcile at least some of the scholarly controversy. The *Fractio Panis* could depict a scene at once funerary and sacramental. In late ancient Rome, all-night funerary vigils appear to have been single-sex for the sake of preserving women's modesty in prayer; they probably also included a Eucharistic banquet as part of the ritual proceedings. Therefore it's possible that the banquet scene at the front of the Greek Chapel commemorates *both* a Eucharist *and* a funerary banquet—just as it is likely (indeed, proper!) that all the celebrants would be female, rather than a combination of both sexes. But that the scene could represent a purely idealized funerary banquet with Eucharistic associations also seems likely, given the number of figures in the scene and the seven baskets beside them—a lot of bread for only seven people! If the veiled woman is the central figure here as I suspect, then she becomes the visual focus, presiding over the meal. Still, questions remain: was she the one who commissioned the Greek Chapel, who then chose to have an image of herself presiding over the funerary banquet of a lost loved one? Or did one of her loved ones have an image of her dining in paradise painted over her grave to commemorate her? Who are the other figures? And who was she?

To begin to penetrate the meaning of the *Fractio Panis* fresco we need to place it in its broadest possible context. This means we need to see it in relation to its immediate surroundings in the so-called Greek Chapel, to the Catacombs of Priscilla, to its sociohistorical setting in third- or fourth-century Rome. We need to see what contemporary literary sources say about the issue of women's active participation in ancient Roman Christianity, and if there is any comparative visual or epigraphical evidence for this aspect of

Roman Christian women's lives. Only then can we even approach the question of meaning.

Let's start with the room that houses the image, because it is a bit of a curiosity. One of its mysteries concerns when precisely it was built. Dating features from the catacombs—including its frescoes—is extraordinarily difficult. Many Catholic scholars maintain that the Greek Chapel and the larger room off which it lies, called the atrium or cryptoporticus, constitute one of the archaic hearts of the Priscilla catacombs. One theory is that the cryptoporticus and Greek Chapel once formed part of the substructures of a suburban Roman villa that belonged to a wealthy family, perhaps as a sort of underground dining room in which to escape Rome's oppressive summer heat. Later—perhaps in the third century—the area was taken over by Christians, who modified the architecture and added the frescoes. Others, however, maintain that the area has always been Christian, dating from perhaps as early as the end of the second century.[32] The dating of the Greek Chapel's paintings has been particularly fraught; the tendency of Catholic scholars has been to date them early—as early as 170–180 CE—in large part to support an implicit argument that sacramental Catholic Christianity (best represented by the *Fractio Panis* painting) took root in Rome early and definitively. Still, certain influential scholars continue to suggest that the paintings—if not necessarily the room itself—date to the end of the third century or later, in the Constantinian period. For our purposes, it hardly matters *when* precisely the space was painted, for it was certainly executed during the first four centuries, when women's participation in the church was being most hotly debated.

Unlike *cubicula* housing the burials of entire families, the Greek Chapel originally contained only a single burial in a sarcophagus sited directly under the main apse—at least so claimed Joseph Wilpert.[33] The sarcophagus has long since disappeared. According to Wilpert, the space prepared for burial was only large enough to have accommodated the bones of a child. But who would have prepared such an elaborate chamber only to house the bones of a child, without preparing spaces for the parents? Two arched niches lie to either side of the main "apse," but the niches themselves were evidently never prepared as burial sites. It remains a mystery why no other family members were ever interred alongside.

We do have, however, two burial inscriptions in Greek—the language of the earliest Christian communities in Rome up until the fourth century. In fact, they are why the Greek Chapel is called "Greek." Painted in tall red letters, in a script typical of this catacomb (thus known as Priscillian), they sit almost awkwardly on the curved ceilings of these side niches. Crude and off-center, they were clearly not executed by the artists responsible for the wall paintings. There's no way to be sure whether they are contemporary with the Greek Chapel or provide clues to its use or dedication. The names, however, are otherwise unknown to us. In one of the inscriptions, a man named Obrimus commemorates his "sweetest" (*glukutatos*) friend Palladius, a cousin and schoolmate (*synscholaste*).[34] The term *synscholaste* indicates that Palladius had reached at least his teenage years; he could not have been the young child whom Wilpert reported was buried at the front of the space.[35] In the second inscription, the same Obrimus commemorates a woman, the happy (or "blessed," *makaria*) and sweetest Nestoriana.[36] The last line of this second inscription is illegible. The Greek names may indicate that Obrimus and his companions were immigrants from farther east, although it was also common for native-born Roman slaves and persons of low status to have single Greek names. What is certain, however, is that the names do not indicate senatorial or other highborn status. It would seem, too, that they do not correspond to the single original burial in this space, so were perhaps added as a separate, pious commemoration by an individual to his loved ones at a later date, when other burials were performed here. This hypothesis is also supported by the inscription's lack of relationship, visually, to the otherwise meticulously adorned chambers.

Few, however, have argued that the Greek Chapel, with its meal scene, was primarily a burial chamber. Instead, many scholars since the nineteenth century have agreed that it was used for early Christian worship services. But if it were, this set of two rooms was hardly well suited for the range of activities that would have been performed by a Christian community. The space accommodates scarcely a dozen adults, making it highly unlikely that it was used as a public or semi-public area for prayer or liturgy. The rooms contain no altar or area for baptism, and the burial area at the front is a focal point in the room. Lacking both the space and the facilities of other extant Christian banquet halls used to celebrate feasts in honor of the dead, it would be difficult to celebrate any meal within such a small, elongated space.[37] But a clue provided for us is the long, narrow stone bench that lines one side of the room. It probably provided seating for prayer or a funerary vigil.[38]

If the architectural features of the room are not particularly illuminating, its wall paintings are more helpful. Like the Via Latina catacombs, the Greek Chapel contains scenes from the Old and New Testaments, from the

The Greek Chapel at the Catacombs of Priscilla, seen from the entrance. The first ceiling arch bears an image of the three Magi visiting Mary and the Christ child; the ceiling arch at the back of the double chamber bears the "Fractio Panis" image. The large "Susanna" cycle can be seen on the left- and right-hand walls closest to the camera. Note the single long, thin bench, which probably provided seating for women during funerary vigils.

Apocrypha—Jewish and Christian texts regarded as authoritative in Catholicism but excluded from the formal canon of the Bible—and additional images more difficult to identify. Its Old Testament scenes include standard early Christian depictions of Moses striking the rock (Exod 17:1–6) and Noah in his ark (Gen 8:8–14). These are still clearly visible when one is standing at the back of the chamber facing the entrance. The sacrifice of Isaac (Gen 22:1–12) is painted on the wall adjacent to the resurrection of Lazarus. These scenes are conventionally and beautifully rendered, but rather commonplace; all are frequently found within the corpus of catacomb art.

The New Testament scenes we find here are all more unusual than the Greek Chapel's relatively standard Old Testament scenes. On the south wall of the vault of the first chamber, barely intact because of peeling plaster, we find the healing of the paralytic from John 5:5–9, carrying his pallet on his back.[39] From our extant corpus of Christian catacomb art, only a few images of this episode are recorded. Over the central arch in the first chamber, a nativity scene portrays three Magi bearing gifts to the infant Jesus on Mary's lap. Although the scene derives from Matthew 2:7–12, the number of the Magi derives from apocryphal tradition, already apparently fixed within artistic conventions by the first decades of the third century. Over the central arch facing the back of the room remains an unusual scene of the raising of Lazarus from John 11:32–44, featuring Mary and Martha with Jesus before Lazarus's tomb.

The Greek Chapel also features scenes from the book of Daniel and its apocryphal additions—short, almost folkloric texts that were composed in Greek within Jewish communities during the Hellenistic period. A standard, though well-rendered, scene of the three Hebrews in the fiery furnace from Daniel 3:15–29 adorns the right-hand side of one wall. Wilpert also identified the remains of a Daniel in the lions' den, but this image is now almost impossible to discern. More noteworthy is a large and elaborate Susanna cycle, which has almost no parallel in our extant repertory of catacomb art. The cycle dominates both walls of the entrance chamber, at eye level with the viewer; the figures identified as Daniel, Susanna, and the elders are easily the largest in the rooms.

Finally, the Greek Chapel also contains two unidentifiable images. Directly above the inside door is a roundel with an unidentified woman's portrait. Portraiture is rare in early Christian catacomb painting, but this image may commemorate the room's founder. On the left-hand central wall when an observer is facing the back of the space, a small male figure—still clearly discernable—points directly toward the entrance, or possibly toward the image of the three Hebrews in the fiery furnace across the entrance. The identity of this figure remains a mystery. It is possible that he represented an important member in the community or a significant ritual moment within the space; he points directly at whatever person walks through the entrance of the Greek Chapel and stands in the very center of the room.

At first glance, the images in the Greek Chapel seem to float, disconnected from one another. Yet, like most sacred spaces, the room has its own elegant logic. It speaks in a particular symbolic or typological language, and it tells a specific story about those who used it. We need only to listen attentively. We know at the outset that those who used it were Christian. Unlike many other catacomb *cubicula* (including Proba's), we find no provocative juxtaposition of pagan and Christian images that might lead us to conclude that both Christians and pagans used this space together. The non-Christian elements that are employed, such as the paintings of four seasons that once adorned each corner, are purely decorative space fillers. Beyond this, two prominent themes run throughout the Greek Chapel's paintings. The first theme is God's deliverance of the faithful from peril: Noah, Moses striking the rock, Abraham and Isaac, the three Hebrews, Daniel in the lion's den, and Susanna all provide examples of individuals whom God rescues in their hour of need. It was natural for Christians, in their own times of need, to draw upon in their litanies and prayers these same figures from the Old Testament. This listing of the afflicted and delivered, at once ritualized and heartfelt, soon became in the Catholic tradition connected with prayers offered up for the dying or dead. In the early Middle Ages, Christians developed a set of prayers for the dying, the *Commendatio animae*, which invokes the examples of Moses, Daniel, the three Hebrews, and Susanna; the *Commendatio* may in fact have had its genesis much earlier in Christian Rome.[40]

A second unifying theme in the iconography of the Greek Chapel is perhaps even more apparent: many of the room's scenes feature women prominently. In terms of figural art, we have a rare portrait of a woman over the entrance. In terms of biblical iconography, an unknown artist appears to have deliberately selected certain scenes and figures to emphasize the role of women in salvation history—the story of Susanna dominates the space, and the early nativity scene featuring the Magi visiting Mary with Jesus on her lap is suspended over the central arch in the room; it is one of the first, most visible, and most recognizable scenes visitors see as they approach. Besides these, one of the artists who painted the biblical scenes appears to have literally refigured traditional iconography to highlight or emphasize women's activity in the early church. Though the scene of the raising of Lazarus is one of the most common in catacomb art, with more than seventy-three surviving examples, the one we find in the Greek Chapel is the only one to include Mary and Martha, standing as quiet, veiled presences behind Jesus.

And then there are images, such as the meal scene, where women have been misinterpreted—mis-seen—as male. Intriguingly, one of the other images that scholars have interpreted as featuring a male figure—the painting Wilpert identified as Daniel in the lion's den—I suspect has been most often and badly misidentified. The image features a lone figure standing before a cityscape. It is badly faded, but even in Wilpert's reproductions it is clear that the figure wears a long garment that reaches to the ground. To the right of the figure, a lion—barely visible—crouches at the figure's feet. The combination of lion plus human figure almost always signals the telltale characteristics of early Christian paintings of Daniel in the lion's den, which is why Wilpert identified this scene in the way he did.[41]

But there are significant problems with this identification. First, the scene features only one lion, although all other scenes of Daniel in the lion's den place Daniel between two lions. It's possible that the first lion has merely faded away. More puzzling, though, is a second feature: the scene clearly takes place outdoors; there is a cityscape in the background, and no indication of anything that might resemble a cave or den. Third and most curious of all, the sole figure is clothed. In every other image of Daniel in the lion's den in catacomb art, Daniel is naked or wearing a loincloth. Why would Daniel be wearing a long *stola*—the ancient dress of Roman *women?* And why, upon closer inspection, would he have his hair carefully arranged in a bun? What kind of Daniel is this?! Perhaps the artist deliberately clothed a usually nude Daniel in women's clothing. Or perhaps the figure is not Daniel at all. If not, then who would it be?

There *was* a story popular in early Christian circles that fits with the iconography of this scene. By the third century, many Christians knew the story of the brave virgin Thecla. Her story circulated with a group of ancient Christian legends or romances known as the Apocryphal Acts of the Apostles. Thecla's story, in particular, is told in the third-century *Acts of Paul and Thecla*. It starts in the Mediterranean town of Iconium, where the maiden Thecla was engaged to a prominent young man, Thamyris. One day, Paul appears in Iconium to preach his gospel. For Thecla, it is love at first sight. Hearing him preaching in the town forum from her window perch, she is rooted to the spot. Thecla heeds Paul's message of sexual continence and celibacy, immediately breaking off her engagement with Thamyris to follow Paul as a chaste virgin. But Thecla is not the only woman taken by Paul. Such a potent effect has Paul, in fact, that the men conspire to have him thrown into prison and then expelled from the city for corrupting the labile minds of Iconium's women. When she hears of his arrest, Thecla races to visit Paul in prison, only to discover he has already been removed from Iconium. In a remarkable scene, she flings herself upon the ground where Paul had lain in his cell and rubs her body in the dirt, as if desperate to soak up any last bits of his presence. But even with Paul far away, the damage had been done. Thecla continues to refuse Thamyris's hand and is eventually sent to the amphitheater to face the beasts for her rebelliousness.

Three prominent modern scholars—Stevan Davies, Virginia Burrus, and Dennis R. MacDonald—have observed that the *Acts of Paul and Thecla* may have particularly appealed to an ancient female audience.[42] It features female heroines confronting situations that likely evoked strong feelings of empathy from women listeners. Indeed, it's difficult not to see the *Acts of Paul and Thecla* as a story explicitly designed for Christian women. As Thecla faces the beasts in the amphitheater, the women present in the stadium cry out—a virtual Greek chorus—condemning the evil judgment on Thecla; at one point they throw heavily scented flowers onto the sands of the amphitheater to lull the savage beasts into a torpor and save Thecla from being torn to shreds. But even female *beasts* are on Thecla's side. At the climax of the tale, Thecla faces a lioness. The lioness does not devour her; rather, it crouches at her feet in submission, "and the crowd of women raised a great shout." Thecla cannot be martyred—certainly not for her steadfast faithfulness and innocence, nor for her refusal to participate in a marriage arranged by men according to the laws of men, not God.

Thecla's story was well known and well loved in late ancient Christianity.[43] We know, for instance, that there is a fourth-century Catacomb of Thecla in Rome. And prayers for the dead such as the *Commendatio animae,* while conspicuously lacking in female figures, include Thecla with only a small handful of other women who received divine favor. Indeed, that privileged group includes only Thecla, the Virgin Mary, and Susanna—and we already find the Virgin Mary and Susanna on the walls of the Greek Chapel. Still, no image from the catacombs has ever been identified as a scene from the *Acts of Paul and Thecla*—at least, not until now. The cityscape, the clothed figure with a woman's hairstyle, and the presence of a single lion crouched at its feet suggest that far from representing Daniel in the lion's den, the image is the earliest depiction of Thecla and her lioness at the amphitheater of Iconium. The focus on a woman's story, too, fits much better with the overall theme of the Greek Chapel than does Daniel. That the painting illustrates a scene from a book popular among female audiences but rejected as spurious by centuries of male ecclesiastics brings us a long way toward understanding why a nineteenth-century male Catholic viewer like Wilpert would so steadfastly see Daniel where ancient women viewers (and perhaps some modern viewers) would see Thecla. Women's iconography is invisible in a male world of symbols and meaning.

There is one final set of images in the Greek Chapel that reveal the artist's (and the commissioner's) desire to create a space where women's roles and activities were considered both primary and sacred. Strikingly, the Chapel's so-called Susanna cycle is virtually unparalleled in early Christian art.[44] The Susanna images in the Greek Chapel are, after the central meal scene, its most extraordinary feature. They dominate either side of the wall just as a visitor enters, and their scale is immense by comparison with others. Whereas the figures in the *Fractio Panis* scene are diminutive—perhaps only ten inches high—the Susanna figures are comparatively huge, more than two feet tall. They have been interpreted as scenes from the little-known apocryphal book of Susanna, which tells the harrowing tale of the matron Susanna. The story recounts how the comely Susanna, bathing one day in her own enclosed garden, is spied upon by two town elders. Aroused by lust, the elders approach her, but Susanna spurns their sexual advances and flees. The elders retaliate. They combine forces and stories, compile lie upon lie, and publicly accuse Susanna of sexually shameful behavior—the very thing in which they themselves had engaged. With no witnesses to preserve her honor and those in the highest positions of power falsely accusing her, Susanna raises her arms to the heavens and begs for God to send an intercessor. Daniel appears—as if from nowhere—and speaks to her innocence; on the power of his testimony, Susanna is released.

What interested a third-century Christian audience in this ancient Jewish tale? First of all, it was a colorful story of God's mercy that Christians might draw upon to articulate their own experience of persecution during the Roman Empire. The third-century Roman bishop Hippolytus writes:

> Susanna prefigured the Church; and Joachim her husband, Christ; and the garden, the calling of saints, who are planted like fruitful trees in the Church. And Babylon is the world; and the two elders are set forth as a figure of the two peoples that plot against the Church—the one, namely, of the circumcision, and the other of the Gentiles. (*Commentary on Daniel* 6.7, ANF 5.192)

But this interpretation leaves no room for the significance of Susanna's gender. To Hippolytus, Susanna may have been a symbol for the church as a whole, but did Christian women as individuals ever particularly identify with her predicament? The art historian Janet Huskinson notes that the story "involves sexuality as well as gender, and the abuse and assertion of power, moral and social."[45] If Susanna's presence at the Catacombs of Priscilla indicates anything, it is that few women role models existed from the scriptures of a woman who expressed her faith neither domestically through having children (Sarah, Rebecca, Rachel), nor as ancillary to a male (Miriam), nor martially (Judith), but independently and publicly. Recently, Huskinson has demonstrated persuasively that the figure of Susanna appears in the art of late antiquity as a symbol of the learned woman; on sarcophagi, Susanna figures are fully clad (as here) and carry a scroll. The toga—but even more so, the scroll—served as important status markers in Roman art. Huskinson continues, "This scroll has no place in the textual narrative, and so it is of major interest here as a signal to the viewer that Susanna should be identified with Christian women who have been empowered by their learning to live according to the precepts of their faith." She contrasts this virtue with the weakness of the men in Susanna's narrative who had abused their positions of authority and, worse, failed to control their sexual impulses.[46]

The Greek Chapel's Susanna cycle offers a fine example of what we might call *polysemy*—a range of meanings contained within visual text. The image of Susanna may, on one level, simply stand for the church, as Hippolytus averred. To women viewers, Susanna may have represented a type more familiar and accessible: the model of the learned woman. And perhaps—although we cannot be sure—Susanna also provided a subtly veiled allusion to women's struggles against male domination. Perhaps, most simply, Susanna peers at us from the walls of the Greek Chapel because there were so few examples of holy women there, in that space, where women would once gather in silent prayer.

Let's make Susanna's polysemy still more complex. What if scholars have mistakenly identified these frescoes as scenes from Susanna? How can we be so sure of the attribution? In fact, we can't. First, since the images are not labeled (as was done occasionally), the attribution can be made only on the basis of comparison with other early Christian images of Susanna, or by pointing out a clear relation to biblical text. The problem is, we have nothing in early Christian artistic depictions of Susanna that looks even remotely like the ones in the Greek Chapel. This is noteworthy, because early Christian art is extraordinarily visually consistent. All images of Adam and Eve look virtually identical, as do images of Noah in his ark or Daniel in the lion's den. One image identified as Susanna from another set of catacombs off the Via Labicana—the Catacombs of Peter and Marcellinus—shows the heroine as an *orante* in a garden standing between two elders, not with the two elders standing either together or on either side with their hands on her head, as we find here. Another Susanna image, from the Catacombs of Praetextatus, is, by contrast, purely figurative and actually depicts a lamb surrounded by wolves. We know the figure is Susanna only because the lamb and wolves are labeled "Susanna" and "the Elders" (*seniores*), respectively.

We also encounter problems when we try to match the images on the wall of the Greek Chapel to the book of Susanna. In one wall panel, an *orante* Susanna is surrounded by three male figures, two of whom raise their hands in her direction as if pointing; the lone male (usually identified as Daniel) stands next to a structure that scholars take to represent a garden but that looks very much like a temple or tomb of the type we find most commonly in images of Christ raising Lazarus. Although Susanna's narrative takes place in a garden, there is no temple or tomb there. But it seems unlikely that this obviously skilled artist would have painted a tomb (or some sort of edifice) when he meant to paint a garden. The other scenes in the Greek Chapel's Susanna cycle are just as vexing. In one, a man and woman (presumably Susanna and Daniel) are twin *orantes,* looking at one another even as they raise their hands heavenward. The scene does not correspond to any moment in the book of Susanna. In the other scene, Susanna stands between two men who place their hands on her head, perhaps an illustration of the apocryphal book Susanna, chapter 34. But perhaps there is a better explanation of what is going on in these scenes.

Just as the Greek Chapel's Thecla image has been misidentified as Daniel in the lion's den, I suspect that the Susanna image has been similarly misidentified. There are two options that seem to make at least as much sense. The first is that the female figure is Mary Magdalene, and the scene represented is from the end of John's Gospel. In chapter 20 of this gospel, Mary Magdalene goes first to the tomb, and sees that the stone covering the tomb had been rolled away. She tells Simon Peter and another follower of Jesus (known here as the Beloved Disciple) that Jesus's body has been taken, and the two men race each other to the tomb (20:4). Mary, weeping outside the grave, turns to see Jesus standing there, but he is in a physical form she does not recognize until he calls her by name (20:15–16). Reaching to touch him, he chastens her: "Do not hold me, for I have not yet ascended to the Father, but go to my brethren and say to them, I am ascending to my Father and your Father, to my God and your God" (20:17 RSV). In Latin, the

One of two images of a so-called Susanna cycle from the Greek Chapel. On the right, two elders raise their hands in judgment. In the center stands Susanna, in archaic dress (stola and palla), raising her hands in prayer and supplication. At left stands a lone male figure identified as Daniel. But there are significant problems with this identification, beginning with the prominent tomb structure painted on the far left of the fresco.

phrase "Do not hold me" is "*Noli me tangere,*" and thus *Noli me tangere* has become the broad title for this scene, one of the more popular in the entire corpus of medieval and Renaissance Christian art. It has been thought to be entirely absent from early Christian art. But the attribution makes sense of many of the puzzles in the fresco. It explains why we find a tomb structure in a garden when there is no tomb in Susanna's but there is in the Gospel of John. It explains, too, the curious "staging" of the scene which does not exist in Susanna but does in the Gospel of John. If I am right that this scene in the Greek Chapel may illustrate John 20, this would fit both with the room's emphasis on women's iconography and with its emphasis on the Gospel of John, since we also find on the walls other scenes from John rarely depicted in early Christian art—the paralytic with his pallet (John 5:9) and the raising of Lazarus in the presence of Martha (John 11:20–44).

One final possibility remains. The so-called Susanna cycle may not be an illustration of a biblical scene at all, but a multipaneled *cursus vitae* or series of illustrations from the life of the person buried in the chamber such as the one we saw in the last chapter in the cubiculum of the Velata. Indeed—the two chambers lie only a short distance from one another along the same level of the Catacombs of Priscilla. Frescoes representing the occupation of the deceased are commonplace in funerary art; we find in the Catacombs of Priscilla, for instance, depictions of barrel-makers, millers, and bakers.[47] Could, then, this cycle depict moments in the life of the same Christian woman depicted on the roundel? Could the images indicate her special significance to an early Christian community? Of particular interest here is the east wall of the first chamber, with its two scenes: one in which Susanna and Daniel stand as twin *orantes*, the other in which two men place their hands on Susanna's head, ostensibly in judgment. A third-century viewer, I suspect, would likely interpret this gesture rather differently: ordination—reserved for bishops, presbyters, and deacons—was conferred by a laying on of hands and a prayer to the Holy Spirit. The verb "to ordain" (*chirotonein*), in fact, means literally "to lay on hands."[48] The practice had started early in Christianity, as references from various writings of the New Testament make clear. Canons 2, 3, and 4 (for ordaining presbyters and elders, respectively) of the Synod of Carthage (257 CE) describe the process of laying on of hands in the ordination ceremony: two bishops pronounce blessings over the head of the one being ordained.[49]

Although the text is unclear, it appears from Hippolytus's third-century *Apostolic Tradition* that the ordination of a deacon required that a bishop lay his hand on the shoulder of the one to be ordained.[50] Could this image, then, record a woman's ordination to the deaconate? If so, the second scene of the veiled "Susanna" and "Daniel" as twin *orantes* might make more sense; they are commemorated in the act of public prayer that customarily followed an ordination ceremony, indicating their roles as community leaders. Although this is purely speculative, they may have been a husband-and-wife team; it is provocative that although they raise their arms to heaven, they gaze at one another. The "two-step" scene on the wall, therefore, reads as two identifiable moments in a third-century ritual; together, the cycle may record the significant moment in the life of the Greek Chapel's founder which inaugurated her career as a deacon. This may be a more plausible reading than is afforded by reading the painting as an unparalleled scene from an apocryphal text to which our images clearly do not easily correspond.

However we interpret the Greek Chapel's extraordinary and unparalleled Susanna cycle, the room's focus on women's tales and sacred history seems to suggest that physical space in late ancient Christianity could be gendered—that space designed for women's use actually looked different from space used by men and women together. In the Greek Chapel, we may have one of our earliest examples of ancient Christian women's sacred space. That it has never before been recognized or acknowledged as such speaks volumes about the nature of the modern Catholic Church.

Who used the Greek Chapel? If we read its iconographic program as a whole, we can infer that the space was meaningful to a community that knew of and likely read the gospels, particularly the Gospel of John. It also may have considered authoritative the book of Daniel and its apocryphal additions. This broad profile offers at least some clues into the nature of the community that used it: they were Christians who drew upon Jewish scriptural traditions. They were also Greek-speaking, wealthy, and probably relatively few in number. So far, then, there is nothing here to indicate that this group was in any way unusual from other Christians commissioning catacomb art, apart from some curious design choices in their sacred space. All Christians drew upon Jewish scriptural traditions in the third century; there was no New Testament until after the fourth century. Greek was the official language of the Roman liturgy until the time of Pope Damasus (366–384 CE), and the second language of many immigrant communities; perhaps, then, this community was not itself native to Rome, but consisted of members who had emigrated from more eastern parts of the empire. We may speculate, too, that this community may have selected scenes of deliverance from peril to symbolically mark—and give thanks for—their own persecution and subsequent deliverance. Again, however, this would not be unusual, and it rests purely upon speculation.

One tantalizing hypothesis would be that the Greek Chapel had been commissioned by a small community of Roman Montanists. The Montanists were an alternative Christian movement that first emerged in Asia Minor (modern-day Turkey) and quickly spread throughout the Roman Empire. Certainly they had arrived in Rome by the late third century.[51] The Montanists were not an altogether disreputable bunch—they held austere doctrines of chastity, for instance—and they attracted a large following, including, for a time, Tertullian. What set the Montanists apart from what would become Catholic Christianity (and what eventually turned Tertullian off) was the emphasis they laid upon the active roles of women in their community. Two of their most revered founders were women—the prophetesses Maximilla and Prisca (or Priscilla, for which Prisca is a nickname).

Certainly Montanists scandalized the more orthodox Roman clergy for their willingness to let women serve as prophets, elders, and even presbyters. Could the Greek Chapel have served a community of Roman Montanists? It is at least plausible that an unorthodox community that privileged the role of women might establish a small vigil chapel here at the Catacombs of Priscilla—perhaps especially because the name of their founder matched the name of the catacomb's own founder, the noble Priscilla.

On the other hand, the Montanist theory assumes that women's sacred space in early Christian circles—virtually by definition—had to be un-orthodox. It ties women's concerns and women's activity in salvation history with a community of heretics, because it presumes that women played no significant roles, nor had any significant place to call their own, in early Catholicism. But there is nothing explicitly heretical about the iconography we find in the Greek Chapel, and indeed, the chambers themselves are found inside a catacomb administrated by the Catholic Church since the third century. The orthodox pedigree of the Catacombs of Priscilla is hardly in dispute. Thus we can think of the Greek Chapel as one geared to-ward use by and for Christian women, probably in the proto-Catholic (what we call also "orthodox") tradition. But we are still left with some mysteries. What was it used for? Women's prayer and vigils? Did it commemorate any specific woman? If so, who?

Since this was a privately commissioned burial chamber, a family may have had it built to honor a dead child; the emphasis on women's iconogra-phy may have conveyed the interests of a wealthy matron who had lost a beloved child whom she had buried at the front of the Greek Chapel—much the way that the woman I named "Proba" in chapter 2 commemo-rated her only, lost daughter. But another possibility exists: perhaps the grave at the front of the room was tiny not because it held a child's bones. Rather, it may have functioned as a sort of ossuary or secondary burial for a martyr's bones.[52] In this case, the room was actually what is known as a *martyrium*. In fact, the Greek Chapel may have been designed as such. It was built to house only one body, because that body was the focal point of devotion. But in the time after it was designed and completed, numerous bodies were buried in the space too—these are what we call *ad sanctos* buri-als—because later Christians wished to be buried as close as possible to a holy person (*sanctus*) or to a martyr's relics. The presence of so many *ad sanctos* burials in this region tells archaeologists that people of late antiq-uity—from the fourth through the sixth centuries—believed that a very holy person indeed was buried there, and they wanted to clamor close, even in death. At some point in late antiquity, a hole was punched through the back wall of the Greek Chapel, and the space became a *confessio* or martyr's shrine; the faithful would, on their itineraries through the catacombs, insert small pieces of cloth to be sanctified by touching the martyr's bones, sopping up their holiness like bits of bread in soup.

Whose bones once sanctified the Greek Chapel? We can only speculate. The overwhelming emphasis on women's imagery suggests that the holy person of the Greek Chapel burial was herself a woman. She may have been a leader of a Christian community of the third century—a wealthy *patrona*. The family who founded at least one core section of the catacombs—a noble Roman family from an ancient clan called the Acilii Glabrioni—may have had in their ranks a female teacher or patroness who had a substantial following. Her leadership of the community in word and deed, through Eucharists and sacred meals and public prayer, were recorded on the walls of her burial chapel for posterity so that those in her family and community might come to pay their enduring respects to her. Over time—and we cannot know how much time—her images were misunderstood and misrepresented by a male clergy anxious to efface real women from history. The images of her at prayer or in the act of being consecrated were reinterpreted as biblical scenes of a victimized Susanna appealing to heaven and a male God who sent his male emissary Daniel to vindicate her shame and vouch for her chastity. The central roundel portrait of her above the door of her own tomb was disregarded as an uninteresting and meaningless smudge. And the central meal scene at which she sat in the place of honor—presiding over a Eucharistic banquet which she herself led—came to be seen, by centuries of patriarchal, clerical "readers" as a gathering of men, presided upon not by our unnamed woman, but by the by-now unambiguously male figure to her right. Patriarchal memory obliterates women.

That is one way of reading the evidence, anyway. It has its plausibilities and its attractions, particular for those of us to wish to reinstate women to a history of Christianity that has been predominately androcentric. But it's not the only way to read the evidence. Nothing is ever so simple.

The painting of the Greek Chapel—and significantly, its meal scene—took place at a time in the church's history when the active participation of women in Christianity was heatedly contested. One central issue considered women's proper place in running a church. Was influence best exercised through women acting in official capacities—as, let's say, deacons or even presbyters—or was it more appropriate for them to be silent in the churches, even as they worked behind the scenes as patrons, fundraisers, organizers, and enthusiastic congregants? We can find in third-century documents substantial evidence that some women still exercised clerical power in certain congregations. This authority included the right to teach and to baptize. Those women drew on certain figures in Christian history to justify their activities—and Thecla was one of them (Tertullian, *On Baptism* 1.17).[53]

But before we imagine that we might have discovered the burial chamber of a lost woman priest or deacon in ancient Christian Rome, there are some fundamental suppositions and terms of reference that need to be brought forward. To say that women exercised authority in the church is not the same as saying that they acted as priests. In fact, the word "priest" was not used in early Christianity for women or for men; instead, terms for ecclesiastical leaders included *episcopos* "overseer" (which we now translate most frequently as "bishop"), *diakonos* ("server" or "minister"), and *presbyter* ("elder"). Women, at various times and places, were certainly deacons. Whether they were ever elders or overseers is more controversial.[54]

Second, we must also accept that if women celebrated the Eucharist, this does not mean that they did so as consecrated priests. There is some evidence that in the early Christian church, consecrated virgins may have had this privilege, particularly in exclusively female communities. It's also the case that although women may never have served in positions of authority in the first Christian centuries, they clearly did within rival Christian groups such as the Montanists. Indeed—in Rome, it could well have been the case that prominent or powerful women chose not to become Catholics because their leadership options in Catholic communities were severely limited; they turned instead to other Christian communities where their leadership would have been welcomed. To put it differently, women may have been early Christian priests, but they would not have been Catholic priests. Still, there is absolutely no textual or inscriptional evidence for a female Christian priesthood in third- or fourth-century Rome and, as we have seen, the visual evidence is tricky to interpret.

Women's roles within Christian communities were different in different parts of the empire at different times. Historians cannot use the evidence of women serving Eucharists in rural southern Italy (let's say) to claim that women in Rome were doing the same. Wherever there was a shortage of men, women likely filled in with sacramental services and privileges out of necessity. Rodolfo Lanciani cites a list of church possessions seized during Emperor Diocletian's persecution in the early fourth century at a small assembly in Cirta, now in modern Algeria. The itemized list included eighty-two tunics for women, sixteen tunics for men, thirteen pairs of men's boots and forty-seven pairs of women's shoes.[55] This is not proof of women serving in formal ecclesiastical offices, but it does point to a fascinating disparity in the number of men and the number of women active in one church community. We do have proof of women presbyters, though, in fifth-century Bari, an Italian city on the Adriatic coast.[56] On March 11 of 494 CE, Pope Gelasius I dispatched an angry epistle to three local dioceses around Bari:

> Nevertheless, we have heard to our annoyance that divine affairs have come to such a low point that women are encouraged to officiate (Latin: *ministrare*) at the sacred altars and to take part in all matters delegated only to the offices of the male sex, to which they do not belong.[57]

The presence of women ministers around Bari has been bolstered by the discovery of a tomb inscription there from a husband to his wife: "Sacred to her good memory. Leta the presbyter lived for forty years, eight months, and nine days, whose husband set up this tomb. She preceded him in peace on the day before the ides of May."[58] Only seventeen years later, far away in Gaul, three bishops censured two priests, Lovocatus and Catinernus, for allowing women to hold the Eucharistic chalice and distribute the Eucharist during a service. Evidently, suitable men were in short supply, both in southern Italy and Gaul.[59]

The city of Rome was different, however, and never suffered a shortage of men—even at times of wars and epidemics. The population was simply too high, and there was always the influx of new immigrants from other parts of the Empire. But then there could be other reasons for women to serve as presbyters. A sarcophagus inscription from the eastern city of Salona in Dalmatia, dated to 425 CE, records that the owner of the sarcophagus, Theodosius, had purchased his own burial spot for three gold solidi from a *presbytera* there named Flavia Vitalia. Interestingly, Flavia Vitalia had an official function as the administrator of cemetery lands—probably not too far from her Roman female counterparts, the lost bone gatherers, who saw to it that Christians received a decent burial on their lands.[60]

The problem with the reconstruction I've suggested here—that the Greek Chapel commemorates the life and death of an illustrious female deacon of the third century—is that not a single piece of textual or epigraphical evidence proves that women of third- or fourth-century Rome were ordained.[61] We do know a little about what the Roman ecclesiastical structure of the time looked like. A letter of Pope Cornelius (251–253 CE) to the bishop Fabius of Antioch records that Cornelius had under his authority in the middle of the third century one hundred and fifty-five priests.[62] These priests, in turn, ministered to a community of about thirty thousand.[63] The city also boasted seven deacons and seven subdeacons for the seven established ecclesiastical areas under Cornelius's immediate predecessor, Pope Fabian (236–250 CE). Under the deacons served forty-two acolytes and forty-six other registered priests.[64] Could any of these two hundred priests have been women? Almost certainly not—not in Rome, and not in the third century. That already would have been unthinkable.

Under the bishop of Rome—the pope, at that time, although he was not yet the uncontroverted head of the church—served a legion of lesser clergy arranged in a rigid hierarchy. The eighth-century *Liber Pontificalis* or *Book of the Popes* lists under Pope Gaius (283–296 CE) the positions of deacon, subdeacon, *sequens* (acolyte), exorcist, lector, and gate-porter or *ostiarius* (comparable to a "greeter" or usher in modern church congregations).[65] There were also something like ecclesiastical bureaucrats, the *notarii* and *exceptores,* whose job it was to keep records, take notes, and write shorthand. We might add to these various positions attested from funerary inscriptions, including *mansionarii,* clerics, *pueri, staurophoroi* ("cross bearers"), cantors, *famuli, servi,* ministers, *cubicularii, primiscrinii, actuarii, fossores,* and *vestiarii.* We're not even sure what all these people did, but all were apparently male, given the names on the inscriptions. We have no inscriptional evidence that any of these positions included women in their ranks. Occasionally, though, wives left behind epitaphs for their office-holding husbands. A lector's wife, for instance, commemorated her beloved spouse:

> To a most pleasing husband and sweetest soul Alexius, a lector at the church near the fullery, who lived with me for sixteen years and was joined with me for sixteen [more] years, a virgin to a virgin . . . rest in peace among the saints, among whom you merit. He departed this life on the 8th of the Kalends of January.[66]

The absence of evidence of female Christian officeholders might provoke the skeptic to insist that perhaps the Catholic Church engaged in a conspiracy of silence; perhaps women deacons and priests *did* practice in late ancient Rome, but they were not commemorated, or their existences were intentionally and systematically obliterated. This is within the realm of possibility, certainly. But in truth, by the fourth century patriarchalism had long been a core feature of the Roman church, and a public Christian cemetery run by the church would hardly have been the sort of place where one might have advertised a woman's having infiltrated the ecclesial ranks. Were the Greek Chapel a private burial site like the Via Latina catacombs, we might expect the unexpected. But it was not.

A different answer to the question of why women could not, and did not, serve as priests involves the movement of Christianity from house churches or the private domain to the public domain of the Constantinian and post-Constantinian world, where they could hold little power.[67] Yet in recent debate, church historians such as Carolyn Osiek have questioned the degree to which this private/public dichotomy was really operative in late ancient Christianity.[68] The house church was in effect liminal space, as was the catacomb. The rise of Constantinian churches did not mean the replacement of these private spaces. At the same time, it is certainly the case that with Constantine's endorsement and patronage of what was to become the Catholic Church, certain movements or communities that may have relied upon private, wealthy female donors may have been confined to households. Of concern to male clerics, therefore, was the alternative movement of Christian teachings through private networks and avenues of these female sponsors. It brought about one sort of bifurcation of Christianity—one male, clerical, imperial, and centralized, and the other more fluid, lay, private, and atomized. Only in this second Christianity could women have any direct influence and agency.

If the woman for whom the Greek Chapel was designed and in which her bones lay was not likely to have been a third-century female deacon or presbyter, who could she have been? Here, early medieval pilgrims' itineraries provide some intriguing clues. These itineraries were travel guides that pilgrims brought with them to identify points of interest as they moved around the city of Rome in a great circle, visiting cemetery after cemetery to spend a moment in the presence of the holy. They tell us that the Catacombs of Priscilla were the burial place of six popes, three hundred sixty-five unknown martyrs, and a number of named ones, including Crescention, Felix, and Philip. We also know from these texts that significant women were buried in the Catacombs of Priscilla, including the senatorial noblewomen Praxides and Pudenziana. Of these, the most important was the Roman martyr Prisca. Visitors to her grave would have descended the central staircase from the mortuary chapel on the surface and entered a subterranean area (the itineraries call it a *spelunca* or "cave") for prayers, to be in the presence of her tomb.[69] This we know from the ancient itineraries, but we don't know precisely where this particular subterranean area would have been. As it happens, we find one such area directly adjacent to the Greek Chapel. To reach the Greek Chapel in antiquity, a visitor would descend a staircase from the mortuary chapel above and enter an impressive bricked chamber with a high vaulted ceiling. Once upon a time, modern scholars surmised that this chamber was a sort of basement (*criptoporticus*) for an impressive Roman villa that had once graced the surface directly above.[70] But in the 1960s, excavations by the Vatican engineer Francesco Tolotti revealed something surprising: no Roman villa had ever stood on these grounds; rather, the first structures built there were funerary chapels, probably for the wealthy Roman family of the Acilii Glabriones.[71] Their own mortuary chapel and funerary inscriptions are still found a short distance underground from the Greek Chapel. An unknown member of the Acilii Glabriones—a Christian, but whether male or female is uncertain—constructed this atrium, probably in the fourth century, as a family mausoleum and a martyr shrine or *martyrium*.[72] The main burial in the atrium had its own heavy marble sarcophagus that nestled into a niche in one of the room's antechambers. Who was buried there, we do not know. I would surmise that it was the *paterfamilias* of the clan.

The six or so chambers leading off this atrium—of which the Greek Chapel is by far the most impressive—would have held the bodies of other martyrs. At the opposite end of the atrium from the Greek Chapel, for instance, lies a small, bare cubiculum. The presence of a *forma* or *ad sanctos* burial set into the floor in front of the *arcosolium* grave in this cubiculum lets us know that ancient visitors considered the grave there to hold the body of someone of great sanctity. Some have identified that small room as the burial place of an early pope—all we know is that others, at some point, clamored to be buried close to whoever was first interred there. The room was certainly a *martyrium*—but curiously, it was never fully painted, certainly never as elaborately finished as the Greek Chapel on the other side of the atrium. If this room was important, the Greek Chapel was even more so.

Francesco Tolotti suggested that the Greek Chapel functioned as an anteroom for the atrium, which he viewed not as a family crypt but as a larger *martyrium* that held only one body: that of an important female martyr by the name of Prisca or Priscilla.[73] But it is curious that of all the anterooms leading off the atrium (and including the atrium itself), the Greek Chapel is by far the most elaborately decorated. If, then, one were to speculate on the *spelunca* that ancient pilgrims' guides insisted held Prisca's bones, my choice would not be the atrium, but the Greek Chapel itself. The atrium, by contrast, would have held the bones of the patriarch of the family—whose name we do not know. But the most significant burial in the complex was not his; it was another member of the same clan, buried in an ancillary chamber of the family complex. This member, I'm guessing, was Priscilla (Prisca) of the Acilii Glabriones.

So who was this Priscilla? Unfortunately, it's unclear. Ancient history is murky, and all we know for sure is that a number of historical and legendary Priscillas were eventually combined in pious memory into the one figure of Saint Priscilla (or Saint Prisca). There was certainly a Roman noblewoman by the name of Priscilla. We know, because we have her gravestone from the Catacombs of Priscilla. There's no indication from her epitaph that she was Christian. It may be this woman—or another Priscilla from the same family, since Roman noblewomen all tended to have the same name—who gave her name to the catacomb complex. She, therefore, was likely its *patrona;* she donated her own lands to Christians for their burials, and was rewarded by having her name attached to the catacombs for the rest of time.

But time confuses all things. There were also other Priscillas/Priscas who came to be associated with the burial complex. A fifth-century source mentions a neighborhood Roman church called the *titulus Priscoe* that was established, probably in the fourth century, on the Aventine hill overlooking Rome's great Hippodrome. In fact, the church there—Santa Prisca—still thrives today on the same sleepy street on which it has sat for sixteen centuries. There is a possibility that the Prisca associated with the Aventine church was a descendant of Pudens Cornelianus, a man of senatorial class whose name was found on a bronze tablet discovered near the *titulus* bearing the date 224 CE. As a *patrona* of the Roman church, she would have given up a portion of her property for Christians to have used for their worship services. Some say, instead, that Priscilla was the mother of the senator Pudens, who according to tradition welcomed Saint Peter into their home near Rome's Viminal hill, where today stands the church of Santa Pudenziana.[74]

We can't fathom the symbolic relationship between the *patrona* Prisca who established the church on the Aventine hill, the Priscilla associated with Santa Pudenziana, and the woman Priscilla of the Acilii Glabriones family whose grave tablet was discovered in her family crypt at the Catacombs of Priscilla; several women were probably conflated over time into one single "Priscilla." We do know, however, that the Prisca mentioned by seventh-century pilgrim's itineraries as buried in the Catacombs of Priscilla was venerated on January 18. A later legend relates the martyrdom of one thirteen-year-old Christian girl named Prisca, who was beheaded at the tenth milestone on the Via Ostiensis for refusing to denounce Christ. Her body was collected by Pope Eutychianus (275–283 CE) and translated to the church of St. Prisca on the Aventine. Although this Prisca seems to have been different from the Prisca buried at Priscilla, she too was venerated on January 18. In summary, what we appear to have in the case of the catacombs is one Priscilla of the Acilii Glabriones family who may have donated her cemetery lands to Christians for burial, a second Prisca of the Aventine Hill who allowed Christians to meet in her house, and a third Prisca who was a child martyr. All three became hopelessly intertwined into the figure of one martyr buried at the catacombs named in her honor, to whom crowds of pilgrims came to focus their devotions.

There is one other Prisca, however, associated with the Catacombs of Priscilla, and it's time to meet her.

For a moment, let's go back further in time, earlier even than Rome's Greek Chapel, to the city's earliest Christian communities—that is to say, to around the year 50 CE, when the apostle Paul wrote to the fledgling community of Christ-followers there. Those committing themselves to a life in Christ met in house churches. We should imagine these as fairly small, simple accommodations where the noncitizens (that is, people of lower status than the elites) of Rome lived.

What did Christian worship look like within a house church? We know that there was prayer, preaching, and a celebration of the Eucharist (Acts 2:46; 20:7). We also have good reason to believe that women exercised positions of leadership within these domestic worship spaces.[75] The domestic realm tended to be the one in which women ran the show. References in Paul's letters, the book of Acts, and other early sources make explicit the connection between women, house churches, and authority. Acts 12:12 refers to a prayer meeting in the house of Mary, the mother of the apostle John Mark. In Colossians 4:15 we find a woman by the name of Nympha who runs a "church in her house." In Philemon, verse 2, Paul greets a leader of a house church, Apphia, in the eastern city of Colossae (now in modern Turkey). Women would have founded and led these communities, provided the physical space and food for meetings, led prayers, and instructed new converts.

In Rome, Christianity was established early. The conversion of the city's first Christ-followers is attributed to Jesus's disciple Simon Peter, who remains Rome's primary patron saint. Rome's Jewish community, strong and ancient, likely provided a sort of base or source of potential converts.

We also know that the city's Christ-followers—the term "Christian" had yet to be coined in the first century—had organized into communities already by the time that Paul visited. The community to which he wrote was not one that he founded; his letter to the Romans, preserved in the New Testament, lays out his ideas for an audience unaccustomed to Paul's particular brand of theology. But it provides a few significant details about the nature of this particular Roman community. One thing that strikes a careful reader is the importance of women in this community: of thirty-six people Paul mentions by name, as many as sixteen were women.[76]

At one key point in his letters to the Romans, Paul mentions a couple by the name of Prisca and Aquila who had organized a "church in their house" (Rom 16:3–5; see also Acts 18:2, 2 Tim 4:19, and 1 Cor 16:19). The fact that Paul mentions Prisca's name before her husband's may be an indication that she held more authority than him. Prisca and Aquila had, so Paul tells us, "risked their necks" to save Paul's life. They had welcomed Paul into the church that met in their house (Rom 16:4). Prisca was hardly Paul's disciple; she did not serve under him. Rather, she was an independent patron and leader on the same level as Paul, who refers to her as a *synergos*, a "coworker" in the Lord (Rom 16:3). This Prisca, along with her husband or partner, Aquila, welcomed Christians into their home to share gospel and table fellowship. Paul held her in great respect, great enough to intimate that she was one of the heads of the Roman church—a teacher, a leader, and a deacon.

The medieval pilgrims who journeyed to the Catacombs of Priscilla came not to see the bones of Priscilla of the Cornelii or Acilii Glabrioni clan but the holy relics of Prisca, the Roman woman with whom the apostle Paul stayed when he visited the city in the middle of the first century. Her bones rested there until the ninth century, when Pope Leo IV translated them to a place now lost.[77] I myself wonder if medieval pilgrims located those bones in the Greek Chapel, deep underground, following the swift staircase from the surface into the cavelike, labyrinthine catacombs. They first found themselves in a large atrium—a martyr's shrine of floor-burials and oil lamps and vaulted ceilings—and pressed forward, the darkness closing around them, into the Greek Chapel. The most finely decorated space in the area, it lured visitors with its warm reddish glow then as it does now —a memory box of color and image. From its walls shone the faces of women from Christianity's most hallowed history. There in the Greek Chapel, groups of pious, everyday women gathered on sacred occasions for overnight funerary vigils. The men were not welcome here, not in this place. The women took their places, silently, along the long, narrow bench specially cut to be women's seating.[78] Their backs rested against the cool, damp walls as they gazed up at the images of sacred women that floated out from the white and blood-red backgrounds of the walls. There they meditated on the salvific work and examples of every significant woman in early Christian history: Jesus's disciples Mary, Martha, the Virgin Mary, and Mary Magdalene, and two of the most holy women associated with the apostle Paul: Thecla and Prisca.

The women who sat in silent vigil in this room never held substantial power in the Roman church. But they had found a place of their own; it was a space for reverential glances backward to perhaps what some considered a more potent age. There, in that space, powerful female teachers still left a residue, a sacred vapor trail of sanctity. Prisca's bones were there, and the images of her sisters were almost as indelible as bone. Their traditions and memories still thrived, in the hearts of Rome's ordinary Christian women, sitting in subterranean darkness.

CHAPTER 5

PETRONELLA GOES
TO PARADISE

*The central collision of the post-Constantinian church . . . was not between pagan
and Christian per se, but rather between alternate notions of familia, one based on
the bonds of kin and dynasty, and the other on a chosen kinship, that of the Christian ecclesia, whose ties were as durable as those of blood.*
—Kate Cooper, "The Martyr, the Matrona, and the Bishop"

On a different side of the city from the Velata and Proba—possibly at
precisely the same time—lived another one of Rome's pious citizens.
Unlike the Velata and Proba, however, we know her real name: Veneranda.
In Latin, her name was a strong one, carrying the force of an imperative:
"woman needing to be venerated." It was a name of considerable dignity,
and our only surviving portrait of Veneranda shows her wearing it well.
Veneranda died middle-aged in a city that too was approaching middle
age. During her lifetime, she saw Rome become a Christian city, of a sort.[1]
By the middle of the fourth century, Rome had taken on a distinctly "late
antique" face. Long gone were the days of classical Rome, of togas and
marble-clad monuments. Men and women garbed in tunics of rich color and
imported silks replaced those in undyed woolen or linen togas on the streets.
The monuments of the past still stood, and Christian emperors and bishops
only added new Christian monuments to a venerable, urban landscape.

Proba had chosen a private burial complex in the southeast sector of the
city. Veneranda, like the Velata (and most Christians of their day), chose a
more "public" site, albeit an exclusive area within it. Her tomb was prepared

for her in a coveted section of the Catacombs of Domitilla, one of the largest and oldest of the church's cemeteries.[2] We can guess why it appealed to her; it was not Domitilla's antiquity that drew Veneranda, nor was it merely that she lived in the appropriate district of the city to warrant a more or less automatic right to interment there.[3] The catacombs held the bones already of countless anonymous Christians, but most important of all, they held the bones of the saints Nereus, Achilleus, and Petronella in a special basilica chapel built around the first half of the fourth century.[4] What drew Veneranda was the numinous lure of these holy martyrs. During the last decade of her life, Veneranda had witnessed the extension of Domitilla's catacombs so that as many people as possible could be buried close to the partially subterranean basilica dedicated to the three saints.[5] *Fossores* strained to hew three new regions west of the basilica, adding monumental staircases to lead masses of visitors swiftly into the darkness of the martyrs' shrine.[6] The graves in this new region were predominantly *arcosolia* and cubicula— that is to say, the region was exclusive, expensive, and coveted. Although Christian catacombs provided burials for all Christians, they were far from democratic spaces. Mile upon mile of galleries teemed with the bodies of Rome's urban poor, but those of means purchased "luxury suites" from the catacombs from the *fossores,* who became powerful enough by the third century to constitute a minor category of clergy. Not any humble Christian might aspire to be buried tucked in so close to the holy.[7] But this is where we find Veneranda: in a sort of luxury suite featuring a painted lunette over her carefully constructed masonry grave. There are no other paintings in the cubiculum. The year of her burial remains a mystery, but most scholars date it to 356 CE.[8]

Like so many of Rome's ancient women, Veneranda becomes visible to us only upon her death. She died alone, apparently, separated from her family. Although over the centuries her cubiculum came to hold the bodies of at least ten or twelve other adults, these were later burials. The chamber was commissioned for her alone, and hers is the only *arcosolium* or arch grave in the chamber. Such dislocation from earthly family is, as we have seen in the case of the Velata, hardly unusual for a fourth-century Christian woman. She had with her in paradise a new family and the friendship and "matron-age" of a saint. What use had she, after all, for an earthly family if she was in the arms of her heavenly martyr-sister?

The lunette fresco carefully painted with Veneranda's likeness is rela- tively small—small enough that to view it is a relatively intimate act. Pil-

Saint Petronella (right) leads the pious matron Veneranda to heaven. Their names are painted next to their heads. Note the book and basket of scrolls to the right of Petronella. This lunette fresco adorns Veneranda's grave, behind the basilica of St. Petronella (now the Church of Saints Nereus and Achilleus) at the Catacombs of Domitilla.

grims passing through the catacombs to reach the graves of the martyrs might catch a glimpse of it as they walked through, but to see it fully, one would have to stop and linger.

Veneranda is depicted here much the same way that other pious Christian women of the fourth century were portrayed.[9] She stands with her arms upraised, her eyes averted. Although the pose she assumes is highly conventional in early Christian art, there is no question of that the image constitutes portraiture, not some symbolic representation of piety. We have here a portrait, however idealized, of a wealthy woman, elegant in her full-length, resplendent saffron dalmatic with dark purple or deep red stripes (*clavi*) on the sleeves. The dalmatic's stripes match the interior wrapping of a heavy veil that covers her hair, but not her face. Her slippered toes barely peek out from the bottom of her hem. The anonymous artist carefully recorded in red painted letters the precise day she died—the seventh of the ides of January (January 7)—next to her name on the fresco that adorned her grave. It was on this day ever after that Veneranda's family or friends would descend to the catacombs to visit her, the woman needing to be venerated. Behind her and to her left, a second woman guides her, her arm on Veneranda's shoulder. She, too, has her name and "title" written above her head: PETRNEL·MAR or "Petronella, martyr."[10] Petronella is not veiled; instead, her hair is up tidily; she wears not the long dalmatic but the more formal and archaic *stola* and *palla*. The lack of veil may indicate that she is already in heaven where no earthly sign of modesty is necessary, but the space is intimate and gendered: we see her unveiled, as only a family member might.

As I look carefully at the painting of Veneranda, I am struck by how I, as viewer, am drawn into the scene. I become a participant in her world, not merely a spectator. The historian Margaret Miles attributes the participatory quality of some ancient paintings such as this one as a consequence of what she (and other art historians) call "frontality": "In the small chambers of the catacombs," notes Miles, "frontality 'spoke' to the viewer, *facie ad faciem*, the better to communicate a strong message of hope and comfort in the face of the ever-present threat of physical death."[11] The painting could salve the cruel wounds of grief and loss. At the same time, the frontality of the figures that draws us in is balanced by our exclusion from the scene's self-contained focus: the women gaze at each other, not at us. Our presence is ignored, or perhaps allowed, at best, within the intimacy of their world. It is not *our* world; we are not yet fully in it, although we may have it to look forward to when our own time comes.

Veneranda's grave allows us to learn the stories of two women—one real and one conjured, imagined. There is an irony to this: about the real woman, Veneranda, we know little except that which we might unearth, as we put her together piece by piece from her burial. About Petronella, we know simultaneously far more and far less; as a holy martyr and virgin of the church, she leaves behind a wake of passed-on tradition, partial images, and inferences cloaked in the certainty of Catholic piety. But even these quickly disintegrate with a gentle prod, like human bones that crumble when exposed to air after millennia encased in stone. A quick search of Petronella's name in Catholic encyclopedias and biographies of the saints reveals the contours of a compressed, conflated history: she is "a virgin, probably martyred at Rome at the end of the first century."[12] But the more one reads, the more unsteady seem the details. Was she a martyr or a holy virgin? Did she live in the first century or the second? Was she of Jewish Palestinian ancestry, or was she a noble Roman scion of a powerful family?

When Giovanni Battista De Rossi, the great archaeologist of the early Roman church, discovered the Catacombs of Domitilla's subterranean basilica dedicated to Petronella (and, nearby, Veneranda's grave) in 1873, he sought to rescue the saint from the obscurity into which she had fallen. Veneranda, a rich and pious laywoman from the fourth century, interested him far less. Petronella, by contrast, could serve the Roman Catholic Church very well. The discovery of her grave—and her cult—might demonstrate the antiquity and authority of the Roman church, reifying its ties with powerful members of the imperial families. De Rossi set about composing six separate short articles on Petronella's chapel, relics, and Veneranda's painting of her for the Vatican's *Bulletino di archeologia cristiana*, which he published from 1874 to 1879.[13]

Let's start with what De Rossi knew. To late ancient Christians as, presumably, to Veneranda, Petronella was the virgin daughter of Saint Peter. We can read an early version of Petronella's legend in an ancient collection of stories known as the *Acts of Peter*. Here, Peter does the unthinkable: he refuses to use his powers to heal his own daughter from a palsy that renders her severely handicapped. One from the crowd of faithful collected around Peter requests an explanation: "Why have you not helped your virgin daughter, who has grown up beautiful and has believed in the name of God? For she is quite paralyzed on one side, and she lies there stretched out in the corner helpless" (*Acts of Peter* 1.128). For the questioner, Peter's refusal could only be a case of perverse obstinacy: "We see the people you have healed; but your own daughter you have neglected" (Ibid.). As a vivid illustration of his own powers, Peter bids his daughter to "rise up . . . and walk naturally before them all and come to me" (1.130). The daughter does as she is commanded, and the crowds marvel. The point having been made, however, Peter then orders her back on her bed: "Go to your place, lie down and return to your infirmity, for this is profitable for you and for me" (1.131). The disease is a true blessing in disguise, Peter explains: it preserves her virginity and saves both her and the men around her from falling into the sins of the flesh.[14] Her beauty had tempted men since she was only ten years old, but the Lord himself had preserved her "from uncleanness and shame" by afflicting her with disease (1.135).

There are later legends as well, no less chilling. In the *Acts of Nereus and Achilleus,* which dates to perhaps the fifth or sixth century, Petronella's great beauty leads a count by the name of Flaccus to fall in love with her.[15] He comes to her house with his soldiers to take her by force. But she rebukes him: if he wants her for his wife, forced entry into her home with a band of soldiers is hardly the way to win the heart of a bride. Rather, she intones, the sanctity of her chamber ought only to be penetrated by women. She bids Flaccus to wait three days, then to send a group of matrons and virgins to conduct her to his house. Flaccus complies, and Petronella passes the three days with her foster-sister Felicula in prayer and fasting. On the third day, after receiving the Eucharist but no other sustenance, Petronella dies, her hunger strike swiftly successful. Flaccus's female attendants arrive not to escort a new bride to her new home but to serve as part of her funeral *cortège.* They bear her body back to the Via Ardeatina in the south of the city, where they bury it in the cemetery grounds of her kinswoman Domitilla.[16]

Petronella's narrative, as horrifying as it is, is not (strictly speaking) a martyrology. An account of a martyr's death has certain stock features: an arrest, a formal interrogation, imprisonment, torture, another interrogation before a tribunal, a death judgment duly handed down, and the final, spasmodic (even vaguely pornographic, as we shall see in the next chapter) spatter-fest of an execution. Petronella's death in this account, by contrast, is of another, related genre: the heroic death of a young woman who chooses chastity over marriage, even at the cost of her life. It was a lesson that the late ancient Roman church rehearsed over and over again, each time with new heroines but the same central drama. All these legends expressed precisely the same conviction: a fight to the death for one's chastity offered women the surest route to heaven. Marriage and family were only dead ends: disastrous, mundane distortions of human potential. A woman's spiritual possibilities were inextricably linked with her ability to avoid the complicated, even polluting ties of domestic life and to establish for herself a place in paradise, where she might live as sexlessly as the angels.

But we are moving away from De Rossi, who, though a nineteenth-century man of the church, did not truly believe that Petronella had been the daughter of Saint Peter. He was also a man of science—most moved by the palpable evidence of the catacombs' material remains. Concerning Petronella, he had at his disposal more reliable pieces of information than the simple legends of the pious. He rejected the idea that Petronella was Peter's daughter, but resolutely maintained (as the late ancient *Acts of Nereus and Achilleus* made explicit) that she had lived sometime in the second century, a scion of the powerful Flavian family—the same family that produced the Roman emperors Domitian and Vespasian. He knew from his studies of the Catacombs of Domitilla's funerary chapel to Nereus and Achilleus that all the old medieval topographies of Rome placed Petronella's grave next to theirs. The discovery of Veneranda's painting only supported what the medieval sources made explicit. He also knew from ecclesiastical documents that Petronella's remains were no longer in the basilica; they had been moved or "translated" to the Vatican in their original sarcophagus during the papacy of Paul I (757–767 CE). This sarcophagus had come to light at the Catacombs of Domitilla sometime in late antiquity; an ancient excavator— perhaps one of the church's own league of grave robbers, the so-called *corpisantari* who raided catacombs to remove the bones of the dead to circulate and sell as relics—came across it, fully intact. It bore only a wistful, laconic inscription: AVR. PETRONELLAE FILIAE DVLCISSIMAE, or "For a most sweet daughter, Aur. Petronella."

Armed with the knowledge that Petronella's sarcophagus had been removed from the Catacombs of Domitilla more than a thousand years earlier, De Rossi then identified the place in the chapel dedicated to Nereus, Achilleus, and Petronella where this very sarcophagus must once have lain in its own richly decorated niche. The archaeologist priest had helped another holy martyr to move from being "just a legend" to a flesh-and-bones reality. It was a thrilling moment for the Catholic Church.

De Rossi's enthusiastic bulletins on Petronella's burial eventually came to unsettle later generations of Vatican archaeologists. Umberto Fasola, another archaeologist priest who undertook extensive studies of the Catacombs of Domitilla, remarked that it was odd that Petronella's *passio* had her die in own bed when Veneranda's painting identified her so clearly as a "martyr."[17] This minor puzzle Fasola revealed to one of his students at the Pontifical Institute of Christian Archaeology, Philippo Pergola. It burned in Pergola's mind, until in 1982 at a conference and following a course with another Vatican archaeologist, Patrick Saint-Roch, Saint-Roch expressed his own controversial opinions: he believed that Petronella had really existed, but that she had not been Peter's daughter. Nor had she ever been martyred, Saint-Roch averred. After all, the sole testimony to her status as a martyr was Veneranda's brief description on her tomb. None of the many official church documents mentioned anything of Petronella's martyrdom. And unlike De Rossi, Saint-Roch disputed that Petronella was a scion of the Flavian clan who had starved herself to avoid an infelicitous marriage with a fictitious count named Flaccus. No—she was someone else entirely. It was left to Pergola to publish the hypothesis. For eight more years Pergola remained silent, until he finally, tentatively, shared their surprising secret of who Petronella probably was.

If we can unravel the puzzle of Petronella—who she really was—we can go a long way in understanding the powerful intersection of faith, history, and memory-making in the Catholic Church. To uncover what we can about her, we might work backward, from the Italian Renaissance. During renovations to Petronella's chapel at St. Peter's in the year 1574, two witnesses saw Petronella's sarcophagus for the last time before it was disassembled to be used as part of the chapel's floor. The architect in charge of the project, Tiberius Alpharano, and another humanist of the period, Pietro Sabino, both noted that the sarcophagus was decorated in a simple style called "strigilated," derived from the strigil or curved scraper that made long wavy decorative marks along its sides.[18] The style is typical of ancient Roman sarcophagi—most of them pagan—that were reused by resourceful Christians in late antiquity. Because sarcophagi were so often reused, we can't use the sarcophagus to date Petronella's death. But what about its inscription, duly recorded by Alpharani and Sabino? As learned men, they read the AVR in the inscription AVR PETRONILLAE FILIAE DULCISSIMAE differently than it had been read in antiquity. Christians of the early Middle Ages, moved by the optimism of a sure faith, understood the abbreviation "AVR" not as part of her name, but as the adjective "golden" (*aureae*), as in the "golden Petronella." They even believed that the steady hands of Saint Peter himself had carved the very words on the sarcophagus's heavy marble sides, as he grieved for his sweetest child. Alpharani and Sabino, by contrast, understood that AVR stood not for *aureae*, but was the short form of the name "Aurelia." The inscription was therefore a standard funerary inscription, like tens of thousands of others that commemorate lost daughters in Rome. It could not have been Peter, the grieving father of the first century, decrying the loss of his "golden" daughter.

What Alpharani and Sabino saw destroyed in Petronella's chapel that day in 1574, then, was the ordinary sarcophagus of an ordinary girl, Aurelia Petronella. Her name tells us that she could have been a freedwoman—Aurelius was the most common *nomen gentile* or surname in Rome after the third century for freed slaves—or it might have been aristocratic. We have no way of knowing for sure. As for her second name, Petronella is, like Priscilla and Domitilla, what is known as a *cognomen* and, typically, a diminutive: a fond and familiar form of another noble name, Petronia. It's tempting for some to link Aurelia Petronella with Titus Flavius Petronius, an ancient ancestor of the Flavian clan whose daughter, Domitilla, had donated the lands where Petronella herself would be buried. If this were the case, then Petronella was of noble birth, buried in the cemetery lands of her own family. This, at least, might explain why Petronella was buried in such a fine place in the Catacombs of Petronella. But the connections to these ancient families are tenuous. Either way, there is good cause to think that late ancient Christians sanctified not the virgin daughter of Christ's disciple and leading apostle, but an ordinary if well-to-do Roman woman who happened to bear a common name.

Pergola's revelation—buried in a brief article in French published in an obscure volume by the Vatican—overturned the older Catholic consensus on Petronella as the daughter of Saint Peter and a saint: she was no martyr, only a Christian woman who had received a "privileged inhumation" sometime after the "Constantinian Peace"—that is, after 313 CE.[19] Pergola concluded, "All these arguments make me think that [what we have here is] a privileged inhumation . . . of a holy woman of great merit, who died at the moment of, or a little bit after, the construction of the basilica."[20] He wondered if Petronella had been a "donatrice-évergète," that is, a *patrona* who had contributed financially to the construction of the basilica to Nereus and Achilleus.[21] If she had sponsored the basilica, it made sense that she would have been richly installed, after her premature death, in one of the basilica's three finely decorated apses. But to the faithful who thronged to her tomb some twenty-five to fifty years after her death, Petronella was remembered and celebrated as a martyr, the little golden daughter of Saint Peter, not as a scion of the Aurelian or Petronian clans. Language—and faith—sometimes have the power to make ordinary daughters into saints.

There is more to say here about how an ordinary woman, perhaps a donor to the church, becomes remembered as someone else entirely. For this, we need to return to Veneranda, and to whom she believed, fervently, Petronella to be: a holy martyr, one fully worthy of paying dearly to ensure eternal proximity to her bones. Here, Veneranda was hardly alone. In the context of the middle to late fourth century when Veneranda lived, Petro-

nella wielded considerable power. In late antiquity she was greatly venerated. Her name appears in later martyrologies under the calendar day May
31. In 395, Pope Siriacus (384–399 CE) recognized her cult and renovated
her grave at the Catacombs of Domitilla along with those of Nereus and
Achilleus.[22] His builders sank the floor of the church down into the catacombs to literally enclose all three sacred martyrs' graves at the front of the
apse. Other, older graves were destroyed or moved to make room for
crowds of devout pilgrims entering the basilica. Veneranda was fortunate;
her grave remained intact, tucked as it was down behind Petronella's
bones.[23] There was an irony to it: had Veneranda been wealthier and gotten
herself still closer to Petronella's bones, her own grave would likely not
have survived.

By the sixth or seventh century, Petronella's name was included in
official documentary lists of Rome's most important martyrs, including the
Epitome libri de locis sanctorum martyrum that listed all the city's sacred martyr shrines.[24] But the church that Pope Siriacus had built in her honor became known simply as the Church of Saints Nereus and Achilleus. The
disappearance of Petronella from her own ancient sanctuary was hardly an
atypical fate—particularly for a female saint. The cult of the saints was both
agonistic and experimental; some saints fared better than others. Nereus and
Achilleus continued on; Petronella gradually faded away.

Part of the problem was that Petronella was only partially integrated
into the later sacred history of Rome—and never as seamlessly or ardently
as Rome's chief patron saints, Peter and Paul. Her name originally became
detached from her church because—ironically—she had become too important to reside there. When, in 757 CE, Paul I transferred her sarcophagus
to an old circular building—an imperial mausoleum dating from the end of
the fourth century near St. Peter's—he had intended to reunite Petronella
with her father, placing her back under his *aegis*. This building now housing
her bones was subsequently altered to become the Chapel of St. Petronella
at St. Peter's basilica.[25] And with that, Petronella became the special patroness of the treaties sworn in her chapel between the popes and the Frankish kings of the eighth and ninth centuries. Since the Franks styled their
rulers the spiritual sons of St. Peter, Petronella became, too, the spiritual sister of the first Holy Roman Emperor, Charlemagne. But with the decline of
the Frankish kingdoms, Petronella's cult fell into decline. An altar dedicated
to her—her bones resting beneath—is still there today at St. Peter's, but
hardly any one notices anymore or cares to find out who she was.

Why did Veneranda choose Petronella as her special spiritual *patrona*?

What invisible threads connected them? Was there some aspect of Petronella's legend that made Veneranda declare: "Yes: she is my protector?" Was it a question of some temporal connection? Did they share the same *dies natalis?* Or was it a spatial connection? Was Petronella the saint for people of one particular region of Rome, so that if you happened to live there, you were more or less "assigned" a neighborhood protector? Or, since the faithful believed that Petronella protected her devotees from vicious fevers, had she once spared Veneranda's life, brushing away a fever from her as a mother brushes a fly from her child's cheek? There's no way to penetrate Veneranda's logic. But she surely stood to benefit in some way, perhaps unfathomable to us, from her choice of Petronella as her special saint. To imagine what this benefit might have been, we need to know more about the martyr cults of Rome.

Fourth-century Rome witnessed a shift from respecting or reverencing the ordinary dead to venerating the extraordinary dead. This shift required the confluence of a variety of different modalities for thinking about death, about space and place, and even about time itself. We find it anticipated in part by the tendency of many Romans to apotheosize or divinize their deceased beloveds. For Proba, for example, her daughter had become no less than a goddess—however human she might have been during her short life on earth. The custom of visiting graves, too, was ancient and unforgotten; Christians borrowed it directly from traditional Roman practice. In the third century, Tertullian noted that Christians observed death anniversaries; indeed, these anniversaries became the new "birthdays" (*dies natalis* in the Latin, or "natal day" in English) of the deceased: "when the anniversary of their death comes around, we make ritual offerings to the dead as birthday honors" (*oblationes pro defunctis, pro nataliciis, annua die facimus*) (*de Corona militis* 3.3). These ritual offerings (*oblationes*) might be a few drops of wine or oil, trickled down into the grave through holes or pipes placed there for just such a purpose. Christians and pagans alike used them widely.

Before it was the exclusive prerogative of the saints to benefit the living by standing as their witnesses and protectors before God, it fell to the ordinary dead, including women and children: "Anatolius erected this monument to his well-deserving son, who lived 7 years, 7 months and 20 days. May your soul rest well in God. Intercede for your sister."[26] Even infants in heaven were fully capable of intercession: "Matronata Matrona, who lived for one year and one day. Pray for your parents."[27] The family grave was a point of contact between realms, with the deceased standing ready to deliver up to the powers that be the prayers heard from their families. In the third century, Cyprian, the bishop of Carthage, had written of the sure power of one's beloveds as intercessors: "There a great number of our dear ones is awaiting us, and a dense crowd of parents, brothers, children, is longing for us, already assured of their own safety, and still solicitous for our salvation" (Cyprian, *De mortalitate*, 26, 5.475). Countless Christian epitaphs from the catacombs preserve families' entreaties to their beloved: "Januaria, may you be well refreshed [in heaven] and pray on our behalf."[28] Or, "Attica, pray for your parents!"[29] So frequent are the calls to the dead that they sing a mournful refrain: "Remember me" (*in mente nos habeto*).[30] The plea of those left behind not to be forgotten inverts the traditional Roman calls to readers from the grave: "You who read this as you pass by, remember me!"[31]

In the latter half of the fourth century, the intercessory power of deceased family members was eclipsed by the more powerful spiritual clout of the martyrs. Of all the things that Veneranda might have chosen to convey about her life, her relationship with a saint was the most precious: the gentle surety of that moment of awakening into the presence of her angel. But what is the unspoken narrative this catacomb image conveys or assumes? *Why* does Petronella wait for Veneranda in paradise? Having family in heaven—no matter how much you loved and missed them—got you only so far in terms of finding real favor. As Jaś Elsner observes, Christianity's "best claims lay in the bones of those whose passage to sainthood had been aided by the city's executioners."[32] At the Catacombs of Cyriaca at the Basilica of San Lorenzo fuori le mura, an elaborate inscription made evident the power of the saints: "The holy martyrs shall be advocates for all before God and Christ."[33] Sometimes these imprecations to the martyrs for intercession were engraved on funerary epitaphs, but more commonly, they were more spontaneous and heartfelt, chicken-scratched onto the plaster walls of the martyr shrines.

The practice of honoring the dead with food on their natal days not only continued unabated into the fourth century, it expanded to include visits to the tombs of the martyrs. As a young man, Jerome passed weekends making the rounds at local martyr shrines: "On Sundays," he reminisces, "I was accustomed to tour the sepulchers of the apostles and martyrs" (*Comm. in Ezech.* 12.40; PL 25, col. 375). Such activity prompted his contemporary, the outspoken fourth-century pagan Libanius, to decry Christians contemptuously as "those around the tombs" (*Oration* 62.10). The pagan emperor Julian "the Apostate" (361–363 CE) complained to the Christians, too: "You have filled the whole world with tombs and sepulchers, and yet in your scriptures it is nowhere said that you must grovel among tombs and pay them honor" (*Against the Galileans* 335C, LCL, 415). The year was 361 CE, and he might well have been speaking of Veneranda and her own choice to venerate the sacred bones and dust of long-dead saints.

This newfound preoccupation with the holy dead precipitated a marked alteration in urban horizons, as many of Rome's Christian citizens shifted their devotions from churches within the city walls to cemeteries outside them. What held power for them were not the marble monuments and temples of the Roman Forum at the city's core, but the cemeteries, catacombs, funerary basilicas, and martyr sites of the city's periphery. The church father Jerome commented of Rome that the city had "changed address" (*movetur urbs sedibus suis*) (Letter 107). On a visit to the city, the fourth-century Spanish poet Prudentius wrote admiringly of the pious crowds thronging to the grave of the martyr Hippolytus: "The majestic city disgorges her Romans in a stream; with equal ardor patricians and the plebeian host are jumbled together, shoulder to shoulder, for the faith banishes distinctions of birth" (*Peristephanon* 11.199–202). A resolutely urban population thus turned the city inside out, assembling in droves in the countryside, bringing the clatter of the city into the silent, subdued subterranean shrines of the dead. Veneranda herself was caught up in this shift, leaving for us a sure measure of the power of the dead in the mind of one fourth-century woman.

Veneranda's particularized loyalty to Petronella, so evident from her choice of painting, had broad implications—for others in her community who were not in the financial position to broadcast their devotional allegiance on their graves, and for the ecclesiastical hierarchy that chose in the fourth century to promote the apostles Peter and Paul as twin bearers of Roman Christian identity.[34] The foremost historian of late antiquity, Peter Brown, reminds us that a grave like Veneranda's could be a "zone of conflict."[35] He observes, "Family piety could lead to a 'privatization' of religious practice, whether through ostentatious forms of celebration at the family grave, or by the extension to the graves of the martyrs of practices associated with strong private family loyalties."[36]

Veneranda's grave, then, is poised in exquisite tension between the private obsequies of a family mourning its dead, and the broader, more locally or civically based worship of a saint. What is remarkable about the painting we find there is that *both* an ordinary woman *and* a saint are commemorated, within the context of a private family burial site in a bigger public complex. What an image of Petronella meant there in Veneranda's private grave was therefore different from what her image meant in a basilica where it was freely accessible and unambiguously iconic—that is, something meant to be venerated. The tension was one between the construction and perpetuation of "private" versus "communal" memory. Whose story came to mind, as passers-by moved through Veneranda's cubiculum: Veneranda's own, or Petronella's? Or, with this image, did the two become immediately fused into one particular narrative of a woman's entrance into paradise at the hands of another?

There are two different but related elements in play in the "backstory" to Veneranda's grave. One element is Petronella as, most likely, herself an active participant in the late antique economy of relics. She (or her family, we cannot tell) likely actively participated in the cult of the saints through establishing a reliquary chapel for the saints Nereus and Achilleus. She was, then, a bone gatherer. Armed with money and influence, women such as Aurelia Petronella could literally broker the holy by owning, moving, and housing relics, placing themselves between the awesome power of the saints and the worldly community. The second element to the backstory is Veneranda, who as a woman of lesser means could not herself broker the holy, but who nevertheless could place herself in a position of proximity: she was not so much a patroness like Petronella as she was Petronella's spiritual client.

The hidden issue behind the choice of saint one promoted was one of patronage, the chief load-bearing social system in the late empire. "Patronage," broadly defined, was part of a socioeconomic system by which elites gained respect and authority from financial benefaction to people of lesser means. It was a system by which both the patron and her client stood to gain different types of social "capital." Because elites did not work for a living, their money could only slowly dwindle. One might at least spend extravagantly and for the public good. Public buildings and works—from bread doles to circus games—were subsidized through private interventions on a wide-ranging scale, from the emperor himself to the relatively low-placed but wealthy freedmen, the *petit bourgeoisie* of the city.

Women, who could exercise no active and public political role in Rome (or even much of a religious one), found patronage one of their only paths to public recognition and status. They could run burial societies and other *collegia* of workers and priests—even if the majority of their clients were male. And they could build things—or more accurately, they could have things built. Ascribing their names on works they funded became a rare chance for women to gain enduring visibility and palpable influence in a man's world. Women could own things; more powerfully still, they could give things away. Both were necessary to broker the holy. Yet both women's ownership and women's largesse could prove divisive and threatening to an all-male ecclesiastical hierarchy that was both dependent on and ambivalent toward the heady connection between wealth and power.

As the empire Christianized, so did the patronage system. In a newly Christian city, the saint came to displace the earthly patron. Her (or his) beneficence could be bought, owned, and meted out to others in the form of physical remains or relics. This required the creation of a second tier of patrons who might throw their weight behind the saintly patron as a sort of human viceroy. Thus the power of a saint came to be resolutely privatized or, if opened up to others, made available through the largesse of lay patrons—powerful, wealthy Romans unaffiliated with the church in any official capacity. More often than not, these lay patrons were women. We can look to the evidence to see that women—even more than men—duly recognized the potential of lay patronage for acquiring or wielding power and authority. In his classic study *The Cult of the Saints* (1981), the historian of late antiquity Peter Brown offers two examples of powerful *patronae*, both from outside Rome. The noblewoman Pompeiana in 295 CE obtained the body of the martyr Maximilianus, even though she was not his kin, and buried it next to another martyr, Cyprian, in Carthage. When she herself died ten days later, she too was buried in the same spot. In Salona, the first known martyr's shrine was established by the *matrona* Asclepia above the grave of the martyr Anastasius, in a building that she had commissioned to hold her own body. Through such acts of ownership and proximity, women maintained a strong upper hand in mediating access to the holy. What is still more remarkable is that on the issue of Christian *male* lay patrons, the sources largely fall silent. This can mean only two things: either male lay patrons were uncontroversial and thus no one bothered to write much about them, or else the practice of Christian patronage tended to be the special and characteristic prerogative of noble and wealthy Christian women alone.[37]

So what issues pressed women to be active in the cult of the saints? Unable to show their piety through ecclesiastical roles reserved for them (the only significant roles were registered widows or consecrated virgins), married noblewomen apparently made the best of their ability to acquire relics or, at least, proximity to the holy. Most likely, women's involvement with the late antique relic trade within the patronage system was deeply and hotly contested. We see shadows of this contestation in late antique debates concerning women's scope within activities such as public preaching, teaching, and prophesying. Whether it was proper for women to endow public buildings or own relics presented still new territories for debate. Christians entered these territories with markedly differing notions of what constituted appropriate and respectable behavior. Women might perform these acts of public good privately and more or less invisibly. Or they might choose an unlikely venue—such as their own funerary monument—to make a subtle but acerbic statement about whose friends the saints really were. This, at least, was Veneranda's way. It may, too, have been Petronella's way.

There is a doubleness, a "next chapter-ness" to the story of Petronella and Veneranda, seen as a whole. In the early fourth century, Petronella spent her money on the church—perhaps financing a burial chapel for the relics of Nereus and Achilleus on the cemetery grounds of one of her kinswomen, Flavia Domitilla. The chapel—and her richly decorated grave—broadcast her benevolence and her piety. A few generations later, the historical Petronella had been forgotten, and people came to the Church of Saints Nereus and Achilleus to revere the bones of the "martyr" Petronella. And then, just as Petronella had paid to be buried close to the remains of Nereus and Achilleus, so people paid to be buried close to Petronella's bones. There is, indeed, another "step" to the dance, as Veneranda's own tomb was transformed into a sort of shrine in late antiquity; the slab covering her humble masonry grave became an altar from which the Eucharist was served to the pious who came to wonder at the image of Petronella leading Veneranda to paradise.

Although she had herself depicted as a sister and friend to the holy martyr Petronella, Veneranda was not wealthy and powerful enough to have owned Petronella's relics. But she could signify her wealth and influence through the proximity of her own body to Petronella's. In her day, when it came to a choice for burial, location mattered, even more than ostentation. *Ad sanctos* or *retro sanctos* ("behind the holy") burials were sold off as final resting places of considerable prestige. These were the graves of those who could claim the saints as their personal friends and intercessors. The burial locations guaranteed not only a front-row seat at the Resurrection, but they spoke eloquently to those who visited the saint's shrines, to those who passed scores of "ordinary" graves as they clamored to press close to the holy. Physical space became the currency of fourth-century piety. Those fortunate enough to procure for themselves tombs next to the saints even recorded their status on their epitaphs: "We, Januarius and Britia, purchased for ourselves from the gravediggers this spot in front of the martyr [*domna*] Emerita";[38] or "Filicissimus and Leoparda bought this double-grave at the entrance to the martyr Criscention's shrine."[39] Proximity to the saints was common enough (and prestigious enough) to be reduced to simple formulae; many funerary inscriptions bear explicit indicators of their locations, as if words somehow made more concrete the indelible presence of their graves: *ad sancta martyra* ("at the grave of the holy female martyr") or *ad domnum cornelium* ("at the grave of the martyr Cornelius") or *at ippolitu* ("at the grave of Hippolytus").[40] Proximity to the holy body, as Peter Brown notes, "mapped out in a peculiarly blatant manner . . . the balance of social power within the Christian community."[41] The grave cozied close to the martyr's shrine was, as the author of one inscription recognized, "desired by many, but obtained by few."[42] Veneranda—or her family, for we don't know who commissioned her grave—was canny enough to recognize the power of the saints in making a lasting and evocative statement. So, too, was Petronella and her own family. In this world, women, too, could claim to be the friends of the saints, to draw from them their own power.

Veneranda's holy city of Christian martyrs was no idealized, idyllic, unified City of God. It was rife with local factionalism: protracted power struggles between popes and emperors, popes and anti-popes, lay patrons and clerics. If the topography of Rome changed during the fourth century—that is, if the city came to look different and more Christian—this was because of the strenuous efforts of local members of the clergy to promote their own communities, neighborhoods, parishes, and even cemeteries as centers of Christian worship. In short, Christianity of fourth-century Rome was profoundly agonistic and competitive.[43] What was at stake in this battle between rival Christian groups was the continuity of civic and, in a sense, religious patterns: Who—which people—were the true friends of the saints? Was it the ancient dynasties and lay members of noble families? Or coalitions of clerics and bishops, some of whom had just arrived in Rome? Who was responsible for imposing new Christian rhythms of time on an ancient city, or building new monuments, or administrating the vast necropoleis for Roman Christians awaiting the day of Resurrection? Who was now closer to the holy?

Veneranda knew the answer to this question, and she asserts it on the painting that carries her name. Her devotion to Petronella put her under the patronage not of unstable and vain human powers but of the "Very Special Dead."[44] It didn't seem to matter much to her that Petronella was at that point excluded from the formal, ecclesiastical record of the saints. By the middle of the fifth century, Petronella's name had still not yet been added to Catholicism's official list of martyr's feasts, the *Martyrologium Hieronymianum*. Her name was not read aloud during any part of the church services. Yet as Veneranda shows us, she had been actively venerated in the city already for at least a century. Thus this painting stands as emblematic of what historian Lucy Grig has called "*private* rather than ecclesiastical piety."[45] This is not to say that the church did not actively promote the cult of the martyrs. Rather, in the catacombs we find individual Christians—laywomen specifically—constructing the meaning of the saints for themselves through devotional acts that included commissioning inscriptions and paintings—or else, if they were able to write, leaving behind graffiti at the martyrs' graves.

Sometimes, the meaning women imparted to the saints differed considerably from that of the standard church liturgy or official lists of the saints. It was Veneranda's personal devotion to Petronella, I suspect, that made her choose the scene she had for her tomb. The intimacy of the women's pose—and the fact that only two figures fill the visual frame—highlights the potent intercessory powers of a martyr that shattered the boundaries between heaven and earth.[46] And it is significant that the saint whom Veneranda chose was not one of the apostles whom the Roman church had claimed for itself—Peter and Paul—nor any other of the more famous male martyrs. In fact, Veneranda's grave painting is our only complete image from the early church of a martyr leading one of the faithful to heaven. It is indeed interesting, then, that both figures are female.[47]

Who saw the image of Veneranda and Petronella, and what did it mean to him or her? The question of audience for any human production in the past is notoriously difficult to penetrate. We cannot presume one single response, one single ideal viewer.[48] Certainly, the painting underscores that women venerated martyrs. Yet we know this simply because this is what Veneranda is doing in the image, not because we know how ancient viewers responded to the image itself. It is not possible to say generally, on the basis of this image, whether women venerated martyrs in greater proportion than men or whether their experiences of visiting and viewing the martyr's shrines differed qualitatively from men's. We certainly cannot be so naïve as to imagine that women chose to venerate women martyrs exclusively or disproportionately just because we find a single surviving example of it here. And unlike the catacomb of Priscilla's Greek Chapel, Veneranda's cubiculum shows no evidence of having been gendered space. It was the private grave of a respectable and well-to-do matron—not a shrine or an oratory or a chapel.

The question "Who saw the image of Veneranda and Petronella?" is further complicated by a related one: For whom was the fresco intended to be seen? The cubiculum's later use as a sort of satellite shrine to Petronella was probably largely unintended—although it might not have been wholly displeasing to Veneranda. But the image was created primarily for the benefit of Veneranda's community. It relies on a combination of words and portraiture to convey a specific, unambiguous meaning designed to comfort her intimates. Images with words on them become more and more common in catacomb art of the fourth century and beyond, although seen in relation to the corpus of Christian funerary art and the sheer volume of graves in the catacombs, they are quite rare. Combinations of words and images presume a literate audience, which most visitors to the catacombs were not. And the words—specifically the names of the women—ensure the correct identification of the scene above the grave. Without them, it would be difficult to know just what the women were doing, and whether they were meant to represent real people or biblical figures. The words act to fix meaning for posterity. It's also telling that next to Petronella sits a large container of scrolls, and a codex or book floats, upside down, next to her left arm.[49] Like the words themselves, the book and scrolls point to a literate audience.[50] They also signify Veneranda as learned, or at least give her the aura of learnedness—she herself could probably read, although many nonelite women could not.[51] Finally, the appearance of a book alongside a scroll helps us to date the painting to the period after Constantine, when the scriptures began to circulate widely in book format. The post-Constantinian era brought a renewed respect, even awe, for the power of the Word.

By the year 354 CE, the city's churches and cemeteries were spokes in a great wheel of Christian holy sites linked around Rome's periphery. Pilgrims trudged well-trodden routes to each of these sites in patterns governed not by relative location, but by the sacred time of liturgical celebration. What this meant, practically speaking, is that 354 CE saw an empire in transition, keeping two sacred calendars: one that traced out a pagan past, and one that was committed to creating a new Christian history marked by the martyrdoms of the faithful. Later, the rhythm of secular or civic festivals, or the endless elections of civic officials, would come to be deemed irrelevant to the church's growing identity as a sacred institution. What was important to commemorate was not a pagan festival or a new consulship, but the endlessly circular time of the martyrs.

The creation of these martyr calendars also made work for the church. Peter Brown observes, "The careful noting of the anniversaries of the deaths of martyrs and bishops gave the Christian community a perpetual responsibility for maintaining the memory of its heroes and leaders."[52] Initially, the tales, or *gesta,* of the martyrs along with their dates had to be gathered from the local neighborhoods that preserved the memories of local saints. The act of collecting martyr stories, not incidentally, coincided with the institutionalization of the city's Christian catacombs. By the middle of the third century many of the larger catacombs came to be administrated by the church. At around the same time, during the episcopacy of Fabian (236–250 CE), a special clerical office known as the *notarius* or "record keeper" was devised to keep track of local martyrs within the city's diaconal structure. The office of the *notarius* marked a shift in the way that the church viewed the catacombs; no longer was the emphasis on private, family-based cemeteries providing workaday burials for the ordinary dead; instead, the importance of the catacombs lay in their sanctity as shrines of the holy martyrs.

As part of this switch, the practice of marking individual death dates on epitaphs came to be seen as less consequential than remembering the death dates of the catacomb's martyrs. There were instances when both coincided. Some rare individuals were fortunate enough to be buried on a saint's natal day: "The grave (*locus*) of Felicitas, who was placed here on the natal day of saint Thecla"[53] or "[The grave of] Studentia, deposited [here] on the natal day of Marcellus, during the consulship of Sallius."[54] Others fell just short of the crucial day: "Pascasius, deposited (here) in peace. He lived twenty years, more or less. His fate was to die on the 4th of the ides of October, eight days before the natal day of Saint Asterius."[55] But others were more blessed: "Euskia, the blameless one, who lived a life of goodness and purity for twenty-five years, died on the feast of our lady (saint) Lucia, for whom no praise is adequate. She was a perfect Christian, well-pleasing to her husband, and endowed with much grace."[56] But the process of privileging saint's days over individuals' natal days happened only slowly. A hundred years after Fabian's appointment of the city's first *notarii,* when Veneranda was buried, the picture bearing her image alongside her favorite martyr's was painted with only a sole date. The date is not Petronella's natal day—her *dies natalis*—but Veneranda's. At Veneranda's grave, the rhythm of this sacred space is still marked by the death of human kin.

Let us return to the curious conjunction of space, place, body, and image that made Veneranda's grave into the secondary martyr shrine that it became. In the middle of the fourth century, an image might function as a relic. In the case of Veneranda's grave painting, the fresco of the two women in heaven extended the imagined, sacred parameters of Petronella's bones beyond her own grave into a secondary but no less venerated area *retro sanctos*, where Veneranda's grave lay. The sacred image painted over Veneranda's bones lessened the distance between the two women's graves —a mere twenty yards or so, although separated by a warren of tunnels and cubicula. The fresco not only placed the two within the same intimate corner of paradise, but it also, significantly, showed the women touching. There was little concern with conveying the sanctity of the martyr over the humility of an ordinary woman; Petronella has no halo or crown to signal her special status, and both are similarly and richly attired. The visual impression is one of harmony, horizontality, and analogy; Veneranda is the visible and human *patrona* beside (not beneath) the otherworldly *patrona* Petronella. The imagery brought Petronella's power out of the grasp of the Christian community as a whole, and placed it instead within the parameters of a single woman's grave. At some later date, another sturdy grave was added directly in front of Veneranda's own *arcosolium* and lunette, so that someone else might also soak up the blessings to be derived from proximity even to Petronella's likeness. Still later, when the first altars or *mensae* were established in the catacombs to celebrate the feasts of the martyrs, this later grave in Veneranda's cubiculum became a sort of offerings table, the focal point for ardent acts of piety directly before the powerful presence of the martyr. The pilgrims had come to rest, to pause in their devotions, in the course of their pilgrimages, at Petronella's own grave, and then at Veneranda's, where they might again gaze on Petronella anew. One wonders if one site was better than the other, or if the power of the martyr simply lived in its fullness at both.

Veneranda's grave painting is a sort of way station in Roman Christianity's development of what art historian Cynthia Hahn has termed a "visual rhetoric of sanctity." It is a rhetoric that, ultimately, "condenses the holy past and the sacred present within the particularities of a given space."[57] Few images from early Roman Christianity more effectively illustrate the pull of the immediate present of the ordinary dead into the mythical space of the sacred dead. Petronella who, as Veneranda understood it, had three hundred years earlier forfeited her life for her faith, is made fully present there in her devotee's grave. There, in the intimate space of the grave, the two women could be made holy sisters together. The magical "bivalency of presence and absence" put them at once on the Via Ardeatina, their bones pressing close to one another, and also in heaven, far removed from the charnel house of the catacombs.[58]

But Veneranda's presence in the fresco also undermines its relevance, its use, as an icon of Petronella. The painting is not (merely) of or about Saint Petronella; therefore it cannot truly be a devotional image—an icon—to her. Petronella may intercede between God, Christ, and the people, but Veneranda stands between the martyr and the viewer. She interrupts. The painting tells us, as viewers, what Petronella can do for Veneranda—by extension what she can do for us, yes, but primarily and most immediately, what she has done for one particular woman. Later images of the saints would, literally, take the worshiper out of the picture. Having her in there could only complicate the direct line of power that stretched, taut, from image to devotee.

What we do *not* see in Veneranda's grave painting is also telling: the complicated dance between text and image that together comprised the cult of the saints in Rome. The image is an example of what Jaś Elsner terms "visual hagiography"—literally, a pictorial writing about a saint.[59] But it hovers disconnected from our contemporary martyr texts: other hagiographies. The earliest one—contained in the Codex Calendar of 354—never mentions Petronella in its enumeration of venerated saints and their natal days. Petronella's absence from the church's official sanctioned list of martyrs reveals a fundamental disconnection between whom people actually venerated and whom Rome's bishops advocated venerating. Part of this may have been gendered. The official list is dominated by male saints, with only four of forty-six recognized martyrs being women, and only two of those—Agnes and Bassilla—being Roman women.[60] Veneranda's painting suggests that even in 354, memory traditions of "unrecognized" martyrs such as Petronella still lay in the hands of women. That was soon to change.

Petronella's painting in Veneranda's *retro sanctos* grave teaches us how in early Christian Rome, image and pilgrimage worked in concert, mutually reinforcing one another with notions of the city as a holy sanctuary that rivaled even Jerusalem, that holiest of cities. Lucy Grig writes evocatively of the power of martyr texts and martyr images for creating a powerful performance of the holy:

The Christian community hoped to *make present* the martyr in the performance of the martyr's story on his or her "birthday," perhaps on the site of the martyrdom, or at the tomb, over a relic—or even without these things, the story, the prayer, and the commemoration being sufficient. Each re-telling of the martyr's story (re)enacted the martyr's victory, the victory of the Church.[61]

Grig reminds us that there is a bigger way of thinking about images: how they organize ritual space and order time. And yet, for all their power, images of the martyr did not manage to come close to the immeasurable impact of martyr texts. Part of this had to do with what Grig recognizes as the "evocativeness, lyricism of expression" of later martyrs' *gesta*.[62] But it was not only their evocativeness or lyricism of expression; it was also, frankly, the paradoxical capacity of these texts to convey *more graphically than image* the glorious suffering of the martyrs. Martyr texts speak of the martyrs' uncanny and unflinching capacity for enduring unimaginable pain. Yet we do not find in early Christian art any paintings of these martyr acts, nor any attempts to render their ghastly details with paint and pigment. When the martyrs do appear on the walls of the catacombs in the fourth century, crowned and irenic, they appear shining out from heaven, leading the dead to a place they have prepared for them.

CHAPTER 6

THE SILENT VIRGIN AND
THE PALE CHILD

That is the hour when they are holy,
the silent virgin and the pale child.
Then they are again as before all suffering
and sleep deep sleep and have no glory
and their souls are as white silk,
and from the same longing both tremble,
and are frightened by their heroism.
—Rainer Maria Rilke, "Martyrs"

Nestled in a quiet part of Trastevere, a neighborhood in Rome across the Tiber from the historical center, sits in quiet dignity the ancient basilica complex of Santa Cecilia. Its high, elaborate façade conceals the peacefulness of a quiet, grassy inner courtyard crisscrossed by stone paths that intersect at a small fountain made out of an ancient stone vase. Toddlers watched over by mothers and grandmothers practice their first unsteady steps in the grass; nervous couples, holding hands, rehearse for their weddings. The church sits at the end of this courtyard, a heavy, imposing, eighteenth-century stone and marble edifice.

You hear the church of Santa Cecilia almost before you see it. White-garbed Benedictine nuns cloistered inside its convent sing the church offices in Gregorian chant several times a day; their voices soar out of the convent's large open windows and into the courtyard, mingling with the sonorous clangs of the medieval campanile's bells. It is a musical place, and this is intentional, since Santa Cecilia (the Romans even pronounce her name musically: "She-shilia") is the patron saint of musicians and, so the story goes, the inventor of the organ. In most images of the saint, you can recognize Cecilia from the organ or other musical instruments figured with her.

Passing through Santa Cecilia's peaceful atrium toward her church, you pass into the cool pale gray hall of the main basilica. It's a tranquil, hushed spot, often festooned with fragrant lilies for the many weddings celebrated there. But what immediately catches your eye when you enter the church is its luminous apse mosaic. Dating from the ninth century, it features a large image of Christ raising his hand in a gesture of blessing. God's hand, plump and sure, reaches down from the top of the apse to crown him. To one side of Christ stands Saint Peter with the martyrs Cecilia and Valerian; to the other side stands Saint Paul between another martyr, Agatha, and the pope who commissioned this particular magnificent mosaic, Paschal I (817–824 CE). Paschal even adorned the bottom of the mosaic with a long, elaborate Latin inscription. The last words are particularly sonorous:

> Serene in the love of God,
> He joined the bodies of Saint Cecilia and her companions;
> Youth glows red in its bloom.
> Limbs that rested before in crypts:
> Rome is jubilant, triumphant always, adorned forever.

The unnamed "he" of this inscription was Paschal himself, who had transformed an earlier, humbler church associated with Cecilia into a handsome basilica. Paschal, whose papacy fell just after the time of Charlemagne and the beginning of the Holy Roman Empire, was a builder and an iconophile; that is to say, his papacy is remembered best for its spasm of church-building and mosaic-making. In the Byzantine East, the iconoclastic controversy raged; zealous monks slashed and burned their way through hundreds of years of precious Christian art. In the West, Paschal promoted in Rome a new, jeweled style of Byzantine art and architecture. On Santa Cecilia's glorious, sparkling apse mosaic, you can see him standing holding a small, scale model of the church—a visual record of his donation and patronage of Santa Cecilia.

Paschal was an active promoter of local Roman cults, some of which in the ninth century were still centered on the worship of women saints and martyrs. First of all, there was his work at Cecilia. Then, close to the important Basilica of Santa Maria Maggiore, Paschal renovated another small church dedicated to Santa Prassede. Prassede and her sister, Pudenziana, were said to be the saintly daughters of an influential Roman senator, Pudens.[1] Together, the two women were bone gatherers—of a sort. Prassede and her sister, so it is said, gathered not the bones of martyrs but their blood, sopped up into sponges and collected to consecrate the living. Their images sometimes show them standing with sponge and urn in hand. The church of Santa Prassede still today preserves a circle of dark red porphyry on the floor, where according to legend, the well once stood that contained the blood and bones that the sisters had gathered.

As Prassede had supposedly done centuries before him, Paschal sanctified the church of Santa Prassede and its golden chapel with bones: the relics of the martyrs. By the ninth century, the catacombs had fallen into obscurity and ruin; they had even been ransacked by plundering barbarians. So Paschal ordered countless cartloads of holy remains to be removed from the catacombs and brought within the circuit of the city walls. The bones were likely merely those of the ordinary dead, but over time, people fervently believed that they were martyrs' bones, possessing the ability to make a church still more holy by their presence. Paschal was one of these people. A stone plaque near Santa Prassede's altar records the names of twenty-three hundred "martyrs" whose bodies found rest in this church's vault in what is known as Paschal's "Great Translation" of July 20, 817. Paschal accomplished on a grand, papal scale what the legendary bone gatherer Prassede had done with her sister for the love of the martyrs. He trafficked in the holy, gathering into one community the scattered remnants of the lost and forgotten.

Paschal sanctified the church of Santa Prassede, but he took particular interest in the basilica of Santa Cecilia. There had long been a church in that part of Trastevere—one that bore Cecilia's name. The part of Rome on which the earliest church of Santa Cecilia was built was once a densely settled commercial district where you could still catch sight of the jetties, storehouses, and shipbuilding workshops that lined both banks of the nearby Tiber. You could even see, quite clearly, the Colosseum and the imperial palaces of the Palatine hill, far on the opposite side of the river. The lands on which Santa Cecilia's basilica now stands were once mixed commercial and residential property. In fact, under the west end of the church's north aisle, visitors can pay a small fee to gain access to the remains of the private Roman houses of the second century that are hidden beneath the immense weight of the basilica. Some will tell you that at least one of the houses was Cecilia's. Perhaps, indeed, a woman by the name of Cecilia had allowed Christians to meet on her lands here by the Trastevere jetties. It is likely, however, that these domestic buildings were transformed by the fourth century into what is known as a *titulus* church, a sort of parish church founded on private lands that catered to the local Christian faithful. These churches were both older in their foundations and more accessible than the huge imperially sponsored basilicas like St. Peter's and St. John Lateran. They were—and remain—neighborhood places and, perhaps more arguably, places where women were more likely to be honored and remembered.

Originally, each *titulus* church in Rome was distinct, not yet part of an overarching, unified Catholic Church. Each had a degree of local autonomy—its own hierarchy, its own character or flavor, and its own set of legends and saints. Rome's fairly small size guaranteed that the *tituli* communities engaged rather strenuously in local political wrangling and competition. Santa Cecilia, for instance, is only a five-minute stroll from San Crisogono, another early church with which it surely vied for local resources and clientele. Each was built partly on a *fullonica* (a place where cloth was dyed); each had its martyr stories. Crisogonus was said to be a Roman official, sentenced to death for his obstinate adherence to Christ. His feast day on November 22—only two days apart from Cecelia's—guaranteed that the Trans Tiber neighborhood would have a festive end of November.

The extent to which people considered Cecilia a holy martyr in Paschal's time is unclear, but one thing is certain: she was important enough that Paschal did not simply move her bones along with those of 2,299 other saints in the Great Translation. Instead, Cecilia's popularity required what's called an *inventio*—a bishop's public, ritualized "discovery" of holy relics. It was a way to publicize a martyr's cult, to celebrate its civic significance. It was not simply a case of a bishop authorizing a cult that might hitherto have been more or less local, or even private. With an *inventio* ritual, a local cult could be moved spectacularly out of the hands of the laity and into ecclesiastical control. The *inventio* of a saint created opportunities for an "orchestrated revitalization ritual" that extended far beyond the narrow streets of Trastevere.[2] It focused people's energies into acknowledging Rome's identity as the spiritual center of the Western world. In this way, the discovery of new martyr relics also benefited relationships between early medieval papacy and other powerful Christian coalitions. Frankish Christians to the north and west, in particular, clamored for the bones of Roman martyrs—

especially those of Cecilia. In the church's quest for an alliance with these formidable Frankish kingdoms, Cecilia's formal arrival into its purview would be no less than a triumphant moment for the Roman papacy.

According to church records, the bones of the powerful martyr Cecilia lay undisturbed in the catacombs. Over a few days one October, then, Paschal sought out Cecilia's remains in the Catacombs of Praetextatus to translate or "repatriate" within the city. But searching through the gloom of the catacomb, he was unsuccessful in finding them. Finally, one night, Cecilia herself visited Paschal in a dream and provided him with precise directions to where her body lay. It was just a little bit beyond where he had given up in frustration. Paschal went again to Praetextatus and this time returned triumphantly. Remarkably, far from being a clatter of earthy brown bones, the body was intact. So in 820 CE, Paschal transferred Cecilia's body from the Catacombs of Praetextatus to her small church in Trastevere near the Tiber, where it now rests under the main altar along with the remains of her husband, her brother-in-law, and two popes. And with that, the *patrona* Cecilia who had donated the lands on which this church sat became the miraculous Roman martyr Cecilia. Her arrival in the city, and into the official record of the church, was late, spectacular, and (seen in retrospect), suspiciously expedient for the emergent papacy.

The *inventio* of Cecilia into Rome offers a classic case of how a saint was made in late antiquity. Through the awesome and indisputable power of a vision, the martyr herself appears to the pope, disclosing to him information to which no one else was privy. His authority—particularly in potent combination with the visitation of a saint from paradise—could not be contested. But there is a problem with the story as we read it in the ecclesiastical records. Even as early as the seventh century—two hundred years before Paschal's "discovery" of Cecilia—pilgrims were *already* visiting Cecilia's grave, not at the Catacombs of Praetextatus where Paschal had searched for her, but far to the south at the Catacombs of Callistus. The early medieval itineraries or guidebooks that they brought with them told them just where it was and urged them not to miss it; for of all of the catacomb's sights, Cecilia's grave was among the more significant. Her body was far from lost; it was long celebrated and venerated. Indeed, these seventh-century itineraries indicate that at Callistus, there was not just a humble grave but a spacious basilica bearing Cecilia's name, where "innumerable" other martyrs also slumbered.[3] Two hundred years before Paschal "discovered" her, then, Cecilia's influence was considerable enough to warrant her own cemetery basilica outside the city walls at the Catacombs of Callistus—a pilgrim's shrine where numerous dead saints slumbered in lands bearing her name. Even in the early sixth century she was known. Her image adorns a mosaic in the chapel of the archbishop of Ravenna; in the same century and in the same city, we find her taking place in the solemn procession of women martyrs that lines one wall of the beautiful, somber basilica of San Apollinare Nuovo.

As it turns out, we can trace back Cecilia's veneration even further. In the fifth century, Cecilia's crypt at Callistus, nestled close to the burial chamber of nine early popes, had already been richly painted, though the images have long ago faded or been painted over. Around the same time, someone compiled the earliest martyrology that listed her feast days, the fifth-century *Martyrologium Hieronymianum*.[4] On the other hand, none of the major ecclesiastical writers of the late fourth century—Jerome, Ambrose, or Prudentius—mentions Cecilia. Nor does she appear in the fourth-century *Depositio Martyrum*, a listing of the city's martyrs along with the cemeteries that held their remains. But this does not mean—as we have seen with the case of Petronella—that Cecilia had no following before the fifth century; it means only that it was at this point that she entered the formal ecclesiastical record.

We also know that Cecilia's church in Trastevere already existed in the fifth century as the *titulus sanctae Caeciliae* or the titular church of Saint Cecilia.[5] In fact, we can witness the moment when the *titulus* associated with a *patrona* named Cecilia became the *titulus* of *Saint* Cecilia. Cecilia's meteoric rise to sainthood happened, in fact, in the year 499. That year, a church meeting or synod was convened in the city; of the clerics who attended, Cecilia's top official, Boniface, signed official synod documents as *presbyter tituli Caeciliae* or "priest of the church of Cecilia," and his colleague Marcianus—probably emboldened by some sort of ecclesiastical power play—chose a more important self-designation: *presbyter tituli sanctae Caeciliae*. In fact, of the twenty-nine titular churches of Rome identified in 499 CE, Cecilia's was one of only three to include the designation "saint" in its name.[6] These titular churches were established by lay donors—many of them women. They originally bore the unelaborated names of those donors. But as the cult of the saints gained momentum, considerable prestige could be gained from associating one's church with a saint rather than with a lay patron. Thus in 499, the matron Cecilia who originally founded the church came to be officially remembered as a holy martyr.[7] Between 499 and the synod of 595 under Pope Gregory the Great—the next time at which we find a comprehensive listing of Rome's parish churches—most titular churches established by women made similar claims of their founders. To "explain" the summary canonization of Rome's female lay donors as martyr saints, the church released over the course of the sixth century a slew of new and wholly fictitious martyr acts commemorating the deeds of saintly women such as Cecilia, Sabina, Susanna, Eugenia, Anastasia, Prassede, and Prassede's sister Pudenziana.[8] Most of these women had once been *patronae* of local churches. Now they were heroines of a very different sort: virgin martyrs of the church.[9]

Cecilia's martyr acts are so thoroughly saturated with the mythical that it is difficult to wring from them any historical veracity. The sixth-century version recounts that she was an aristocrat, a daughter of the senatorial-class Caecilius family. As in most families within Christian legend, her mother is a Christian, but her father is a pagan. Cecilia herself is born and raised an inviolate virgin of the church. But her father urges her into respectable marriage to a young pagan nobleman, Valerian. Cecilia does marry Valerian, but she informs him before their wedding night that it would be foolish—even dangerous—of him to assume that he could expect a normal conjugal life. Her virginity is under guard, she reveals, by an invisible angel to whom she is betrothed; he protects her with an invisible angelic shield of virtue. Valerian could even see the angel for himself—if only he would convert and consent to baptism. Valerian, perhaps implausibly more intrigued by the possibility of seeing angels than having his conjugal right fulfilled, has himself baptized forthwith by Pope Urban. To his amazement, upon his return as a new Christian, Valerian sees the angel in all his glory, who sanctifies his chaste marriage to Cecilia with roses and lilies.

Valerian and his brother Tiburtius devote themselves to works of Christian benevolence, for which they meet the ire of the urban prefect, Turcius Almachius. The prefect has them put to death, and Cecilia becomes a bone gatherer. She collects their remains and has them buried together in her family vault. She begins to preach publicly, turning many toward Christianity before Turcius Almachius orders her death. The process of Cecilia's death given in the official ecclesiastical account is a brutal one. First, she is locked up in the *calidarium* or steam room of her family's bath (each noble family had its own private bath-sauna complex) to be steamed to death. When she emerges unscathed from her ordeal, she faces the executioner, whose hatchet job of a beheading wounds her mortally but fails to dispatch her quickly. It takes three days for Cecilia to die.

Christians of late antiquity disputed when Cecilia's martyrdom had occurred. Had it been in the 230s, under Alexander Severus, as her *passio* or martyr's story reports? Roman historical records, however, prove that no martyrdoms took place under Alexander Severus in Rome. Other versions of the *passio* claim that Cecilia lived and died during the reign of Marcus Aurelius (161–180 CE), Commodus (180–192 CE), Septimius Severus (193–211 CE), Maximinus Thrax (235–238 CE), Decius (249–251 CE), Diocletian (284–305 CE), and Julian (361–363 CE).[10] According to historical records and lists of civic officials, the prefect of the story, Turcius Almachius, never existed. As a historical document of one woman's martyrdom, then, Cecilia's *passio* is entirely wrong. Martyrologies often are. Their point, after all, is not to write history, but to evoke feeling. Her story is one of mythic rather than historical construction. Still, it would be overly cynical to argue that Paschal and the other influential bishops of Rome simply made Cecilia up. Her veneration in the ninth century had likely shaped and moved the people of Rome for more than five hundred years. Paschal surely knew as much.

Who were Rome's women martyrs, and who venerated them? What made a martyr, in the minds of fourth-century Christians? Where did their cults fit into the history of late Roman Christianity? And why did some cults celebrating women martyrs succeed while others did not? Cecilia's cult flourished; Petronella's simply faded away. Petronella remained local, obscure, and an intercessor to lost women; Cecilia burst spectacularly onto papal horizons. Why was this so? Why did some female martyrs come to mean so very much to Roman Christianity—papal Christianity—and others not?

Part of the answer to this last question has to do with the church's campaign against the core component of Roman society: the conjugal unit. The ideals of Christianity sat in uneasy relation to the nature and structure of family. They had since Christianity's inception. In a key passage from the gospels, Jesus rejects the idea that his vision of the kingdom would reflect normative family roles. In the kingdom of God, every family relationship would be set on edge:

Do not suppose that I have come to bring peace to the earth; I did not come to bring peace, but a sword. For I have come to turn a man against his father, a daughter against her mother, a daughter-in-law against her mother-in-law; a man's enemies will be the members of his own household. (Matt 10:34–36)

The apostle Paul, although in less radical terms, had also advocated against marriage; he insisted that not much time remained until the Eschaton, the dawning of a new era in Christ. Marriage provided a concession to those who could not contain their sexual impulses ("It is better to marry than to burn," he famously wrote; 1 Cor 7:9, KJV). But for those who wished to dedicate themselves to the Lord, marriage could only be a form of oblivion:

From now on those who have wives should live as if they had none. . . . An unmarried woman or virgin is concerned about the Lord's affairs: Her aim is to be devoted to the Lord in both body and spirit. But a married woman is concerned about the affairs of this world—how she can please her husband. (1 Cor 7:29, 34)

Highly influential, these scriptural passages had, as the historian Gillian Cloke describes it, "a violently anti-normal effect on Roman family models."[11] As a consequence, she observes, Christianity set "its adherents—and particularly women—against traditional Roman concepts of 'family values.'"[12] Martyr texts of the fourth, fifth, and sixth centuries emphasize the monstrousness of marriage; in these stories, "the ideals of Christian belief were seen as standing in opposition to normative life-choices."[13] The historian Kate Cooper similarly notes that, from the perspective of many fourth- and fifth-century Christians, there was no "religiously positive role for married couples," nor a "socially positive role for married women."[14]

The Roman church's formal campaign against marriage required a number of orchestrated ideological maneuvers. First came a direct appeal to young, nubile, elite women and their pious mothers, in the form of treatises formally lauding virginity as a viable way of life. Next followed the elevation of virgins—male and female—as people invested with considerable spiritual power. Third came the progressive devaluation of wives, mothers, and women operating within the confines of family structures—even if these women were active lay supporters of the church. Fourth, powerful lay *patronae* were transformed within Christian memory. Women such as Cecilia, Priscilla, and Petronella—regardless of their origins as real and influential women—became imagined, constructed, misremembered, and reinvented as martyrs. None of these women faced martyrdom; they were martyrs who were made, sewn together from scraps of tradition and memory. The new, uncontested female "heroine" of Roman Christianity thus became the virgin martyr. As it happens, the most revered of these virgin martyrs in Rome was Agnes, at once the "silent virgin" and the "pale child." Her history—and her influence—was rather different from Cecilia's, so it's constructive to compare the two.

Like Cecilia, Agnes is a "quintessentially Roman saint," one "tightly embedded into the history and topography of the city of Rome."[15] The fifth-century poet Prudentius lauded Agnes in his work on martyrdom, the *Peristephanon* (ca. 400 CE):

> The tomb of Agnes is in the home of Romulus
> Brave girl and glorious martyr.
> (*Peristephanon* 14.1–2)

She was one of the earliest martyrs to be venerated in the city. By the fourth century, when Cecilia was probably yet to be considered a saint, Agnes's devotees included emperor's daughters and Roman nobles. The earliest Roman calendar of saints from 354 CE lists her feast day (the twelfth of the kalends of February; according to my reckoning, January 21), along with twenty-three other martyrs, only three of them female.[16]

As with Cecilia, many accounts of Agnes's martyrdom exist, each one different. Few agree on when she met her death: perhaps it was under emperor Decius (250 CE), or else under his successor Valerian (257 CE) or, most usually, under Diocletian, the last imperial persecutor of Christians (304 CE). The sources agree only that she was ultimately decapitated, and that at the time of her death, she was unmarried—still a child, really, only twelve or thirteen years old. Her fifth-century martyrology recounts that at the age of thirteen, this beautiful girl was already steadfast in her devotion to Christ. As she innocently makes her way home one day, the son of the city prefect catches sight of Agnes and instantly desires her. He offers her jewels and more, if only she will consent to his hand in marriage. Agnes retorts that she already has all that she desires—the devotion of her "lover," Christ. Rejected, the prefect's son runs to his father to effect a counter-humiliation. The prefect, Aspasius, summons Agnes to a tribunal, where it is suggested that she become a vestal virgin if her desire to live inviolate was so steadfast. Agnes declines. Aspasius, enraged by Agnes's impudence, demands that she sacrifice to the gods or be sent to a brothel.

Agnes's public humiliation commences with her forced stripping at the brothel; but God intervenes to preserve her virtue: first, her hair grows prodigiously to cover her nakedness; a bright light occludes her, and then a shining vestment appears. When the prefect's son shows up to rape her, he is struck dead. Chaos ensues, whereupon Agnes is charged with murder and hauled out for her public execution. Again, she is interrogated; she prays and restores the young man to life. But she is still to face death. Sentenced to be burned alive, the flames fail to consume her. Finally, Agnes is decapitated.

Tradition holds that Agnes faced her executioners in the Stadium of Domitian. Most visitors to Rome have stood on the spot, probably unwittingly; it is now one of Rome's most acutely romantic places: the Piazza Navona in the heart of the historical center. Tourists and modern Romans make their way around its oblong circuit, where chariots once clattered up dust and sand. In the center of Piazza Navona, eclipsed behind Bernini's magisterial fountain of the four rivers, stands the Baroque church of Sant'Agnese in Agone with its somber façade. "Agone," here, doesn't mean "agony." It is the same word of which "Navona" is a garbled corruption— from the Greek *agon* or athletic contest. In this place, gladiators and athletes once contested for their lives; and here, so the story goes, Agnes fought her final battle, the ultimate *agon*. The heavy gray-black church marks the place traditionally identified as the site of Agnes's death. It holds under its main altar a gruesome relic: Agnes's decapitated head.

Though Agnes's head still rests in downtown Rome, the rest of her body resides under the main altar in the church of Sant'Agnese fuori le mura, about two kilometers from Rome's city walls. Minus her head, Agnes is the only martyr to have been buried *in praediolo suo* (at a cemetery complex on what had been her family estate). The site today lies off the busy Via Nomentana. This was an ancient consular road, later used by long lines of pilgrims who snaked their way from the Capitoline hill through the city gates at what is now Porta Pia and out the long, straight road to Agnes's church. This burial complex on Via Nomentana—including a fairly small catacomb—was significantly enlarged in the fourth century, when it received imperial patronage: in the 340s, Constantine's daughter Constantina erected a massive funerary basilica dedicated to Agnes, setting up a dedicatory inscription:

> I, Constantina, venerating God and dedicated to Christ,
> Having provided all the expenses with devoted mind
> At divine bidding and with the great help of Christ,

Consecrated this *templum* of Agnes, victorious virgin,
Because she has prevailed over the temples and all earthly works,
[Here] where the loftiest roof gleams with gold.
(*ICUR* 8.20752, lines 1–6)[17]

The shining gold-roofed basilica was matched in beauty by an elegant ring-shaped mausoleum that Constantina had built on the same site to house her own remains.[18] When she died in 354, far from Rome, her body was carried back in solemn procession and laid to rest in a massive porphyry sarcophagus that nestled into the back niche of this mausoleum (Ammianus Marcellinus, *History* 14.11.6). Now the church of Santa Costanza, it is open to the public. It is an ancient, exquisite site. Lively mosaics shimmer in the light; they provided inspiration for Proba's artists, who set to painting her own, much humbler grave on the Via Latina, far away across a crowded and chaotic city.

What affinity the emperor's daughter felt with Agnes would be interesting to know; imagination sufficed for later ecclesiastical writers, who turned it into the stuff of romance. According to them, Constantina had been struck by leprosy until her earnest imprecations to Agnes cured her. With such imperial backing, Agnes the virgin martyr acquired unassailable prestige and power. Unlike many other prominent sites and shrines in the late-fourth-century city, Agnes's complex was resolutely connected to empire and the continuing authority of the imperial family. It was the sole imperially sponsored site to honor a Christian female saint. By her intervention at Agnes's site, Constantina became one of the most literal and powerful of Rome's bone gatherers, one of the most formidable of the female *patronae* of the church.[19] In turn, her custodianship of Agnes transformed the humble martyr shrine into a golden palace commemorating a child's lost beauty and innocence.

But imperial patronage of Agnes's shrine had some dire consequences. It made the site infinitely more alluring to those seeking power than, let's say, a neighborhood *titulus* could ever be. This is why, later in the fourth century, Agnes's basilica would become a major center of ecclesiastical wrangling. Conflicts within the Roman church had reached such a flash point in the second half of the century that two popes held office simultaneously, Liberius I (352–366 CE) and Felix II (355–365 CE). Their competing camps carved up the city, each hunkering down in specific neighborhoods.[20] Agnes's complex held a special significance for Liberius; it was in her shrine that he ensconced himself in 358 CE.[21] Like Constantina, he adorned

Agnes's grave, adding marble revetments and renovating her basilica once again—a scant four years after Constantina's death. Were we to guess a reason for Liberius's investment in Agnes, we might well look to her site's imperial patronage and the considerable esteem in which many of Rome's citizens held it. Unlike many of the sacred sites in Rome, Saint Agnes had it all: imperial patronage, prestige, and beauty, plus (most important) the bones of a member of the imperial family alongside the relics of a saint.

A generation later, in the next major conflict between bishops for primacy, two new figures enter our story: the dual(ing) popes Ursinus (366–367 CE) and Damasus (366–384 CE). Liberius's successor, Ursinus, chose the church of Agnes as his base. The Ursinians favored the site not because of Agnes per se—not because of their devotion to her, anyway—but because Liberius had favored the site. But Ursinus proved no match for Damasus, one of late antiquity's most brilliant and ruthless popes. In 368 CE, on the grounds of Rome's most revered martyr-shrine, Pope Damasus trapped his rivals and slaughtered them savagely.[22] He took Agnes by force. This was another way a pope might own the body and the legacy of a virgin martyr. What Damasus did to Agnes—and how it reflected distinctive concerns of the papacy in relation to the gendering of Christianity—will be the subject of the last chapter.

Around two rather different Roman women martyrs, Agnes and Cecilia, emerged two rather different sacred sites. One was local; one was more definitively "catholic" in the word's broadest sense of "universal." One came to the attention of a pope in the fourth century, one only five centuries later. One woman was a matron who turned relatively late into a martyr in pious memory; one was a young virgin whose only existence in historical memory was as a saint. And this one, Agnes, outshone Cecilia in the size and importance of her cult. Why?

Like most female martyrs of Roman martyrologies—and as the first and best developed of these martyrs—Agnes rebelled against the demands of a pagan empire by withholding the only possession it demanded of her: her body, for breeding future pagan aristocrats. Virginity, therefore, represented more than abstinence from sex; it represented the only means available to women by which they might remove themselves from a political and social system they had been cultivated since childhood to regard as demonic. To some, virginity and martyrdom were interrelated forms of resistance, which is why they came to be irrevocably joined in the figure of Agnes. Thus, on Agnes's name day in 377 CE, Ambrose, the bishop of Milan, composed his treatise on virginity, *De virginibus,* in which he inscribed virginity with seductive elements of martyr legend. To fully understand the significance of the female virgin martyr figure in late antiquity, we need to reflect more on how virginity and martyrdom came to be associated, and why.

Martyrdom simultaneously compels and repels us. Classic studies of martyrdom usually begin with the sporadic but repeated persecutions of Christians that began as early as Nero in 64 CE only to proliferate in size, scope, and horror.[23] These attacks against Christians culminated in the Great Persecution under Diocletian, the last pagan emperor of Rome before Constantine. But martyrdom in the Roman Empire was always a phenomenon both Roman and non-Roman. Our earliest court records of martyrdom do not come from the city of Rome itself, but from parts of the empire where the tensions between Christians and Roman authorities were drawn more tightly as acts of resistance to Roman colonialism. Martyrdom was not what we might call a "religious" issue in an empire where a certain degree of religious autonomy was taken for granted. Rather, most modern scholars understand martyrdom as a form of political resistance against Rome's relentless imperialism. The act of honoring the emperor as a god was set deliberately on edge against Christianity's (and Judaism's) steadfast rejection of idolatry; Jesus's advice to "render unto Caesar" meant, in the late Roman purview, to serve the greater aims of empire: to pay taxes or perhaps to offer a modicum of civic obedience. But many Christians refused to elide civic obedience into the blasphemy of emperor worship.

In one sense, martyrdom offered equal opportunities to women and men. Although both sexes had an equal ability to imitate Christ through voluntary death and to suffer whatever tortures the Roman authorities might devise, men and women differed in the sorts of activities that might provoke Roman magistrates. In the court transcripts of male martyrs, the crimes with which they were charged were most often *lèse majesté* or treason. Men, caught between an allegiance to the service of the one true God and to the emperor, might refuse to honor their civic duties. In the later martyrologies, male protagonists frequently serve, prior to their conversion, in the military, or else they are somehow associated with the administration of the empire—as with Cecilia's husband, Valerian, son of an urban prefect. The drama in men's martyr stories revolves around the conflicting religious and social obligations in which men find themselves mired; only their voluntary death can "resolve" the conflict. Women, by contrast, initially fall afoul of authority within more intimate circles, by refusing arranged marriages or abandoning (invariably pagan) husbands and children—this is the model we see in Agnes's rejection of her young suitor. It is the shattering of these socially mandated domestic bonds and obligations that brings opprobrium (or worse) to women. Cloke observes wryly, "antifamilial feeling is not an accusation hurled at the male martyrs and confessors."[24]

What it meant to be a "bad citizen," then, differed by gender, with the sphere of female transgression more closely limited—at least initially—to the family. What obeisance to empire meant to Christian men was different from what it meant to Christian women. Christianity unraveled the gendered social fabric of Rome, picking insistently and consistently at its loose threads. It made most headway at those points where this social fabric was at its weakest: unmarried women at both ends of the age scale, from the unruly adolescent girls like Agnes to the widows emancipated from male control and therefore likely to bring the full bore of their life experience and worldly resources into power negotiations. Central to the drama of women's martyrdom accounts is the refusal of these women to capitulate to the social demands of marriage and a subsequent sexual existence.[25] As Francine Cardman observes, "conversion to Christianity, especially by women, begins the dismantling of the patriarchal household; impending martyrdom hastens its disintegration."[26] Classicist Mary Lefkowitz notes the same dynamic: women in martyr narratives are "in noticeable isolation from their families, in defiance of, rather than loyalty to, their husbands and fathers."[27] The Christianity of martyr stories, then, provides for women's sexual emancipation on the one hand, and the fundamental destabilization of the traditional Roman family on the other. Such emancipation bore a heavy cost, even if female martyrs seem to have borne it lightly. According to our martyr texts, women eagerly embraced a fate that offered an alternative to the marriages (and ensuing childbirth) that brought them a step closer to death.

To imagine that this situation represented reality, however, is to oversimplify and devalue Roman marriage as oppressive, loveless, and unequal. In reality, Roman marriage conferred considerable (and highly desirable) respectability; it even allowed for a certain balance of power between a married couple. It channeled sexual desire into activities both licit and at least potentially mutually satisfying, brought legal and financial rights to women, and assured the continuation of one's family and traditions. By no means, therefore, did all Christians of the fourth century condemn marriage. We can detect no general decline in the numbers of ordinary Christians marrying. But there are indications that those who opposed marriage became increasingly more vocal. Christianity's continuing, cathectic doctrines on virginity and marriage ensured that the voices of those moderates encouraging marriage were preserved less often than those who found it monstrous. The martyr tales come down squarely on the side of those who found it monstrous.

In 320, Constantine introduced legislation to end the legal penalties that faced those who wished to remain unmarried. He addressed the people with an edict:

> Those who were classed by the old law as *caelibes* (unmarried) shall be freed from the looming terrors of the laws: let them live as if included among the married and supposed by the treaty of matrimony: let all be equally able to inherit what they deserve. And let no one be classed as childless; the losses prescribed for this name shall do no harm. (*CTheod.* 8.6.1)

Constantine emphasized that release from the old law was extended to women as well as men: "We think this also with regard to women, and we release all alike from the yoke imposed upon their necks by the commands of the law" (*CTheod.* 8.16.1). The reprieve from what had been, earlier in the empire, mandatory marriage for all eligible citizens brought unintended consequences; young girls choosing chastity now had the backing of the law to hold against the threats and pleas of their family.[28]

By the late fourth century, the question of whether Christians ought to marry resonated through the city. Arguments were made on both sides. On the one hand, Roman marriage represented a significant venture into respectability; thus certain Christians bolstered their social conservatism with earnest appeals to scripture starting with God's injunction in Genesis to "be fruitful and multiply."[29] On the other hand, powerful clerics denounced marriage as merely "a garment fit for mortals and slaves" (Chrysostom, *On Virginity* 14.5.6). The debates grew ugly. One presbyter, Jovinianus, had been teaching that in heaven, in the sight of God, wives were valued no less than virgins. His writings caught the attention of a Christian senator by the name of Pammachius, then of Pammachius's friend Jerome, and then of the pope, Siricius. Jovinianus was summarily excommunicated, and Jerome worked to mop up the damage that Jovinianus caused by teachings that Jerome considered "nauseating trash." Around 493 CE, Jerome composed a special treatise, *Against Jovinianus,* emphasizing that no one who was truly committed to Christianity would consider anything other than a celibate lifestyle. He even composed a second treatise, *Against Helvidius*, for a female audience, in which he extended his denigration of marriage:

> Then come the prattling of infants, the noisy household, children watching for her word and waiting for her kiss, the reckoning up of expenses, the preparation to meet the outlay. On one side you will see a company of cooks, girded for the onslaught and attacking the meat; there you may hear the hum of a multitude of weavers. Meanwhile a message is delivered that the husband and his friends have arrived. The wife, like a swallow, flies all over the house. She has to see to everything. "Is the sofa smooth? Is the pavement swept? Are the flowers in the cups? Is dinner ready?" Tell me, pray, where amid all this is there room for the thought of God? (22)

In this passage, we see the late flowering of Paul's teachings on marriage in 1 Corinthians 7:31–34: How could a married woman give her full heart to her heavenly Lord, when her earthly lord has her bound so tightly to the mundane world with his demands of sex, childbearing, and childrearing?

Treatises or letters such as Jerome's, directed at impressionable young women and their mothers, may have had considerable influence.[30] On the other hand, they may simply indicate that women needed more convincing; it's difficult to say. But some of the stories from the fourth century remain compelling. Ambrose tells of a girl in his congregation whose family refused to heed her desire to be consecrated as a virgin. In the middle of Mass, the girl rushed the altar, grabbed the altar cloth and wrapped it around her head like a veil, begging Ambrose to consecrate her immediately. Shocked and shamed, a female family member remonstrated her, invoking the memory of the girl's recently deceased father: "Do you think your father would allow you to remain unmarried if he were alive?" "Perhaps he died so that no one could prevent me," the girl shot back (*Concerning Virgins* 1.12.63–65). The unstated assumption that the girl, though impudent, was nevertheless in the right was underscored by the chilling postscript to Ambrose's story: the family member who questioned her was dead within a week.

Let's return to the martyr stories themselves. Ambrose's story suggests that the scenario of a woman spurning the husband her family had chosen for her had at least a whiff of historical plausibility to it; a woman's prime responsibility was to accept the marriage arranged for her by her family, and to make the best of a union in which she had little choice but a great deal of personal investment in terms of her (and her family's) honor.[31] The high tension between the church's calls to virginity and the social obligations of marriage ensured that, as Cloke puts it, "in the closing centuries of the Western Roman empire, the family circle became something of a battle-ground."[32] Then again, the "spurned suitor" motif in our martyr acts is also the point in the narrative at which the martyr stories of women become their most novel-esque. Surely most spurned fiancés did not run crying to local magistrates—or in some instances, even to the emperor himself—to protest having been cuckolded by their fiancée's fanciful engagement to Christ. That the refusal of a suitor became in these stories grounds for beheading a woman suggests a rush to judgment and a male hysteria both unreal and histrionic.

To "rebel" against the constraints of empire, martyrs such as Petronella, Cecilia, and Agnes all chose the path of virtue. Yet the models of virtue open to them were not exclusively Christian; they were also Roman, tradi-tional, and conservative. The men who composed their stories were well aware of this. Tertullian deliberately invokes for his readers the "well-known" example of the Roman heroine Lucretia, who stabbed herself in the chest rather than bear the desecration of her chastity. Other women through history fought just as vigorously and heroically for their virtue, he reports:

> For even women have despised the flames. Dido did so lest, after the death of a husband very dear to her, she should be compelled to marry again; and so did the wife of Hasdrubal, who, Carthage being on fire, that she might not see her husband a suppliant at Scipio's feet, rushed with her children into the conflagration. (*Ad martyras*, 4)

The fourth-century poet Prudentius, too, makes Agnes a classical virgin in the style of Polyxena, the "fortunate virgin" who escapes rape through her sacrificial death at the tomb of Achilles.[33] Polyxena, in classical litera-ture, was no passive victim; she was a "brave and death-defying spirit" who turns toward the sword "with savage and fierce expression" (Seneca, *Troades* 1131–1164). Agnes's defiance matches Polyxena's: "You may stain your sword with blood as you will—but you will not stain my limbs with carnal lust" (Prudentius, *Peristephanon* 14.36–37).[34]

The model woman who preserves her chastity at all costs, in other words, did not begin with Christianity. She represented the best form of self-control that any Roman, male or female, might display in the face of cruel fortune. The Christian woman martyr, in her sexual continence, becomes at once a gladiator and a philosopher. These two were not so far apart as one might imagine.[35] Tertullian, in his treatise on martyrdom, provides counsel to both men and women as if they were gladiators (*Ad martyras*, 1). As for the philosopher, citizens were still much impressed in late antiquity by the ideal of holding one's passions with tight reins. For Prudentius, the tortures of martyrdom only set in high relief the essential pure impassivity of the soul: "There is another, within the body, whom no one is able to rape [. . .] free, undisturbed, unharmed, exempt from grievous pain" (*Peristephanon* 5.157). Historian Peter Brown gives the example of the young Spanish martyr Eulalia from Prudentius's *Peristephanon:* although she was "painted scarlet with blood" from the tortures that she suffered, "that blood . . . touched her hidden, inner self as little as a wash of red paint affected the cool, smooth surface of a wall down which it dripped."[36] This non-participation in the external sufferings of a demonically driven world Brown calls the "miracle of impassivity."[37]

Both these models of self-control and discipline—the philosopher and the gladiator—were gendered male. Resistance to sexual intercourse was the highest form of courage that a woman could exhibit, and to exhibit it was, literally, to be man-like. The Greek word for "courage" is *andreion*, which derived from the root word *aner*, "man." The exhortation from early Christian literature, "Have courage!" meant also "Be a man!" The gendered implications of martyrdom and sexual continence also appear in the word "virtue," which literally means the power of a man (*vir*). It was in the fourth century that the word "*virtus*," male power, became transformed into "virtue," the power of the chaste maiden. In the first century, the Stoic philosopher Seneca had defined *virtus* as

> free, inviolable, immovable, unshaken, and so steeled against the blows of chance that it cannot even be bent, much less toppled. It looks straight at the instruments of torture and does not flinch; its expression never changes, whether adversity or prosperity comes into its view. (*On Constancy*, 5)

The fourth century saw the concept of virtue deconstructed and reassembled, from Seneca's masculine *virtus* to the female virgin's power to remain chaste in the face of overwhelming forces of corruption. Eusebius maintained that a virtuous life would be for a woman to surrender to death impassively rather than to face sexual violation. He writes about one brave mother:

She exhorted both herself and her daughters that they ought not to submit even to listen to such a thing [the threats of rape]; For she said that to surrender their souls to the slavery of demons was worse than all deaths and every form of destruction. She set out that to flee to the Lord was the only way of escape from it all. And after they had listened, after arranging their garments carefully around them, on coming to the middle of the road they quietly requested the guards for a little time to rest, and threw themselves into the river that flowed by. Thus they became their own executioners (*HE* 8.12)

Self-martyrdom becomes, in the eyes of Eusebius and his fourth-century colleagues, the only form of glory and power affordable to women. But this theme had little to do with a state-led persecution of Christianity; it had everything to do, rather, with male constructions of idealized virginity, which included a discomforting connection between the despoliation and torture of women and the deep, mythological pull of an ancient theme: the sacrificial death of a female virgin. Ambrose describes Agnes as "ripe for martyrdom, but not yet ripe for marriage" (*Matura martyrio fuit, matura nondum nuptiis*) (*Hymn*, 65.9–12).

The tales of the virgin martyrs are not reading for the faint of heart. They delve deeply into the dark potential for the male desecration of the female body. Accounts of the lives of late ancient Roman martyrs betray their authors' obsession with the *cruciabiles poenae* or "excruciating torments" of the martyrs (Ammianus Marcellinus, *History*, 21.11.10). Peter Brown describes the late-fourth-century imaginative world of the church as "awash with blood."[38] But it was not male sacrificial blood that fourth-century audiences were compelled to hear about in sermons and homilies; it was the spatter tales of dismembered women. Eusebius describes for his audience an elderly virgin by the name of Apollonia. Her torturers

broke out all her teeth with blows on her jaws, and piling up a pyre before the city threatened to burn her alive, if she refused to recite along with them their blasphemous sayings. But she asked for a brief space, and, being released, without flinching she leaped into the fire and was consumed. (*HE*, 6.41.7)

Eusebius never shied from graphic details. He continues to tell the story of the women martyrs in Thebais, Egypt:

Women were fastened by one foot and swung aloft through the air, head downwards, to a height by certain machines, their bodies completely naked with not even a covering; and thus they presented this most disgraceful, cruel and inhuman of all spectacles to the whole company of onlookers. Others, again, were fastened to trees and stumps and so died. For they drew together by certain machines the very strongest of the branches, to each of which they fastened one of the martyr's legs, and then released the branches to take up their natural position: thus contriving the rending asunder all at once of the limbs of those who were the objects of this device. (*HE* 8.9)

When it came to devising tortures for women, there was no end to limits of human inventiveness. Men poured boiling pitch drop by drop on a woman named Potamiaena before burning her to death (Eusebius, *HE* 6.5.4–5). A late church chronicle, the *Chronicon Paschale*, describes how torturers disemboweled Christian virgins alive, stuffed their guts with grain, and then set them out for the pigs to devour in a gluttonous feast of degradation and horror (92, cols. 741–742). Jerome writes of a woman who survived seven blows to her neck at a botched beheading not unlike Cecilia's (Jerome, Letter 1.3–7). These accounts of unthinkable violence reflect what Brown has called "strong fantasies of disintegration and reintegration."[39] They were not the fantasies or fears that might plague women. They are male-generated fantasies and terrors.

This "despoliation anxiety" of women being violated provoked another aspect of the virgin martyr archetype: the fantasy of beauty. Again and again in the martyr stories, the virgin martyr is physically beautiful. The martyr Agathonica, when she removes her garment before being led to the stake, causes the audience to swoon and grieve that such beauty will be immolated.[40] The description of the virgin as beautiful hints that despite her purity, she is perceived as a sexual object. This is particularly evident in Ambrose's and Prudentius's heavily sexualized depictions of Agnes. The young, beautiful Agnes rejects her suitor not because she wants to preserve her chastity per se; it is because—as she tells the suitor—she *already has Christ as her lover*. And at the climax of Prudentius's poem about Agnes, male despoliation anxiety manifests as an execution that is at once a defloration. As Lucy Grig observes, Agnes wills penetration in the form of the executioner's naked sword.[41] Ambrose, discussing the story of Agnes in his treatise on virginity, even wonders: 'Was there room for a wound in that small body?' (*Fuitne in illo corpuscolo vulneri locus?*) (*Concerning virginity*, 1.2.7). Furthermore, this defloration of the virgin by sword is not seen as a violation so much as something that Agnes herself desires, as she is made to reveal in a remarkable, climactic speech in Prudentius's *Peristephanon:*

> I revel more a wild man comes,
> A cruel and violent man-at-arms,
> Than if a softened youth came forth,
> Faint and tender, bathed in scent,
> To ruin me with chastity's death.
> This is my lover, I confess,
> A man who pleases me at last!
> I shall rush to meet his steps
> So I don't delay his hot desires.
> I shall greet his blade's full length
> Within my breast; and I shall draw
> The force of sword to bosom's depth.
> (*Peristephanon,* 14.69–78)

Martyrdom is here a "death-marriage," the moment at which Agnes becomes, as she declares herself, the "bride of Christ."[42]

At face value, Agnes's is a blood-curdling story of male domination, intransigence, and cruelty. It is a world in which women face a sort of "double martyrdom": first, sexual debasement in a culture that revolved around notions of honor and shame, followed by a sadistic death.[43] Grig explains this account as "a patriarchal discourse engaged in both the control of women and the construction of a Christian masculinity."[44]

The archetype of the virgin martyr was powerful enough to occlude the veneration of women martyrs in other types of family relationships. We have no evidence from the fourth century that any of the city's female martyrs venerated at that time were revered simultaneously as wives and martyrs. Of the four women saints who appear in the earliest martyr calendars—Agnes, Bassilla, Perpetua, and Felicitas—the last two were young mothers at the time of their deaths, but their decision to give up their children to choose martyrdom was lauded as a feat of self-control and spiritual foresight. Of Perpetua and Felicitas, we have no evidence for how they were venerated in fourth-century Rome. They had no oratory or cult site, and no images remain of them. We cannot look to them for any indications that in fourth-century Rome, it was acceptable to be at once a martyr and a matron. For all intents and purposes, the two were mutually exclusive terms. Given that the martyr narratives posed the chief conflict for young women as the choice between marriage and death, this is hardly surprising. Any woman who had chosen marriage had by implication failed in her quest to become a saint.

In the fifth century, however, the church had promoted its ideology of virginity successfully enough that only a few Roman martyrs who became popular in this period slipped through the requirement that they be virgins. But there are not very many of these. For example, Concordia, the wife of Saint Hippolytus, was tortured along with her husband and tossed into a sewer.[45] More frequently in martyr stories, though, wives were sympathetic to Christians without choosing to die for their cause. These include Tryphonia, the (fictitious) wife of the emperor Decius, who dies of natural causes and is therefore not, herself, a martyr (although her virgin daughter, Cyrilla, is), and Dafrosa, the pious mother who buries her martyred virgin daughter, Bibiana.[46] Matrons, in martyr literature, are largely powerless figures, removed from any human agency but to mourn the horrific deaths of their loved ones.

Although the matron or martyr wife in Roman Christianity is very rare indeed, there were a number of women venerated as martyr mothers. Saint Hilaria was the wife of a city tribune, Claudius, and the mother of martyrs Maurus and Jason;[47] she was commemorated as a martyr, a bone gatherer, and a patroness of the church, an owner of cemetery lands north of the city that still bear her name. Saint Sinforosa, the mother of seven sons, was drowned in the Annio just north of Rome. She was significant enough in the eighth century that her bones were moved inside the city walls to the church of Saint Angelo in Pescheria near the Tiber, although Paschal, too, claims to have moved them into Prassede during his Great Translation.[48] Then there was the matron Sophia, who was venerated at catacombs south of the city along with her martyr daughters, Faith and Charity.[49] The Catholic Church's discomfort with these martyr mothers, however, is well demonstrated in the thirteenth-century *Golden Legend* by Jacobus de Voragine, which retells the story of Sophia and her daughters. When Faith is tortured, she is beaten by thirty-six soldiers, then her breasts are torn off, and "all [the assembled people] saw milk flowing from the wounds and blood from her severed breasts." This curious inversion of milk where blood should issue and blood where milk should issue reveals a deep masculine ambivalence toward the uneasy mixing of "mother" with "martyr."[50]

The most successful of the Roman martyr mothers was Saint Felicita, whose remains were housed in an oratory commissioned by Pope Boniface I (418–422 CE). By all accounts, Felicita was well known and highly revered in Rome in late antiquity.[51] Her story is recorded in the early-fifth-century *Passio Felicitae,* where she appears as the widowed mother of seven sons, all martyred for their faith. But Felicita was hardly a historical person; rather, she was a local, late Roman retelling of perhaps the very oldest martyr story: the suffering and death of the unnamed and aged Jewish mother of 2 Maccabees 7:20–41 who witnesses the grotesque torture of her seven sons and encourages them to hold fast to their religion in the face of their persecutors. Although not a virgin martyr, the loosely Romanized, Christianized figure Felicita nevertheless had considerable importance; her small catacomb has a disproportionately high number of children's graves—perhaps because some Roman Christians imagined Felicita as the eternal mother looking after their sons and daughters in heaven. But as an archetypal figure, she worked effectively enough in late Roman ecclesiastical ideology. In the fifth century, Pope Boniface adorned her oratory with a touching inscription lauding maternal sacrifice.[52] Still, the social values that Felicita the devoted mother represented—values such as commitment to family and the upholding of traditional Roman social codes—no longer resonated much as the highest "goods" to which Roman Christians could aspire.[53]

There was also a third option, as martyr stories about women came to be composed: historical women later remembered as martyrs—for instance, Cecilia—could be recast as ex post facto virgins. The martyr Candida—who was once highly venerated at the oratory that bore her name in the Catacombs of Ponziano in Trastevere—plays different roles in different *passios;* in the *Passion of Pimenius* she is a bone-gathering matron who buries the martyr Pimenius at the catacombs located "by the Capped Bear."[54] In another *passio,* she is the wife of Artemisius and the mother of Paolina, both of whom were martyred on the Via Aurelia.[55] But in later ecclesiastical memory, Candida became a virgin martyr.[56]

A different way to handle the difficulty of a married martyr was to deny her involvement in the sexual life of a marriage. Although Cecilia herself probably was a powerful married benefactor of the church, she was formally commemorated as a woman who had successfully negotiated a marital existence that excluded sexual intercourse. Since the real Cecilia was no virgin martyr, she could only be commemorated as a married woman; but since most fourth-century clerics of the post-Constantinian church eschewed marriage, the best they could do is claim what no one beside Cecilia and her husband would have known: that they continued married but celibate—arguably enjoying the best of both worlds. We find other examples of Roman Christian matron martyrs living in chaste or "spiritual" marriages. The converted vestal virgin Daria, for example, lived chastely with her husband, Chrysantius; though both were legendary, not historical figures, they were hugely popular in the Middle Ages, and pilgrims came in droves to visit their tomb north of the city.

The assurance that the few married martyrs promoted by the fourth-century church had practiced sexual abstinence provided a workable model to which ordinary Roman Christians might reasonably aspire. Women, in particular, suffered the "burden of Eve," the inherent unworthiness of the (female) flesh; it was an innate, biological weakness not just of the flesh, but of the will, the fatal flaw of femininity. The constraints of Roman marriage imposed limits—a shape—on the amorphous threat of womanness; with this inherited and scripturally imposed ancestral Eve complex, marriage worked for Christians even more effectively and attractively than for pagans. Yet the practical problem was, evidently, the bipolar seduction of marriage and celibacy. The Christianity of martyr texts offered only a stark choice between the two: one way (marriage) led to spiritual deficiency, to being locked out of the community of the blessed; the other way (virginity) led to death but everlasting glory. The lived, everyday, practical Christianity, by contrast, provided room for both in the form of married but sexually chaste couples.[57]

Postmarital celibacy was an attractive option for laypeople.[58] The Christian catacombs of Rome contain a large number of epitaphs from couples living a chaste life together: "Eucarpius made this [epitaph] while still living for himself and his well-deserving wife, who lived twenty-eight years, more or less; and who remained in virginity for eight years, six months and seventeen days," or "Flavius Urbicus and Victoria Nicene, his virgin, made this [epitaph] for themselves and their people, while still living." Ordinary men like Eucarpius and Flavius Urbicus noted that they had purchased their graves during their lifetimes for themselves and their virgin spouses.[59] Others proudly broadcast the long duration of their celibate unions: "For Florentius, who lived for forty years, eight months and twenty days, from his virgin Firmina with whom he lived for eighteen years and four months; he departed in peace on the nones of May,"[60] or "Deposited here in peace is the well-deserving Onesima, who lived for twenty-seven years and two months; she completed ten years [living] with her virgin Basilides."[61] "Spiritual marriages" such as these provided for ordinary Christians an alternative and more practical lifestyle than the sort of Christian extremism spearheaded by aristocratic women of Rome under Jerome.[62] Both men and women could benefit from such an arrangement. Still, if we didn't have the evidence from the catacombs that preserves the voices of those who chose both marriage and virginity simultaneously, we would be left with the impression that in the end, celibacy and extramarital asceticism dominated the Roman Christian church in the fourth century.

It is worth thinking, for a minute, about what becoming a martyr got for women in the fourth century. In the earlier centuries of persecution, for those women about to meet their deaths, it could bring them extraordinary power. For the noblewoman Perpetua—living at the end of the second century in Carthage—the experience of death's proximity made her a "living martyr"—that is, a human being endowed with the unique ability to intercede between God and his people. But this is in part because Perpetua probably adhered to a sect of Christianity known as the New Prophecy; within this sect, which spread from the wilds of Phrygia in Asia Minor to North Africa, such "living martyrs" were held in high esteem within their assemblies. But this was not necessarily the case in Catholic Christianity. The New Prophesy—the influence of which was certainly felt in Rome— differed sharply in certain points of theology and practice, and because it ordained women, the sect met with derision from the Roman ecclesiastical hierarchy. Attitudes toward martyrs, too, were different in Catholic circles. Eusebius, the first and best of the nascent Catholic Church's ideologues after Constantine, is notably stingy with his use of the title "martyr" for married women. Revealing is his account of the unnamed Roman matron who stabs herself rather than face rape: she is a moral exemplar—a model of virtue—but Eusebius never calls her a martyr.[63] When we see women being venerated as martyrs in the city of Rome—at least from the formal ecclesiastical sources—they are already legendary and idealized; in other words, the church was free to elevate their memory as vastly powerful women without having to make room for "living martyrs" as real women of power in Christian assemblies. In a brief article on female martyrs, Stuart Hall speculates what might have happened if a high-profile woman had survived martyrdom and shown up in a Roman congregation in the third century: Would she have been seated with the presbyters? he asks. He answers in the negative: "Presumably not, since the sexes were normally sharply separated. She could be given the same portion of the offerings. . . . She might have sat with the official Widows. Clearly the charisma she is endowed with does not match the rising codes of ecclesial order."[64] By the middle of the

The dead Cecilia, by Stefano Maderno (1576–1636). Maderno emphasizes in an accompanying oath that his sculpture is a true likeness of Cecilia's preserved body, exhumed about thirteen hundred years after her death. Note the marks of the executioner's sword on her neck, and the gesture of her fingers.

fourth century, the only action that might confer status on a woman was her rejection of a sexual existence. It was a lesson that young women were taught aggressively, though an orchestrated campaign of text, preaching, and example.

Let us return, though, to the basilica of Cecilia in modern Rome. The quietness and beauty of the site as women's space—filled by the song of black-and-white-clad, cloistered Benedictine nuns—does not prepare the visitor for the church's most remarkable—many would even say disturbing—sight: the statue of Santa Cecilia by Stefano Maderno. Almost life-size, it rests behind a panel of glass under the main altar. Of finely polished, cool white marble, it is so finely rendered as to make us feel as if Cecilia's body were still warm. Maderno did not conjure this image from his imagination or from listening to martyrologies. He was present when Paolo Cardinal Sfodrati, head priest of the church in the late sixteenth century, reopened her tomb in 1599 to find her body—as had Paschal eight hundred years earlier—still undecayed. Maderno's goal was to engage the viewer's emotions, to have him or her experience the horror of witnessing the body as if the martyrdom had just happened moments before. She lies on her side, her knees drawn up. Her loose garment covers a lithe and youthful body; her feet are bare. Her head is veiled, but twisted away from the viewer, so that we cannot see her face. The veil, too, falls up over her head, revealing her neck and its ghastly deep slash. Her hands are bound together in front of her. Upon close examination, she appears to be gesticulating, even in death: on one hand, her thumb and first two fingers are extended, on her other, only her index finger. Some say it was Cecilia's last message: of the three persons of the Trinity, God is only One.

We cannot know how close to "reality" is Maderno's Cecilia; part of its allure is the plausibility of the story, the artwork's careful pedigree of verisimilitude: *this is how she looked when she was exhumed.* Maderno supports this with an oath carved in stone beside her:

Behold the body of the most holy virgin Cecilia, whom I myself saw lying incorrupt in the tomb. I have in this marble expressed for you the same saint in the very same posture.

The oath contains the verb "to see" twice: once in the past tense, and once as an imperative. Maderno saw her; then he compels us verbally to behold her. Together, we become witnesses to the martyr whose very title, *martus*, means "witness." Here, as at the close of the sixteenth century, we are *made to look.* But looking directly at martyrs in the ancient world was far more dangerous. For Ambrose of Milan, the gaze (understood to be male) was transgressive; men looked at the virgin Thecla's nakedness with "immodest eyes" (*impudicos . . . oculos*) (*Concerning Virginity* 2.19). In the *Peristephanon*, the crowds look away out of respect for her modesty except for one who, "not fearing to look at her fearful place [*verendum locum*, a euphemism for her genitals] with a lustful eye" is struck down and blinded (*Peristephanon* 14.40–45). "In both these stories [*Concerning Virginity* and *Peristephanon]*," Grig comments, "the body is sexualized and exposed, but at the same time it is sacralized and forbidden to us. The voyeuristic gaze of the audience is both provoked and denied."[65] The dangerous ambivalence of looking upon a martyr, the act at once sacred and transgressive, begins to explain why, in the late Roman world, there were no visual images of the martyrs which conveyed martyrdom for what it was: at once monstrous and pornographic, for we are unable to avert our eyes. The small cool marble body of a dead Cecilia, her mangled wound left gaping open for us to look inside, is a product of early-modern sensibilities, not ancient ones.

CHAPTER 7

POPE DAMASUS, EAR TICKLER

I f there is a villain in this book—and one period in which things changed—it would be the ruthless, visionary pope Damasus (366–384 CE), who transformed, unified, and focused the Catholic Church of Rome. Damasus knew well the life of a Roman ecclesiastic. Son of a priest from the parish of San Lorenzo in the eastern quarter of the city, he was, in a sense, "to the manor born." He inherited a city riven by Christian factionalism, and, driven by his vision of a unified Christian Rome, he brought the city together under his sole leadership. It was a formidable task, and Damasus gained enduring fame within the Catholic Church for it. But such centralization bore a heavy cost: I suspect that Damasus's transformation of Rome in late antiquity was to the detriment of its female sponsors and patrons. Indeed, Damasus's deliberate invocation of glorious Rome threw into shadow the cults of venerated female martyrs and the patronage of powerful women.

To understand what drove Damasus, we need to start further back, at the very beginning of his episcopacy. There was no single, united, and Catholic Rome in 366 CE. The city roiled under the control of not one but two legitimate popes, Liberius (352–366 CE) and Felix II (355–365 CE). The many years of two simultaneous popes reflected the political complexity of a city not yet fully Christianized and a Christianity that had not yet consolidated into a solitary identity. Felix would die first, leaving Liberius holding the papal see alone, but only for a year. The phenomenon of two popes disastrously complicated the problem of papal successor. Which of the two men would have an official successor? Was there one man who would return the papacy to a solitary head? Certainly Damasus believed he was that man. He had served as a trusted and faithful deacon under Liberius and had followed the pope into exile. But later, in 355 CE, he had ingratiated himself with Liberius's rival, the "anti-pope" Felix, only to switch allegiances yet again to Liberius upon the latter's return to Rome in certain triumph. Damasus, then, understood both men, and possessed an insider's knowledge of the pope's job that was both cunning and sanguine. He set about securing for himself what had not been officially conferred on him by the emperors: the sole leadership of the Catholic Church.

The death of Liberius on September 24, 366 CE, was met by the bloodiest outbreaks of Christian violence that Rome had ever witnessed. His body was laid to rest, with due honors, at the Catacombs of Priscilla—close to the martyr shrine of Prisca. Liberius's followers quickly chose a successor, Ursinus, electing him at the basilica built by Pope Julius I (352–366 CE) on the city's Esquiline hill near the present-day Santa Maria Maggiore.[1] Felix's followers elected Damasus at a small titular church near his home neighborhood in Rome's low-lying Campus Martius, now known as San Lorenzo in Lucina. He had come far, even for the son of a church official. Yet his triumphal accession to the papal seat meant nothing without a fuller acclamation. The official seat of the pope—the Constantinian basilica of St. John Lateran—was still out of reach. In truth, neither Damasus nor Ursinus probably possessed enough authority, in the chaos that followed Liberius's death, to occupy a site as large as the Lateran. Both men, however, burned equally for the papal seat (Ammianus Marcellinus, *History* 27.3.11).

Needing a secure base of operations, Ursinus and his backers ensconced themselves in a basilica across the Tiber, in the neighborhood of Trastevere not far from the titular church of Santa Cecilia. Damasus responded as any despot would do: he hired a gang of thugs to storm the basilica and to slaughter any of the Christian clergy they found within.[2] The massacre lasted three days. We do not know precisely how many met their deaths, but other sources indicate that more than a hundred people died. Apparently, Damasus then ordered a second slaughter of the Ursinians at their base on the Esquiline hill.[3] With the Ursinians decimated, Damasus and his thugs easily seized the Lateran. A week later, with the blood of hundreds of Christians slaughtered in a house of God on his hands, Damasus was consecrated at the Lateran, the official Holy See.[4] He had waited until Sunday, the holy day of rest. And then, summarily, he colluded with civic authorities to have Ursinus and two of his surviving deacons expelled from the city.

Ursinus was not kept out of Rome for long. The emperor, Valentinian (364–375 CE), ordered Rome's city prefect, Vettius Agorius Praetextatus, to allow Ursinus and his followers to return. Thus on September 15, 367 CE, a year after their brethren had been massacred by the Damasian faction, the Ursinians reentered the city in triumph. Predictably, the situation quickly deteriorated into open riots. Expelled again from the city core, the

Ursinians set up shop along the Via Nomentana, at the complex of St. Agnese fuori le mura. They favored the site not because of Saint Agnes per se—nor because of their devotion to her—but probably because the site had been favored by Liberius, Ursinus's immediate predecessor. But early in 368 CE, on the grounds of Agnes's revered martyr shrine on the Via Nomentana, Damasus "slaughtered many through the savagery of his devastation," according to a contemporary account.[5]

Damasus's brutal appetites made him history's bloodiest and most despotic pope, but he did succeed in winning the papacy for himself alone. It was a bitter lesson for the developing Christian community: no cost of human life was too great in the greater good of Christian "unity." Chief among Damasus's concerns was to see to it that the bishop of Rome was foremost among all the bishops of the late empire—a position we call "Roman primacy." Because of the city's connection to both Saint Peter and Saint Paul, Damasus was fond of referring to Rome as the "apostolic see." He was thus the first of the bishops of Rome to claim that of all the bishoprics of the late empire, his was the most important. In effect, he began the process by which the pope became the unquestioned head of the Roman Catholic Church, not merely the bishop of Rome among a coalition of other powerful bishops reaching across a newly Christian Empire, from Gaul to Syria, the Danube to North Africa. How remarkable a success this was tends to be lost on modern audiences, many of whom assume that the papacy has been the papacy since Peter arrived in Rome. In reality, the concept of a chief bishop—what we now call a pope—had to be developed and asserted. Given that Constantine—the first emperor to promote Christianity—had shifted the empire's power base from Rome to his new capital, Constantinople, a more seamless and logical choice for chief bishop might have been the bishop of Constantinople. The bishop of Jerusalem might have been an obvious choice, too—presiding as he did over the holiest Christian city—or even the bishop of Alexandria, who commanded a powerful, ancient, and substantial Christian flock. Given the strength of the competition, then, Damasus had to become an ardent promoter of those apostles of Jesus who had found their new base in his ancient city.

By the 360s, devotion to the city's twin apostolic saints, Peter and Paul, had reached a peak under Damasus's direction. His carefully orchestrated propaganda campaign promoting the newly minted Roman citizens featured images of the two saints everywhere—in catacomb paintings, even on medals and medallions that the devout could pick up for a few coins from vendors stationed outside the city's holy martyr shrines. No longer were these apostles associated with the backwaters of Palestine and Asia Minor. They were purveyors of a new civic identity—the founding fathers of a new *Roma Christiana*. Then, on February 27, 380 CE, the emperor Theodosius I issued an edict making Christianity not just a legal religious option (as had his predecessor Constantine) but the official religion of the empire. At the summit of that newly Christian empire was not Theodosius himself— or not merely Theodosius, anyway—but Damasus, as the heir to a primacy that Jesus had bestowed upon Peter according to church teachings (Matt 16:18). There was now in place a direct and continuous thread of "apostolic succession" extending from Peter, now remembered formally as the first bishop of Rome, to each man who held the bishop's *kathedros* or seat.

But it was not just Peter and Paul who emerged as twinned emblems of Christian unity. Curiously, Damasus favored a number of "twinned" male saints. He also elevated and celebrated the Roman jailers of Peter and Paul, two soldiers by the names of Processus and Martinian. He introduced the martyr cult of the brothers Protus and Hyacinth, and that of the soldiers Nereus and Achilleus. At the Christian cemetery *ad Duas Lauros* he built a diminutive L-shaped chapel dedicated to the martyred exorcist Peter and a companion, the priest Marcellinus. At the Catacombs of Commodilla, Damasus lauded the martyred priest Felix and the bystander who accompanied Felix to his death, Adauctus; at the Catacombs of Priscilla, he celebrated Felix and Philip, two of seven martyred sons of the pious matron Felicita.[6] This curious and consistent pairing and elevation of male saints some have explained as an attempt to emphasize concord in a deeply divided city.[7] Still, if Damasus's goal was to put forward a new public image of Concordia through his elevation of the twinned Peter and Paul (or other twinned men, for that matter) we might remember that Concord had been represented in Roman art since the time of Marcus Aurelius by the image of the marital couple. In Damasus's Rome, by contrast, the church once again chose to emphasize unity through nonfamilial or nonspousal bonds. In the Damasan vision of the church, the female half of Rome's ancient Concordia equation was suddenly absent in a new, masculinized reformulation of a classical past.[8]

We might ask, at this point, what Rome's matrons thought of Damasus's ambitions. Certainly no sources preserve their words and thoughts. It seems fair to imagine, however, that women of means did not take kindly to Damasus. They had problems of their own: no matter how wealthy or powerful, they could play no public role within official Christianity or within urban social networks, many of which were still substantially pagan. This is not to say that women held no social power whatsoever; rather, their sphere of influence was limited—as it had been since Christianity's beginnings in Rome—to the household. Women exercised power solidly within the confines of the *domus*. The question to be raised, then, is to what extent the *domus* (or the family grave within the public cemetery which was, in its way, a sort of continuation of private domestic space) stood opposed to more public dimensions of Damasan Christianity.

The church historian Harry O. Maier has recently argued for the existence of what he terms "two Christian topographies" in Rome in late antiquity.[9] These existed simultaneously as private and public ecclesiastical space, and the legitimacy claimed between those who inhabited one realm or the other was deeply contested. The division occurred between private Christian study circles operating out of households, many of them led by women, and larger, imperially funded churches run by an all-male clergy— in other words, those churches that came, later, to make up what we now call the Catholic Church. In this dichotomy between private and public domains of Christian power and authority, the household became, in Maier's view, "a kind of frontier dividing orthodox and heterodox topographies."[10] To put this differently, proponents of nascent Catholicism characterized any Christian study circles in which women played prominent roles as "heterodox" (from the Greek word meaning "a different opinion") or, worse, "heretical."

In fourth-century Rome, private space was still apt to be women's space. This threatened the church—not just because women were women, but because in the insistence of patristic writers, ecclesiastical activities around the *domus* seeded invisible communities of heresy in which women were free to indulge their perverse theologies. The prejudice had started as early as the late-first-century Pastoral Epistles. One alludes darkly to heretical teachers who "work their way into households and capture gullible women burdened with sins, led by various desires, always seeking and never able to arrive at knowledge of truth" (2 Tim. 3:6–7). Indeed, the threat of domestic infiltration appears to have been real. In northern Italy, for instance, small groups of traveling Christians visited the homes of domestic virgins, working to convert them privately to their own forms of Christianity (Jerome, Letter 22.34). In an attempt to subvert such potentially dangerous home visits, Eusebius points out in his *Life of Constantine* (3.65) that "heretics" were not only forbidden to meet in any public assembly, but even "in any private house or place whatsoever." Another ancient historian of the period, Theodoret, noted that the infamous arch-heretic of the fourth century, Arius, proselytized from house to house; the heretic Socrates, too, read his works to followers in their homes. Jerome, clearly threatened, castigated clergy who visited rich widows in their home and who, at the end of their visit, kissed the women on the forehead and stretched out their hands—not to bless, he says, but to receive money. The women, too, he charged with hypocrisy: they may have appeared pious, but their real intentions were revealed when after a lavish dinner the women "retired to dream of the apostles" (Letter 22.16).

Home visits from charismatic and influential Christian teachers outside the fold of proto-Catholicism necessitated action. Prominent "orthodox" churchmen intervened to undo the damage caused by an undermining of power they found insidious. Jerome, for instance, faced a challenging mop-up job with his friend Marcella after she received a home visit from a convincing Montanist preacher (Letter 41). Considering that Montanism encouraged asceticism and (perhaps more enticingly) the active ministry of women, it's hardly surprising that a powerful aristocrat like Marcella might have been attracted to its cause. Considering, too, that Jerome was on Damasus's payroll, it's hardly surprising that he was called upon to rein in the spiritually ambitious women of his own circle. Jerome had his hands full, too, with the priest Pelagius, who frequented the households of elite women to spread his ideas on the proper place of marriage and celibacy (Letter 133.11). Jerome's other nemesis, Jovinian, likewise trolled Roman women's households, bringing a message that actively recognized the place of marriage and the potential contributions of women to Christianity without having to first embrace a more continent or ascetic lifestyle. But even outside Rome, we find similar cases. In Spain, the aristocratic matron Lucilla brought a Christian sectarian movement known as Donatism from North Africa, setting up a community for them on her private estate (Optatus of Milevis, *Libri VII*, 1.16). One female patron of Priscillian, a Spanish "heretic," was executed along with him in 385 CE, the first Christians to be martyred by Christians.[11]

Potent anti-Catholic or non-Catholic theologies traveled from household to household rather than by pulpit, spurring anxiety among male Catholic clerics. "Rogue" forms of Christianity—so many of which included active roles for women as teachers, leaders, or patrons—could scarcely be stopped without active attempts to shut down home visits and to discredit the female vectors of unsanctioned teachings. Thus for the author of the late-third-century *Didascalia Apostolorum*, a woman had to stay at home "and not waste her time running from one house to another . . . to obtain gifts, to spread gossip, and to stir up quarrels." The text concludes its diatribe on home visits with a wicked play on words: "These are not widows, but wallets" (*non viduae, sed viduli*). The sense of the wordplay—largely untranslatable—was that these women had their wallets as their god; that is, they turned the ministry into a home business (*Didascalia Apostolorum*, 15).[12]

The repeated insinuation in early Christian texts that Christian women were evidently going door to door soliciting money to support their own pet projects for their church points to interesting tensions between Damasus's male clerics (who were increasingly forbidden from visiting the houses of women) and Christian female fundraisers. Although these women did ecclesiastical work soliciting money from other women, their work was denigrated as meddling and manipulative, just as the Christian teachings they disseminated through domestic networks of women were disdained as nothing more than gossip. Damasus, for his part, grew fat and rich on the spoils of the church, living indulgently enough that some priests dedicated to lives of Christian austerity bitterly complained to the emperor about the pope's plump, bejeweled fingers and glittering buildings of gold.

Different church ideologues under Damasus responded differently to the infiltration of women's domestic space by roving male ecclesiastics, developing what we might call, following church historian Elizabeth Clark, "strategies of containment."[13] One technique involved the deliberate denigration of women in the creation of a wholly negative ideology of gender that suffused patristic anthropology. In shutting down private networks of female patronage and leadership, the church embarked upon a full-fledged ideological campaign to impugn women's character. Since women exercised power that ran counter to the aims of this patriarchal ideology, fathers of the church turned primarily to the scriptures to close the gap between a present they found abhorrent and a past that set the ideals for feminine behavior. Eve provided the model par excellence of a woman who had used her willful independence to condemn the human race. In a passage remarkable for its venom, Tertullian railed against women who dared to wear fine garments and show themselves as public leaders and intellectuals:

> *You* are the devil's gateway: *you* are the unsealer of that (forbidden) tree: *you* are the first deserter of divine law: *you* are she who persuaded him

whom the devil was not brave enough to attack. *You* so easily destroyed God's image, man. On account of *your* punishment—that is, death— even the Son of God had to die. And you even *think* about adorning yourself over and above your "tunics of skins" (Gen. 3:21)? (*De Cultu Feminarum,* 1.1)

It didn't end with Tertullian. Again and again, fourth-century Christian writers denounced women (powerful or not) as weak, gullible, and tellingly, garrulous. These slanders could be employed to different ends. The *topos* of female weakness could put women back in their "natural" place, but it worked rhetorically for male audiences as well, challenging the masculinity of those men who associated with women teachers. Jerome, for instance, was not above ridiculing itinerant male teachers who dared enter the households of uneducated and "weak" women, insinuating that if their knowledge of Aristotle and Cicero were more acute, they might choose more challenging (read: male) peers to whom to present their teachings (Letter 50.1, 5). Meanwhile, from his base in Antioch, John Chrysostom offered a damning laundry list of supposedly female behaviors directed at those men who lived chastely with women. Such an association put men in jeopardy of being infected with feminine qualities that would render them "hot-headed, shameful, mindless, irascible, insolent, importunate, ignoble, crude, servile, niggardly, reckless, and nonsensical" (John Chrysostom, *subintr.* 10, *PG* 47.510; trans. Clark, "Woman," 167).

Even more than being inherently weak, women posed a danger to men for their loose tongues. All women's speech was merely gossip, the church fathers insisted, and gossip was certainly not the purpose of church meetings. Our sources evince a fascinating tension between the controlled and stylized rhetoric of the church fathers and their horror of uncontrolled speech that, they insisted, characterized meetings of "bad" Christian women. Tertullian emphasized that to be "good," Christian widows had to avoid "lazy, gossipy, inquisitive, and dipsomaniacal friends" (*Ad Uxorem* 1.8.4). He borrowed his words from a Pastoral Epistle that condemns younger Christian widows as "gossips and busybodies" who "wander about from house to house" (1 Tim 5:13). Jerome, too, expressed curled-lip contempt for an unnamed Roman woman he dismisses unkindly as a *garrula anus,* a "yakky old woman" (Letter 53). He was clearly unsettled by this woman's effrontery; he hints that she actively taught the gospel to women and, indeed, even dared to teach men, drawing on the words of Virgil to teach the ways of Christ. We don't know who she was, but some speculate that she was the highborn Roman Christian poet Faltonia Betitia Proba, whose writings had been, in their day, bestsellers. [14]

The patristic denigration of women as weak, loose-lipped Eves coalesced in the church's construction of the "heretical" woman, or rather, in the association of women with "heretical" Christian movements and sects. The fourth-century writer Epiphanius advocated skepticism: "Do not believe a vulgar woman; for every heresy is a vulgar woman" (Epiphanius, *Panarion* 79.8). Jerome, too, had a ready litany of examples:

> It was with the help of the whore Helena that Simon Magus founded his sect; troops of women accompanied Nicholas of Antioch, that inventor of pollutions; it was a woman that Marcion sent as his precursor to Rome, to undermine the souls of men in readiness for his traps; . . . Montanus . . . used two wealthy noblewomen, Prisca and Maximilla first to bribe and then to subvert many churches; . . . when Arius was determined to lead the world into darkness, he commenced by deceiving the Emperor's sister; it was the resources of Lucilla that helped Donatus to pervert many people throughout Africa with his filthy version of baptism. (Letter 133.4)

So effective was the association of powerful, wealthy women with heresy that only recently have feminist historians of the church successfully moved beyond the assumption that late ancient women were natural-born heretics.[15] In fact, church historian Virginia Burrus has argued persuasively that the association of women with heresy was deliberately crafted in reaction to the financial and religious autonomy of some women living in late antiquity. Women emerged within church ideology not as living *individuals* but as symbols of licit and illicit Christian *communities*. For that reason, we must not mistake what we find described in the pages of patristic writings as portraits of "real" women; rather, male anxieties of influence largely effaced "real" women, only to refract them into mere variations on a single trope: the "heretical woman." The "heretical woman," Burrus argues, "represents a church, the internal structure of which is perceived negatively as chaotic and anarchic." On the other hand, a church that is "properly ordered according to the traditional model of the separation and subordination of the private sphere to the public sphere and of women to men" emerges in patristic writings as symbolized by the Wise and Temperate Virgin who carefully guards herself from male influence.[16]

The heretical woman is monstrous, Burrus argues, because she violates all the symbolic social and somatic boundaries between herself and the world: she listens indiscriminately, babbles and gossips, and fails to guard the gateways of her body, whether through loose speech or sexual autonomy. She refuses to limit herself to the private realm of the *domus*, as she refuses to subordinate herself publicly in the world of men. Worst of all, Burrus observes, the heretical woman is a "gadabout."[17] By contrast, the ideal woman of the orthodox church guards her body:

> The virgin is typically described as maintaining the enclosure or privacy not only of her sexual parts, but also of her mouth (she is silent, diligently guarding the received tradition), of her physical location (she rarely leaves home or receives visitors) and of her social location (she does not presume to enter the public sphere of men or to challenge their hierarchical superiority).[18]

Burrus's analysis brilliantly parses out the symbolic language that emerged from one half of Rome's dual topographies of the sacred. One of these topographies was male-driven, ecclesiological, and rhetorically shaped by male anxieties of influence. The second topography was relatively or cautiously "egalitarian" in that both men and women worked actively in the dissemination of ideas and teachings; it lacks a surviving rhetoric, because voices from this side were either destroyed, suppressed, or discredited as mere "gossip." This other Christianity was doctrinally diverse and moved fluidly through social networks of women. It was misrepresented by those who came to dominate the voices left to us from late ancient Christianity—the fathers of the church—as comprised of wholly illicit, even perverse, communities led by heretical women. The construction of the "heretical woman" was itself a direct response from those male ecclesiastics who longed for a clearer, more conservative social world when, to their horror and dismay, everything around them seemed to have gone hopelessly awry.[19]

To address the problem of women exercising influence within networks of home churches or assemblies, the church fathers employed effective strategy after effective strategy. They shored up the perceived threat to the stability of family structures by reiterating the "natural" order of marriage: woman was submissive to man. As Augustine remarked in the late fourth century, "It is the natural order of things for mankind that women should serve men, and children their parents, because this is justice itself, that the weaker reason [*ratio*] should serve the stronger" (*Quaest. In Hept.* 1.153

[CCSL 33.59]). Reflecting on proper natural order in the household, Augustine noted that if a wife were subdued to her husband's *dominium,* there reigned a *pax recta* (a sort of "right" or "just" peace) in the household; if not, and the wife dominated, its opposite: a *pax perversa.* Even before Augustine's time, the Roman Christian writer now known as Ambrosiaster actively participated in the masculinist, clerical discourse of late-fourth-century Rome. He emphasized that women should be submissive to men, but most especially to bishops.[20] Ambrosiaster's work shared much with his likely inspiration: Milan's powerful bishop, Ambrose (340–397 CE). In terms of gender politics, Ambrose's teachings were carefully conservative: a man should "direct his wife, as if he were her governor [*gubernator*], to honor her as a partner of his life" (Letter 14[63].107 [CSEL 82.3.293]). Indeed, the church's stance on the sanctity of marriage and the naturalness of a relationship in which women were subordinated to men was the order of the day; even the more ascetic Jerome, when pressed, extolled the virtues of the ancient Greek writer Xenophon's *Oeconomicus,* which laid out traditional household rules.[21]

Not all arguments for social conservatism came from the pens of male clerics. There is abundant evidence that late ancient Roman Christian women found in their marriages a secure sense of a life lived in proper relation to both the social and the spiritual order. This is manifest from literally thousands of Christian epitaphs from wives to their husbands—particularly those that proudly record the length of marriage down to the very hour. The same view is reflected in Christian writings of the same period. The *Cento,* an epic poem by Faltonia Betitia Proba, the best-selling fourth-century poet mentioned earlier, reveals that traditional values were not simply the rallying cry of male clerics. Proba's seven-hundred line poem—not so much fully her own composition but, in keeping with the conventions of a cento, a collection of verses from Virgil rearranged and augmented—sings Christ's virtues in the traditional meter of ancient worlds. Proba used her *Cento* to emphasize traditional family values—including Mary's maternity—against those more extreme Christian philosophies that promoted lifelong virginity and denigrated family life. Rather than extolling Christ as a model of celibacy, the *Cento* offers that Christ's teaching included devotion to family. Adam and Eve are even refigured as an idealized Roman couple with a full, blissful sexual existence. It comes as no surprise that Proba dedicated her poem, in its final lines, to her "sweet husband" (*dulcis coniunx*), the powerful Adelphius, who served the city's highest political office—the urban prefect—in 351 CE.[22]

A minority of very vocal Roman Christians, however, took issue with the sort of social conservatism evinced by countless women such as Proba. To control the power relations between women in the *domus* and the men they supported, these Christians waged a fierce ideological campaign against family. Thus, around the year 370 CE, the Roman aristocrat Melania forsook her opulent lifestyle and her last remaining child to sail to Egypt. Her kinsman, the prominent bishop Paulinus of Nola, vividly describes the scene from her last day, as she bade farewell to her youngest child along the banks of the Tiber:

> She joyfully threw off the burdens of human love along with the ropes of the ship, while we all wept . . . she "loved her son by neglecting him and kept him by relinquishing him" . . . once Melania had torn her only son from her breast and set him in Christ's bosom, so that he might be nourished by the Lord himself, she herself gave him no more personal care, thinking it a sinful lack of faith to still devote attention to one whom she had entrusted to Christ. (Paulinus, Letter 29.9–10)

Melania's abandonment of her son was met with open hostility from her pagan relatives, who worried that her callousness toward her own family would damage their good family name.[23] But other aristocratic women apparently followed Melania's lead. In 385, Paula—one of Jerome's closest friends—took her youngest daughter Eustochium with her to the Holy Land. As she was leaving, her son Toxotius "howled with the terror and aching sorrow of being abandoned by his own mother from the shore of the Tiber, stretching his arms out to her." Few descriptions of the fourth-century world strike so much pathos in the hearts of modern readers. Paula remained unmoved by her small son's suffering; she kept in mind the gospel, "He who loves his son or daughter more than me is not worthy of me" (Matt 10:37), then "raised dry eyes to heaven, overcoming her devotion as a mother that she might prove herself worthy as a handmaid of God" (Jerome, Letter 108.6).

Melania and Paula's brand of Roman ascetic Christianity dramatically inverted traditional Roman family values; for hundreds of years, these values dictated that a woman marry young (according to her father's choice of husband for her), make love with her husband, raise children, and then remain within the limits of the household to see to the elementary education of those children. Instead, late Roman ascetic Christianity insisted that, as Gillian Cloke puts it, "to desert one's family was to look for their care, and to impoverish them was to look to their heavenly wellbeing."[24] As the martyr mother Agathonice calmly informs her accusers, "My children have God who watches over them."[25] There developed, for an influential few, the profound, anarchic realization that a commitment to God could require, for both men and women, an abandonment of duties to both family and Rome.[26] As Jerome advocated to the young virgin Furia, "Honor your father, but only if he does not separate you from your True Father" (Letter 54.3).

The popularity of home visits from Christians of various stripes and allegiances, as far as the church was concerned, rendered not just marriage but also the home itself dangerous to women. It was incumbent upon the clergy, therefore, to dissolve these home meetings and to redirect worship and study in the more closely monitored forum of the basilica. It is also not surprising that in the absence of women's monasticism (it had not yet developed), such removal of women from the attractions of the world to a closely guarded "closed" ecclesiastical space ensured a sort of doctrinal "orthodoxy" that domestic asceticism could never structurally bear. In other words, it was not enough for fourth-century Roman Christianity to actively promote virgins and virginity to diffuse the dangerous, fissile powers of the matrons and the priests they financially supported. It was necessary to remove these virgins from the domestic networks and settings that still provided them with too many opportunities to throw their considerable financial resources behind the teachings of those whom they favored.

Both the negative assessments of women in fourth-century ecclesiastical ideology and imperial legislation against home visits by clerics underscores the reality of powerful women within elite networks of Roman Christianity. Within these networks, women functioned actively as patrons and scholars. Far from marginal figures, they were critical participants in late ancient Christianity, as they funded, translated, and interpreted a new Christian culture. Paula and her daughter Eustochium, for instance, became proficient enough in Hebrew and Greek that Jerome came to them for translation assistance. For such women, "literacy" consisted not in the ability to compose or author works but in activities that might be useful in the support of male clerics: translation, copying, and disseminating texts—activities that garnered fame for women such as Melania the Younger.[27]

By the end of the fourth century, the church had become, in Elizabeth Clark's words, "a primary outlet for female patronage."[28] To draw on an example from Asia Minor, the rich heiress Olympias supported not just the prominent theologian Gregory of Nyssa, but also Nectarius, the patriarch of Constantinople. Indeed, the list of prominent fathers of the church actively supported by female patrons includes Augustine, Jerome, John Chrysostom, Gregory of Nazianzus, Palladius, and Rufinus.[29] These great men were directly—and generously—supported by "relays of women."[30] Indeed, as historian Gillian Cloke wryly observes, "These great men of their age were bought and sold by women."[31] Often enough, too, the women outclassed the Christian men they supported. Jerome, John Chrysostom, and Augustine came from families that were no match socially and economically for those of the women on whom they depended.[32] Nevertheless, these Christian women were expected to give over both their money and their authority to men. Clark comments, "The idea, it appears, was for a committed virgin or widow to donate her entire substance to the Church" and to "willingly to submit herself to the control of ecclesiastical authority."[33] Thus we find the curious phenomenon of aristocratic Roman women such as Paula and Eustochium seemingly bent on creating, through charity, their own financial destitution.[34]

On July 30, 370 CE, during Damasus's pontificate, the emperor Valentinian I issued an edict read aloud in all the city's churches: members of the clergy were now forbidden from entering the homes of widows.[35] The cause of this prohibition was apparent: the clergy had been accepting gifts or inheritances from wealthy Christian widows who were legally entitled to dispose of their wealth as they saw fit.[36] From the perspective of the Roman state, such ties between private noblewomen and the church constituted a dangerous form of influence peddling. Christianity could become merely opportunistic—a religious movement designed to separate wealthy Roman aristocrats from their money. Up to this point, after all, civic aristocrats played a crucial role in urban patronage; the city's infrastructure—the baths, assembly halls, aqueducts, grain dole, and other crucial social services—were all underwritten by private (rather than imperial) benefactors.[37] Women had their own money, with which they might reasonably be induced to part, following ancient traditions of patronage—providing that their donations were duly recognized as part of a complex ritual of civic display. Given their inability to hold government office, in fact, women were all the more likely to participate in local benefaction.[38] The issue was not so much acquiring (or broadcasting) power as it was garnering honor— a deeply desirable form of social capital equally attractive to men and women, pagans and Christians.

Although they supported some fathers of the church, late Roman Christian women excelled, above all, in supporting major building projects that enhanced the church's prestige and swelled its coffers. The rich Christian divorcee Fabiola built a hospital and a guesthouse in Rome's nearby port city Ostia, partly with the help of a senator, Pammachius (Jerome, Letter 77:10). Paula spent the lion's share of her inheritance building a monastery in Bethlehem (Jerome, Letter 108). These women usurped roles more customarily assumed by male aristocrats long expected to establish themselves and build their family's honor by adorning ancient cities. Roman Christian women of the fourth century differed from their male forebears by confining their benefaction to buildings that directly benefited Christians and the growth of Christianity. Rather than building aqueducts or bathhouses, women like Paula built monasteries and hospices.

The art historian Leslie Brubaker has recently demonstrated how elite women—particularly imperial women—financed building projects in honor of Helena, Constantine's mother and Christianity's first imperial patroness. Helena had changed the face of Christianity. It was she who discovered, in Jerusalem in 326 CE, the True Cross on which Jesus had reputedly hung; she who built Jerusalem's famed Church of the Holy Sepulcher and adorned it with her money; and she who then brought the precious relic of the True Cross to Rome to house it in her large basilica, the Basilica Heleniana. She also donated a large tract of her land—the *fundus Laurentus*—for Christian use as the cemetery complex of *ad Duas Lauros*. She even built a special basilica there for her own interment. Like other generous laywomen, she was rewarded for her largesse by being transformed into a saint; by the ninth century, her cemetery basilica had become known as the *basilica beate Elene,* the basilica of the blessed Helena.

Just as Helena's basilica once bore her name, other fourth-century titular churches dispersed among the residential quarters on Rome's seven hills were named after their women founders. The church of Anastasia nestles between the Palatine and the Circus Maximus. On the Aventine hill where Ceres' temple still stood in the fourth century, worshipers had a choice between the titular churches of Tigrida (also called Balbinus), Prisca, and Sabina; in Trastevere across the Tiber stood the *titulus* of Cecilia; in the Campus Martius, the "field of Mars" where soldiers had long trained, was the *titulus* of Lucina. On the Cispian hill, we still find the small churches of the highborn sisters Prassede and Pudenziana. On the Caelian hill not far from the Colosseum, the church of Aemiliana (now called the Quattro Coronati) is still home to a small community of cloistered nuns. Near the Quirinal hill stood the *titulus* of Susanna on the site of an ancient pagan temple. Between the Quirinal and the Viminal hills on the long road or *vi-cus longus*" that stretched through the city, the *titulus* of Vestina welcomed Christians long before it received its current name, the church of San Vitale. And far out on the Via Appia stood the church of Crescentiana, now the chapel of Saint Sixtus. All in all, at least twelve of Rome's twenty-five *tituli* bore names of their women founders and donors—although only seven are still known by those names today.[39]

Women patrons funded these building projects across several genera-tions, through family lines that Leslie Brubaker calls "matronage chains."[40] Grand acts of matronage were more visible outside Rome, in part because empresses wealthy enough to build truly extravagant churches were no longer based in the city after the fourth century. The fifth-century Byzantine empress Aelia Eudoxia, for instance, sent to Gaza in 402 CE money, archi-tectural plans, and columns to build a church in the form of a cross; it came to be called the Eudoxiana, in her honor.[41] An imperial princess, Galla Placidia, built in Ravenna the church of Santa Croce and the chapel of San Lorenzo around the year 425 CE. The church historian Sozomen reports that the empress Aelia Pulcheria excavated the shrine of St. Thyrsos in Se-baste and discovered the relics of forty martyrs between 434 and 446 CE— probably a carefully staged *inventio* ritual meant to replicate Helena's discovery of the True Cross.[42] In fact, Helena's legacy remained potent for imperial women. Brubaker writes that Helena represented a "matrix of val-ues" that included traditional Roman social codes, political power, civic pa-tronage, and elite female piety. In this way, the memory of Helena validated those pious late Roman women who chose to operate within a female struc-ture "based on continuity rather than disruption."[43]

Women patrons worked with the construction of a past, observes Brubaker, "in ways defined by gender, though with the resources defined by class."[44] Although Brubaker writes primarily about imperial women *pa-tronae*, the financial donations of some aristocratic laywomen in late antiq-uity were also substantial. Olympias's donations to the church have been calculated as equivalent to about $900 million.[45] The Roman aristocrat Melania the Younger's annual income could support twenty-nine thousand people; she once fed five thousand monks in one day. It's no surprise why priests and bishops courted these ladies—they provided their crucial finan-cial base. At the same time that wealthy donations lined the church's coffers, though, the rechanneling of funds away from a patron's family could have severe financial implications. It's little wonder that Theodosius I (379– 395 CE) attempted to force Olympias into a contracted marriage with one of his relatives, from which the family would have reaped a considerable profit. As for Melania the Younger, she was forced into a marriage to consolidate family wealth, from which she repeatedly attempted to escape; her struggle to retain control over her fortune so that she could donate it to the church required legal intervention (*Vita Melaniae Junioris,* 10–12). Later, in fact, Rome's city prefect attempted to confiscate her property to offer it as a bribe to the Visigoth leader Alaric as he prepared to sack the city in 410 CE (101–109). The consequences of this transfer of money from private women to public institutions was profound; rather than supporting descendants, the money would pass irrevocably into public use. Elizabeth Clark likens this bleeding off of money from the aristocracy to the withdrawal of the female body from the duty of breeding future aristocrats.[46]

As a response to this massive transfer of funds away from families and into the proto-Catholic Church, late Roman emperors attempted to shore up political support by issuing a series of edicts aimed at stopping the erosion of aristocratic family fortunes. Various imperial laws issued during Damasus's papacy prevented women from giving money to the church, but these were evidently neither fully effective nor quite specific enough; twenty years after Valentinian I's edict, on June 21, 390 CE, another imperial law formally forbade deaconesses from donating or bequeathing any part of their family estate to either a cleric or a pauper. Remarkably, two months later, the law was revoked. But why? If the church emerged as triumphant in having this law struck from the books, the ones to lose were the male aristocrats of Rome, who watched with alarm as their inherited fortunes were siphoned into the church's coffers. Surely they were not the likely candidates for lobbying against a law that clearly placed them back in control of some of the city's movable wealth. The church itself, then, stood to gain most—practically and financially—from having such laws repealed.

On the other hand, these laws limiting clergy protected women and families from being "suckered" by underhanded clerics primarily concerned with separating wealthy women from their money; the laws militated against their exploitation. Still, social historian Michel Verdon claims that late ancient Roman women teamed up with the clergy to have the laws restricting their distribution of wealth revoked. "It could only have been the women," he argues, "who were defending, not their clergy, but their right to dispose of their own property at their own free will, against the very men who had obviously expressed their interests in female property by having the law passed in the first place."[47] These women were well aware that if they did not redistribute their wealth to the church, it would fall into the hands of men anyway: their male kin, who may or may not have espoused Christianity. Bound by a mutual contract of expediency, women and the male clergy stood to gain. The clergy saw their authority expanded and secured. Their women patrons—although given no direct, ecclesiastical positions of power—won the right to control their own money; to win earthly admiration and divine favor by constructing churches, hospitals, and hospices for the poor; to buy, circulate, and revere holy relics; and finally, to refuse the burden of marriage and childbearing. It was a devil's wager—but perhaps women struck the better bargain.

But let's return to Damasus, under whose episcopacy the struggle between the generosity of women lay patrons of Christianity, the active effort of women to remain on the frontier of clerical activity and teaching, and the ideological devaluation of women as Eve's daughters combined in disturbing crescendo. How much this suppression of women's activity and their negative valuation can be directly attributed to Damasus himself remains unclear. Nevertheless, Damasus's actions reveal that at the summit of institutional Catholicism, there was an intentional effort to sideline, even suppress, women's Christianity. Nowhere is this more evident than in Damasus's stunning masculinization of Rome's sacred space.

In his quest for the ideological domination of *Roma Christiana*, Damasus's strategy was to control all the Christian sites in the city. That is, he wanted not merely to create a unified Catholic Church (the word "catholic" is from the Greek *kat'holos* or "according to the whole") but to prove definitively his authority over all Christian factions and sites in the city. He flooded Rome with Christian places of worship, including new buildings in areas associated most clearly with pagan Rome; in the Campus Martius—sacred territory where soldiers trained and temples to the gods had long stood—he built the modest church of San Lorenzo in Damaso, dedicated to Rome's foremost martyr, Saint Lawrence. And along the western flank of Rome's pagan heart, the Palatine hill, Damasus built (or perhaps enlarged) the church of Saint Anastasia.[48] Before Damasus, Christians had scarcely dared to make their presence known in a landscape so powerfully sacred for the city's pagans. Only then, after he had enhanced the city's churches, did the pope turn to Rome's suburban cemeteries and catacombs—already sites of local factionalism—to transform them into ecclesiastically controlled, subsidized martyr shrines. To do this, Damasus took advantage of the popularity of the new "cult of the saints"—the veneration of the relics of the Very Special Dead.

Damasus's work elevating the catacombs to martyr shrines was at once brilliant and revolutionary. In the eighteen years that he held the papal seat, he profoundly transformed the topography of Rome. He changed late antiquity's Roman Christianity definitively and irrevocably. Catacombs—many fallen into disrepair by the late fourth century—became, under his guidance, public pilgrimage sites enlarged to incorporate large numbers of devout pilgrims. In many cases, Damasus commissioned new, wide staircases that led throngs of devoted Christians down into the bowels of the cemeteries, so that people might clamor close to the bones of the martyrs. New air wells and light wells in the catacombs flooded chambers with filtered sunlight and stirred the stale air; cubicula and galleries were broadened and deepened to create new elite spaces for those who wished to be buried *ad sanctos,* close to the living presence of the saints.[49]

Damasus's lasting and most characteristic contribution to Roman Christianity's redrawn cityscape was at once concrete and ethereal; the pope commissioned his friend, a skilled calligrapher named Furius Dionysius Philocalus, to set into stone lofty poems of praise that Damasus himself had composed, the so-called *epigrammata* or *elogia* of Damasus. Philocalus obligingly designed a new script—called Philocalian to this day—to carve out Damasus's long, hexameter verses onto large marble plaques. Each of these approximately sixty *elogia* Damasus ordered erected as part of his renovations of martyrs' shrines.[50] Each major route out (or in) of Rome had its own martyr shrine or shrines, each marked with Damasus's own words in a hand that evoked the Dreamtime of the classical era.

The Ursinians and other rivals of Damasus despised the pope not so much for those martyrs he promoted, but for those he willfully neglected: Damasus blotted out many of the city's local martyr traditions.[51] He cannily picked and chose which martyrs had to be venerated following a logic that served his own ends. Remarkably, with the exception of Agnes—and we will return to why Agnes might have remained important for Damasus—*virtually every single martyr promoted was male.* In effect, Damasus manipulated and created an official Christian collective memory and self-identity that obliterated powerful women from Roman Christian imaginative horizons.

Damasus's masculinization of Roman Christianity started early. He was elected pope in a small titular church along the Via Lata called, in the ancient sources, *in Lucinis;* that is, it likely derived its name from a patron named Lucina. Most likely, this Lucina was the same woman who became the bone gatherer of later Christian narrative. Damasus did not formally recognize her, and after the fifth century her church was reconsecrated as San Lorenzo, dedicated to Rome's popular martyr Lawrence. It is now known as the church of San Lorenzo in Lucina. There is no need to assert that Damasus knowingly obliterated the memory of Lucina. Nevertheless, we find a similar pattern emerging again and again in his pattern of commemoration and renovations of church property. Let's return, with Damasus, to some of the sites we've seen already.

As he began his monumental task of renovating saints' shrines in the city, Damasus turned at some point to the small Catacombs of Bassilla on the Via Salaria. The catacombs had received their name from a female patron of the church, Bassilla, who had donated a portion of her lands for Christian burials. Over time, Bassilla came to be remembered not as a wealthy donor but as a young virgin martyr. The veneration of Bassilla had already reached full flower by the time that Damasus reached the site. She is one of only two female Roman martyrs—the other is Agnes—mentioned in the Codex Calendar of 354. Bassilla's presence in the Codex Calendar indicates one of two things. Either she was a martyr with a cult popular enough to have merited special mention in the Codex Calendar, or the rich patron who commissioned the Codex had some particular reason to promote her cult. Both, in fact, could be true. What's clear is that Bassilla was recognized as a prominent Roman martyr immediately prior to Damasus's papacy. Her popularity among pious laity is still attested by two moving inscriptions from her catacombs that entreat Bassilla to take care of deceased infants in the afterlife. "[Here lies] in eternal slumber Aurelius Gemellus, who lived for one year . . . a most innocent and well-deserving son. I commend to the innocent Bassilla a most innocent and well deserving child." And another: "Lady Bassilla, we Crescentinus and Micina commend to you our daughter Crescentia, who lived for ten months."[52]

Given that Bassilla was apparently widely venerated as a martyr and intercessor in the second half of the fourth century, it is not surprising that Damasus ordered erected at the catacombs in her name one of his famous *elogiae*. But the inscription never once mentions Bassilla. Instead, it commemorates the twinned male martyrs, Protus and Hyacinth ("[Damasus] preserves the bodies of the pious"), along with another local martyr, Hermes. Unlike Bassilla, none of these other martyrs is mentioned in the Codex Calendar. The graffiti left by the pious to the three male saints, scratched into the walls of the catacombs near the *ad sanctos* graves, all date after the

Damasan intervention. Through Damasus's efforts, then, three new male saints suddenly appeared on fourth-century horizons. Bassilla's memory, by contrast, fell into eclipse.

The pattern continues. At the Ponziano catacombs near the Via Portuense in the leafy modern Roman neighborhood now known as Monteverde Vecchio, we find remnants of three fourth-century tombs for the martyrs Pollio, Candida, and Pigmenius. Their martyrologies are found in the much later *Acts of Saints Peter and Marcellinus*. Recent archaeological work undertaken by the Pontifical Commission on Sacred Archaeology reveals that in the decades after 313 CE, two separate oratories were set up here. This time—for a while, anyway—it was the male saints Pollio and Pigmenius who were forgotten. Saint Candida, however, continued to be venerated at one of these two oratories. Still, it was at *another* oratory, the martyr shrine to the eastern saints Abdon and Sennen, that Damasus set up his inscription. The inscription has not survived, but from what we know from copies of it, Damasus did not see fit to mention Saint Candida; instead, it glorifies the memory of the twinned male saints Abdon and Sennen. Then, for reasons left unexplained, he allowed Candida's oratory to fall into disuse.

There was more. At the Catacombs of Priscilla, as we have seen, the most significant woman associated with the complex—either as Prisca (of Prisca and Aquila fame) or as Priscilla, the founder of the catacombs—appears to have had a recognized and substantial following throughout late antiquity. In 1981, the engineer and archaeologist Francesco Tolotti identified a portion of the catacombs as a *martyrium* that may have held the relics of various martyrs, the most significant of whom was probably Prisca herself.[53] Medieval guidebooks or *itineraria* agree that Prisca had a small shrine in her honor in one cave-like area of the catacombs. Like Bassilla in her own catacombs, Priscilla also was the recipient of graffiti from the pious; one, for instance, appeals to the salvific power of the "martyr" Priscilla's prayers.[54] Yet in Priscilla's catacombs, Damasus chose to elevate not Prisca / Priscilla, but two arguably lesser-known martyrs, Felix and Philip. These brothers were (according to legend) two of the martyr Felicita's seven sons, although the only two to be buried in Priscilla.[55] About Prisca—a leader of the church mentioned twice in the New Testament who possessed the potential to tie Damasus back to the apostolic age in Rome and to his beloved hero Saint Paul—Damasus remained entirely silent.

Damasus continued doggedly with his ambitions. At the Catacombs of Domitilla on the Via Ardeatina south of the city, the pope set his workers to increasing the areas there devoted to *ad sanctos* burials. The catacomb had already been subjected to extensive renovations in the middle of the fourth century. Here, in one of the luxury suites, we find Veneranda. At Domitilla —at least in the fourth century—the martyrs venerated were Nereus and Achilleus, as well as Petronella. Damasus renovated the area, marking it with a long inscription—to Nereus and Achilleus alone. In the end, of Damasus's sixty flowery inscriptions in honor of the martyrs, only one commemorates a woman martyr. Not a single one acknowledges the foundations of a holy site by a woman patron—not even in her later, mythicized form as a bone gatherer.

Damasus's *epigrammata* or inscriptions themselves merit some attention, for they offer remarkable insights into one fourth-century pope's imaginative horizons. Father Antonio Ferrua's 1942 edition of the *epigrammata* provides copious evidence of the masculinizing language that Damasus favored.[56] Of the twinned male saints Nereus and Achilleus, for instance, we learn that these brothers, soldiers under the Great Persecution of emperor Diocletian, converted suddenly and dramatically and deserted the camp and the trappings of military service. A portion of the inscription now set up at what used to be the Chapel of Saint Petronella reads:

> An amazing thing to behold!
> All at once, they let fall their fury,
> Converted, they abandoned the impious camps of their general.
> They rejected shields, decorations and regalia
> Confessing Christ, they rejoiced to carry their (new) spoils
>   of Christ. (*ED*, 8)

Similarly, the martyrs Felix and Philip of the Catacombs of Bassilla win the coronas of Christ for their *virtus*—their power of maleness (*ED*, 39)— and Felicissimus and Agapitus are twinned *comites* in the unconquered cross (*hi crucis invictae comites*) who win the triumphs of Christ by standing by their *dux* or leader, the pope Sixtus.

These inscriptions underscore that times were changing. Damasus's deliberate invocation of glorious Rome imposed a discourse of masculinity on a city full of revered female martyrs. His heroes were resolutely male: they were popes, deacons, and apostles, not labile Christian maidens coyly resisting their pagan suitors. His choice of language and imagery was enduringly masculinizing and martial, conceiving Christianity not as a stroke of grace but as conquest: thus in his epigrams the protomartyr Stephen carries off "the trophy from the enemy" (*ex hoste tropaeum*)—language subverted from Rome's finest poet, Virgil. Felicissimus and Agapitus carry off the "triumphs of Christ" (*Christi meruere triumphos*) as comrades (*comites*) under the unconquered cross (*crucis invictae*) to win the Kingdom of the Pious (*regna piorum*) (*ED*, 25). In the papal crypt at the Catacombs of Callistus, the martyred *comites* of Sixtus once again carry off the enemy's trophy (*ex hoste tropaea*) (*ED*, 39). As the historian Dennis Trout observes, Damasus's martyrs reveal themselves as exemplars of "deeply embedded notions of manly excellence."[57]

Women are virtually entirely occluded from Damasus's muscular Christianity, save for five *elogia* he composes to honor women: one to Agnes; one to his mother, Laurentia; one to his sister Irene (a consecrated virgin by the age of twenty); one to the young Roman noblewoman Projecta, the daughter of a male friend; and one to the chaste Afrodite, wife of his friend Evagrius. Four of the five inscriptions to women were ordinary epitaphs—if a tad flowery—to ordinary women he knew, of the sort that any Roman man of means might erect for those close to him. But we must not be moved by his familial devotion to the point that we fail to recognize Damasan family ideology: family is important, but those roles his women play best are securely of the fourth-century church: his mother's chief virtue commemorated in her epitaph is her widowhood; his sister's and Projecta's, their consecrated virginity. In other words, it was not the Damasan women's embeddedness within the structure of the family that Damasus saw fit to eulogize, but their success in standing aloof from it. Damasus highlights these nonfamilial roles for women even as he pushes female martyrs into eclipse. And in these *elogia* to women, the language of Christianity by conquest is markedly absent. Agnes and Projecta are marked not by their valor but by their *pudor*—their "shame." Women, inasmuch as they appear on Damasan horizons at all, retain or exert no agency. They vow their bodies to chastity, and they bear in their bodies the heavy weight of shameful sexuality. It is no wonder that in Damasus's account of Agnes, the virgin martyr is protected from the male gaze by a miraculous profusion of hair that sprouts to conceal her.

Damasus's *elogium* to Agnes, however, was still heartfelt: "You whom I must venerate, holy heroine of chastity (*pudor*)," he writes, "hear favorably the prayers of Damasus, I beg, noble martyr."[58] So why did Agnes escape Damasus's masculinization of Rome? Three reasons, I suspect. First, her site had become an Ursinian stronghold; Damasus's use of her cult, then, was probably more about the reconquest of Catholic Christian space than about Agnes herself. Slaughtering his opposition and taking over Agnes's shrine, Damasus won over Agnes's cult as part of the spoils of his own holy war. Controlling the worship of Agnes's cult ensured that he had won a certain victory over the Christian factions that controlled this northwestern part of the city. Second, Agnes's site—like St. Peter's and St. Paul's—was directly associated with the Constantinian dynasty, and Damasus was eager to align himself with imperial power. Third, as a virgin martyr, Agnes stood alone as a powerful iconic figure. It was a power to which Damasus might yield without losing anything of his own. By contrast, other sites such as the Catacombs of Priscilla and Bassilla were associated with lay patrons who also happened to be female. It was not their gender as much as it was their patronage (and the implications such patronage brought to the exercise of power and authority) that Damasus likely sought to subvert.

The masculinizing crisis of conversion so prominent in Damasus's program to male soldier saints provides the flip side to popular Christian narratives such as the *Acts of Paul and Thecla*. In these stories, women dominate the action. Conversion becomes a women's drama—a central event that sets the young heroine against her betrothed and her earthly family. In this book, we've seen shades of this in Thecla's attraction for Paul and her scorning of her fiancé Thamyris; we've seen it, too, in Cecilia's attraction to Christianity despite her family's wishes and in Agnes's rejection of her suitor. These popular stories—and literally dozens of such stories circulated in late Roman Christianity—may have spoken directly to the concerns, anxieties, and aspirations of young Christian women. These stories, too, were recounted in spaces associated with their eponymous virgins and martyrs, thus creating powerful dramas enacted in pilgrimages to Rome's sacred sites.

By drawing on a discourse at once masculinist and martial, however, Damasus gendered space in the catacombs and *martyria* to emphasize male activities and male concerns. The lessons to be learned from the *elogia* direct themselves at an audience assumed to be male. They speak to male anxieties concerning the retention of status after men's conversion by assuring martial victory under the new banner of Christ, and ensuring a divine apotheosis for those men who die for the Christian cause. In Damasus's inscriptions, Christianity grows not through the *domus* and the strident efforts of women to maintain chastity and devotion to Christ through refusing to marry, but through the sudden and dramatic defection of men from the largest and most troubling social demand of the late Roman empire: military service.[59] The *elogia* address a potent male anxiety of conversion to

Christianity as perhaps inherently emasculating, in that it required turning away from the late Roman army and the civic and imperial duty of military service. They speak directly to the concerns of the all-male clergy, which was poised in exquisite tension with the late Roman army in competing pools of talent and interest.

But let us return to Damasus's martyr shrines. In a sense, Damasus re-intellectualized the experience of viewing the saints. It was not all the pure experience of gentle spectacle. It was not enough, in the Damasan universe, just to admire and wonder at the holy relics, to pass through the catacombs to the *martyria* in childlike and wide-eyed devotion. Damasus created of the catacombs a spectacle, a theater of the saints. Unlike the uncontrolled bursts of feeling on display at unsanctioned shrines, his theater of the saints carried the considerable heft of explicit clerical approval. Martyr shrines offered feasts for the senses—from the shouts and tears of the visitors, the air made heavy with incense, the flicker of lamps—a pilgrim could ensure that all her senses would be fully engaged. And yet the Damasan universe was one of measured control, from the constraining of the diffusely numinous holy relics into queer, boxy square shrines he designed and built, to the sobriety of long *elogia* which required, in many cases, a studied attempt and several minutes' attention to read or hear. The point of his *elogia* was, most potently, to teach the faithful to see—to make meaningful the chiaroscuro of subterranean bone and stone. As in any official tour, what visitors saw was carefully controlled and portioned out for maximum dramatic effect. Damasus controlled the "cone of vision," the very way in which the catacombs and tombs of the saints were viewed. Through this Damasan lens, certain elements of Christian identity and focus were willfully suppressed. The remainder were crafted to conform to his aims and vision of a universal church.

As much as it may seem that Damasus brought the saints closer to the people, his goal may have been to distance them—to bring them tantalizingly close but yet ultimately out of reach. The flights of stairs he commissioned to bring the devout down to the graves increased, not lessened, the double-edged sense of distance. The approach was direct, and yet heightened the sense of physical space between realms. His martyr shrines enclosed their graves in roofed boxes; the relics themselves were locked away behind stone grilles. And thus Damasus, and the church under his control, developed complex rituals of access: worshipers had to visit the sacred through designated and gate-controlled itineraries plotted for maximum dramatic effect. The visit might culminate in revealing a visible shrine, but relics were just out of reach. Those prepared could bring with them *brandea*, little pieces of cloths that could be inserted into the tomb's openings to absorb and render portable the saints' sanctity. But even those who donated these relics—many of them women—would no longer have direct access to the holy.

Although he renovated the martyrs' tombs, building small shrines featuring cut-stone *transennae* that both marked off the bones as separate and allowed a tantalizing peek inside, the chambers Damasus built to house the shrines were adorned only with plain marble slabs or simple white plaster walls.[60] There were no images, no pictures to inspire nor to take attention away from proximity to the numinous bones. The soft light of visitors' oil lamps must have shone off the marble and white walls, making the entire chamber glow with a gentle but unearthly glow. After all, the pilgrims had entered not the bowels of death but paradise in the eternal presence of the blessed.

It was not merely the visual, the act of seeing, that became central to Damasan Catholicism, but also *speaking*. It is telling that Damasus chose words over images to guide and instruct the visitor. Damasus's fascination with words inscribed *in situ* that explain what we see reveals a distinctly new preoccupation with the power of language. It was Damasus, after all, who hired Jerome to translate the scriptures from Hebrew to Latin. To do so— almost ironically—Jerome worked with his coterie of highly educated noblewomen on the city's Aventine hill. Their knowledge of ancient languages challenged Jerome's own expertise, and yet he alone is credited with the creation of the Vulgate Bible—the definitive Catholic Bible up until Vatican II.

Words can be imperfectly understood, but images were more dangerously opaque. Without words to explain what the viewers were seeing, a plurality of interpretations might be advanced—some less licit, orthodox, or appropriate than others. The *elogia* provided the necessary backstory to evoke proper reverence; they connected the reader to the saints through the direct mediation of Damasus. If all other recourse to a subtlety of interpretation failed, they often enough ended with a stern order: "Venerate the tomb!" And the devout did venerate the tombs. They left behind graffiti— *words*—scratched as prayers into the walls of the catacombs. The response to the visual, even visceral, experience of the martyr's shrine was not to create more images, but to carve words of wonder in handwriting immeasurably less elegant than Filocalius's script, but equally eloquent.

Most saliently of all, Damasus provided his viewers with a script. His emphasis on florid prose inscriptions speaks not only to his ideal audience of educated Roman elites who might appreciate Virgilian resonances in his *elogia* but, more broadly, to the increased importance of text and literature for creating, codifying, and controlling Christian orthodoxy in the late fourth century. The Damasan age was resolutely an age of language. And in the catacombs, words—reading them as well as hearing them spoken— were a necessary component of spectacle. With language as his most effective tool, Damasus rewrote Christian Rome's classical past while simultaneously obliterating women in roles other than chaste widows and virgins. This was a cult of memory at once oppositional and antagonistic, one that excluded women patrons or even their memory. Slicing and eviscerating public memory, Damasus transferred and projected a violence onto the still painful era of persecution of the church—a time that he describes in a number of inscriptions as the age in which "the sword splits open the belly of the Mother" (*tempore quo gladius secuit pia viscera matris; ED* 12, 23, 28, 32, 34). The wound was not to be *healed* by Damasan Christianity, but to be *avenged* by its male martyrs—sons of the Mother Church—and their conquests under the banner of the unconquered cross.

I began this book with the matron Lucina, who gathered the pope Cornelius's broken and ragged body and took it to her lands to be buried. She commemorated him only with a simple epitaph: "Cornelius, bishop and martyr." And in this book about the invisibility of women in Christianity, we will end without her. Damasus, as it turns out, also left his mark on Cornelius's tomb. In the last year of his life, sick and aged from the weight of the ambitions of empire, Damasus set up his last *elogium*, to the same Cornelius:

> Behold: a descent to the crypt has been built: darkness has been expelled: you can behold the memorial of Cornelius and his resting-place. The zeal of Damasus has enabled him, though careworn and ailing, to accomplish the work and make your pilgrimage easier and more efficacious. If you are prepared to pray to the Lord in purity of heart, entreat Him to restore Damasus to health; not that he is fond of life, but because the duties of his mission bind him still to this earth.

Prayers did not buy Damasus the time he begs here from pious pilgrims. He died before the carved inscription was finished, and it fell to his successor Siricius to complete the *elogium* and have it erected in place. But here, at Cornelius's grave on the lands that had once been Lucina's, Lucina herself is invisible—both from Damasus's account of the site and from the act of bone gathering, of memorializing. Instead, Damasus takes the role for himself. In words carved in stone, Damasus literally reinscribed Christianity with meaning while simultaneously obliterating the role of the women bone gatherers. What remains is only Damasus himself.

By the end of the fourth century, the Catholic Church based in Rome had its own bone gatherers, and these were not women. In contrast with the action of the bone-gathering women of later Christian literature—private, agonized, pious, intimate—the activity of male bone gatherers was papal, public, celebratory, antagonistic, theatrical, and miraculous. Indeed, the translation, repatriation, and consecration of the bodies of the martyrs became the papal acts *extraordinaire* of power, patronage, and piety. The disjuncture is striking: when women move and bury bodies, it is because they are sentimental, pious, and dutiful. When popes move and bury bodies, the act constitutes a highly orchestrated revitalization ritual of the church, carefully commemorated and duly attributed.

So why did Damasus leave out Lucina and her sisters? Was it only because they were women? Probably not. More likely, Lucina played a role in the mythologies and competing ideologies of different Christians factions active in Rome between the third and the sixth centuries. She was a heroine, but for the wrong side. Damasus largely extirpated women from this sacred landscape not necessarily because he was misogynist, but because as he sought to promote a new, papal Christianity, women played a greater role in the Christianity of his rivals than he would acknowledge. Women simply lost out, secondhand victims in struggles for power between a masculinized, "Catholic" or papal Christianity and the more lay-oriented, democratic, and local Christian communities of the city. In this papal hierarchy, there were simply no roles for women except as idealized, mythologized, and symbolic succors to male interests.

What the Christian women of Rome thought of Damasus's masculinizing Christianity remains unrecorded. One intriguing note is Damasus's nickname in a rare, surviving pro-Ursinian tract, where he is called the *auriscalpius matronarum* or the "matron's ear-tickler"—presumably because the close relationships he entertained with Rome's wealthy Christian women were perceived by his enemies as influence-peddling.[61] And yet one wonders at the nickname, for there is scarce evidence of much fondness between fourth-century Roman noblewomen and the bishop. It is certainly difficult to see how Damasus served their ambitions. One account is thought-provoking, though. Two presbyters, Faustinus and Marcellinus, charged that Damasus had become fat and debauched on wealth and power. It is difficult to imagine that those very matrons who supposedly supported him—the first representatives of Roman asceticism who created for themselves a "desert in the city"—were not profoundly uncomfortable with the bishop's excesses.[62] Perhaps this is why, at the close of the fourth century, so many of Rome's elite Christian women quitted Rome for new destinies in the Holy Land. In Jerusalem, as in Egypt, Rome's wealthy Christian *patronae* were free to pursue a spiritual existence far different from anything Damasan Rome would either see or countenance.

EPILOGUE: TURTURA'S VEIL

One last catacomb visit awaits. Deep in the Catacombs of Commodilla, south of the city, lies a small subterranean basilica dedicated to two of Damasus's beloved twinned male saints, Felix and Adauctus. Despite Damasus's promotion of their cult, the space as it remains today was largely financed not by him, but by a lay patron sometime after Damasus's renovations had worn thin from too many visitors. As it stands now—humble, bare, and less a basilica than a dim, dusty passageway where throngs of modern visitors amble through without much stopping to look—we get little sense of this as sacred space. Once, though, it stood fine and proud—and the lay patron, as a final touch, commissioned a huge wall painting featuring the Virgin seated with the infant Jesus on her lap, the saints Felix and Adauctus, and—for good measure, her own likeness between them all, standing in quiet joy alongside her new, heavenly family.[1]

This lay sponsor was a widow by the name of Turtura. She lived to be around sixty. Her name in Latin means "turtle dove," which, according to a long, painted prose inscription at the bottom of the panel, suited her gentle disposition. In terms of the broad history of Roman Christianity, Turtura is a nonentity. In the formal, written history of Roman Catholicism, with its records of theological disputes and letters and annals and tables, Turtura's is a nonpresence. In the modern historical studies even of women in late ancient Christianity, Turtura's is still a nonpresence. And yet we find her here, her image stretching three or four feet across a wall fresco, standing amid exalted company: Mary, Jesus, Felix, and Adauctus. Her donation of money won her the privilege of being buried close by the martyrs just after the shrine's construction.[2] Hers was one of the very last burials in the catacombs.

Turtura died sometime in the late sixth century, in the days after Rome's back had been broken by marauding Visigoths and Lombards and even long after the last of the Roman emperors, a child named Romulus Augustulus, had been mercifully relieved of his post. Under the force of repeated assaults, the city had contracted, yielding up its treasures to its invaders and

Turtura, a pious widow, stands with the saints Felix and Adauctus and the Virgin and Child in a fresco commemorating her life and her family's donation to the church. Note the austerity of her dress and demeanor—the new late ancient ideal for pious Christian women.

retreating within its stout walls. These incursions had changed burial patterns, as Romans sought to protect even the dead by crowding them up to their saints and intercessors in funerary basilicas rather than laying them, shroud-clad and wrapped in the exquisitely visceral vulnerability of death, along the hollow canals of the catacombs' galleries. Since Damasus's time, constructing these funerary basilicas had been the special responsibility of popes, part of their sacred duty to care for their flock even after death. So Turtura and her family did what we might expect a pope to do: they gave others access to her favorite saints by renovating their *martyrium*. Then Turtura's only surviving child, a son, placed her image directly before the faithful, before the sightless eyes of the dead buried in their shallow graves and the reverent gaze of Felix's and Adauctus's devotees as they pushed through the candlelight toward them.

Turtura's image powerfully underscores how much had changed between Christianity of the mid-fourth century and Christianity of the late sixth. In her large, red-framed fresco we find the full flowering of Christian devotional art—the steady forward gazes, the resplendent golden halos around the Virgin and Child, Felix and Adauctus, and the hieratic frontality of bodies and gestures. We have here something that looks more familiar to us than the small, faded images of Veneranda or the "Fractio Panis." This painting has the quality, the feel, of a Byzantine icon. The Virgin sits upon a crimson-colored pillow on a heavily jeweled throne, holding on her lap the child Jesus clad in a golden tunic and *pallium*. Felix and Adauctus, in their long white togas, flank them. And, remarkably, Turtura stands slightly to the front of them all, her hands covered by a diaphanous white veil as she proffers two books, as a young, beardless Adauctus rests his hand, almost casually, on her right shoulder. As the historian Dennis Trout observes, Turtura's painting collapses time; it makes her the midpoint in a holy continuum that begins when Jesus was a child, continues on to the age of the saints Felix and Adauctus, and comes to rest in the timelessness of heaven.[3]

Let's look at the fresco carefully. The anonymous artist's use of symmetry and the painting's limited palette gives a pleasing balance to the picture—the men flanking the Virgin are dressed in white, but the women, in heavy black. Visually, these contrasts and similarities simultaneously strike and soothe the eye. Both the Virgin and Turtura are veiled and hold white cloths; indeed, their dress is identical; the women are analogous, familial. They're not sisterly as much as they stand in some undefined, shifting filial relationship to one another; they have very similar features, as if one were mother and one were daughter. But it's hard to say which one is which. The Virgin may be the Mother of God, but Turtura's face is aged, betraying the wear of mortality, while the Virgin's is resplendent, youthful. Turtura, one senses, is the true mother of the assembly.

By the time we reach the late sixth century, the problem of images in late Roman Christianity had become acute. How do we know how an image such as Turtura's was interpreted? Was it iconic? Representative? Votive? Didactic?[4] To put this differently, when pilgrims saw Turtura's image at the grave of Felix and Adauctus, how did they read it? Did they see it as something to revere in the same way that they revered Felix's and Adauctus's physical remains? Was it iconic in the same way that the Virgin and Child sitting next to Turtura are clearly iconic? Did they read it as a story of intercession of the saints Felix and Adauctus—or of the Virgin—in Turtura's life? Was it narrative? Was it an image that could be universally read by all Roman Christians, or did it convey a resistant localism against other prominent Roman martyr cults? Or was it all of these?

What is clear from my viewing of it is that by the sixth century, things had changed. Unlike Veneranda, who stands with her saint Petronella richly attired in saffron-colored garments and the finery reserved for the wealthy, Turtura adheres to an aesthetic of austerity. By the fifth century, coarse black cloth and the absence of decoration for clothing became what historian Gillian Cloke calls "reverse status indicators."[5] "Christians who renounced the world," she observes, "wore black precisely because it onnoted dirt and deprivation: it was the colour of mourning, and poor people wore dark clothes. Black, worn by the ascetic, said 'I am a poor sinner.'"[6] For women, black indicated not just an espousal of poverty but also the vow of virginity; thus John Chrysostom described the ideal virgin as recognizable from her "messy hair, downcast eyes, and dark cloak" (*On Virginity*, 7). It was the dress not of a highborn Roman matron, but of the renunciant who gained power, paradoxically, from her willingness to give power up.

Turtura's show of austerity had significant precedents. From the late fourth century onward, families of aristocratic ascetic women actively opposed their conversion, if only because it strained against Roman notions of marriage and family as crucial ways to bind people to ancient tradition.[7] Around the 370s, the heiress Melania left Rome, taking with her an almost inestimable fortune. She had faced sure opprobrium from her relatives for rejecting the responsibilities, along with the visual markers, of her class and status. Some thirty years later, Melania returned to Italy from her sojourn in the Holy Land. Her grand entrance provided a striking spectacle of new, Christian authority: she rode on a donkey's back surrounded by other holy women who, like her, wore the somber robes that are the precursors to the monastic habit of medieval nuns. Around her, Melania's now-adoring relatives, in their full finery, were borne along in their litters and carriages. The parade resembled the triumphant *adventus* or arrival of the emperor into a city; yet this was an *adventus* turned on its head: not only did a mere woman displace an emperor, but poverty and humility took the place of glittering costumes, jewels, prancing horses, and gilded chariots. Melania's friend, the powerful bishop Paulinus, witnessed the spectacle. He was well aware of the full significance of the status inversions: "The world (was) in a turmoil fit for God's eyes, crimson silk and gilded trappings playing servant to old black rags" (Paulinus of Nola, Letter 29.12).

In the lost worlds of third-, fourth-, and fifth-century Rome, most nonelite women had not yet given up their saffron garments to keep playing at what was becoming, increasingly, a man's game. By the sixth century, however, Turtura epitomized the new woman of the church. Still, what she did was not so very different from what her spiritual grandmothers and great-grandmothers had done. *Patronae* had always stood apart for their attempts to retain a social presence even as avenues for this presence were being systematically shut down for women. Bejeweled or black-clad, they continued to muddy the line between private and civic visibility because patronage, as a civic virtue, had always been inherently a male activity; the very word "patronage" stems from the Latin noun for father, *pater*. Accordingly, the *patrona* was more public than private. Public display and civic recognition are the very currencies of patronage. Women patrons accommodated themselves to this system by ensuring that they marked their civic benevolence with inscriptions and images that emphasized their private (that is, domestic) virtues. In their dedicatory inscriptions, women were still defined by their relation to men and to families. Turtura's epitaph, carefully painted in an early medieval Latin script, is no different from that which a devoted son might have left for his mother in the days of Virgil:

> Now take up your tears, mother, and a surviving son's lamentations that, lo, he pours out in your praise.
>
> After father's death, thus widowed, you chastely preserved for thirty-six years your husband's trust in you. You performed the duty of father and mother for your son; your husband, Obas, lived on for you in your son's face.
>
> You are named Turtura, but you were a true "turtle dove," for whom there was no other love after your husband's death.
>
> There is a single reason why a woman draws praise, because you show that you devoted yourself to your marriage.
>
> Here rests in peace Turtura, who lived for sixty years, more or less.[8]

Some of these sentiments move us, still. We feel Turtura's son's bone-wracking sorrow at losing a parent. We know the experience of wonder as we look into our children's faces and see written in them the features and mien of our loved ones, for the living comfort us as the dead cannot. But other words chafe against our modern sensibilities, as a son defines his mother only by her devotion to his father. Still, what catches us up here in this inscription is the distilled relationship of a dutiful, grieving son to his mother. We can just discern from it the invisible but almost subversive power of the mother in the late ancient family. It is often the mother, behind the scenes, who molds her sons into ideal, active members of society; thus Cloke speaks wryly of the rise in late antiquity of "middle class Hausfraus planting ideological trip-wires in the consciences of their children and turning out priests, monks and bishops by the seminary-load."[9] Peter Brown writes, too, not just of the role of late ancient women in crafting notions of Christian masculinity in this period as they raised their often fatherless sons, but of the rise of the indomitable *nonna,* the wise and influential grandmother who knew, as Turtura surely did, precisely how to cultivate proper and vigorous Christian piety in their young charges.

And yet in the end, despite her donation to the church and her lifelong devotion to her family, modern visitors to the Catacombs of Commodilla encounter Turtura, the turtle dove, present without a presence. Few notice the tension between what is said about her, what is shown about her, and what she herself was actually doing by having that subterranean basilica rebuilt. She stands today as she has for fourteen hundred years, in the basilica paid for out of her family's money, wearing her coarse black robe that denoted, paradoxically, her poverty. There is paradox, too, in the factness of her submission to the patriarchal authority of the church—she is, after all, wearing her black ascetic robe of chastity and poverty rather than her jewels and elaborately dyed and woven garments—read against her active, nearly smug presence standing ever so slightly in front of two male saints, looking like nothing less than the mother of the Mother of God. She is there to remind us of her existence and all the complexity of being that she comes to represent. And there is paradox, finally, in the elaborate inscription under the fresco that vaunts Turtura's demure nature even as it exalts her status: it tells us nothing about the figures we are seeing in the painting except for her, the patroness. She served her husband chastely and meekly, a proper Roman. Her virtues are uxorial and domestic. Her achievements usurp Roman notions of maleness, but in word and image, only Turtura's womanliness is remembered.

The medieval historian Jo Ann McNamara argues that the Gregorian Reform of the eleventh and twelfth centuries aimed to transform the Catholic Church into a "woman-free space"—a "church virtually free of women at every level but the lowest stratum of the married clergy."[10] In fact, the church of Rome had become virtually a "woman-free space" centuries earlier, and in the fourth century we see the last signs of powerful women working within church networks the way they had for three centuries in the city before the final avenues of authority were cut off from them. These signs were visual and inscriptional, and their very transience and liminality makes them poignant. Visual images of laywomen started to appear in early

Christian art in the beginning of the fourth century, but by the sixth, they had disappeared.

By the end of the fifth century—notably after a synod held on March 1, 499, Rome was fully Christianized. At this point, the number of clergy in the city swelled considerably. The church had become a "woman-free zone," at least when it came to women serving official positions. But a few powerful laywomen continued to have influence in the ecclesiastical politics of the fifth and sixth centuries, and the cult of women martyrs and saints redoubled in the seventh, eighth, and ninth centuries. This is the age when Agnes's basilica is renovated, the glittering mosaics added to her church, to Cecilia's church, and to Pudenziana's. This is the age in which martyr acts—especially those of women martyrs—proliferate. The fourth-century martyr calendars, the *Depositio Martyrum* and the *Depositio Episcoporum,* contain the feasts of forty-six martyrs and bishops, of whom only four are women. By the ninth century, there are dozens.

In broad social terms, of course, men were also uprooted within the Catholic Church; they no longer aligned themselves with their earthly families but with their new heavenly brothers. Nevertheless, being uprooted from domestic and dynastic lines had always meant for women something different from what it meant for men. Women stood to gain from being freed from their domestic constraints: the obligations to marry men they did not love or choose; to engage in a sexual existence for which they were usually ill prepared and, often enough, ill considered; to endure failed pregnancies or labors gone terribly wrong; or to birth child after child only to bear the jagged, cut-glass grief of a child's death. Christianity could bring relief to women from biological burdens, but the cost of that relief was their utter abnegation—a systematic and thorough devaluation of most of what it meant to be female. It had not always been so, but as the fourth century progressed, the best a woman might hope to bring beyond a silent acquiescence to a man's world was the sacrifice of everything else that defined her: her money, her status, her voice. Their images that remain from this time are like flashbulb pops that temporarily sear these women onto our retinas even as they fade permanently into the darkness. Even when we reenter the catacombs and shine our flashlights onto their pictures, real women have become such active nonpresences in the church that we don't acknowledge them—they are merely symbols of higher realities, or they are visual clutter in the iconography of the saints, or else we see them as men, not women, sitting down to dine in the presence of the Divine.

ACKNOWLEDGMENTS

This book began to take shape in the philosopher's stone of Princeton University, in both the Department of Religion and the Program in the Ancient World. I feel more fortunate than I can express to have been nourished intellectually during my graduate studies there by so many outstanding scholars, but a special acknowledgment is due to Elaine Pagels, John Gager, Peter Brown, Robert Lamberton, Ted Champlin, and Garth Fowden. Those who had finished their studies at Princeton soon before me but who still visited often—particularly David Frankfurter and Kate Cooper—set the bar very high indeed, and I continue to aspire to it daily. I am grateful for their ongoing support and enthusiasm. Groups in which I have actively participated, including Peter Brown's Group for the Study of Late Antiquity and the Society of Biblical Literature's Late Antique Pieties group, provided a stimulating group of colleagues and topics that have stayed with me for many years. Foremost among those who inspired me was the late Keith Hopkins of Cambridge University, whose work on Roman demographics and whose wonderfully macabre essays on death in ancient Rome kindled in me a deep fascination for dead Roman women.

In the summer of 2002, I was fortunate enough to participate in a summer seminar on Roman religions in their cultural context funded by the National Endowment for the Humanities held at the American Academy in Rome. Special thanks are due to our seminar director, Karl Galinsky of the University of Texas, Austin, but also to Vincenzo Fiocchi Nicolai for taking us into the Catacombs of Ponziano, and to Darius Arya, who made many things possible. Colleagues from that summer who particularly focused on catacomb-related issues with me were Georgia Frank, Jeffrey Brodd, Barbette Spaeth, Alice Christ, and Greg Snyder. I owe a special thanks to Georgia, who acted as an inadvertent midwife for her incisive questions at the Catacombs of Domitilla that initiated this particular project, and who volunteered her precious time to read parts of this manuscript. Thanks, too, to Edward Gutting and the Department of Classics at the University of Mississippi for their graciousness and hard work reconvening us in the fall of 2004, enabling us to continue our discussions. Chapters 2 and 3 would have been impossible without Barbette's work on Ceres and Greg's work on the Via Latina catacomb; both have inspired me immeasurably, and I thank them for their numerous corrections on these chapters. Any errors which remain are mine entirely. Alice Christ helped to show me what a fine critical reader of the catacomb material might look like, and I thank her for her insight and clear-headedness.

In Rome, I am indebted to the Vatican Museums and the Pontifical Commission for Sacred Archaeology for private access and special permissions, to Sandro Luciani at the Catacombs of Priscilla, and particularly to Sister Martha of the Benedictine Sisters of Priscilla for her patience, good cheer, and astonishing knowledge of the Catacombs of Priscilla. Olof Brandt of the Swedish Institute at Rome generously shared with me his unpublished work on Roman *tituli* and his excavations of San Lorenzo in Lucina.

I also want to thank Christine Thomas, Stephen Davis, and Kim Bowes for their invitations to present papers at their Society of Biblical Literature sessions; I am grateful for their support, feedback, and the opportunity to share some of the material in this book in an untested form. Linda Sue Galate, Sharon Salvadori, and Janet Tulloch—my fellow women of the tombs—were all invaluable resources. Joan Branham provided encouragement and inspiration. Kristina Sessa saved me from many an embarrassment with her sage comments and edits of the introduction and chapter 5. Roberta Panzanelli, senior research specialist at the Getty, lent me the ear of a skilled art historian early on.

Financial support for this book was provided by the NEH and by a 2004–2005 individual research grant from the American Academy of Religion. A generous individual subvention grant from Bowdoin College in 2005–2006 helped defray expenses for the map and the photographs in this book. At Bowdoin, I found congenial colleagues in the Departments of Religion, History, and Classics. Dallas Denery kindly read portions of the manuscript, as did Molly Swetnam-Burland. James Higginbotham shared with me a small but tremendously useful portion of his knowledge of Roman *triclinia*. The undergraduates enrolled in my Late Antique Women's Piety seminar in the spring of 2006—Youree Choi, Jessica Stirba, Vanessa Palomo, Dan Yingst, Lydia Pillsbury, Annie Cronin, Rebekah Muller, Margot Bunn, Katie Mitterling, and Jason Riley—heard much about dead Roman women and responded with good cheer and wonderful sagacity. Dan

Yingst provided additional, invaluable last-minute research and biblio-graphical assistance.

Parts of this book were delivered as public lectures between 2004 and 2005 at the Episcopal Divinity School, the University of Mississippi, Harvard Divinity School, Princeton University, and Brandeis University. I want to thank Elaine and John again here and acknowledge the much-needed encouragement I received in Princeton from Martha Himmelfarb, Jeff Stout, and Shawn Marmon. In particular, I must single out Bernadette Brooten at Brandeis for her unflagging support and Larry Wills at Episcopal Divinity School for his invitation to present a paper to his Christian Origins working group.

This book would never have been written without the generous support of Harvard Divinity School's Women's Studies in Religion Program, for which I was fortunate enough to have been selected to be a Research Associate for 2004–2005. Huge thanks are due to the program director Ann Braude; our faculty assistant Tracy Wall; and my sister fellows for their most useful feedback: Shawn Copeland, Elora Shehabuddin, Tonia Sharlach, and Susan Zaeske. The program gave me the financial support to devote myself full-time to researching and writing, as well as immeasurably useful *amicitia* and intellectual engagement. Also at Harvard Divinity School, the support and encouragement of my colleagues Laura Nasrallah and Karen King were much needed and much appreciated. My graduate students at the divinity school—Darcy Hirsh, Robyn Walsh, Heidi Wendt, Laura Randall, Christy McKearney, Crystal White, and John McCarthy —pushed me on important questions and always provided a thoughtful, stimulating forum. Our Women's Studies in Religion research assistants, Jennifer Pavelko and Levi Bjork, got me out of a scrape or two. A special thanks to Heidi, Robyn, and John Robichaux for following me to Rome just to look at and photograph long-dead women. Last—but first—on the list of influential students would be my undergraduate advisee Sarah Madole for her Skidmore senior thesis on the Greek Chapel (2000) that got us both thinking about women's space in the catacombs.

Heartfelt thanks go to all those at Beacon who helped with this book, especially my skilled and sage editor at Beacon, Amy Caldwell, and her assistant, Tracy Ahlquist; and to Joel Thomas Walker for introducing me to the wonders of Rome in 1992—the trip that changed my life in many unexpected and wonderful ways. Finally, I thank my mother, sisters, nieces, and daughter, Lola—the Denzey women—and Patrick Rael, for sacrifice of his own research time in potent combination with his remarkable editorial astuteness. And, last of all, I need to convey my deepest gratitude to Tal Lewis, my partner in all things, who has taught me so much about how to get past "98 percent done," and how to begin again with clear sight and an open heart.

NOTES

Introduction

1. For a description of the discovery of Cornelius's epitaph, see Rodolfo Lanciani, *Pagan and Christian Rome* (New York: Houghton Mifflin, 1892), 215–216. It is, of course, not clear that the stone was engraved under Lucina's orders; some have attempted to link it to the late-fourth-century epigrapher Furius Dionysus Philocalus.

2. No archaeological evidence has been discovered; for early reports, see J. Stevenson, "L'area di Lucina sulla Via Ostiense" in *Nuovo Bulletino di Archeologia Cristiana* (1898): 68ff.

3. Generosa's name is known from the sarcophagus inscription when the bones of the saint were transferred to the church of St. Bibiana. See O. Marucchi, *Manual of Christian Archaeology,* 4th Italian ed., translated and adapted by Hubert Vecchierello (Paterson, N.J.: St. Anthony Guild Press, 1935), 152; see also Lanciani's version of the story in Lanciani, *Pagan and Christian Rome,* 332–334.

4. *AA.SS,* Oct. XI (Paris, 1870), 482; Augostino Amore, *I martiri di Roma* (Rome: Augustinianum, 1975), 56.

5. For the text, see the *Passio Polychronii* 29 (BHL, 6884); and H. Delehaye, "Recherches sur le légendier romain: la passion de S. Polychronius," *Analecta Bollandiana* 51 (1933): 93; Amore, *Martiri,* 96.

6. Marucchi, *Manual,* 147.

7. For Cecilia's story, see my chapter 6.

8. R. Krautheimer, S. Corbett, and W. Frankl, eds, *Corpus Basilicarum Christianorum Romae,* Vol. 2 (Vatican City, 1959), 192–193.

9. Matt 27:61–28:20; Mark 16:1–8; Luke 23:55–24:11; John 20.

10. Mark 14:9. For a groundbreaking, feminist theological interpretation of the passage, see Elisabeth Schüssler Fiorenza, *In Memory of Her: A Feminist Theological Reconstruction of Christian Origins* (New York: Crossroads, 1983), esp. xliii–xliv.

11. Richard Saller, *Personal Patronage under the Early Empire* (New York: Cambridge University Press, 1982); Stanislaw Mrozek, "Les bénéficiares des distributions privées d'argent et de nourriture dans les villes italiennes à l'époque du Haut-Empire," *Epigraphica* 34 (1972): 30–54; Jean Andreau, "Fondations privées et rapports sociaux en Italie romaine (Ier-IIIe s. ap. J.-C.)," *Ktema* 2 (1977): 157–209.

12. Robin Lane Fox, *Pagans and Christians* (New York: Knopf, 1986), 53.

13. See the comments of historian Elizabeth A. Clark: "Insofar as patronage was one of the few ways in antiquity for women to assume a public role, Christian women of means simply employed the existing social structures to advance their church's cause—and probably their own personal causes as well." E. Clark, "Early Christian Women: Sources and Interpretation," in *That Gentle Strength: Historical Perspectives on Women in Christianity*, ed. Lynda L. Coon, Katherine H. Haldane, and Elisabeth W. Sommer (Charlottesville: University Press of Virginia, 1990), 24.

14. Patrick Geary, "Sacred Commodities: The Circulation of Medieval Relics," in *The Social Life of Things: Commodities in Cultural Perspective*, ed. Arjun Appadurai (New York: Cambridge University Press, 1986), 169.

15. *Passio Sebastiani* 88 (BHL 7543) (*AA.SS*, Ian. II, p. 278).

16. As Kate Cooper points out in her excellent article, at stake behind these martyr stories is the question of where the relics of Peter and Paul lay: in the catacombs along the Via Appia where they had a shrine? Or in their shrines at the Vatican and the Via Ostiensis? The second locations are more closely affiliated with the church factions that later came to be the historical "winners" in Catholicism. Cooper points out that from the sixth century it was "papal policy to assert that the apostles were no longer on the Via Appia." See Kate Cooper, "The Martyr, the Matrona, and the Bishop: The Matron Lucina and the Politics of the Martyr Cult in Fifth- and Sixth-Century Rome," *Early Medieval Europe* 8 (1999): 311.

17. Marucchi, *Manual*, 153.

18. *Passio Processi et Martiniani* (BHL 6947); Marucchi, *Manual*, 148.

19. Cooper, "The Martyr, the Matrona, and the Bishop," 300.

20. "FALTONIAE HILARITATI/DOMINAE FILIAE CARISSIMAE/QUAE HOC COEMETERIUM/A SOLA SUA PECUNIA FECIT/ET HUHIC RELIGIONI DONAVIT." The stone is reproduced and transcribed in Vincenzo Fiocchi Nicolai, Fabrizio Bisconti, and Danilo Mazzoleni, eds., *The Christian Catacombs of Rome: History, Decoration, Inscriptions*, trans. Cristina Carlo Stella and Lori-Anne Touchette (Regensburg: Schnell & Steiner, 1999), 23 fig. 18.

21. Cooper, "The Martyr, the Matrona, and the Bishop," 308.

22. Eusebius, *HE* 2.25.7. On the *tropaion,* see John Curran, *Pagan City and Christian Capital: Rome in the Fourth Century* (Oxford: Oxford University Press, 2000), 108.

23. Margaret Miles, *Image as Insight: Visual Understanding in Western Christianity and Secular Culture* (Boston: Beacon, 1985), 11.

24. For works about or works that use the history of response, see David Freedberg, *The Power of Images: Studies in the History and Theory of Response* (Chicago: University of Chicago Press, 1989); John R. Clark, *Art in the Lives of Ordinary Romans: Visual Representation and Non-Elite Viewers in Italy, 100 BC—AD 315* (Berkeley: University of California Press, 2003); Jaś Elsner, *Art and the Roman Viewer: The Transformation of Art from the Pagan World to Christianity* (New York: Cambridge University Press, 1995).

25. On this, see most outstandingly Curran, *Pagan City;* and Jaś Elsner, "Inventing Christian Rome: The Role of Early Christian Art," in *Rome the Cosmopolis,* ed. Catherine Edwards and Greg Woolf (New York: Cambridge University Press, 2003).

26. The bibliography on fourth-century ascetic women is substantial. See, for instance, Joyce Salisbury, *Church Fathers, Independent Virgins* (London: Verso, 1991); Gillian Cloke, *This Female Man of God: Women and Spiritual Power in the Patristic Age, AD 350–450* (New York: Routledge, 1995); G. Clark, *Women in Late Antiquity: Pagan and Christian Lifestyles* (Oxford: Clarendon Press, 1993); Anne Ewing Hickey, *Women of the Roman Aristocracy as Christian Monastics* (Ann Arbor: UMI Research Press, 1987); M. R. Salzman, "Aristocratic Women: Conductors of Christianity in the Fourth Century," *Helios* 16, 2 (1987): 21–34; Hagith Sivan, "On Hymens and Holiness in Late Antiquity: Opposition to Aristocratic Female Asceticism at Rome," *JAC* 36 (1993): 81–93; Hagith Sivan, "Anician Women, the Cento of Proba, and Aristocratic Conversion in the Fourth Century," *VC* 47 (1993): 140–157; Anne Yarbrough, "Christianization in the Fourth Century: The Example of Roman Women," *Church History* 45 (1976): 149–164.

27. See, among these, Karen Jo Torjesen, *When Women Were Priests: Women's Leadership in the Early Church and the Scandal of Their Subordination in the Rise of Christianity* (San Francisco: Harper San Francisco, 1993); Elisabeth Schüssler Fiorenza, *In Memory of Her: A Feminist Theological Reconstruction of Christian Origins* (New York: Crossroads, 1994); Elisabeth Schüssler Fiorenza, "'You Are Not to Be Called Father': Early Christian History in a Feminist Perspective," *Cross Currents* 29 (1979): 301–23; Elaine Pagels, *The Gnostic Gospels* (New York: Random House, 1979), esp. chap. 3, "God the Father, God the Mother."

Chapter 1. Death Takes a Bride

1. Lanciani, *Pagan and Christian Rome*, 301.

2. Lanciani, *Notes from Rome*, ed. Anthony L. Cubberly (London: British School at Rome, 1988), frontispiece.

3. Interesting tensions with the Vatican are revealed in Lanciani's *Notes from Rome*, a collection of short monthly newsletters that he wrote for the *Athenaeum*, a British journal of the fine arts, between 1876 and 1913. See esp. no. 8: 22–27; and no. 23: 71–74. For a brief discussion of late-nineteenth-century tensions between church and state from the Catholic perspective, see W. H. C. Frend, *A History of Early Christian Archaeology* (Minneapolis: Fortress, 1996), 80–81.

4. Lanciani, *Pagan and Christian Rome*, 302.

5. For a full archaeological account of the find, see the monograph by A. Bedini, *Crepereia Tryphaena. Le scoperte archeologiche nell'area del Palazzo di Giustizia* (Venice: Marsilio, 1982).

6. For the social significance of freedman family groupings in funerary reliefs, see the comments and sources in B. D. Shaw, "The Cultural Meaning of Death: Age and Gender in the Roman Family," in *The Family in Italy from Antiquity to the Present*, ed. D. I. Kertzer and R. P. Saller (New Haven, Conn.: Yale University Press, 1991), 66–90.

7. Perseus, *Satire* 2.70; Varro, as cited in Nonius, *De compendiosa doctrina* 863.15L.

8. Andrew Oliver, "Jewelry for the Unmarried," in *I, Claudia II: Women on Ancient Rome*, ed. Diana Kleiner and Susan Matheson (New Haven, Conn.: Yale University Art Gallery, 2000), 115–124.

9. Lanciani, *Notes from Rome*, no. 29: 94.

10. The seminal article on the topic is A. D. Nock, "Cremation and Burial in the Roman Empire," *HTR* 25 (1932): 321–359.

11. Ibid., 323. As Nock makes clear, the Christianization of the empire was apparently not a significant factor in the shift from cremation to inhumation. Christians preferred burial, on the whole, because the practice was an ancient one used by the Jews of Palestine and well attested in the New Testament. On this, see Minucius Felix, *Octavius* 11.4ff, 34.10; see also Macrobius, *Saturnalia* 7.7.6. At any rate, it would be an overstatement to say that Christians always buried their dead; the catacombs contain the occasional cremated human remains in urns set into *loculi* burials, and sarcophagi may have contained ashes as well as bones.

12. Rodolfo Lanciani, *Ancient Rome in the Light of Recent Discoveries* (Boston: Houghton Mifflin, 1888), 64.

13. Ibid., 65.

14. See Richard Brilliant, *Visual Narratives: Storytelling in Etruscan and Roman Art* (Ithaca, N.Y.: Cornell University Press, 1984), 164; Paul Zanker and Björn Christian Ewald, *Mit Mythen leben: die Bilderwelt der römischen Sarkophage* (Munich: Hirmer, 2004); Paul Zanker, *Die mythologischen Sarkophagreliefs und ihre Betrachter* (Munich: Verlag der Bayerischen Akademie der Wissenschaften, in Kommission bei C. H. Beck, 2000); Michael Koortbojian, *Myth, Meaning, and Memory on Roman Sarcophagi* (Berkeley: University of California Press, 1995); Hellmut Sichtermann and Guntram Koch, *Griechische Mythen auf römischen Sarkophagen* (Tübingen: Wasmuth, 1975); and Guntram Koch, *Römische Sarkophage* (Munich: Beck, 1982).

15. For a discussion of the Penthesileia "type" and the repression of its narrative meaning, see Zanker and Ewald, *Mit Mythen leben*, 52–54; the example they discuss is cat. no. 3, 285–288, fig. 36 (photo, p. 286). The acquisition number for the sarcophagus is Musei Vaticani, Cortile del Belvedere Inv. 933.

16. "The mythology on the sarcophagi did not only fill space; it plunged viewers into an unprosaic, nonrealistic atmosphere. It matters little which myth is represented; the point is that the Romans fled death through myth. The beautiful imagery of mythology (so unlike the pathos in the portrait art of the same period) was a way of aestheticizing death, of avoiding melancholy." Paul Veyne, *A History of Private Life, Vol. 1: From Rome to Byzantium*, trans. Arthur Goldhammer (Cambridge, Mass.: Belknap, 1987), 233.

17. A. D. Nock, "Sarcophagi and Symbolism," in *Essays on Religion and the Ancient World*, ed. Zeph Stewart ,Vol 2 (Cambridge, Mass.: Harvard University Press, 1972), 615.

18. Lanciani, *Pagan and Christian Rome*, 302. On biographical sarcophagi, see N. Boymel Kampen, "Biographical Narration in Roman Funerary Art," *AJA* (1981): 47–58.

19. The minimum age for marriage under Roman law from the first century until 530 CE was set at twelve for girls and fourteen for boys (*CJ* 5.4.24 [530 CE]). There is evidence, however, that these laws were sometimes ignored. See M. K. Hopkins, "The Age of Roman Girls at Marriage," *Population Studies* 18 (1965): 313; Hopkins cites 12 of 145 pagan funerary inscriptions in which a girl's marriage took place between the ages of ten and twelve. On the other hand, see the response by Brent Shaw, "The Age of Roman Girls at Marriage: Some Reconsiderations," *JRS* 77 (1987): 30–46, which notes that the working poor population probably married later, and that the usual age of marriage for girls of less than noble status was somewhere between twenty and twenty-five.

20. For an outstanding account of women's bodies in Roman medical theory, see Aline Rousselle, *Porneia: On Desire and the Body in Antiquity*, trans. Felicia Pheasant (Oxford: Blackwell, 1993).

21. Veyne, *History of Private Life*, 34–35.

22. Walter Scheidel, "Roman Age Structure: Evidence and Models," *JRS* 91 (2001): 6.

23. Hopkins, "Age of Roman Girls," 264; for other studies (but similar numbers) see A. R. Burn, "*Hic breve vivitur:* A Study of the Expectation of Life in the Roman Empire," *Past and Present* 4 (1953): 1–31; Bruce W. Frier, "Roman Life Expectancy: Ulpian's Evidence." *Harvard Studies in Classical Philology* 86 (1982): 213–264; W. R. MacDonell, "On the Expectation of Life in Ancient Rome, and in the Provinces of Hispania and Lusitania, and Africa," *Biometrika* 9 (1913): 366–380; H. Nordberg, "Biometrical Notes" in *Acta Instituti Romani Finlandiae* 21:2 (1963): 1–76; Brent Shaw, "Seasons of Death: Aspects of Mortality in Imperial Rome," *JRS* 86 (1996): 100–138.

24. Some of these data are from my own research (2004). They essentially corroborate Shaw's findings in "Seasons," and Nordberg's in "Biometrical Notes." Nordberg claims that Christians set up more tombstones to children between the ages of ten and fifteen than did pagans, but he intimates that this may have had to do with cultural differences, not biometrical realities ("Biometrical Notes," 40). Note that these numbers do not reflect deaths of infants under the age of one, for which we have no solid data.

25. Scheidel, "Roman Age Structure," 8.

26. Nordberg, "Biometrical Notes," 58, gives July to October as the most fatal months of the year. Shaw, "Seasons of Death," 111–117, concurs. Scheidel ("Germs for Rome," in *Rome the Cosmopolis*, ed. C. Edwards and G. Woolf [New York: Cambridge University Press, 2003], 162) calculates that 38 percent of all deaths in Rome occurred from August to October, 1.8 times as often as usual.

27. Scheidel, "Roman Age Structure," 9.

28. See R. Sallares, *Malaria and Rome: A History of Malaria in Central Italy in Antiquity;* and Scheidel, "Germs for Rome," 163–164.

29. Malaria was still a problem in Lanciani's day. In *Notes from Rome*, no. 6 (p.18), he notes that the railroad workers laying down new lines in the city were given free rations of quinine and a decent burial in the case of their premature death from malaria.

30. Scheidel, "Germs for Rome," 17.

31. Scheidel, "Roman Age Structure," 9.

32. Ibid.; William McNeill, *Plagues and Peoples* (Oxford: Blackwell, 1977), 132.

33. "Measles," pamphlet from the Centers for Disease Control. Online at www.cdc.gov/nip/publications/pink/meas.pdf.

34. Figures for 2003 released by the Centers for Disease Control, Atlanta: "Deaths: Preliminary Data for 2003." News release, April 2003.

35. W. V. Harris, "Child-Exposure in the Roman Empire," *JRS* 84 (1994): 1–22; and J. E. Boswell, "*Expositio* and *oblatio:* The Abandonment of Children and the Ancient and Medieval Family," *AHR* 89 (1984): 10–33.

36. Scheidel, "Roman Age Structure," 10–11.

37. A. R. Hands, *Charities and Social Aid in Greece and Rome* (Ithaca, N.Y.: Cornell University Press, 1968), 113 ff.

38. Walter Scheidel, "Emperors, Aristocrats, and the Grim Reaper: Towards a Demographic Profile of the Roman Elite," *CQ*, n.s., 49, 1 (1999): 275 n. 64. For the epigram, see Martial *Epigrams* 10.63.

39. Nordberg, "Biometrical Notes," 40. Later demographic historians, starting with Keith Hopkins, have persuasively dismantled and dismissed the idea that average ages of death can be reliably calculated from epigraphic material; see M. K. Hopkins, "On the Probable Age Structure of the Roman Population," *Population Studies* 20 (1966): 245–264. Comparative evidence from the provinces indicates that Romans tended to record ages at death only if they were tragically low; thus Nordberg's "averages" tell us only the median age at death from among the selective, skewed samples given on epitaphs. They do not, therefore, accurately represent the average age of death within the Roman population. This figure cannot be calculated, only guessed at based on comparative data such as UN Life Tables. Nevertheless, scholarly reconstructions all point to a shorter female life expectancy and a general median age of death for inhabitants of Rome at somewhere around twenty-five years.

40. Gillian Clark, "Roman Women," *Greece and Rome*, n.s., 28, 2 (1981): 197. See also S. Dickison, "Abortion in Antiquity," in *Arethusa* 6 (1973): 159–166; E. Eyben, "Family Planning in Antiquity," *Ancient Society* 11–12 (1980–1981): 5–82; and K. Hopkins, "Contraception in the Roman Empire," *Comparative Studies in Society and History* 22 (1980): 303–354.

41. This view presents a corrective to the controversial claims of Rodney Stark, *The Rise of Christianity: A Sociologist Reconsiders History* (Princeton, N.J.: Princeton University Press, 1996), 95–128, esp.119–121. Some of this material is reproduced in his article, "Reconstructing the Rise of Christianity: The Role of Women," *Sociology of Religion* 56 (1995): 229–244.

42. Nordberg, "Biometrical Notes," 66. Furthermore, Nordberg observes that eight of these women were twenty or younger at the time of their deaths.

43. On Carmenta: Aulus Gellius, *Attic Nights*, 16.16.4. The list of the other deities is modified from Lanciani, *Ancient Rome*, 69. See the list of partum and postpartum deities from Varro through the pen of Augustine in Peter Garnsey, "Child Rearing in Ancient Italy," in *The Family in Italy from Antiquity to the Present*, ed. David Kertzer and Richard P. Saller (New Haven, Conn.: Yale University Press, 1991), 54; the list includes Vaticanus to preside over the infant's first cry, Opis to place her on the ground, and Levana to raise her up again. To Intercidona, Garnsey adds Pilumnus and Deversa; the three gods guard over the house of the newborn with ax, broom, and pestle. Cunina watches over the cradle, Rumina over breast-feeding, Potina and Educa over feeding and drinking, and so on. See, too, V. French, "Midwives and Maternity Care in the Roman World," *Helios* 13, 2 (1987): 69–84.

44. See Amy Richlin, "Carrying Water in a Sieve: Class and the Body in Roman Women's Religion," in *Women and Goddess Traditions*, ed. K. King (Philadelphia: Fortress, 1993), 352.

45. Garnsey, "Child Rearing in Ancient Italy," 54.

46. Scheidel, "Grim Reaper," 276; H. Lindsay, "A Fertile Marriage: Agrippina and the Chronology of Her Children by Germanicus," *Latomus* 54 (1995), 3–17.

47. Scheidel, "Grim Reaper," 277.

48. M. I. Finley, "The Silent Women of Rome," in *Sexuality and Gender in the Classical World: Readings and Sources*, ed. Laura K. McClure (Oxford: Blackwell, 2002), 153.

49. On Cicero's letters of consolation, see Amanda Wilcox, "Sympathetic Rivals: Consolation in Cicero's Letters," *American Journal of Philology* 126, 2 (2005): 237–255. Wilcox correctly points out the masculinist edge of reproach and rivalry in the Roman consolatory genre. See also Andrew Erskine, "Cicero and the Expression of Grief," in *The Passions in Roman Thought and Literature*, ed. Christopher Gill and S. M. Braund (Cambridge: Cambridge University Press, 1997), 36–47. For Roman notions of shame and honor, see C. A. Barton, *Roman Honor: The Fire in the Bones* (Berkeley: University of California Press, 2001).

50. The *tollere* or *suscipere* was the ritual moment at which the *paterfamilias* picked up the newborn infant laid at his feet by the midwife, if he chose to accept it and raise it as his. If he chose to let the child lie there, it would have to be killed or exposed.

51. Nordberg, "Biometrical Notes," 42.

52. Toynbee, *Death and Burial*, 43–61.

53. Lanciani, *Pagan and Christian Rome*, 295–301.

54. Ibid., 298.

55. S. C. Humphreys, *The Family, Women, and Death: Comparative Studies* (London: Routledge & Kegan Paul, 1983), 144.

56. Marucchi, *Manual*, 195.

57. *SEG* I.567, 16; and *Samm.* 6178, 3 (trans. Lattimore, 185).

58. *ILS* 8751 (trans. Fant/Lefkowitz, 257–258).

59. Humphreys, *Family, Women and Death*, 195.

Chapter 2. Proba and the Piglet

1. On the *porca praesentanea* sacrifice to Ceres, see the late Roman writer Sextus Pompeius Festus, *De Verborum significatione quae supersunt*, "*praesentanea porca,*" 250; and Barbette Stanley Spaeth, *The Roman Goddess Ceres* (Austin: University of Texas Press, 1996), 53–56.

2. On the necessary slaughter of a pig to consecrate a tomb, see Cicero, *de Legibus* 2.55–57. It is not mentioned in late Roman law (composed in a Christian Empire), but Justinian's *Digest* says that a tomb is not considered a *res religiosus* unless a body is interred within: *non totus qui sepulturae destinatus est locus religious fit, sed quatenus corpus humatum est* (11.7.2.5). It is not clear when the pig sacrifice died out as a requirement of interment as the empire became Christian.

3. On the ban on nocturnal sacrifices: *CTheod* 16.10.5 (353 CE).

4. Could women sacrifice in ancient Rome? More and more scholars are now pointing out the ritual opportunities for women. See, in particular, the evidence presented by Amy Richlin, "Carrying Water," 356–357. On the priestesses of Bona Dea, see Henk Versnel, "The Festival for Bona Dea and the Thesmophoria," *Greece and Rome* 39 (1992): 32, 43, and 48. More conservative is John Scheid, "The Religious Roles of Roman Women," in *A History of Women I: From Ancient Goddesses to Christian Saints*, ed. Pauline Schmitt Pantel, trans. A. Goldhammer (Cambridge, Mass.: Belknap, 1992), 377–408, esp. 378–381.

5. Festus, *de sig*, "*everriator,*" 77. On pagans as the "Romans of Rome," see Peter Brown, "Aspects of the Christianisation of the Roman Aristocracy," *JRS* 51 (1961): 4.

6. *Twelve Tables* 10.1; see E. H. Warmington, *Remains of Old Latin*, Vol. 3, LCL 1956.

7. On the switch from cremation to inhumation: Nock, "Cremation and Burial,"

321–359. More generally, see J. Toynbee, *Death and Burial in the Roman World* (Baltimore: Johns Hopkins University Press, 1971).

8. See F. De Visscher, *Le droit des tombeaux romains* (Milan: Giuffrè, 1963), 43–63, and R. Düll, "Studien zum römischen Sepulkralrecht," *Festschrift Fritz Schulz* (Weimar: Hermann Böhlaus, 1951), 194–199.

9. According to Jocelyn Toynbee, there actually were in the Roman Empire professional undertakers (*libitinarii*) and assistants (*pollinctores* and *vespilliones*). Cremations of the earlier period were carried out by *ustores*. There were also professional mourning women (*praeficae*) and the *dissignatores*, who delivered funerary orations and acted as masters of ceremonies at funerary events. See Toynbee, *Death and Burial*, 45. It's not clear how many of these positions continued in Christian Rome; evidence seems to indicate that the *fossores* and other church officials replaced these earlier, secular roles.

10. Guido Clemente, 'Il patronato nei collegia dell'impero romano," *Studi Classici e Orientali* 21 (1972): 142–229; Lelia Cracco Ruggini, "Stato e associazioni professionali nell'età imperiale romana," *Akten des VI. Internationalen Kongresses für Griechische und Lateinische Epigraphik, München 1972* (Munich: C. H. Beck, 1973), 298, esp. #101.

11. Reproduced in Marucchi, *Christian Epigraphy*, trans. J. Armine Willis (Chicago: Ares, 1974), 29.

12. Frank M. Ausbüttel, *Untersuchungen zu den Vereinen im Westen des Römischen Reiches* (Kallmünz: Lassleben, 1982), 82, 42; Mary Beard, John North, and Simon Price, eds., *Religions of Rome*, Vol. 1 (Cambridge: Cambridge University Press, 1998), 297.

13. Mark Johnson, "Pagan-Christian Burial Practices: Shared Tombs?" *JECS* 5, 1 (1997): 41.

14. See the evidence provided by Johnson, "Burial Practices," 40.

15. On mixed pagan-Christian burials, see Johnson, "Burial Practices," 37–59; L. Pani Ermini, "L'ipogeo detto dei Flavi in Domitilla," *RivArcC* 45 (1969): 119–173; P. Pergola, "La region dite des 'Flavi Aurelii' dans la catacombe de Domitille," *MEFRA* 95 (1983): 183–248; Umberto Fasola, "Un tardo cimitero cristiano inserito in una necropoli pagana della via Appia; L'area 'sub divo': La catacomba," *RivArcC* 60 (1984): 7–42.

16. See Jean Guyon, *Le cimetière aux deux lauriers: recherches sur les catacombes romaines* (Rome: Ècole française de Rome, 1987), 30–33.

17. See, on this, C. Carletti, "Pagani e cristiani nel sepolcro della 'Piazzola' sotto la Basilica Apostolorum a Roma," *Vetera Christianorum* 18 (1981): 287–307.

18. *ILCV* 3877: *D(is) m(anibus) Aurelius Niceta Aureliae Aelianeti filiae bene merenti fecit. Fossor, vide, ne fodias! Deus magnu oclu abet, vide, et tu filios abes.*

19. *ICUR* 8.21396: *male pereat, insepultus iaceat, non resurgat, cum Iuda partem habeat si quis sepulcrum hunc violaverit.* For others in a similar vein, see Carletti, *Iscriɀioni cristiane di Roma: testimonianɀe di vita cristiana (secoli III–VII)* (Firenze: Nardini, 1986), 127–131.

20. On the sale of tombs in fourth-century Rome, see J. Guyon, "La ventes des tombes à travers l'épigraphie de la Rome chrétienne (IIIe–VIIe siècles): Le rôle des *fossores, mansionarii, praepositi* et prêtres," *MEFRA* 86 (1974): 549–596.

21. The story was widely reported in various media outlets; see, for instance, Nick Pisa, "Bones in Togas Puzzle Vatican Archaeologists," *(Chicago) Telegraph,* May 21, 2006.

22. William Tronzo, *The Via Latina Catacomb: Imitation and Discontinuity in Fourth-Century Roman Painting* (University Park: Pennsylvania State University Press, 1986), 21, thinks the hypogeum of Via Latina was purely a "commercial venture," so that families buried in adjoining rooms did not necessarily have a relationship to one another.

23. Six million dead: see Shaw, "Seasons of Death," 101.

24. On this chamber as a "special order," see Beverly Berg, "Alcestis and Hercules in the Catacomb of Via Latina," *VC* 48, 3 (September 1994): 221.

25. For site plans, see Idoia Camiruaga, *La arquitectura del hipogeo de Via Latina en Roma* (Burgos: Colegio Oficial de Arquitectos de Castilla y León Este, Demarcación de Burgos, 1994) which replaces the older and more rectilinear one in A. Ferrua, *Le pitture della nuova catacomba di Via Latina* (Vatican City, 1960) and A. Ferrua, *Catacombe sconosciute: una pinacoteca del IV secolo sotto via Latina* (Firenze: Nardini, 1990), published in English as *The Unknown Catacomb. A Unique Discovery of Early Christian Art,* trans. Iain Inglis (New Lanark: Geddes & Grosset, 1991).

26. To avoid confusion with other hypogea that have been discovered on Via Latina, the hypogeum or catacomb of Via Latina is now officially known as the Catacombs of Via Dino Compagni. I use the old name here to avoid confusion for modern readers, since most of the scholarship done on this catacomb up to now has referred to it as "Via Latina," and the new name is both slow to catch on and clumsier.

27. I follow the chronology of Tronzo, *Via Latina Catacomb,* 10–17, which is later than that of Ferrua. Tronzo's work supports the claims of Marcel Simon, "Remarques sur la Catacombe de Via Latina," in *Mullus. Feschrift Theodor Klauser,*

ed. Alfred Stuidber and Alfred Hermann (Münster: Aschendorff, 1964), 327. The dating is supported by André Grabar, *The Beginnings of Christian Art 200–395*, trans. Stuart Gilbert and James Emmons (London: Thames & Hudson, 1967), 231.

28. The bibliography on Constantine is immense. Recent studies include Charles Odahl, *Constantine and the Christian Empire* (London: Routledge, 2004); Michael Grant, *Constantine the Great: The Man and His Times* (New York: Scribner, 1994); Timothy Barnes, *Constantine and Eusebius* (Cambridge, Mass.: Harvard University Press, 1981); and A. H. M. Jones, *Constantine and the Conversion of Europe* (Toronto: University of Toronto Press, 1978).

29. Antonio Ferrua, *Unknown Catacomb*, 42–43. The inscriptions are published in their entirety in *ICUR*, 6 (1975): 38–41.

30. Against the hypothesis that Christians and pagans were both buried in Via Latina, see F. P. Bargebuhr, *The Paintings of the New Catacomb of the Via Latina and the Struggle of Christianity against Paganism* (Heidelberg: C. Winter, 1991), esp. 69. Bargebuhr saw the entire catacomb as belonging to a syncretizing Christian "brotherhood." Others have agreed that the pagan images in the catacomb must be interpreted as "Christian" or "Christianizing," properly read as allegories and types of Christ. See here also Josef Fink, *Bildfrömmigkeit und Bekenntnis: das Alte Testament, Herakles und die Herrlichkeit Christi an der Via Latina in Rome* (Cologne: Böhlau, 1978), 29–34, 94–98. For a very different interpretation, see Josef Engemann, "Altes und Neues zum Beispielen heidnischer und christlicher Katakombenbilder im spatantiken Rom," *JAC* 26 (1983): 129–151.

31. Ferrua, *Unknown Catacomb*, 169 n. 10.

32. Michael Mauss, "Isis in the Via Latina Catacomb" (paper presented at the Third Annual Byzantine Studies Conference, New York City, December 1977).

33. Ferrua, *Unknown Catacomb*, 132 n. 6.

34. On an Etruscan urn ca. 600 BCE found at Falerii (outside Rome) that mentions Ceres, see Spaeth, *Goddess Ceres*, 1.

35. Richard Krautheimer, *Rome: Profile of a City, 312–1308* (Princeton, N.J.: Princeton University Press, 1980), 13–14.

36. Curiously, there appear to have been four burials in Cubiculum N, not two. The identity of the people buried in the two other graves is unknown. Berg, "Alcestis," 228, notes that the cubiculum appears to have been designed "for a second pair of occupants." Usually, double graves (*bisomi*) held married couples. So it appears that there were two sets of married couples in Cubiculum N, but the relationship between them isn't clear.

37. We must be careful to interpret the term "family" here as different from our notion of a "nuclear" family. Family vaults contained the bodies of a husband and wife, any children to die past the age of a few months, family slaves, and, occasionally, freedpeople associated with the family. Graves were not prepared in advance for the living children of a couple, since it was imagined that they would be buried with their own spouses later on. Family graves were thus restricted to one generation and their retainers, rarely carrying on to a second or, even more rarely, a third generation. On Roman family structure, see R. P. Saller, "Familia, Domus, and the Roman Conception of the Family," *Phoenix* 38 (1984): 336–355; Suzanne Dixon, "The Sentimental Ideal of the Roman Family," in *Marriage, Divorce, and Children in Ancient Rome*, ed. Beryl Rawson (Oxford: Clarendon, 1991), 99–113; K. R. Bradley, *Discovering the Roman Family: Studies in Roman Social History* (New York: Oxford University Press, 1991); Beryl Rawson, *The Family in Ancient Rome: New Perspectives* (Ithaca, N.Y.: Cornell University Press, 1986); D. I. Kertzer and R. P. Saller, eds., *The Family in Italy from Antiquity to the Present* (New Haven, Conn.: Yale University Press,1991).

   On family graves, see Keith Hopkins, "Death in Rome," in *Death and Renewal*. Sociological Studies in Roman History 2 (Cambridge: Cambridge University Press, 1983), 201–256. On Christian family structures as reflected in burials, see Brent Shaw, "Latin Funerary Epigraphy and Family Life in the Later Roman Empire," *Historia* 33 (1984): 457–497.

38. Spaeth, *Roman Goddess Ceres*. For Ceres as a protector of wives, see Henri Le Bonniec, *Le Culte de Cérès à Rome* (Paris: Klincksieck, 1958), 86–88.

39. William Tronzo has recently suggested that the Via Latina catacomb contains not the burials of Rome's top-drawer nobility, but rather upwardly mobile freedpeople or *liberti*. Indeed, freedpeople had by the fourth century a long history of ostentatious funerary monuments in Rome, many of which still stand, such as the Pyramid of Gaius Cestius outside the Porta Ostiensis or the monumental tomb of Eurysaces the baker outside the Porta Maggiore.

40. On the Roman "memory theater," see Bettina Bergman, "The Roman House as Memory Theater: The House of the Tragic Poet in Pompeii, " *Art Bulletin* 76, 2 (1994): 225–256; Marjorie Venit, *Monumental Tombs of Ancient Alexandria: The Theater of the Dead* (Cambridge: Cambridge University Press, 2002), esp. 37–67.

41. For images as a sort of text and visual narratives or storytelling in Roman art, see Rchard Brilliant, *Visual Narratives*, particularly 15–20 and 124–165.

42. See H. Gregory Snyder, "Pictures in Dialogue: A Viewer-Centered Approach to the Hypogeum on Via Dino Compagni," *JECS* 13, 3 (2005): 349–86.

43. On decorative elements in catacomb painting as stock-in-trade: Paul Corby Finney, *The Invisible God: The Earliest Christians on Art* (New York: Oxford University Press, 1994), 206.

44. *ILS* 1259–1261. Since they were not usually "authors," Roman women often become visible to us only through their commemoration at death. Note, however, the work of Michele Salzman, who analyzed the epitaphs of late Roman aristocrats and discovered that in her sample of sixty-two aristocratic women, only eleven were pagan ("Aristocratic Women," 21–34). Salzman observes: "The predominance of Christian women as compared to pagan women is probably due . . . to the fact that pagan women rarely put their names and vows on stone. This anepigraphic habit also accounts for the far smaller proportion of pagan women to pagan men as compared to the proportion of Christian women to Christian men that occurs in the sample" (211).

45. See, for instance, Anne Ewing Hickey, *Women of the Roman Aristocracy;* and Gillian Cloke, *Women in Late Antiquity.* For articles, see H. Drijvers, "Virginity and Asceticism in Late Roman Western Elites," in *Sexual Asymmetry,* ed. J. Blok and P. Mason (Amsterdam: Gieben, 1987), 241–273; E. Clark, "Ascetic Renunciation and Feminine Advancement: A Paradox of Late Antique Christianity," *ATR* 63 (1981): 240–257.

46. Brown, "Aspects of the Christianisation." Following and commenting on Brown's hypothesis, see Jan Bremmer, "Why Did Christianity Attract Upper-Class Women?" in *Fructus Centesimus: Mélanges offerts à Gérard J. M. Bartelink* (Dordrecht: Kluwer, 1989), ed. A. A. R. Bastiensen, A. Hilhorst, and C. H. Kneepkens, 37–47; and Anne Yarbrough, "Christianization," 149–165. A thoughtful and interesting challenge to Brown's hypothesis is posed by Salzman, "Aristocratic Women," 21–34, and *The Making of a Christian Aristocracy: Social and Religious Change in the Western Roman Empire* (Cambridge, Mass.: Harvard University Press, 2002), esp. 138–177.

47. Tronzo, *Via Latina Catacomb,* 69.

48. Ibid., 70.

49. See Tronzo, *Via Latina Catacomb;* and Elsner, *Art and the Roman Viewer,* 271–280.

50. For examples, see *LIMC* 4, 858 #122, 859 #138, 140, 143; 862 #140–141. M. Bieber, *Ancient Copies: Contributions to the History of Greek and Roman Art* (New York: New York University Press, 1977), 155, figs. 648–649, documents how these seated Ceres images become models for later Christian images of the seated Madonna.

51. M. Bieber, "The Copies of the Herculaneum Women," *Proceedings of the American Philological Society* 106 (1962): 111–134.

52. On the patristic literature that employs the grape as a symbol for Jesus, see Otto Nussbaum, "Die Grosse Traube, Christus," *JAC* 6 (1963): 136–143. But we must not make the mistake of seeing the grape as a purely Christian symbol. The cult of Ceres, Liber and Libera in Rome also regarded the grape as the attribute of Liber, a form of Bacchus, the Roman god of wine. It is also intriguing that the Greek myth of Demeter and Persephone (= Ceres and Libera/Proserpina in the Roman context) is a form of a much more ancient Near Eastern myth of Dumuzi and his sister Geshti-Nanna. Geshti-Nanna, like Proserpina, spends a portion of the year in the underworld. Her emblem is the grape. I thank my Women's Studies in Religion Program colleague Professor Tonia Sharlach for this observation.

53. Spaeth, *Goddess Ceres*, 37.

54. See the testimony of Valerius Maximus, *Memorable Deeds and Sayings* 1.1.1, and see Richlin, "Carrying Water," 336. For an enumeration of Ceres priestesses around Italy based on the inscriptional evidence, see Richlin's Appendix A in Richlin, "Carrying Water," 368–374.

55. Richlin, "Carrying Water," 350.

56. See Fabrizio Mancinelli, *Catacombs and Basilicas: The Early Christians in Rome* (Florence: Scala, 1981), 30 fig. 57.

57. For the inscriptions, see *CIL* 6.1151, 31856. Spaeth, *Goddess Ceres*, disagrees; she locates the main temple of Ceres on the Aventine, not the Forum Boarium.

58. Spaeth, *Goddess Ceres*, 29.

59. Susan Wood, "Mortals, Empresses, and Earth Goddesses: Demeter and Persephone in Public and Private Apotheosis" in *I, Claudia II*, ed. Diana Kleiner and Susan Matheson, 88, fig. 5.1, from the Capitoline Museums, inv. 249.

60. On Proba's choices of imagery for Cubiculum N, see Berg, "Alcestis."

61. Spaeth, *Goddess Ceres*, 52.

62. Ibid., 51–79.

63. Festus, *de sig.*, "*mundus,*" 54.

64. Spaeth, *Goddess Ceres*, 65.

65. Walter Burkert, *Greek Religions* (Cambridge, Mass.: Harvard University Press, 1987), 11.

66. The worship of Ceres, like the worship of many other Roman deities, was not centralized into one official cult, but took many forms across the empire—even

in Rome. The cult of Ceres and Proserpina, which allowed only women to join, was different from the cult of Ceres-Liber-Libera, which had a male priest and both male and female adherents, or the cult of Eleusinian Ceres, into which men and women could be initiated. See Spaeth, *Goddess Ceres*, 103–113.

67. *CIL* 6.1779, 1780.

68. *ILS 1259*, 11.2–7. Praetextatus's wife, Aconia Fabia Paulina, had also been initiated into the mysteries (*ILS* 1260; *ILS* 1259).

69. For the theme of "Rape-Elopement" on Roman sarcophagi, see J. Bayet, "Hercule funéraire," *MEFRA* 39 (1921–22): 228ff; and Wood, "Empresses and Earth Goddesses," 77–99.

70. See, for instance, Berg, "Alcestis," 219.

71. An image of Persephone would have been haloed or crowned, in the manner of Ceres. One would also expect Persephone to be substantially younger than the woman portrayed here, who looks to be a matron in her thirties or forties. And her pose in white garments and pearl necklace holding two wheat sheaves does not accord with other Persephone images of the empire. Finally, compare this image with the two other images of young women in Cubiculum O—the Persephone on the ceiling holding the grapes and *thyrsus,* and the haloed girl on the top of the *arcosolium* vault arch, whom I take to be an image of the deceased in the guise of Persephone.

72. Festus, *de sig.*, "*facem*," 87.

73. It is interesting to speculate whether the image conventionally identified as the feeding of the five thousand in Cubiculum O is really the miracle at Cana, which is iconographically very similar. If so, the symbolic associations are of wine (see the grapes of Proserpina directly above this image), water, and the marriage feast—a set of symbols represented elsewhere in the room.

74. Festus, *de sig.*, "*facem*," 87.

75. Kleiner and Matheson, *I, Claudia II,* 9, 12.

76. Wood, "Empresses and Earth Goddesses," 77–99.

77. Noelle Oxenhandler, "Polly's Face," *The New Yorker,* November 29, 1993, 95–96.

78. Spaeth, *Goddess Ceres,* 108.

79. Clifford Ando, "From the Palladium to the Pentateuch," *Phoenix* 55, 3–4 (2001): 383.

80. Ando, "Palladium," 383.

81. Wood, "Empresses and Earth Goddesses," 92–93.

Chapter 3. Waiting in the Afterlife

1. See the outstanding survey of Beard, North, and Price, *Religions of Rome*. Franz Cumont, *Afterlife in Roman Paganism* (Piscataway, N.J.: First Gorgias, 2002) overstates the evidence, as does his tremendously learned *Recherches sur le symbolisme funéraire des Romains* (Paris: P. Geuthner, 1942).

2. T. H. C. Van Eijk, "Marriage and Virginity, Death and Immortality," in *Epektasis; mélanges patristiques offerts au cardinal Jean Danielou*, ed. C. Kannegiesser (Paris: Beauchesne, 1972), 209–211, on Christian transformations of pagan ideas of procreation as immortality.

3. For photographs, see Ferrua, *The Unknown Catacomb*; and Tronzo, *The Via Latina Catacomb*. Far weaker on analysis, but with useful photographs, is Bargebuhr, *Paintings of the New Catacomb* (1991). Carlo Pavia, *Guida delle catacombe romane: dai "tituli" all'ipogeo di via Dino Compagni* (Rome: Gangemi, 2000) has beautiful color photographs of the catacomb toward the end of its (unpaginated) text. Camiruaga, *La arquitectura del hipogeo de Via Latina*, gives a recent site plan. The landmark article on "Proba" and Alcestis remains Berg, "Alcestis." For a study of the catacomb, see also Walter Schumacher, "Die Katakombe an der Via Dino Compagni und Römische Grabkammern," *RivArcC* 50 (1974): 331–372.

4. Berg, "Alcestis," 220, 222. Most commentators before Berg assumed that the choice of images was actually Proba's husband's, not Proba's. See, for instance, the musings of E. R. Goodenough: "Ferrua's suggestion that some widower planned all this only to commemorate his wife's beautiful character seems to me to recall early nineteenth-century romanticism rather than late Roman days" ("Catacomb Art," *JBL* 81 [1962]: 126). But he goes on to say, "Whoever did this was a rich man, for only two burials (without inscriptions) were made in the whole room." Though a male commissioner is certainly possible (as Ferrua and Goodenough assume), the precise nature of the iconography points to the wife as the master exegetical hand, as Berg so effectively demonstrated.

5. Berg, "Alcestis," 222: "The patron here commemorates her own loyalty during her husband's illness—she too would have sacrificed life itself to save him."

6. See the evidence collected in Peter Blome, "Zur Umgestaltung griechischer Mythen in der römischen Sepulkralkunst. Alkestis-, Protesilaos-, und Proserpinasarkophage," *Mitteilungen des deutschen archäologischen Instituts, Römische Abteilung* 35 (1978): 435–457; and Susan Wood, "Alcestis on Roman Sarcophagi," *AJA* 82 (1978): 499–510.

For Roman funerary paintings of Alcestis, see Bernard Andreae, *Studien zur römischen Grabkunst*, Mitteilungen des DAI (R), Erganzungsheft 9 (Heidelberg, Germany: Kerle, 1963): 35–37.

7. The sarcophagus is now on display at the Museo Chiaramonti of the Vatican Museums, inv. 1195. It was discovered in Ostia, a port city very close to Rome, in 1826. For reproductions, see W. Amelung, *Die Skulpturen des Vaticanischen Museums* (Berlin: In Kommission bei G. Reimer, 1903), 1.429–430, #179; Robert, *Die Antike Sarkophagreliefs im Auftrager des Kaiserlich deutschen archaeologischen Instituts* (Berlin: Grote, 1897), 5.3 31–33, #26; H. Sichtermann and G. Koch, *Griechische Mythen auf Römische Sarkophagen* (Tübingen: Wasmuth, 1976), 20–21, #8, pl. 16, 17, 18, 19.

8. Interestingly, Metilia Acte apparently outranked her husband—at least as far as duties toward the gods. Her freedman husband was part of the guild of carpenters at Ostia, but she was a priestess of the goddess Magna Mater, whose cult had reached Rome in the second century from the East. For the funerary inscription, see *CIL* 14.371: *D. M. C.IVNIVS.PAL.EVHODVS.MAGISTER.QQ. COLLEGI.FABR.TIGN.OSTIS.LUSTRI.XXI.FECIT.SIBI.ET.METILIAE. ACTE.SACERDOTI.M.D.M.COLON.OST.COIVG.SANCTISSIM.* "To the sacred spirits of the dead. C. Julius Euhodius of the Palatine tribe, a five-year magistrate of the twenty-first lustrum of the guild of carpenters at Ostia, made this for himself and his wife Metilia Acte, a priestess of the Great Mother of the gods at the colony of Ostia, a most holy woman" (trans. mine).

9. Wood, "Alcestis on Roman Sarcophagi," 500, 506.

10. Diana E. E. Kleiner, "Now You See Them, Now You Don't: The Presence and Absence of Women in Roman Art," in *From Caligula to Constantine: Tyranny and Transformation in Roman Portraiture*, ed. E. Varner (Atlanta: Michael C. Carlos Museum, 2000), 45: "Women are just as adept at twisting the truth and crafting flattering narratives that present a personalized view of reality. Roman women, like Roman men, were myth makers and what makes their behavior so fascinating is how comparable it is to our own."

11. Wood, "Alcestis on Roman Sarcophagi," 503.

12. Antonio Ferrua, "La catacomba di Vibia," *RivArcC* 47 (1971): 7–62 and *RivArcC* 49 (1973): 131–161. Such imagery was common; art historian Diana Kleiner also discusses a funerary altar of Q. Gavius Musicus erected by his wife, Volumnia Ianuaria. The front of the altar bears an image of the married couple. On the side, the couple's slaves are depicted in a funeral procession "led by Proserpina who, as goddess of the underworld, welcomes the deceased to her abode" (Kleiner [1992], 195). For more examples, see D. Boschung, *Antike Grabaltäre aus den Nekropolen Roms* (Bern: Stämpfli, 1987).

13. Blome, "Griechischer Mythen," 435–457.

14. Festus, quoted by Richlin, "Carrying Water," 347.

15. Eva Cantarella, *Pandora's Daughters: The Role and Status of Women in Greek and Roman Antiquity*, trans. Maureen B. Fant, with a foreword by Mary R. Lefkowitz (Baltimore: Johns Hopkins University Press, 1987), 137.

16. See Susan Treggiari, "Divorce Roman Style: How Easy and How Frequent Was It?" in *Marriage, Divorce, and Children in Ancient Rome*, ed. B. Rawson (Oxford: Clarendon, 1996), 31–46.

17. Veyne, *History of Private Life*, 34.

18. Plutarch, *Rom.* 22.3; see also Sarah Pomeroy, "The Relationship of the Married Woman to Her Blood Relations in Rome," *Ancient Society* 7 (1976): 215.

19. See Dixon, "The Sentimental Ideal," 102–111; Veyne, "History of Private Life," 36–45.

20. A fourth cardinal virtue was virtue (*virtus*) itself. But the word *virtus* is a complicated one, changing over the course of the second to the fourth centuries from a word for male power (*vir* = man) to female chastity. On second-century sarcophagi, *virtus* was illustrated with a scene from a hunt or a battle, featuring a heroic male hunter or soldier. See Glenys Davies, "The Significance of the Handshake Motif in Classical Funerary Art," *AJA* 89 (1985): 638.

21. See Veyne, *History of Private Life*, 41, 165.

22. Peter Brown, "Late Antiquity," in *A History of Private Life, Vol. 1: From Rome to Byzantium*, ed. Paul Veyne, trans. Arthur Goldhammer (Cambridge, Mass.: Belknap, 1987), 248.

23. Shaw, "Cultural Meaning," 86.

24. Amy Richlin, "Rituals of the Body: Roman Women's Religion," unpublished paper cited in Ross Kraemer, *Her Share of the Blessings* (New York: Oxford University Press, 1992), 51.

25. See the evidence collected in Cantarella, *Pandora's Daughters*, 152.

26. *ICUR* 10.27046: *Cecilius maritus Ceciliae Placidinae coiugi optime memoriae, cum qua vixi annis X bene sene ulla querella*, from the Christian Catacombs of Bassilla.

27. See the listings in Lattimore, *Epitaphs*, 279, and his n. 107.

28. *L'Année Epigraphique* (1901), 140: "D M S CLODIAE SECVNDAE CONIVGI DVLCISSIMAE ET BENE MERENTI QVAE VIXIT AN XXV MEN X DIEB XIIII IN CONIVGIO MECVM FVIT SINE QVERELLA AN VII M IIII DIEB XVIII L CAELIVS FLORENTINVS (CENTVRIO) COH(OR-TIS) X VRB(ANAE) POSVIT
NAT(A) MAMERTINO ET RVFO COS PRI NON AVG DEF XV KAL IVL APRO ET MAXIMO COSS."

29. *CIL* 6.7581 = *ILS* 7804 (trans. Fant in Fant/Lefkowitz [1982], 161).

30. *ILCV* 2.161: *d. m. Flabiae Sperandae coiugi sanctissimae inconparabili, matri omnium, quae bixit mecu annis n. XXVIII, m. VIII sene ulla bilae. Onesiforus c. f. coiux benemerenti fecit,* from the Catacombs of Domitilla. The *c.f.,* which I have translated here only as "noble," is a status marker that indicates that Flavia Speranda was (unlike her husband) of senatorial class.

31. *ILCV* 1.279 = *CIL* 6.31950: *Aurelio Agapito Dracontio eq. R., coniugi dulcissimo adque inconparabili, qui uixit mecu annis XXX sine illa quaerella, Aurelia Amazonius fecint quiescienti in pace,* from the Christian Catacombs of Priscilla. Here, Aurelia Amazonius appears to be a freedwoman, though her husband outranks her as noble. The *eq. R* indicates that he holds equestrian status—below senatorial class, but still highly prestigious (and relatively unattested in Roman Christian circles).

32. Kleiner and Matheson, *I, Claudia II,* 13.

33. R. Syme, *Roman Papers,* Vol. 4, ed. A. R. Birley (London: Oxford University Press, 1991), 241.

34. See Ramsay MacMullen, "Women in Public in the Roman Empire," in *Changes in the Roman Empire: Essays in the Ordinary,* ed. R. MacMullen (Princeton, N.J.: Princeton University Press, 1990), 162–168. See also Gillian Clark, *Women in Late Antiquity,* 193–212; and R. A. Kearsley, "Women in Public Life," in S. R. Llewelyn, *New Documents Illustrating Early Christianity* 6 (1992): 24–27.

35. This has been borne out by my own research and statistical analysis of funerary epigraphy in the late empire. See the brief comment by Kraemer, *Her Share of the Blessings,* 168, but also the more detailed studies of Hopkins, "Age of Roman Girls," and Brent Shaw, "Reconsiderations," esp. 30–46.

36. See Shaw, "Latin Funerary Epigraphy," 457–497; Saller, "Familia, Domus," 336–355; Dale B. Martin, "The Construction of the Ancient Family: Some Methodological Considerations," *JRS* 86 (1996): 40–60. In my study of commemorative patterns at the Catacombs of Bassilla in Rome, 30 percent of epitaphs were from husbands to wives, 10 percent from wives to husbands, and less than 1.5 percent from children to their mothers.

37. Saller, "Familia, Domus," 336–355; Dixon, "The Sentimental Ideal"; Finley, "Silent Women," 149.

38. *ILCV* 2.4270: *Primitibus Ianuare, coiurgi suae bene[me]renti, que mecu uixit bene annis XX, diebus I, ora prima.*

39. *ICUR* 10.27168: *Silvana Niciati marito benemerenti cum quo vixit annis tribus mesibus duobus oris undecem* and *ILCV* 2.4266 = *CIL* 6. 19646: *Ianuaria Felici, marito*

dulcissimo benemerenti, feci qui mecu uixit ann. XGII, men X, dies XVI, or. GII,
from the Catacombs of Callistus.

40. On Roman marriages, see Susan Treggiari, "*Digna condicio:* Betrothals in the
Roman Upper Class," *Échoes du monde classique/Classical Views*, n.s., 3 (1984):
419–451; and S. Treggiari, *Roman Marriage: Iusti Coniuges from the Time of Cicero to the Time of Ulpian* (New York: Oxford University Press, 1991).

41. *CIL* 6.18817.

42. Hopkins, "Roman Death," 220.

43. *ICUR* 10.27164: ELIA.EBANTIA.FACET.SIPTIMIO / FAVSTINO.COIVCI.
MEO.QV.IFE / CIT.MECV.MIESES.GIII.INILLVSME / SESNOBE.IRINTA.
DIIBVS.SANVS AV / I.ANORV.XXXGI.MESORV.NOBE.DVL / CISANIMA.
FAVSTENE.CONIVGALIS/QVALIS.NEINBENTVR.FAMA.TSQVE.

44. *CIL* 6.15546, translated by Hopkins in "Roman Death," 221. For other examples
of marital anguish and loss, see Lattimore, *Epitaphs*, 275ff.

45. See the comments of Lattimore, *Epitaphs*, 280: "At least we can conclude that
they outline an ideal, and that this ideal concedes considerable importance to the
position of women to the household. They are thought of not as subservient,
but as free partners, and the success of the family is thought of as dependent in
large measure on these qualities."

46. Nordberg, "Biometrical Notes"; Lattimore, *Epitaphs*, 278.

47. See Dixon, "The Sentimental Ideal," 109.

48. Shaw, "Cultural Meaning," 66.

49. Finley, "Silent Women," 148.

50. Ibid., 149.

51. A point made by Davies, "Handshake," 637.

52. Berg, "Alcestis," 222–223, 231; Ferrua, *Unknown Catacomb*, 119.

53. See, for instance, the comments of D. L. L. Kleiner, "A Portrait Relief of
D. Apuleius Carpus and Apuleia Rufina in the Villa Wolkonsky," *Archeologia
classica* 30 (1978), 246–251. For Minerva and Heracles in the *dextrarum iunctio* in
late ancient art, see Janet Huskinson, "Some Pagan Mythological Figures and
Their Significance in Early Christian Art," *Papers of the British School at Rome*
42 (1974): 68–97. For the pose in Christian sources, see Antonio Quacquarelli,
"Le nozze eterne nella concezione e nell'iconografia cristiana antica," *Vetera
Christianorum* 22 (1985): 5–34.

54. We find Minerva and Hercules in an identical pose in a piece of fourth-century
"gold-glass" from the Catacombs of S. Castolo; it was created as a wedding gift.

See Oliviero Iozzi, *Vetri cimiteriali con figure in oro conservati nel Museo Sacro Vaticano* (Rome, 1902), Tav. II. Iozzi claims that Minerva and Hercules are meant to represent here the spouses (11).

55. For this sort of minimalist interpretation, including examples from Roman sarcophagi where a handshake is merely a handshake and not the symbol of a marriage vow, see Davies, "Handshake," 627–640. For Heracles on funerary monuments, see Bayet, "Hercule funéraire." Diana E. E. Kleiner, *Roman Sculpture* (New Haven, Conn.: Yale University Press, 1992), 349, notes that Hercules is particularly popular in funerary art of freedpeople from the third century onward.

56. Wood, "Alcestis on Roman Sarcophagi," 504: "Such a reference would have been highly effective in stressing Alcestis's and Admetus's roles as devoted wife and husband, while expressing the joy of their reunion by analogy with the happiness of their original wedding." See too, Kleiner on the second-century Velletri Sarcophagus, which held the remains of seven adults and two children. It probably features a scene of Alcestis, but it might be the myth of Protesilaus, hero of the Trojan War who was mourned by his wife Laodamia so bitterly that the gods returned him to her for three hours. But, as Kleiner notes, the precise identification of the myth is less important than the values both convey: "Both stories emphasize earthly death and heavenly reunion. In other words, a married couple parted by death will be reunited in the afterlife" (*Roman Sculpture*, 259).

57. Brilliant, *Visual Narratives*, 133.

58. Karl Galinsky, *The Herakles Theme: The Adaptations of the Hero in Literature from Homer to the Twentieth Century* (Totowa, N.J.: Rowman & Littlefield, 1972), 81.

59. Carlin Barton, *The Sorrows of the Ancient Romans: The Gladiator and the Monster* (Princeton, N.J.: Princeton University Press, 1993), 136 n. 146.

60. Ruth Webb, "Salome's Sisters: the Rhetorics and Realities of Dance in Late Antiquity," *in Men, Women and Eunuchs: Gender in Byzantium*, ed. L. James (London: Routledge, 1997), 140.

61. Snyder, "Pictures in Dialogue," 379.

62. It is also known as the Cubiculum of the Velatio, the "Cubiculum of the Veiling." I have chosen "Velata" here since it acknowledges the centrality of the central fresco's dominant figure—a woman—rather than the "Velatio" action that some believe is being depicted.

63. So James Stevenson, *The Catacombs. Rediscovered Monuments of Early Christianity* (London: Thames & Hudson, 1978), 88. Stevenson does think that the other two images are portraits of the deceased, although he doesn't explain what the

Virgin might be doing there, except to say that Ambrose uses Mary as the type of the virgin's state and an example for all (Ambrose, *Concerning Virginity* 2.2).

64. Marucchi, *Manual,* 322. He thinks the left-hand scene is the veiling of a virgin, and the Virgin is there "as her model." He continues, "The painting has been interpreted as a reproduction of a scene of real life, but this is inacceptable [*sic*]. The option above [that the image on the left is the Virgin] is more natural and logical."

65. See, for instance, Marucchi, *Manual,* 179: "In [this chamber], a scene depicting the consecration of a virgin is found, showing a bishop seated on a chair typical of the iconographic tradition of St. Peter."

66. O. Mitius, *Ein Familienbild aus der Priscillenkatakombe mit der ältesten Hochzeitsdarstellung der christlichen Kunst* (Freiburg, 1895).

67. Claude Dagens, "A propos du cubiculum de la 'Velatio,'" *RivArcC* 47 (1971): 119–129.

68. Mancinelli, *Catacombs and Basilicas,* 29. See, too, K. M. Irwin, "Archaeology Does Not Support Women's Ordination: A Response to Dorothy Irvin," *Journal of Women and Religion* 3, 2 (1984): 35.

69. See, for instance, the witness of Tertullian, *De virginibus velandis,* 100.11, and Gregory of Nazianzen, *Epistle* 57.

70. Sandro Carietti, *Guide to the Catacombs of Priscilla,* trans. Alice Mulhern (Vatican City Pontifical Commission for Sacred Archaeology, 1982), 17. He dates the lunette painting early, to the second half of the third century (thus contemporary with Tryphaena).

71. Margot G. Houts, "The Visual Evidence of Women in Early Christian Leadership," *Perspectives* 14, 3 (March 1999): 14–18; C. Vogt, "The Role of the Liturgical Celebrant in the Formation of the Marriage Bond," in *Marriage Studies: Reflections in Canon Law and Theology,* ed. T. Doyle (Washington, D.C.: Catholic University of America Press, 1982), 2.73.

72. Clement of Alexandria, *Paedagogus* 3.11.63 (GCS 12.271); see also J. Crehan, "Marriage," in *A Catholic Dictionary of Theology,* Vol. 3 (London: Thomas Nelson, 1971), 244.

73. Carietti, *Guide to Priscilla,* 17–18.

74. Augustine, *Sermo* 37.6. See, too, Treggiari, *Roman Marriage,* 165.

75. Dixon, "The Sentimental Ideal," 65.

76. *ICUR* 10.27053: "SEM EVNOMIVS COCCIAE RVFINAE COIVGI B M CVM QVA BIXI PM ANN XXI; INCOMPARABILI; CVIVS TANTA ANIMOSITAS (FVIT) TRAHENDO, AD VTILITATEM COMMUNEM,

IVGVM QVOD DECEBAT FEMINAM; IN QVOD TANTA PRECE AB OLIM EXORATVS SVM VNVM EX VTERO EIVS SIMILEMQVE TENERE MIHI. VALE IN PACE."

77. For the finest evidence and studies, see Diana Kleiner, *Roman Group Portraiture: The Funerary Reliefs of the Late Republic and Early Empire* (New York: Garland, 1977); and Diana Kleiner, *Roman Imperial Funerary Altars with Portraits* (Rome: G. Bretschneider, 1987).

78. Philip Rousseau, *The Early Christian Centuries* (London: Longman, 2002), 96–97.

79. Ibid.

80. See Pierre Du Bourguet, *Early Christian Painting*, trans. Simon Watson Taylor (New York: Viking Press, 1965), 76; André Grabar, *Christian Iconography: A Study of Its Origins*, trans. Terry Grabar (Princeton, N.J.: Princeton University Press, 1968), 188.

81. Janet Huskinson, "Gender and Identity in Scenes of Intellectual Life on Late Roman Sarcophagi," in *Constructing Identities in Late Antiquity*, ed. Richard Miles (London: Routledge, 1999), 208–209.

82. Ibid., 209.

83. Ibid., 203.

84. Berg, "Alcestis," 220.

Chapter 4. Praying with Prisca

1. The dating of the Greek Chapel has been hugely controversial—in part because of the Catholic Church's desire to locate ritual practices such as the Eucharist to a time as close as possible to the Apostolic Age. Catholic scholars, therefore, have consistently dated the chapel earlier—sometimes, centuries earlier—than others. For the (Catholic) dating, see L. De Bruyn, "La cappella greca di Priscilla," *RivArcC* 46 (1970): 291–330.

2. Lanciani, *Pagan and Christian Rome*, 8.

3. J. Wilpert, *La fede della chiesa nascente* (Vatican City: Pontificio Istituto di Archeologia Cristiana, 1938), 97–99.

4. James A. Francis, "Verbal and Visual Representation: Art and Text, Culture and Power," forthcoming in *Blackwell's Companion to Late Antiquity*, ed. Philip Rousseau (Oxford: Blackwell, 2007).

5. The award-winning study was undertaken by Daniel Simons and Christopher Chabris of the University of Illinois at Urbana-Champaign. You can watch the

video clip used for the experiments through a variety of Internet sites, including the University of Illinois site at http://viscog.beckman.uiuc.edu/media/ig.html.

6. Torjesen, *When Women Were Priests,* 52.

7. See Houts, "Visual Evidence," 7; Dorothy Irvin, "The Ministry of Women in the Early Church: The Archaeological Evidence," *Duke Divinity School Review* 45 (1980): 83.

8. Joan Morris, *The Lady Was a Bishop: The Hidden History of Women with Clerical Ordination and Jurisdiction* (New York: MacMillan, 1973).

9. Thomas F. Torrance, *The Ministry of Women* (Edinburgh: Handsel, 1992), republished as an article in *Touchstone* 5, 4 (1992): 5–12.

10. Irvin, "The Ministry of Women."

11. Irwin, "Archaeology."

12. Patrick Henry Reardon, "Women Priests: History and Theology," *Touchstone* 6, 1 (1993): 24.

13. Janet H. Tulloch, "Art and Archaeology as an Historical Resource for the Study of Women in Early Christianity: An Approach for Analyzing Visual Data (from Late Antiquity)," *Journal of Feminist Theology* 12, 3 (2004): 277–305; and Janet H. Tulloch, Women Leaders in Family Funerary Banquets," in Carolyn Osiek and Margaret Y. MacDonald, *A Woman's Place: House Churches in Earliest Christianity* (Minneapolis: Fortress, 2006), 164–193. See also Dennis Smith, *From Symposium to Eucharist: The Banquet in the Early Christian World* (Minneapolis: Fortress, 2003).

14. Vatican specialist Fabrizio Bisconti calls the scene "probably only funerary in nature" ("Decorations," in *The Christian Catacombs of Rome: History, Decoration, Inscriptions,* ed. Vincenzo Fiocchi Nicolai, Fabrizio Bisconti, and Danilo Mazzoleni [Regensburg: Schnell & Steiner, 1999], 126). He concurs with the much earlier conclusions of H. Matthaei, *Totenmahldarstellungen in der altchristlichen Kunst* (Magdeburg, 1899), 3–22, 43.

15. *Apostolic Constitutions* 8.42. See Paul-Albert Février, "La mort chrétienne," in *Segni e riti nella chiesa altomedievale occidentale, 11–17 aprile 1985,* Settimane di studio del centro italiano di studie: sull'alto medievo 33 (Spoleto: Presso la sede del centro, 1987), 929.

16. The best evidence is from Rome's nearby port town, Ostia, which preserves a fine necropolis and many outdoor dining spaces. For the most recent work, see C. Pavolini, *Ostia* (Bari: Lateria, 1983). The classic study is Guido Calza, *Necropoli del Porto di Roma nell'Isola Sacra* (Rome: La libreria dello stato, 1940).

17. Peter Duckers, "Agape und Irene: Die Frauengestalten der Sigmamahlszenen mit antiken Inschriften in der Katakombe der Heiligen Marcellinus und Petrus," *JAC* 35 (1992): 147–167.

18. See, for instance, *CIL* 6.3413: *ne quis hic urina(m) faciet,* as cited by Snyder, "Pictures in Dialogue," 359.

19. Josef Wilpert, *Fractio Panis: Die alteste der eucharistischen opfers in den 'Capella greca'* (Freiburg im Breisgau: Herder, 1895), 5.

20. This is the interpretation of Robert Milburn, *Early Christian Art and Architecture* (Berkeley: University of California Press, 1988), 25, and Grabar, *Christian Iconography,* 98–99. Agreeing with Milburn and Grabar are, for instance, Michael Gough, *The Origins of Christian Art* (New York: Praeger, 1973), 46; and Brent Shaw, "Women in the Early Church," *History Today* (February 1994): 28. For the official line of the Pontifical Commission for Sacred Archaeology, see, for instance, Marucchi, *Manual,* 291–292: "The fresco . . . represents the liturgical act of the breaking of bread. At the left can be seen the priest or bishop who divides the bread; in front of him stands a chalice. Six other persons, including a feminine figure, are seated around the table." Marucchi goes on to suspect that this is a symbolic scene because of the baskets of bread but also because "the priest has raised his feet to the height of the table, a thing certainly inadmissible in reality" (292).

21. Milburn, *Early Christian Art,* 24.

22. Bisconti, "Decoration," 110–113. Robin A. Jensen, "Dining in Heaven: The Earliest Christian Visions of Paradise," *Bible Review* 14 (1998): 32–39, 48–49.

23. Bisconti, "Decoration," 110.

24. Ibid., 126.

25. Jensen, "Dining," 48–49. Robert Milburn, similarly, sees the scene as more "representative" or idealized than actual: "It would be unwarranted to maintain that this scene literally and directly portrays the Christian liturgy, but its eucharistic overtones would remind the faithful that the sacraments are appointed means to bring about divine assistance" (*Early Christian Art,* 36). The conclusion that the Cappella Graeca banquet commemorates a celestial *convivium* is already in place in the work of M. F. J. Liell, *"Fractio Panis" oder "Cena coelestis,"* eine Kritik des Werkes "Fractio Panis" von Wilpert (Trier, 1903).

26. Jensen, "Dining," 35.

27. For more observations on their "upswept" hair, see part 1 of Houts's "Visual Evidence," 9; and Morris, *The Lady Was a Bishop,* 8, who claims from her close-up investigation that the "hair on top of the principal celebrant's head seems to have been sandpapered down." Houts observes that "the volume of the hair

does seem to be significantly less on several figures in the 'reproduction' published in *DACL* 1932" ("Visual Evidence," part 1, 9).

28. See Craig S. Keener, *Paul, Women and Wives: Marriage and Women's Ministry in the Letters of Paul* (Peabody, Mass.: Hendrickson, 1992), 22–31. See also Houts, "Visual Evidence," part 1, 9. An extended discussion of veiling practices can also be found in M. Levine, "The Gendered Grammar of Ancient Mediterranean Hair," in *Off with Her Head! The Denial of Women's Identity in Myth, Religion, and Culture,* ed. Harold Eilberg-Schwartz and Wendy Doniger (Berkeley: University of California Press, 1995).

29. Wilpert, *Fractio Panis,* 8–9. The figure is gendered male, too, in Sandro Carietti's guidebook put out by the Vatican: "In the place of honor, a bearded man is seated, clad in tunic and pallium"; see Carietti, *Guide to Priscilla,* 30, and the survey of Elisabeth Jastrzebowska, "Les scènes de banquet dans les peintures et sculptures chrétiennes des IIIe et IVe siècles," *Recherches Augustiniennes* 14 (1979): 28, and *DACL,* Vol. 2, 2092.

30. Walter Lowrie, *Monuments of the Early Church: A Handbook of Christian Archaeology* (New York: MacMillan, 1901), 229, describes the outfit as "ecclesiastical garb," although there was no standard outfit for members of the clergy for perhaps another century. See also John Beckwith, *Early Christian and Byzantine Art* (Harmondsworth: Penguin, 1970). For different arguments on the long garment, see Irvin, "Archaeological Evidence," 83; and Irwin, "Archeology," 37.

31. For the arguments, see Wilpert, *Fractio Panis,* 8–17; Mancinelli, *Catacombs and Basilicas,* 29; Irvin, "Archeological Evidence," 85.

32. This is the conclusion of Lucien de Bruyne, "La cappella greca di Priscilla," *RAL* 46 (1970): 291–330.

33. Frend, *History of Christian Archeology,* 248; Lowrie, *Monuments,* 229.

34. *ICUR* 9.26122: "OBRIMOS PALLADIŌ GLUKUTATŌ ANEPSIŌ SUNSCOLASTĒ MNĒMĒS CHARIN" (Obrimus for the most sweet Palladius, a schoolmate, in blessed memory).

35. Wilpert, *Fractio Panis,* 17. He gives the grave's dimensions as 70 centimeters long by 17 centimeters deep. It was completely empty at the time that Wilpert discovered the Cappella.

36. ICUR 9: "OBRIMOS NESTORIANĒ MAKARIA GLUKUTATĒ SUMBIŌ MNĒMĒS CHARIN" (Obrimos for Nestoriana, a blessed and most dear wife, in blessed memory).

37. For an example of an early Christian banquet hall, see the marble-paved room in the catacomb of Saints Pietro and Marcellino that dates from the post-Constantinian period. A photograph appears in Fiocchi Nicolai, Bisconti, and

Mazzoleni, *Christian Catacombs* (84, fig. 94). See also the second-century *triclia* or dining hall under the church of San Sebastiano, which comprised a roof shelter with an open loggia. For the evidence, see Richard Krautheimer, "Mensa— Coemeterium—Martyrium" in *Studies in Early Christian, Medieval, and Renaissance Art* (New York: New York University Press, 1969), 35–58. Banquet accouterments were also common in *cubicula*, although after the post-Constantinian period. See Fiocchi Nicolai, "History," in *The Christian Catacombs of Rome: History, Decoration, Inscriptions,* ed. Vincenzo Fiocchi Nicolai, Fabrizio Bisconti, and Danilo Mazzoleni (Regensburg: Schnell & Steiner, 1999), 44.

38. For illustrations and photographs, see Wilpert, *Fractio Panis,* plates 2 and 3; Paul Styger, *Die römischen Katakomben* (Berlin: Verlag für Kunstwissenschaft, 1933), plate 27. The idea that the area was used for worship and/or a funerary meal has now been replaced with the understanding that it was primarily a burial chamber; see Philippe Pergola, *Le Catacombe Romane: Storia e topografia* (Rome: Carocci, 1999), 133.

39. Wilpert, *Fractio Panis,* 7, fig. 2; and plate 12.

40. For a recent critical edition, see Karl Stüber, *Commendatio animae: Sterben im Mittelalter* (Bern: Herbert Lang, 1976).

41. The interpretation is still stubbornly held. See Philippe Prigent, *L'art des premiers chrétiens: L'héritage culturel et la foi nouvelle* (Paris: Desclée de Brouwer, 1995), 196 fig. 91, where Prigent identifies the image as "Daniel (dans la fosse?) aux lions." Note even this author can't bring himself to say that Daniel is in a den here where there is clearly only a cityscape. He never questions, though, why Daniel is wearing a dress.

42. Stevan L. Davies first argued in 1980 that the Apocryphal Acts may have been written by women—specifically, by women in the order of widows. See Davies's *The Revolt of the Widows: The Social World of the Apocryphal Acts* (Carbondale: Southern Illinois University Press, 1980); Virginia Burrus, *Chastity as Autonomy: Women in the Stories of the Apocryphal Acts* (Lewiston, N.Y.: Edwin Mellen, 1987); and Dennis Ronald MacDonald, *The Legend and the Apostle: The Battle for Paul in Story and Canon* (Philadelphia: Westminster Press, 1983). For a direct rebuttal of Davies's thesis that the acts were written by women, see Dennis Ronald MacDonald, "The Role of Women in the Production of the Apocryphal Acts of the Apostles," *Iliff Review* 41, 4 (1984): 21–38.

43. See Stephen Davis, *The Cult of Saint Thecla: A Tradition of Women's Piety in Late Antiquity* (New York: Oxford University Press, 2001) on the Thecla cult; the conventional dating for the Greek Chapel is early for Thecla imagery, but not beyond the realm of possibility, especially if the Greek Chapel actually dates

to the post-Constantinian era. That Thecla was already known in Rome is argued by Léon Vouaux, *Les Actes de Paul et ses letters apocryphes: introduction, texts, traduction et commentaries* (Les apocryphes du Nouveau Testament) (Paris: Librairie Letouzey et Ané, 1913), although his evidence from textual sources is not as strong as it might be.

44. For a survey, see H. Schlosser, "Die Daniel-Susanna-Erzählung in Bild und Literatur der christlichen Frühzeit," in *Tortulae: Studien ʒu altchristlichen und byʒantinischen Monumenten,* ed. W. N. Schumacher, Römische Quartalschrift 30. Supplementheft (Rome: Herder, 1966), 243–249. The Susanna image as lamb is from the *arcosolium* of Celerina, dating to the reign of Liberius (352–366 CE); see A. Provoost, "Il significato delle scene pastorali del terzo secolo D.C.," CIAC.*Atti* (1978), 414. Stevenson, *Catacombs,* 80, lists Susanna images at six separate catacombs, including Praetextatus and Thecla.

45. Huskinson, "Gender and Identity," 210.

46. Ibid., 205.

47. The Roman catacomb evidence has been assembled in a recent study: Fabrizio Bisconti, *Mestieri nelle catacombe romane: appunti sul declino dell'iconografia del reale nei cimiteri cristiani di Roma* (Vatican City: Pontifical Commission for Sacred Archaeology, 2001).

48. For the ritual gesture, see Acts 6:6 and 13:3 and 1 Tim 4:14. The textual evidence has been gathered by Francine Cardman, "Women, Ministry, and Church Order in Early Christianity," in *Women and Christian Origins,* ed. Mary Rose D'Angelo and Ross Shepherd Kraemer (New York: Oxford University Press, 1999), 306.

49. The synod dates perhaps to the fourth century. The canons are recorded in Charles Hefele, *A History of the Councils of the Church,* Vol. 2 (Edinburgh: T. & T. Clark, 1896), 411.

50. Hippolytus. *On the Apostolic Tradition,* 8.1.

51. Christine Trevett, *Montanism: Gender, Authority, and the New Prophecy* (New York: Cambridge University Press, 1996); William Tabbernee, *Montanist Inscriptions and Testimonia: Epigraphic Sources Illustrating the History of Montanism* (Macon, Ga.: Mercer University Press, 1997); Nicola Denzey, "What Did the Montanists Read?" *HTR* 94, 4 (2001): 427–448.

52. This suggestion was, in fact, first made in Wilpert, *Fractio Panis,* 18.

53. The Montanist women Priscilla and Maximilla traced their example back to Ammia of Philadelphia and the daughters of Philip. See Eusebius, *HE* 5.17.4.

54. The bibliography on the topic is substantial. See Karen Jo Torjesen, "The Early Controversies over Female Leadership," *Church History* 17 (1988): 22–23; Torje-

sen, *When Women Were Priests*. For the claim that women were never presbyters, see (for instance) Roger Gryson, *The Ministry of Women in the Early Church* (Collegeville, Minn.: Liturgical Press, 1976), 78ff.

55. Lanciani, *Pagan and Christian Rome*, 42.

56. There's quite a bit of inscriptional evidence for Jewish women presbyters. See the landmark work of Bernadette Brooten, *Women Leaders in the Ancient Synagogue*, Brown Judaic Studies 36 (Chico: Scholars Press, 1982).

57. *Nihilominus impatienter audivimus, tantum divinarum rerum subisse despectum, ut feminae sacris altaribus ministrare firmentur, cunctaque non nisi virorum famulatui deputata sexum, cui non competent, exhibere* (Gelasius, Letter 14, in A. Thiel, *Epistulae Romanorum pontificum genuinae* [New York, 1974; first edition, 1867], 376–77). For Christian women officeholders, see Kevin Madigan and Carolyn Osiek, eds., *Ordained Women in the Early Church: A Documentary History* (Baltimore: Johns Hopkins University Press, 2005).

58. *CIL* 10.8079 = *ILCV* 1192: B(onae) m(emoriae) s(acrum). *Leta presbitera / vixit annos XL, menses VIII, dies VIIII / quei bene fecit maritus / Precessit in pace pridie / idus Maias*. On the significance of this evidence, see Mary Ann Rossi, "Priesthood, Precedent, and Prejudice: On Recovering the Women Priests of Early Christianity. G. Otranto's 'Notes on the Female Priesthood in Antiquity,'" *JFSR* 7 (1991): 73–94. A photograph of the epitaph is reproduced in Madigan and Osiek, *Ordained Women*, 194.

59. Kraemer, *Her Share of the Blessings*, 184.

60. The inscription, cited by Otranto, ("Priesthood, Precedent and Prejudice," 87) was first published by F. Bulic, "Iscrizione inedita," in *Bolletino di Archeologia e Storia Dalmata* 37 (1914): 107–111.

61. There is, however, a possible epitaph for a deaconess by the name of Anne in the city of Rome, but the dating is late (sixth century): "By the gift of God and of the Blessed Apostle Paul, Dometius, the deacon and controller of the monies of the holy, apostolic and papal chair, together with Anna the deacon[ess], his sister offered this vow to the blessed Paul." See the evidence of Madigan and Osiek, *Ordained Women*, 144, and Ute Eisen, *Women Officeholders in Early Christianity: Epigraphical and Literary Studies* (Collegeville, Minn.: Liturgical Press, 2000), 183.

62. Eusebius *HE* 6.43.11; Cornelius, Letter 9.3 (*PL* 3 col. 765–769); Adolf von Harnack, *Die Mission und Ausbreitung des Christentums* (Leipzig: Zentral-Antiquariat der Deutschen Demokratischen Republik, 1965), 589–611, 806.

63. Harnack, *Die Mission und Ausbreitung*, 806.

64. Victor Saxer, "L'utilisation par la liturgie de l'espace urbain et suburbain: l'ex-

emple de Rome dans l'antiquité et le haut moyen âge," in CIAC.*Atti* (1986), Vol. 2, 920.

65. Marucchi, *Christian Epigraphy,* 213, says there's only one *ostiarius* inscription from Rome.

66. Marucchi, *Christian Epigraphy,* 213: *Dilectissimo marito anime dvlcissimae Alexio lectori de fullonices qvi vixit mecvm ann. XVI ivnctvs mihi ann. XVI virgo ad virgine cvics nvmqvam amaritvdinem habvi cesqve in pace cvm sanctis cvm qvos mereris dep VIII x kal. ianv* (from the Cemetery of Balbina).

67. Torjesen, *When Women Were Priests,* esp. 53–178.

68. A great deal had been written on house churches. For a fine article, see Carolyn Osiek, "Women in House Churches," in *Common Life in the Early Church: Essays Honoring Graydon F. Snyder,* ed. Julian Hills (Harrisburg, Va.: Trinity, 1998), 300–316; and, more recently, Carolyn Osiek and Margaret Y. MacDonald, *A Woman's Place: House Churches in Earliest Christianity* (Minneapolis: Fortress Press, 2006). For a broader study, see L. Michael White, *Building God's House in the Roman World: Architectural Adaptation among Pagans, Jews, and Christians* (Baltimore: Johns Hopkins University Press, 1990).

69. For the medieval itineraries, Ethel Ross Barker, *Rome of the Pilgrims and Martyrs: A Study in the Martyrologies, Itineraries, Syllogae, and Other Contemporary Documents* (London: Methuen, 1913).

70. For instance, Carietti, *Guide to Priscilla,* 11.

71. F. Tolotti, "Le cimetière de Priscille: synthèse d'une recherche," *RivArcC* 3–4 (1970): 291–314.

72. Ibid.

73. Ibid.

74. Marucchi, *Manual,* 178.

75. Osiek and MacDonald, *A Woman's Place;* Torjesen, *When Women Were Priests,* 53–87.

76. On the first Roman Christians, see A. Dutoit, "The Ecclesiastical Situation of the First Generation Roman Christians," *Hervormde Teologiese Studies* 53 (1997): 498–512; for an overview of these women: Elisabeth Schüssler Fiorenza, "Word, Spirit, and Power: Women in Early Christian Communities," in *Women of Spirit: Female Leadership in the Jewish and Christian Traditions,* ed. Rosemary Ruether (New York: Simon & Schuster, 1979), 29–70.

77. Marucchi, *Manual,* 88, 178.

78. Stevenson, *Catacombs,* 96–97, claims that the Greek Chapel's bench is for the remembrance of the martyrs and that the space is specifically for women. A sim-

ilar case of a short bench built into the wall as seating designed for women is in the Chapel of Miltiades in the Catacombs of Callistus; see Marucchi, *Manual*, 104.

Chapter 5. Petronella Goes to Paradise

1. The qualification is necessary; see Curran, *Pagan City*, esp. chap. 4, and Krautheimer, *Rome*, 33.

2. R. Giuliani, "Il restauro dell'arcosolio di Veneranda nelle catacombe di Domitilla sulla Via Ardeatina," *RivArcC* 72 (1994): 61–87.

3. On the correspondence between ecclesiastical regions and the catacombs, see Charles Pietri, "Régions ecclésiastiques et paroisses romaines," in *CIAC.Atti* (1989), Vol. 2, 1035–1062; and Louis Reekmans, "L'implantation monumentale chrétienne dans le paysage urbain de Rome de 300 à 850," in *CIAC.Atti* (1989), Vol. 2, 861–915.

4. P. Pergola, "'Petronella martyr': une évergète de la fin du IVᵉ siècle?" in *Memoriam Sanctorum Venerantes. Miscellanea in onore di V. Saxer* (Vatican City, 1992), 628.

5. The funerary basilica was rediscovered in the modern era by G. B. De Rossi in 1873, who undertook extensive excavations of the area. See G. B. De Rossi, "Scoperta della basilica di S. Petronilla con sepolcro dei Martiri Nereo ed Achilleo nel cimitero di Domitilla" *Bull.Arch.C.*, 1st ser., 3 (1865): 5–35; and G. B. De Rossi, "Pianta della basilica di S. Petronilla nel cimitero di Domitilla," *Bull.Arch.C.*, 2nd ser., 5 (1874): 68–74.

6. On the fourth-century additions to Domitilla, see Fiocchi Nicolai, "History," 54 and 129; U. Fasola, *La basilica dei SS. Nereo ed Achilleo e la catacomba di Domitilla* (Rome, 1965), 23; P. Pergola, "La catacombe romane: miti e realtà (a proposito del cimitero di Domitilla)," in *Società romana e impero tardoantico*, ed. A. Giardina (Roma: Laterza, 1986), 213–215; Giuliani, "Restauro"; Marucchi, *Manual*, 157.

7. For a ground plan, see Fiocchi Nicolai, "History," 53 fig. 60.

8. The date range of 360–370 CE is given in Bisconti, "Decoration," 138. Mancinelli, *Catacombs and Basilicas*, 26, dates the painting to after 356 CE, as does Wladimiro Dorigo, *Late Roman Painting* (New York: Praeger, 1971), 224 and plate 180. Philippo Pergola, "Petronella martyr," 629, suggests a very late date (ca. 430–450 CE). The 356 CE date comes not from Veneranda's grave, but from an epitaph for another grave in her cubiculum, in which a husband, Marcus, commemorates his wife Karisia (*ICUR*, n.s., 6499).

9. For the plates, see Josef Wilpert, *Die Malereien der Katakomben Roms* (Freiburg

im Breisgau: Herder, 1903), plate 213; Pavia, *Guida delle catacombe*, 223; Aldo Nestori, *Repertorio topografico delle pitture delle catacombe romane* (Vatican City: Pontificio Istituto di Archeologia Cristiana, 1975), 120 n. 15. For more on the art history, see Umberto Fasola, *Die Domitilla-Katacombe und die Basilika der Märtyrer Nereus und Achilleus*, 3rd ed., revised by Philippo Pergola (Vatican City: Pontificio Istituto di Archeologia Cristiana, 1989), 33–34.

10. The words, still faintly visible, are published as *ICUR*, n.s., 6963.

11. Miles, *Image as Insight*, 54.

12. *The Catholic Encyclopedia* (1911), Vol. 11, available at www.newadvent.org/cathen/11781b.htm.

13. De Rossi, *Bull.Arch.C* (1865), 46; (1874), 1, 68, 122; *Bull.Arch.C* (1875), 1–77; *Bull.Arch.C* (1878), 125–146; *Bull.Arch.C* (1879), 1–20, 139–160; *Bull.Arch.C* (1880), 169.

14. Augustine, *Adimantum*, xvii. Op. viii. (PL 42.161).

15. BHL, 2257, 6058–6067, 6067b.

16. *AA.SS: Nereus and Achilleus*. Mai. III 10, 11, VII 420–422. Also published by H. Achelis, "Acta SS. Nerei et Achillei," in *Texte und Untersuchungen zur Geschichte der altchristlichen Literatur* 11, 2 (1893): 1–70.

17. U. Fasola, *La basilica dei SS. Nereo ed Achilleo*, 23–26, 49.

18. Tiberius Alpharano, *Tiberii Alpharani De basilicae vaticanae antiquissima et nova structura*, ed. Michele Cerrati (Rome: Tip. poliglotta vaticana, 1914), 167.

19. Pergola, "Petronella martyr," 633.

20. Ibid.

21. Ibid.

22. See the *Epitome libri de locis sanctorum martyrum*, a medieval Roman topography of graves, listing church of St. Petronella. For the text, see De Rossi, *Roma Sotteranea* I. 180; De Rossi, *Bull.Arch.C* (1865), 46; (1874), 1, 68, 122; *Bull.Arch.C* (1875), 1–77; *Bull.Arch.C* (1878), 125–146; *Bull.Arch.C* (1879), 1–20, 139–160; *Bull.Arch.C* (1880), 169.

23. This church of Cyriacus now serves as a sort of lecture hall during the public tours to Domitilla, is now simply known as the chapel of Saints Nereus and Achilleus.

24. De Rossi, *La Roma sotterranea cristiana*, 1.180–181 (Rome, 1867).

25. *ICUR* 2.225.

26. Marucchi, *Manual*, 221: *Anatolius filio bene merenti fecit qui vixit annis VII mensis VII diebus XX ispiritus tuus bene requiescat in deo petas pro sorore tua.*

27. *ILCV* 1.2337: *Pete pro parentes tuos Matronata Matrona que vixit an. I. D. I. L. II.*

28. Marucchi, *Manual,* 226: *Ianuaria bene refrigera et roga pro nos,* from the Catacombs of Callistus.

29. *ICUR* 3.8452: *Attice spiritus tuus in bonu ora pro parentibus tuis.*

30. See the listings in F. Grossi Gondi, *Trattato di Epigrafia Cristiana Latina e Greca* (Rome: Gregorian University, 1920), 233.

31. See the collection in Lattimore, *Epitaphs,* §63, §64 (pp. 230–235), §68 (243–246).

32. Elsner, "Inventing Christian Rome," 78.

33. *pro vitae sue testimonium sancti martyres apud Deum et Christum erunt advocati* (Marucchi, *Christian Epigraphy,* #118, p. 158).

34. For "particularized loyalty," see Peter Brown, *The Cult of the Saints: Its Rise and Function in Latin Christianity* (Chicago: University of Chicago Press, 1981), 32. For Peter and Paul, see Janet Huskinson, *Concordia Apostolorum: Christian Propaganda at Rome in the Fourth and Fifth Centuries,* BAR International Series 148 (Oxford: BAR, 1982); Lucy Grig, "Portraits, Pontiffs and the Christianisation of Fourth-Century Rome," *Proceedings of the British School at Rome* 72 (2004): 203–230; and Charles Pietri, "Concordia Apostolorum et Renovatio Urbis: Culte des Martyrs et Propagande Pontificale," *MEFRA* 73 (1961): 275–322.

35. Brown, *Cult of the Saints,* 32.

36. Ibid.

37. There are also a number of Roman *tituli* that bear the names of male founders and/or saints, including San Chrysogono, San Clemente, San Cyriaco, San Eusebio on the Esquiline hill, SS. Julio and Callisto on the Via Aurelia, San Marco at the beginning of the Via Lata, San Marcello (also on the Via Lata), San Nicomedis on Via Merulana, San Martino ai Monti, and San Gaio. Richard Krautheimer, *Three Christian Capitals: Topography and Politics* (Berkeley: University of California Press, 1983), 99, discusses several cases of male patrons, including the wealthy senator Pammachius, who establishes the church of SS. Giovanni and Paolo, and the patron Philippus, who founds San Pietro in Vincoli. His point, however, is that the reigning bishop of Rome invariably claims credit for the church founding and building, throwing the status of the lay patron into shadow.

38. *ICUR* 9.25165: *Constat nos emisse ianuarium et britiam locvm ante domna emerita a fossoribus.*

39. *Filicissimus et Leoparda emerunt bisomum at Criscentionem martirem introitu* (Marucchi, *Christian Epigraphy,* #164, p. 178).

40. There are two more: *Petrus et Pancara votum posuent martyre felicitati* and *Corpus.*

Sanctis. commendavi. Irene tibi cum sanctis Quintia vale in pace. The second one is from Capua, though, not Rome. See Marucchi, *Manual,* 220.

41. Brown, *Cult of the Saints,* 34.

42. Marucchi, *Christian Epigraphy,* #166: *sepulchrum intra limina sanctorum quod multi cupiunt et rari accipiunt,* from Velletri, ca. 381 CE.; also cited in Brown, *Cult of the Saints,* 34.

43. Cooper, "The Martyr, the Matrona, and the Bishop," esp. 298.

44. For saints as the "Very Special Dead," see Brown, *Cult of the Saints,* chap. 4.

45. Lucy Grig, *Making Martyrs in Late Antiquity* (London: Duckworth, 2004), 126.

46. See Bisconti, "Decorations," 129.

47. Lucy Grig, *Making Martyrs,* 132, says there are others, although this is the best surviving image; she cites Nestori, *Repertorio,* 69, and Wilpert, *Pitture,* 196.

48. Thus, a critique of Jaś Elsner's landmark contribution to understanding Roman art, *Art and the Roman Viewer* (1995).

49. Pergola, "Petronella martyr," 627–636.

50. On early Christian literacy, see Harry Gamble, *Books and Readers in the Early Church: A History of Early Christian Texts* (New Haven, Conn.: Yale University Press, 1995); and Kim Haines-Eitzen, *Guardians of Letters: Literacy, Power, and the Transmitters of Early Christian Literature* (New York: Oxford University Press, 2000). The early Christian world had an overall literacy rate of about 75 percent; Christianity was spread predominantly through preaching.

51. On evidence for fourth-century women as readers, scholars, and philosophers, see Bremmer, "Why Did Christianity Attract Upper-Class Women?" 42–43.

52. Brown, *Cult of the Saints,* 31.

53. Marucchi, *Christian Epigraphy,* #147: *locus felicitatis qui deposita est natale domnes theclae,* from the Catacombs of Commodilla.

54. Marucchi, *Christian Epigraphy,* #149: *Studentiae depositae die natali Marcelli cons. Sallies,* from the Basilica of San Sebastiano.

55. Marucchi, *Christian Epigraphy,* #148: *Pascasius vixit plus minus annus XX fecit fatu IIII idus octobris VIII ante natale domni Asteri depositus in pace,* from the Catacombs of Commodilla.

56. Marucchi, *Christian Epigraphy,* #144, with Greek original. From Syracuse, Italy.

57. Cynthia Hahn, "Seeing and Believing: The Construction of Sanctity in Early Medieval Saints' Shrines," *Speculum* 72 (1997): 1079.

58. Dennis Trout, "Damasus and the Invention of Early Christian Rome," *Journal of Medieval and Early Modern Studies* 33, 3 (2003): 525.

59. Elsner, *Inventing Christian Rome*, 73.

60. The other two women in the *Depositio Martyrum* are Perpetua and Felicitas of Carthage, commemorated together (as they died together) on the nones of March. Unlike many other foreign martyrs who did, Perpetua and Felicitas are never truly "patriated" or made *cittadine* of Rome.

61. Grig, *Making Martyrs*, 4.

62. Ibid., 19.

Chapter 6. The Silent Virgin and the Pale Child

1. *AA.SS. Maii IV* (1685), 296–301; R. Krautheimer, S. Corbett, and W. Frankl, eds., *Corpus Basilicarum Christianarum Romae*, Vol. 3 (1967), 232–259.

2. The expression "orchestrated revitalization ritual" is from Geary, "Sacred Commodities," 178.

3. *Eadem via ad sanctam Caeciliam: ibi innumerabilis multitudo martirum* and *Nec longe ecclesia Caeciliae martyris et ibi reconditi sunt* (*Codex Topographicus Urbis Romae*, ed. Urlichs), 87, 149, cf. 110.

4. *MH*, 50, 74. The particular recension appears to date from the seventh century; the oldest manuscript is of the eighth century. See the comments of Amore, *Martiri*, 145. In the *MH*, Cecilia is celebrated on four dates: August 11, September 16, and November 17 and 22.

5. For the archaeological survey, see N. Parmegiani and A. Pronti, *S. Cecilia in Trastevere. Nuovi scavi e ricerche*. Monumenti di antichità cristiana pubblicati a cura del Pontificio Istituto di Archeologia Cristiana, II series 16 (Vatican City: Pontificio Istituto di Archeologia Cristiana, 2004).

6. The others were Clement and Sabina. See Amore, *Martiri*, 147.

7. For mention of Cecilia as a *matrona* and founder of her church, see Olof Brandt, *San Lorenzo in Lucina: New Light on the Early Christian Basilica*, chap. 3 (forthcoming).

8. For Cecilia's *acta*, see H. Delehaye, *Étude sur le légendier romain*, Subsidia Hagiographique 23 (1936), 77–96; and E. Josi, "Cecilia, santa, martire di Roma," *Bibliotheca Sanctorum* III (Rome, 1962), 1064–1081.

9. Not all *patronae* got their own *passio;* see the cases of Crescentiana, Vestina, and Lucina, who founded Roman churches but, for whatever reason, never appear in martyr literature.

10. For a discussion of the notorious problem of dating Cecilia's *acta* and the events behind them, see Amore, *Martiri*, 144–156.

11. Gillian Cloke, "Mater or Martyr: Christianity and the Alienation of Women within the Family in the Later Roman Empire," *Theology and Sexuality* (1996): 56.

12. Ibid., 37.

13. Ibid., 38.

14. Cooper, "The Martyr, the Matrona, and the Bishop," 14, 82.

15. Grig, *Making Martyrs*, 79.

16. See the Liberian Calendar, published first by Bucher, *De Doctrina temporum* (Antwerp, 1634). For the Codex Calendar of 354, see Michele Salzman, *On Roman Time: The Codex-Calendar of 354 and the Rhythms of Urban Life in Late Antiquity* (Berkeley: University of California Press, 1990). The other women in the Codex Calendar are the Roman saint Bassilla and the North African martyrs Perpetua and Felicita.

17. Translation given in Curran, *Pagan City*, 128. The first letters of the inscription read from top to bottom form, in Latin, an acrostic: "Constantina in God."

18. A. Frutaz, *Il complesso monumentale di Sant'Agnese e di Santa Costanza*, 2nd ed. (Rome: Tipografia poliglotta Vaticana, 1969).

19. The first of the Constantinian *patronae* was Constantina's grandmother, Helena, the patroness *extraordinaire*. See Leslie Brubaker, "Memories of Helena: Patterns in Imperial Female Matronage in the Fourth and Fifth Centuries," in *Women, Men, and Eunuchs: Gender in Byzantium*, ed. Liz James (London: Routledge, 1997), 52–75.

20. See Curran, *Pagan City*, 129–137, and H. O. Maier, "Religious Dissent, Heresy, and Households in Late Antiquity," *VC* 49 (1995).

21. *LP*, i. 207.

22. *plurimos vastationis suae strage deiecit, Collectio Avellana* 1.12; the translation is in Curran, *Pagan City*, 141.

23. For studies of martyrdom, see Glen Bowersock, *Martyrdom and Rome* (New York: Cambridge University Press, 1995); and Arthur Droge and James D. Tabor, *A Noble Death: Suicide and Martyrdom among Christians and Jews in Antiquity* (San Francisco: HarperSanFrancisco, 1992). An outstanding new book that will change the field is Elizabeth A. Castelli, *Martyrdom and Memory: Early Christian Culture Making* (New York: Columbia University Press, 2004).

24. Cloke, "Mater or Martyr," 47.

25. Ibid., 37.

26. Francine Cardman, "Acts of the Woman Martyrs," *ATR* 70 (1988): 147.

27. M. R. Lefkowitz, "The Motivations for St. Perpetua's Martyrdom," *Journal of the American Academy of Religion* 44, 3 (1976): 417–421.

28. See G. Clark, *Women in Late Antiquity,* 51; and D. Hunter, "Resistance to the Virginal Ideal in Late Fourth-Century Rome: The Case of Jovinian," *Theological Studies* 48 (1987): 45–67.

29. For the phrase "venture into respectability," see Cloke, *Female Man of God,* 105.

30. See Jerome's Letter 22 exhorting the young virgin Eustochium, in which he places virginity in relation to marriage: "I praise wedlock, I praise marriage, but it is because they give me virgins. I gather the rose from the thorns, the gold from the earth, the pearl from the shell."

31. R. Kraemer, "The Conversion of Women to Ascetic Forms of Christianity," *Signs* 6 (1980): 298–307.

32. Cloke, "Mater or Martyr," 49.

33. For Polyxena, see Homer, *Aeneid* 3.321–324; Ovid, *Metamorphoses* 13.455–480.

34. For Agnes as a type of Polyxena, see Virginia Burrus, "Reading Agnes: The Rhetoric of Gender in Ambrose and Prudentius," *JECS* 3 (1995): 39–41; Martha Malamud, *A Poetics of Transformation: Prudentius and Classical Mythology* (Ithaca, N.Y.: Cornell University Press, 1989), 143–144; Andrew Palmer, *Prudentius on the Martyrs* (Oxford: Oxford University Press, 1989), 178–179, 188–193; and Michael Roberts, *Poetry and the Cult of the Martyrs: The Liber Peristephanon of Prudentius* (Ann Arbor: University of Michigan Press, 1993).

35. On the complex psychology of the gladiator, see the brilliant book by Carlin A. Barton, *The Sorrows of the Ancient Romans: The Gladiator and the Monster* (Princeton, N.J.: Princeton University Press, 1993).

36. Peter Brown, "Enjoying the Saints in Late Antiquity," in *Decorations for the Holy Dead: Visual Embellishments on Tombs and Shrines of Saints,* ed. Stephen Lamia and Elizabeth Valdez del Alamo (Turnhout, Belgium: Brepols, 2002), 67.

37. Ibid.

38. Ibid.

39. Ibid., 82.

40. "The Martyrdom of Saints Carpus, Papylus, and Agathonice," in *Acts of the Christian Martyrs,* ed. H. Musurillo (New York: Oxford University Press. 2000).

41. Grig, "Making Martyrs," 82.

42. For the phrase "death-marriage" see Burrus, "Reading Agnes," 39.

43. For the expression "double martyrdom" and a discussion of the sexual humilia-

tion of female martyrs, see Anne Jensen, *God's Self-Confident Daughters: Early Christianity and the Liberation of Women* (Louisville, Ky.: Westminster John Knox Press, 1996), 85. Jensen cites Friedrich Augar, *Die Frau im römischen Christenprozess* (Leipzig: J. C. Hinrichs, 1905), who finds thirteen plausible cases of rape in the martyr processes of early Christian women.

44. Grig, *Making Martyrs*, 83.

45. On Concordia, see *MH* (February 22), 24; Amore, *Martiri*, 101–102.

46. On Tryphonia and Cyrilla, see the *Passio Polychronii;* their dates are October 18 and 28. In the eighth century, their bodies are transferred to the Church of San Silvestro in Capite. On Bibiana and her mother, see Amore, *Martiri*, 297–298; and on Tryphonia and Cyrilla, see Amore, *Martiri*, 102.

47. *MH*, 105; see Amore, *Martiri*, 56–58.

48. Amore, *Martiri*, 103–105.

49. Scholars surmise that the women never existed, but emerged as a literalization of allegorical figures, or perhaps a misreading of an inscription. See the comments in Amore, *Martiri*, 254–255.

50. *The Golden Legend*, #48 (trans. Granger Ryan, Vol. 1, 185). See the discussion by Joyce Salisbury, *The Blood of Martyrs: Unintended Consequences of Ancient Violence* (London: Routledge, 2004), 124–125.

51. Antonio Ferrua, "S. Felicita ed i suoi figli," in *La Civiltà Cattolica*, 118 (1967), 2.248–251, tells of the discovery of a fragmentary epigraph of Pope Damasus to the martyrs, pushing the date of their ecclesiastical recognition slightly earlier; with it, Felicita also becomes only the second female martyr to be formally commemorated by Damasus, along with Agnes. On the other hand, the fragment mentions only the seven brothers, not Felicita herself. For more on Felicita, see Amore, *Martiri*, 43–51.

52. Ferrua, "S. Felicia ed i suoi figli," 251–253; and P. Pergola, *Catacombe Romane: storia e topografia* (Rome: Carocci, 1998), 121.

53. For a similar argument for the figure of the emperor Constantine's mother, Helena, see Brubaker, "Memories of Helena."

54. For the text, see *Analecta Bollandiana* 51 (1933): 263.

55. *AA.SS. Giugno, I* (Paris, 1867), 167–169.

56. Amore, *Martiri*, 228–229.

57. Peter Brown, *The Body and Society: Men, Women, and Sexual Renunciation in Early Christianity* (New York: Columbia University Press, 1988).

58. On postmarital celibacy, see D. G. Hunter, "*On the Sin of Adam and Eve:* A Lit-

tle Known Defense of Marriage and Childbearing by Ambrosiaster," *HTR* 82 (1989): 283–299.

59. *ICUR* 8. 20809; 8. 21010: *Eucarpiati coniugi suae benimerenti se bibu fecit qui b an p ım XXVIII et CV. Virg. fec an VIII m VI D XVII* and *ICUR* 8.2105: *FL Urbicus fecit sibi et Victorie Niceni Virginiae suae et omnibus suis se vibo.* See also *ICUR* 8. 21248 (a bit corrupt, but evidently commemorating a chaste union) and *ICUR* 8.21430 (also corrupt). Curiously, modern Catholic epigraphers offer great resistance to interpreting the words *virginia* and *virgo* as "virgins" within marriage, even though this is surely what was meant; instead, they argue that the term "his virgin" means simply "his wife," and that the term means that the woman was married since the time of her virginity—i.e., that she was a virgin when she married. This is absurd, though, for several reasons: (1) most women were virgins when they married, so there was no need to broadcast this; (2) the stones often distinguish between length of marriage and length of time living with the same spouse as virgin (as in the case of Eucarpiatus above); (3) there are also women who commemorate their husbands as "male virgins," which certainly wouldn't mean that the women were not virgins at their marriage but that their husbands had been. Surely, the simplest explanation is that many married couples chose postmarital celibacy for reasons that clearly suited them and their notion of appropriate and pious behavior.

60. *ICUR* 8.21053: *Florentio qui vixit ann XL VIIII D XX Firmina virginio suo cum qua vixit an XVIII m IIII DP, NON MAI INP.*

61. *ICUR* 8.21210: *DP Onesime qve vixit an. XXVII II fecit cvm virginivm svvm Basilidem an. X bene merenti in p.*

62. Another model of "spiritual marriage" is that which Jerome disdains (Letter 22.14), in which unmarried male and female ascetics live together, ostensibly chastely, but with the possibility always existing that the relationship was merely a socially acceptable "cover" for a relationship that included fornication or other illicit sexual activity.

63. The point made by Stuart G. Hall, "Women among the Early Martyrs," in *Martyrs and Martyrologies,* ed. Diana Wood (Oxford: Blackwell, 1997), 8.

64. Ibid., 15.

65. Grig, *Making Martyrs,* 82.

Chapter 7. Pope Damasus, Ear Tickler

1. Curran, *Pagan City,* 136.

2. J. N. D. Kelly, *Oxford Dictionary of the Popes* (Oxford: Oxford University Press, 2005).

3. A Christian source hostile to Damasus, the *Collectio Avellana* 1.7, reports 160 dead; Ammianus Marcellinus, *History* 27.3.13, reports 137. The question remains whether these were separate events, since Ammianus does not identify the location of the massacres aside from the ambiguous "Basilica Sicininum." See the discussion in Curran, *Pagan City,* 140.

4. *Collectio Avellana* 1.6; Charles Pietri, *Roma Christiana. Recherches sur l'église de Rome, son organization, sa politique, son idéologie de Miltiade à Sixte III (331–440)* (Rome: École française de Rome, 1976), 1.409.

5. *Collectio Avellana* 1.12 : "*plurimos vastationis suae strage deiecit.*" The translation is Curran's, *Pagan City,* 141.

6. J. Guyon, "L'oeuvre de Damase dans le cimitière sur la vie Labicana," in *Saecularia Damasiana, Studi di Antichità Cristiana* 39 (Vatican City: Pontificio Istituto di Archeologia Cristiana, 1986), 227–258.

7. Brown, *Cult of the Saints,* 97.

8. For more on the Concordia Apostolorum, see Janet Huskinson, *Concordia Apostolorum: Christian Propaganda at Rome in the Fourth and Fifth Centuries,* BAR International Series, 148 (Oxford: BAR, 1982); Lucy Grig, "Portraits, Pontiffs, and the Christianisation of Fourth-Century Rome," *Proceedings of the British School at Rome* 72 (2004): 203–230; and Charles Pietri, "Concordia Apostolorum et Renovatio Urbis."

9. Harry O. Maier, "Religious Dissent, Heresy, and Households in Late Antiquity," *VC* 49 (1995): 50.

10. Ibid., 52.

11. Sozomen, *History of the Church* 3.1; see also Ambrose, Letter 20; Jerome, Letter 133.3 on the (male) followers of Priscillian shutting themselves in alone with "little women" and singing Virgil to them "between intercourse and embraces."

12. See Wayne House, "A Biblical View of the Ministry, Part 5: Distinctive Roles for Women in the Second and Third Centuries," *Bibliotheca Sacra* 146 (1989): 47.

13. Elizabeth A. Clark, "Ideology, History, and the Construction of 'Woman' in Late Ancient Christianity," *JECS* 2, 2 (1994): 163.

14. Sivan, "Anician Women," 142.

15. Virginia Burrus, "The Heretical Woman as Symbol in Alexander, Athanasius, Epiphanius and Jerome," *HTR* 84, 3 (1991): 230–231.

16. Ibid., 247.

17. Ibid., 232.

18. Ibid.

19. Ibid., 248.

20. D. G. Hunter, "The Paradise of Patriarchy: Ambrosiaster on Woman as (Not) God's Image, "*Journal of Theological Studies* 43 (1992): 447–469.

21. E. Clark, "Ideology, History," 171.

22. Sivan, "Anician Women," 140–157. Sivan dates the Cento to sometime between the mid-350s and Proba's death around 370 CE. There is also the possibility— explored but rejected by Sivan—that the Cento was composed later, around 380, by Proba's granddaughter, Anicia Faltonia Proba, wife of the politician Sextus Petronius Probus.

23. Sivan, "On Hymens."

24. Cloke, "Martyrs and Matrons," 53.

25. "Acts of Carpus, Papylus, and Agathonice," in Musurillo, *Acts of the Christian Martyrs,* 35.

26. G. Clark, *Women in Late Antiquity,* 139–140.

27. Cloke, *Female Man of God,* 16.

28. E. Clark, "Ideology, History," 179.

29. Jan Bremmer, "Pauper or Patroness: The Widow in the Early Christian Church," in *Between Poverty and the Pyre* (New York: Routledge, 1995), 42.

30. Cloke, *Female Man of God,* 6.

31. Cloke, *Female Man of God,* 6.

32. E. Clark, "Ideology, History," 180.

33. Ibid., 181.

34. See Jerome, Letter 108.15.

35. For the best discussion of the legislation, see M. Verdon, "Virgins and Widows: European Kinship and Early Christianity," *Man* 23 (1988): 501.

36. Bremmer, "Pauper or Patroness," 48.

37. Jill Harries, "'Treasure in Heaven': Property and Influence among Senators of Late Rome," in Elizabeth M. Craik, ed., *Marriage and Property* (Aberdeen: Aberdeen University Press, 1991), 54–70.

38. E. Clark, "Ideology, History," 179.

39. There are many lists of *tituli*. This one is based on Louis Reekmans, "L'implantation monumentale chrétienne dans le paysage urbain de Rome de 300–850," *CIAC.Atti*, Vol. 2 (Rome: Ecole française de Rome, 1989), 867. For an older study giving martyr stories as foundation myths for particular *tituli*, see F. Lanzoni, "I titoli presbyterali di roma antica nella storia e nella leggenda," *RivArcC*

2 (1925): 195–257. Whether all these *tituli* were founded by wealthy female patrons remains controversial. The church of Anastasia, for instance, may have been built by Damasus—or perhaps Damasus only renovated a *titulus* ascribed to one unknown patrona, Anastasia. In any case, secure records no longer exist, and it is only through tradition that these names have been ascribed to female patrons. Still, there is no reason to assume that these traditions are erroneous, particularly since they betray a clear pattern of women's patronage.

40. Leslie Brubaker, "Memories of Helena: Patterns in Imperial Female Matronage in the Fourth and Fifth Centuries," in *Women, Men, and Eunuchs: Gender in Byzantium*, ed. Liz James (New York: Routledge, 1997), 52–75, here 56. For earlier evidence of female patronage, see Suzanne Dixon, "A Family Business: Women's Role in Patronage and Politics at Rome 80–44 BC," *Classica et Medievalia* 34 (1983): 91–112.

41. Brubaker, "Memories of Helena," 61.

42. Ibid., 62.

43. Ibid., 64.

44. Ibid.

45. Elizabeth A. Clark, "Early Christian Women: Sources and Interpretation," in *That Gentle Strength: Historical Perspectives on Women in Christianity*, ed. Lynda L. Coon, Katherine J. Haldane, and Elisabeth W. Sommer (Charlottesville: University Press of Virginia, 1990), 24.

46. Ibid., 29.

47. Verdon, "Virgins and Widows," 501.

48. Curran, *Pagan City*, 146.

49. Vincenzo Fiocchi Nicolai, *Strutture funerarie ed edifici di culto paleocristiani di Roma dal 4. al 6. secolo* (Vatican City: Pontifical Commission for Sacred Archaeology, 2001) and Umbert M. Fasola and Vincenzo Fiocchi Nicolai, "Le necropolis durante la formazione della città cristiana," in *CIAC.Atti* 11.2 (1989): 1153–1205.

50. Many of the inscriptions have since been destroyed, but remain today from medieval transcriptions. For excerpts and translations of some of the most important, see Carlo Carletti, *Damaso e i martiri di roma: anno Damasi saeculari XVI* (Vatican City: Pontifical Commission for Sacred Archaeology, 1985). The entire corpus is edited by A. Ferrua (1942).

51. L. Duchesne, *The Early History of the Christian Church*, Vol. 2 (London: Murray, 1910), 483.

52. *ICUR* 10.27034: *Somno heternali Avrelivs Gemellvs qvi bixit an . . . carissimo be-*

naemerenti fecit in pac . . . conmando Basilla innocentia Gemelli, and *ICUR* 10.27060: *Domina Basilla commandamvs tibi Crescentinvs et Micina filia nostra Crescen . . . qve vixit mens x et dies . . .* [inscription breaks off].

53. F. Tolotti, "cimetière."

54. *citocuncti suscipiantus votis domnae priscille beatae,* Marucchi, *Manual,* 280.

55. Felicita's own story is interesting, too. She is ignored by Damasus, but appears in the space of two lines in a later epigram falsely ascribed to the pope. She also has her own catacombs (also called the Catacombs of Maximus), which appear to have been constructed fairly late, judging from those inscriptions we can date securely. Legend has it that her bones are there, along with those of her youngest son, Silanus.

56. Published by Antonio Ferrua, *Epigrammata Damasiana recensuit et adnotavit Antonius Ferrua* (Vatican City: Pontificio Istituto di Archeologia Cristiana, 1942). Damasus also may have composed an epigram for the virgin martyr Agatha (*ED* 52), whose breasts were cruelly cut off as part of her martyrdom.

57. Trout, "Damasus," 522; on Damasus's military language, see also Grig, *Making Martyrs,* 134.

58. *O veneranda mihi sanctus decus alma pudoris / ut Damasi precibus faveas precor inclyta martyr.* (This last line, "I entreat you, noble martyr, look favorably on Damasus's prayers," is also used *verbatim* on Hermes' grave [*ED* 8].)

59. Interestingly enough, in the fifth-century martyr acts of Nereus and Achilleus, the two martyrs are quite literally emasculated; they are not soldiers but the two eunuch courtiers of the noble lady Flavia Domitilla—she who gave her name to the catacomb. They are exiled along with their mistress to the island of Ponza before their execution at Terracina. In this, the focus of the martyrdom is returned to a domestic realm, and the main emphasis is on the female protagonist, Flavia Domitilla. We are back to the conceptual world of the *Apocryphal Acts.* See *AA.SS.* Maii III and H. Achelis, "Acta SS. Nerei et Achillei," ed. H. Achelis, *Texte und Untersuchungen zur Geschichte der altchristlichen Literatur* 11, 2 (1893): 1–70.

60. Fiocchi Nicolai, "History," 50.

61. For the nickname, see *Collectio Avellana* 1.5–6; 1.9.

62. For the creation of the "desert in the city," Cloke, *Female Man of God,* 8.

Epilogue. Turtura's Veil

1. Scholars debate who financed the renovation. Not surprisingly, a pope claimed credit: the basilica had been renovated by Damasus at the end of the fourth cen-

tury, then redone by Damasus's successor Siricius (384–399 CE) and then again by John I (523–526 CE), around which time Turtura's fresco was added—certainly by a lay patron. For more on the basilica as Pope John's creation, see Dennis Trout, "Saints, Identity, and the City," in *Late Ancient Christianity*, ed. V. Burrus (Minneapolis: Fortress, 2005), 184–186.

2. See Bisconti, "Decoration," 129.

3. Trout, "Damasus," 184.

4. Consider, for instance, Robin Jensen's brief list of the various ends that visual art might serve: decorative, illustrative, didactic, exegetical, symbolic, liturgical, and iconic. See Robin Margaret Jensen, *Understanding Early Christian Art* (New York: Routledge, 2000), 6.

5. G. Clark, *Women in Late Antiquity*, 113.

6. Ibid.

7. Yarbrough, *Christianization*, 154.

8. *ICUR* 2.6018 = *ILCV* 2142.

9. Cloke, *This Female Man of God*, 7.

10. Jo Ann McNamara, "The Herrenfrage: The Restructuring of the Gender System, 1050–1150," in *Medieval Masculinities: Regarding Men in the Middle Ages*, ed. Clare A. Lees, Medieval Cultures 7 (Minneapolis: University of Minnesota Press, 1994), 7.

BIBLIOGRAPHY

Selected Greek and Latin Texts

Throughout this book, I have preferred to use easily accessible English (or bilingual Latin/English) translations of primary sources, when available, for the benefit of readers, should they choose to read more of these authors themselves. In many cases, I have deliberately favored older translations that, although more archaic, are more readily available (including, for the most part, online). I have, in some cases, modified and updated translations for readability and faithfulness to the original language. Where a translation has not been attributed, it is my own.

For ease of reading, citations for ancient sources are given directly in the text of this book without edition or translation information. That information is listed below. Full listings for abbreviated series titles can be found in the Abbreviations section at the front of this book.

All biblical quotations, unless otherwise indicated, are from the New Revised Standard Version.

1 Clement. Translated by Bart Ehrman. In Vol. 1 of *The Apostolic Fathers,* ed. Bart D. Ehrman. LCL, 2003.

Acts of Peter. Translated by James Brashler and Douglas Parrott. In Vol. 2 of *The New Testament Apocrypha.* Rev. ed. Edited by William Schneemelcher. English translation edited by R. McL. Wilson. Louisville, Ky.: Westminster John Knox Press, 1991.

Ambroise de Milan. *Hymnes.* Translated and edited by Jacques Fontaine et al. Paris: Éditions du Cerf, 1992.

Ambrose. *Concerning Virgins.* Translated by H. De Romestin. NPNF Vol. 10. 1896.

———. *Selections from the Letters of Saint Ambrose.* Translated by H. De Romestin. NPNF Vol. 10. 1896.

Ammianus Marcellinus. *History.* Translated by John C. Rolfe. 3 vols. LCL, 1950–1952.

Augustine. *De moribus ecclesiae catholicae et de moribus Manichaeorum.* CCEL Vol. 90. 1992.

———. *Quaestiones in heptateuchum.* CCSL 33. 1954.

Ausonius, Decimus Magnus. *Works.* Translated by Hugh G. Evelyn White. 2 vols. LCL, 1967–1968.

Catullus. *Works.* 2nd ed. Translated by Francis Warre Cornish. Revised by G. P. Goold. LCL, 1988.

Chronicon Paschale. Translated by Michael Whitby and Mary Whitby. Liverpool, England: Liverpool University Press, 1989.

Chrysostom, John. *On Virginity.* Translated by Sally Rieger Shore. Lewiston, N.Y.: Edwin Mellen Press, 1983.

Cicero. *Letters.* Translated by Evelyn Shuckburgh. 4 vols. London: Bell, 1908–1912.

———. *Letters to Atticus.* Translated by D. R. Shackleton Bailey. 6 vols. LCL, 1999.

Collectio Avellana. Edited by O. Günther. CSEL Vol. 35/1, 2. 1895, 1898.

Cyprian. *De mortalitate.* Translated by Ernest Wallis. ANF 5, 1886.

———. *Letters.* Translated by Ernest Wallis. ANF 5, 1886.

Didascalia Apostolorum. Translated by R. Hugh Conolly. Oxford: Clarendon, 1929.

Epiphanius. *Panarion.* Translated by Philip Amidon. New York: Oxford University Press, 1990.

Euripides. *Cyclops; Alcestis; Medea.* Translated by David Kovacs. LCL, 1994.

Eusebius. *Ecclesiastical History.* Translated by Kirsopp Lake. 2 vols. LCL, 1980.

Hippolytus. *Commentary on Daniel.* Translated by S. D. F. Salmond. ANF 5, 1886.

Homeric Hymn to Demeter. Translated by Helen Foley. Princeton, N.J.: Princeton University Press, 1999.

Jacob de Voragine. "Saint Sophia and Her Three Daughters." Vol. 1 in *The Golden Legend.* Translated by William Granger Ryan. Princeton, N. J.: Princeton University Press, 1993. 1.185.

Jerome. "Against Helvidius." In *Letters and Select Works.* Translated by W. H. Fremantle. NPNF, 1893.

———. "Against Jovinianus." In *Letters and Select Works.* Translated by W. H. Fremantle. NPNF, 1893.

———. "Commentary on Ezekiel." PL 25.

———. *Letters and Select Works.* Translated by W. H. Fremantle. NPNF, 1893.

Julian. "Against the Galileans." In *The Works of the Emperor Julian.* Translated by Wilmer Cave Wright. 3 vols. LCL, 1962–1990.

Libanius. "Orations," in *Libanius. Selected Works.* Translated by A. F. Norman. 2 vols. LCL, 1969.

Optatus of Milevis. *Libri VII.* SC Vol. 412.

Palladius. *Lausiac History.* Translated by Cuthbert Butler. Nendeln, Liechtenstein: Kraus Reprints, 1967.

Passio Sanctae Caeciliae. Edited and translated by Filippo Caraffa and Antonio Massone. In *Santa Cecilia Martire Romana: Passione e culto.* Rome: Titulus Caeciliae Centro di Spiritualità Liturgica, n.d.

Paulinus of Nola. *Letters of Paulinus of Nola.* Translated by P. G. Walsh. 2 vols. *ACW* 35 and 36, 1966 and 1967.

Plato. *Symposium: or, The Drinking Party.* Translated by Michael Joyce. London: J. M. Dent, 1935.

Pliny the Younger. *Letters.* Translated by William Melmoth. 2 vols. LCL, 1961–1963.

Prudentius. *Peristephanon.* Translated by M. C. Eagan. Fathers of the Church Vol. 43. Washington, D.C.: Catholic University of America Press, 1962.

Seneca. "On Constancy." In *Moral Essays,* Vol. 1. Translated by John William Basore. LCL, 1963–1965.

———. "Troades." In *Seneca. Tragedies,* Vol. 1. Translated by Frank Justus Miller. LCL, 1968.

Sophocles. *The Burial at Thebes. Antigone.* Translated by Seamus Heaney. London: Faber & Faber, 2004.

Soranus. *Gynecology.* Translated by Owsei Temkin. Baltimore: Johns Hopkins University Press, 1956.

Tatian. *Oration to the Greeks.* Translated by Molly Whittaker. Oxford: Clarendon, 1982.

Tertullian. *Ad martyras.* Translated by S. Thelwall. ANF 3. 1885.

———. "Ad Uxorem." In *Tertullian. Treatises on Marriage and Remarriage.* Translated by William Le Saint. *ACW* Vol. 13. 1951.

———. *De coronis militis.* Translated by S. Thelwall. ANF 3. 1885.

———. *De cultu feminarum* (English title: "On the Dress of Women"). Translated by S. Thelwall. ANF 4. 1885.

———. *De virginibus velandis* (English title: "On the Veiling of Virgins"). Translated by S. Thelwall. ANF 4. 1885.

———. *On Baptism.* Translated by S. Thelwall. ANF 3. 1885.

———. *A Treatise on the Soul.* Translated by S. Thelwall. ANF 3. 1885.

Victor, C. Julius. *Ars Rhetorica*. Edited by Remo Giomini and Maria Silvana Celentano. Leipzig: Teubner, 1980.

Vita Melaniae Juniores (English title: *Life of Melania, the Younger*). Translated by Elizabeth A. Clark. New York: Edwin Mellen Press, 1984.

Additional Secondary Sources

The following list includes books and articles beyond the sources listed in the endnotes to provide additional background for readers interested in women and visual culture in antiquity. Please note that this list is far from exhaustive and can only point the way to further study.

Adcock, F. E. "Women in Roman Life and Letters." *Greece and Rome* 14, no. 40 (1945): 1–11.

Alchermes, J. D. "*Cura pro mortuis* [and *cultus martyrum:* Commemoration in Rome from the Second through the Sixth Century]." Ph.D. diss., New York University, 1989.

Alexandre, Monique. "Early Christian Women." In *From Ancient Goddesses to Christian Saints*, edited by Pauline Schmitt Pantel, translated by Arthur Goldhammer, 407–44. Vol. 1 of *A History of Women in the West*. Cambridge, Mass.: Belknap, 1991.

Ardener, S., ed. *Women and Space*. Providence, R.I.: Berg, 1993.

Arjava, Antti. "Jerome and Women." *Arctos* 23 (1989): 5–18.

———. "Women in the Christian Empire: Ideological Changes and Social Reality." *Studia Patristica* 24 (1993): 6–9.

———. *Women and the Law in Late Antiquity*. Oxford: Oxford University Press, 1998.

Armellini, M. *Il cimitero di S. Agnese sulla via Nomentana*. Rome: Tipografia Poliglotta, 1880.

———. *Gli antichi cimiteri cristiani di Roma e d'Italia*. Rome: Tipografia Poliglotta, 1893.

Bachofen, J. J. *Versuch bei die Gräbersymbolik der Alten*. 2nd ed. Basel: Helbing & Lichtenhahn, 1925.

Barnard, L. W. "Early Christian Art as Apologetic." *Journal of Religious History* 10, no. 1 (1978): 20–31.

Baruffa, Antonio. *The Catacombs of St. Callixtus: History, Archaeology. Faith*. Vatican City: Librerìa Editrice Vaticana, 1993.

Beard, Mary, John North, and Simon Price. *Religions of Rome.* Vol. 1, *A History.* Vol. 2, *A Source Book.* Cambridge: Cambridge University Press, 1998.

Belting, Hans. *Likeness and Presence: A History of the Image before the Era of Art.* Translated by E. Jephcott. Chicago: University of Chicago Press, 1994.

Bianchi Bandinelli, R. *Roma. L'arte romana al centro del potere.* Milan: Rizzoli, 1985.

Bosio, Antonio. *Roma sotterranea novissima: opus postumus nella quale si tratta di sacri cimiterii di Roma.* Edited by P. Giovanni Serani da S. Severino. Rome, 1651.

Brown, Peter. "The Patrons of Pelagius: The Roman Aristocracy between East and West." *Journal of Theological Studies,* n.s., 21 (1970): 52–72.

Burke, Peter. *Eyewitnessing: The Use of Images as Historical Evidence.* Ithaca, N.Y.: Cornell University Press, 2001.

Cameron, Averil. "Neither Male nor Female." *Greece and Rome* 27 (1980): 60–68.

————. "Virginity as Metaphor." In *History as Text,* edited by A. Cameron. London: Duckworth, 1989.

Cantalamessa, Raniero. *Etica sessuale e matrimonio nel cristianismo delle origine.* Milan: Vita e pensiero, 1976.

Carietti, Sandro. *Guide to the Catacomb of St. Callistus.* 3rd ed. Revised by Carlo Carletti. Translated by lmelda Cowdrey. Rome: Pontifical Commission for Sacred Archaeology, 1983.

Castelli, Elizabeth. "Gender, Theory, and the Rise of Christianity: A Response to Rodney Stark." *JECS* 6 (1998): 227–257.

————. " 'I Will Make Mary Male': Pieties of the Body and Gender Transformation of Christian Women in Late Antiquity." In *Body Guards: The Cultural Politics of Gender Ambiguity,* edited by Janet Soskice and Diana Lipton, 62–71. Oxford Readings in Feminism. Oxford: Oxford University Press, 2003.

————. "Virginity and Its Meaning for Women's Sexuality in Early Christianity." *JFSR* 2 (1986): 61–82.

Chadwick, W. *Women, Art, and Society.* New York: Thames & Hudson, 1990.

Cioffarelli, Ada. *Guide to the Catacombs of Rome and Its Surroundings.* Rome: Bonsignori, 2000.

Clark, Elizabeth A. *Ascetic Piety and Women's Faith: Essays on Late Ancient Christianity.* New York: Edwin Mellen, 1986.

————. "Patrons, Not Priests: Gender and Power in Late Antique Christianity." *Gender and History* 2 (1990): 252–264.

————. *Women in the Early Church.* Collegeville, Minn.: Liturgical Press, 1990.

————. "Women, Gender, and the Study of Christian History." *Church History* 70, no. 3 (2001): 395–426.

Clark, Gillian. *Women in the Ancient World*. New York: Oxford University Press, 1989.

Consolino, F. E. "Modelli di sanità femminile nelle più antiche Passioni romane." *Augustinianum* 24 (1984): 84–113.

————. "Santo o patrone? Le aristocratiche tardo antiche e il potere della carità," *Studi Storici* 31 (1990): 969–991.

Corley, Kathleen E. "Feminist Myths of Christian Origins." In *Reimagining Christian Origins. A Colloquium Honoring Burton L. Mack,* edited by Elizabeth A. Castelli and Hal Taussig, 51–67. Philadelphia: Trinity, 1996.

Corrington, Gail Peterson. "The 'Divine Woman': Propaganda and the Power of Celibacy in the New Testament Apocrypha: A Reconsideration." *ATR* 70 (1988): 207–220.

————. "Salvation, Celibacy, and Power: 'Divine Women' in Late Antiquity." *Society for Biblical Literature Seminar Papers* 24 (1985): 321–325.

Cracco-Ruggini, L. "La donna e il sacro, tra paganesimo e cristianesimo." In *Atti del II convegno nazionale di studi su la donna nel mondo antico,* edited by Renaldo Uglione, 243–275. Turin: Regione Piemonte, Assessorato alla cultura, 1989.

————. "Juridical Status and Historical Reality of Women in Roman Patriarchal Society." *Klio* 71, no. 2 (1989): 604–619.

Croke, Brian, and J. Harries. *Religious Conflict in Fourth Century Rome: A Documentary Study*. Sydney, Australia: Sydney University Press, 1982.

Cumont, Franz. *Recherches sur le symbolisme funéraire des Romains*. Paris: P. Geuthner, 1942.

Dagens, C. "A propos du cubiculum de la 'velatio.'" *RivArcC* 47 (1971): 119–129.

Daniélou, Fr. Jean. *The Ministry of Women in the Early Church*. Translated by Glyn Simon. London: Faith Press, 1961.

De Bruyne, Lucien. "Refrigerium Interim." *RivArcC* 34 (1958): 87–118.

Deichmann, Friedrich Wilhelm. "Märtyrbasilika, Martyrion, Memoria, und Altargrab," *Mitteilungen des Deutschen Archäologischen Instituts*. Römische Abteil Band 77 (1970): 144–169.

————. *Archeologia Cristiana*. Rome: L'Erma di Bretschneider, 1993.

Deichmann, Friedrich Wilhelm, G. Bovini, and H. Brandenburg. *Repertorium der christlich-antiken Sarkophage*, Vol. 1: *Rom und Ostia*. Wiesbaden: Steiner, 1967.

De Rossi, G. B. *La Roma sotterranea cristiana,* 3 vols. Rome, 1864–1877.

————. "Scoperta della basilica di S. Petronilla col sepolcro dei martiri Nereo ed Achilleo nel cimitero di Domitilla." *Bull.Arch.C,* ser. 2, 5 (1894): 5–34; 68–74.

Dewey, Joanna. "From Storytelling to Written Text: The Loss of Early Christian Women's Voices." *Biblical Theology Bulletin* 26 (1996): 71–78.

Drake, H. A. *Constantine and the Bishops: The Politics of Intolerance.* Baltimore: Johns Hopkins University Press, 2000.

Duval, Y. *Auprès des saints, corps et âme. L'inhumation (ad sanctos) dans la chrétienté d'orient et d'occident du IIIᵉ au VIIᵉ siècle.* Paris: Études Augustiniennes, 1988.

Dvorak, M. "Katakombenmalerei. Die Anfänge der christlichen Kunst." In *Kunstgeschichte als Geistesgeschichte,* edited by M. Dvorak, 1–40. Munich, 1928.

Eisenstadt, S. N., and L. Roniger. *Patrons, Clients, and Friends.* Cambridge: Cambridge University Press, 1984.

Elliott, John H. "Patronage and Clientism in Early Christian Society." *Forum* 3, no. 4 (December 1987): 40–41.

Elsner, Jaś. *Imperial Rome and Christian Triumph: The Art of the Roman Empire AD 100–450.* Oxford: Oxford University Press, 1998.

Engemann, Josef. "Altes und Neues zu Beispielen heidnischer und christlicher Katakombenbilder im spätantiken Rom." *JAC* 26 (1983): 129–151.

————. *Untersuchungen zur Sepulkralsymbolik der späteren römischen Kaiserzeit.* Münster: Aschendorff, 1973.

Fantham, E., et al., eds. *Women in the Classical World: Image and Text.* New York: Oxford University Press, 1994.

Fasola, U., and P. Testini. "I cemeteri cristiani." *CIAC.Atti* 9.1 (1978), 103–139.

Février, P.-A. "Une approche de la conversion des elites au IVᵉ siècles: le décor de la mort." In *Miscellanea Historiae Ecclesiasticae VI,* Congrès de Varsovie 1978, 22–45. Brussels, 1983.

————. "Le culte des morts dans les communautes chrétiennes durant le IIIᵉ siècle," *CIAC.Atti* 9.1 (1978), 211–274.

————. "Études sur les catacombe romaines." *Cahiers Archéologiques* 10 (1959): 1–26.

————. "Un plaidoyer pour Damase. Les inscriptions des necropolis romaines," *RivArcC* 65 (1989): 105–133.

————. "La tombe chrétienne et l'au delà." In *Le temps chrétien de la fin de l'antiquité au moyen age: IIIᵉ-XIIIᵉ siècles, Paris, 9–12 Mars 1981,* edited by Jean-Marie Leroux. Paris: Éditions du Centre national de la recherche scientifique, 1984.

Fink, J., and B. Asamer. *Die römischen Katakomben*. Mainz: Verlag Philipp von Zabern, 1997.

Finney, Paul Corby. *Art, Archaeology and Architecture of Early Christianity*. New York: Garland, 1993.

Francis, James. "Living Icons: Tracing a Motif in Verbal and Visual Representation from the Second to Fourth Centuries, C.E." *American Journal of Philology* 124 (2003): 575–600.

Frank, G. L. C. "Menstruation and Motherhood: Christian Attitudes in Late Antiquity." *Studia Historiae Ecclesiasticae* 19, no. 2 (1993): 185–208.

Frutaz, A. P. *Il complesso monumentale di Sant'Agnese*. Vatican City: Poliglotta Vaticana, 1976.

Galate, Linda Sue. "Early Christian Iconography." In *Near Eastern Archaeology: A Reader*, edited by Suzanne Richards, 473–478. Winona Lake, Ind.: Eisenbrauns, 2003.

Gardner, Jane. *Women in Roman Law and Society*. London: Croom Helm, 1986.

Gnoli, G., and Jean-Paul Vernant. *La mort, les morts, dans les sociétés anciennes*. Cambridge: Cambridge University Press, 1982.

Gould, G. "Women in the Writings of the Fathers: Language, Belief, and Reality." In *Women in the Church: Papers Read at the 1989 Summer Meeting and the 1990 Winter Meeting of the Ecclesiastical History Society*, edited by W. J. Sheils, and D. Woods, 1–13. Studies in Church History 27. Oxford: Blackwell Press, 1990.

Grabar, André. *Early Christian Art: from the Rise of Christianity to the Death of Theodosius*. Translated by Stuart Gilbert and James Emmons. New York: Odyssey, 1968.

———. *Martyrium. Recherches sur le culte de reliques et l'art chrétien antique*. 2 vols. Paris: Collège de France, 1946.

Guyon, J. "L'église de Rome du IVᵉ siècle à Sixte III (312–432)." In *Naissance d'une chrétienté (250–430)*, 771–798. Vol. 2 of *Histoire du christianisme des origines à nos jours*. Paris, 1995.

Hinard, François, ed. *La Mort, Les Morts et l'au-delà dans le monde Romain*. Caen, France: Université de Caen, 1987.

Hinson, E. Glenn. "Women among the Martyrs." *Studia Patristica* 25 (1993): 423–428.

———. "Women Biblical Scholars in the Late Fourth Century: The Aventine Circle," *Studia Patristica* 33 (1997): 319–324.

Hunter, David G. "Clerical Celibacy and the Veiling of Virgins: New Boundaries in Late Ancient Christianity." In *The Limits of Ancient Christianity: Essays on Late An-*

tique Thought and Culture in Honor of R. A. Markus, edited by William E. Klingshirn and Mark Vessey, 139–152. Ann Arbor: University of Michigan Press, 1999.

Janssens, J. *Vita e morte del cristiano negli epitaffi di Roma anteriori al sec. VII.* Rome: Università Gregoriana Editrice, 1981.

Jones, Chris. "Woman, Death, and the Law during the Christian Persecutions." In *Martyrs and Martyrologies,* edited by Diana Wood, 23–34. Cambridge, Mass.: Blackwell, 1993.

Kampen, N. Boymel. "Gender Theory on Roman Art." In *I Claudia: Women in Ancient Rome,* edited by D. E. E. Kleiner and S. B. Matheson, 14–25. New Haven, Conn.: Yale University Art Gallery, 1996.

———. "The Muted Other." *Art Journal* 47 (1988): 15–19.

Kearsley, R. A. "Women in Public Life." In *New Documents Illustrating Early Christianity,* Vol. 6, edited by S. R. Llewelyn, 24–27. North Ryde, Australia: Ancient History Documentary Research Centre, Macquarie University, 1989.

Kitzinger, E. "The Cult of Images in the Age before Iconoclasm." *Dumbarton Oaks Papers* 7 (1954): 119–146.

Koch, G. *Early Christian Art and Architecture.* London: SCM Press, 1996.

Koloski-Ostrow, A. O., and C. Lyons, eds. *Naked Truths: Women, Sexuality, and Gender in Classical Art and Archaeology.* New York: Routledge, 1997.

Koortbojian, Michael. "*In commemorationem mortuorum:* Text and Image along the 'Street of Tombs'" In *Art and Text in Roman Culture,* edited by Jaś Elsner, 210–232. New York: Cambridge University Press, 1996.

———. *Myth, Meaning, and Memory on Roman Sarcophagi.* Berkeley: University of California Press, 1995.

Kroeger, C. "Bitalia, The Ancient Woman Priest." *Priscilla Papers* 7, no. 1 (winter 1993): 11–12.

La Porte, Jean B. *The Role of Women in Early Christianity.* Lewiston, N.Y.: Edwin Mellen, 1982.

Lattimore, Richmond. *Themes in Greek and Latin Epitaphs.* Urbana: University of Illinois Press, 1962.

Lefkowitz, Mary, and Maureen B. Fant, eds. *Women's Life in Greece and Rome: A Sourcebook.* London: Duckworth, 1982.

Lewis, Naphtali, and Meyer Reinhold, eds. *Roman Civilization.* Vol. 2: *Selected Readings: The Empire.* 3rd ed. New York: Columbia University Press, 1990.

Lightman, M., and W. Zeisel. "Univira: An Example of Continuity and Change in Roman Society." *Church History* 46 (1977): 19–32.

Lother, H. *Realismus und Symbolismus in der altchristlichen Kunst.* Tübingen: Mohr, 1931.

Lowden, John. *Early Christian and Byzantine Art.* London: Phaidon, 1997.

Martimort, Aimé Georges. *Deaconesses: An Historical Study.* Translated by K. D. Whitehead. San Francisco: Ignatius, 1986.

McNamara, Jo Ann. "Sexual Equality and the Cult of Virginity in Early Christian Thought." *Feminist Studies* 3 (1976): 145–158.

————. "Wives and Widows in Early Christian Theology." *International Journal of Women's Studies* 2 (1979): 575–592.

Methuen, Charlotte. "'For Pagans Laugh to Hear Women Teach': Gender Stereotypes in the *Didascalia Apostolorum.*" In *Gender and Christian Religion,* edited by R. N. Swanson, 23–35. Studies in Church History 34. Woodbridge, Suffolk, England: Boydell, 1998.

————. "The 'Virgin Widow': A Problematic Social Role for the Early Church." *HTR* 90 (1997): 285–298.

————. "Widows, Bishops, and the Struggle for Authority in the *Didascalia Apostolorum.*" *Journal of Ecclesiastical History* 46 (1995): 197–213.

Mulhern, Alice. "The Catacombs." *Restoration Quarterly* 26 (1983): 29–38.

Murray, Sister Charles. "Art and the Early Church," *Journal of Theological Studies,* n.s., 28 (1977): 304–345.

————. *Rebirth and Afterlife: A Study of the Transmutation of Some Pagan Imagery in Early Christian Funerary Art.* Oxford: B. A. R., 1981.

Nestori, Aldo. "Qualche osservazione statistica sulla pittura cimiteriale romana." In *Historiam Pictura Refert. Miscellanea in onore de Padre Alehandro Recio Veganzones O. F. M.,* 403–406. Vatican City: Pontificio Istituto di Archeologia Cristiana, 1994.

————. *Repertorio topografico delle pitture delle catacombe romane.* Vatican City: Pontificio Istituto di Archeologia Cristiana, 1993.

Nichols, J. *"Patrona Civitatis:* Gender and Civic Patronage." *Latomus* 206 (1989): 117–42.

Osiek, Carolyn. "The Church Fathers and the Ministry of Women." In *Women Priests: A Catholic Commentary on the Vatican Declaration,* edited by Arlene Swidler and Leonard Swidler, 75–80. New York: Paulist, 1977.

————. "The Widow as Altar: The Rise and Fall of a Symbol." *The Second Century* 3 (1983): 159–69.

Pavia, Carlo. *Il labirinto delle catacombe.* Udine, Italy: Collana archeologica C. Lorenzini, 1987.

Phillips, J. E. "Roman Mothers and the Lives of their Adult Daughters." *Helios* 6 (1978): 69–80.

Pietri, Charles. "Le marriage chrétien à Rome IVᵉᵐᵉ-Vᵉᵐᵉ siècles." In *Histoire vécue du peuple chrétien*, edited by Jean Delumeau, 1.105–130. Toulouse: Privat, 1979.

Prinzivalli, E. "Modelli ideali e vita vissuta della donna cristiana a Roma fra II e IV secolo." *Helikon* 31–32 (1991–1992): 351–373.

———. "Il ruolo della donna nella comunità cristiana di Roma." In *La Comunità cristiana di Roma*, 229–245. Vatican City: Libreria editrice vaticana, 2000.

Rebillard, É. *In Hora Mortis: Évolution de la pastorale chrétienne de la mort aux IVᵉ et Vᵉ siècles*. Rome: École française de Rome, 1994.

———. "Koimeterion et coemeterium: tombe, tombe sainte, nécropole," *MEFRA* 105 (1993): 975–1001.

———. *Religion et Sépulture: L'Église, les vivants et les morts dans l'antiquité tardive*. Paris: Éditions de l'école des hautes etudes en sciences socials, 2003.

Rousseau, P. " 'Learned Women' and the Development of a Christian Culture in Late Antiquity." *Symbolae Osloenses* 70 (1995): 116–147.

Ruether, Rosemary Radford. "Misogynism and Virginal Feminism in the Fathers of the Church." In *Religion and Sexism*, edited by R. Ruether, 150–183. New York: Simon & Schuster, 1974.

Rush, A. C. *Death and Burial in Christian Antiquity*. Washington, D.C.: Catholic University of America Press, 1941.

Rutgers, Leonard. *Subterranean Rome: In Search of the Roots of Christianity in the Catacombs of the Eternal City*. Louvain, Belgium: Peeters, 2000.

Simpson, Jane. "Women and Asceticism in the Fourth Century: A Question of Interpretation, " *Journal of Religious History* 15 (1988): 38–60.

Smith, Julia M. H. "Did Women Have a Transformation of the Roman World?" *Gender and History* 12 (2000): 552–571.

Staples, A. *From Good Goddess to Vestal Virgins: Sex and Category in Roman Religion*. London: Routledge, 1998.

Stuiber, A. *Refrigerium Interim, die Vorstellungen vom Zwischenzustand und die frühchristlichen Grabeskunst*. Bonn, Germany: Hanstein, 1957.

Testini, Pasquale. *Archeologia cristiana: nozioni generali dalle origini alla fine del sec. VI: propedeutica, topografia cimiteriale, epigrafia, edifici di culto*. Bari, Italy: Edipuglia, 1980.

———. *The Christian Catacombs in Rome*. Rome: Ente provinciale per il turismo, 1970.

Thurston, Bonnie. *The Widows: A Women's Ministry in the Early Church*. Minneapolis, Minn.: Fortress, 1989.

Torjesen, Karen Jo. "The Early Christian Orans: An Artistic Representation of Women's Liturgical Prayer and Prophecy." In *Women Preachers and Prophets through Two Millennia of Christianity*, edited by Beverly Mayne Kienzle and Pamela J. Walker, 42–56. Berkeley: University of California Press, 1998.

———. "In Praise of Noble Women: Gender and Honor in Ascetic Texts." *Semeia* 57 (1992): 41–64.

Treggiari, Susan. "Divorce Roman Style: How Easy and How Frequent Was It?" In *Marriage, Divorce, and Children in Ancient Rome*, edited by Beryl Rawson, 31–46. Oxford: Clarendon, 1996.

Van Bremen, R. "Women and Wealth." In *Images of Women in Antiquity*, edited by A. Cameron and A. Kuhrt, 223–243. London: Croom Helm, 1983.

Venter, W. "The Position of the Widow in the Early Church according to the Writings of the Apostolic Fathers." *Ekklesiastikos Pharos* 72 (1990): 11–29.

Verdon, M. "Virgins and Widows: European Kinship and Early Christianity." *Man* 23 (1988): 488–505.

Wagoner, Robert. "Presence and Absence in Early Christian Art." In *Common Life in the Early Church: Essays Honoring Graydon F. Snyder*, edited by Julian Hills, 327–343. Harrisburg, Penn.: Trinity, 1998.

Ward-Perkins, J. B. "Memoria, Martyr's Tombs, and Martyr's Church." *Journal of Theological Studies* 17 (1966): 20–37.

———. *Studies in Roman and Early Christian Architecture*. London: Pindar, 1994.

Wilson-Kastner, Patricia, et al., eds., *A Lost Tradition: Women Writers of the Early Church*. Washington, D.C.: University Press of America, 1981.

INDEX